Discovering Research Methods in Psychology

To JOR
with love and thanks

L. D. SANDERS

DISCOVERING
RESEARCH METHODS IN
PSYCHOLOGY

A Student's Guide

 BPS BLACKWELL

BPS Blackwell is an imprint of Blackwell Publishing, which was acquired by John Wiley & Sons in February 2007. Blackwell's publishing program has been merged with Wiley's global Scientific, Technical, and Medical business to form Wiley-Blackwell.

Registered Office
John Wiley & Sons Ltd, The Atrium, Southern Gate, Chichester, West Sussex, PO19 8SQ, UK

Editorial Offices
350 Main Street, Malden, MA 02148-5020, USA
9600 Garsington Road, Oxford, OX4 2DQ, UK
The Atrium, Southern Gate, Chichester, West Sussex, PO19 8SQ, UK

For details of our global editorial offices, for customer services, and for information about how to apply for permission to reuse the copyright material in this book please see our website at www.wiley.com/wiley-blackwell.

Library of Congress Cataloging-in-Publication Data

Sanders, Lalage D.
    Discovering research methods in psychology : a student's guide/L.D. Sanders.
        p.   cm.
    Includes bibliographical references and index.
    ISBN 978-1-4051-7531-9 (hardcover : alk. paper) – ISBN 978-1-4051-7530-2 (pbk.) 1.   Psychology – Research I.   Title.
    BF76.5.S245 2010
    150.72–dc22
                                                    2009017130
A catalogue record for this book is available from the British Library.

Set in 10.5/13pt Minion by SPi Publisher Services, Pondicherry, India
Printed in Great Britain by TJ International Ltd, Padstow, Cornwall

The British Psychological Society's free Research Digest e-mail service rounds up the latest research and relates it to your syllabus in a user-friendly way. To subscribe go to www.researchdigest.org.uk or send a blank e-mail to subscribe-rd@lists.bps.org.uk.

1   2010

Contents

Contents

Acknowledgements

I would like to begin by thanking the authors on whose work I have drawn in writing this book. Their inspiring choice of material and the rigour of their approach made this book what it is. I am grateful to Dr Christian Jarrett and the British Psychological Society for the excellent BPS Research Digest, which alerted me to many of these studies. Thanks also to the BPS for allowing the reproduction herein of the Ethical Principles for Conducting Research with Human Participants.

I am very grateful to Tim Warren for his illustrations and readiness to tweak his designs in response to my whims. I would like to thank Shirley Hobbis, whose patience and helpfulness with the preparation of this work seemed to know no bounds. I also want to thank Lucie Warren and Amy Sanders for their help in the preparation of the chapters, and, along with Ellie Ford, Andrew Lewis and Barnaby Sanders, for the faith and support they always show me. I must also thank all my family and friends for putting up with my preoccupation with this book during its development.

I am indebted to my students, too, who continue to teach me to see things in new ways. Their questions, over the years, triggered the idea for this book and influenced its style. Thank you, also, to my colleagues in UWIC who are a great team to work with; many of you have helped influence and develop my teaching practice. I particularly would like to mention the late Mary Barasi, whose guidance on matters ethical was invaluable – she is much missed.

Finally I wish to thank the team at Blackwell for their support throughout this project: Andrew McAleer and Elizabeth Johnston and, most recently, Annie Rose, especially for the patience with which she has responded to my stream of questions.

Introduction and How To Use This Book

You have probably been attracted to psychology for the same reason as the rest of us: because you are interested in understanding people or behaviour or both. Many of us find the subject matter of psychology intriguing, and these days it is a popular course to study at university. It can be a bit of a surprise to discover that studying psychology also means studying research and statistics. Sometimes it is hard to see the reason for this in the early days. It can feel like an unnecessary imposition, no matter how hard tutors try to persuade you otherwise. With time, the link between psychology and research becomes clearer, but at first it can seem inexplicable!

There are three main types of research that we can use in psychology. We can watch what people do – observation. We can see if we can manipulate events to change individual responses – experiments. Or we can ask people – survey methods. I confess that there is no real consensus about exactly what constitutes survey methods; some researchers would restrict the use of the term to large-scale questionnaire studies, while others use it in its broadest sense, meaning any type of research that involves asking people questions. To complicate matters further, some people, usually not psychologists, use the term 'survey' for an observational study. This text has used this term in the broadest sense to incorporate all interrogative research strategies, thereby including all research that is neither observation nor experimentation.

The main purpose of this book is to introduce the reader to the principles and terminology of research in a way that makes them easy to understand. It is also to illustrate how research methods contribute to the building of our chosen discipline and why they are important. The chapters are based around the subject matter of psychology, and are intended to make the most of your natural curiosity about and enthusiasm for the subject to help you through some of the complexities of research techniques.

There are three sections to this book. Each of the following chapters (2–19) tells the story of one particular piece of research. These chapters draw on studies from different types of research in diverse areas of psychology. The first of these tackles the issue of ethics in research. Often, ethics tends to be a bit of an afterthought, when it should be the foundation of all research, hence its primary position in this text. There are then seven chapters on experimentation, the first three describing single experimental designs; later chapters tackle the more complex ones. The next five chapters are about different observational techniques, followed by four on survey methods. The penultimate chapter is an example of cross-cultural research providing an illustration of how different research methods can be successfully combined. Chapter 20 is an overview of the preceding narratives comparing the methodologies and techniques employed.

If you want to know how a particular study design works, then reading the relevant chapter will show you the pros and cons of that design. Each chapter begins with a familiar topic and considers why it might be worth investigating, leading into the chosen study for that chapter. The study is then briefly outlined: what was done and what was found. Then three questions about the study are reviewed: How safe is the conclusion? How effective is the design? and How appropriate is the research method? These are questions that are useful to bear in mind when reading about any research study. The last question allows us to consider how other research methods might be used to explore the same issue.

Although there are cross-references between the chapters, this is simply to enable the reader to follow things up should they wish. Each chapter is self-contained and does not require the reader to read them in sequence. The only chapter where this is not the case is the final chapter, which draws on the material of the preceding narratives.

If you want to know about some of the general issues you encounter in research, Key Topics (p. 246) describes and summarises some fundamental issues underlying research (including how to write reports and referencing) which require more detailed explanation than is appropriate in the preceding sections.

If you want to find about particular research terminology there is a Glossary on page 275. This is an alphabetical ready reference, and can be used either to check the meanings of terms given in the narrative chapters in **bold** or, alternatively, as a general dictionary of research. Research terminology can seem confusing to the beginner – and to the experienced researcher for that matter! There are different terms for the same phenomena, and there are very similar terms for very different phenomena. It can be really difficult to follow. The terms in the glossary are cross-referenced to increase the chances of the reader being able to find, recognise and then decode any research terms they encounter in their reading elsewhere.

Much of this book concerns quantitative methods, although qualitative methods are included. The reason for this imbalance is not that quantitative methods are superior or more important. The trouble is that they seem more off-putting. To do qualitative research properly, skills and experience are needed just as much as they are for quantitative methods. Yet newcomers to research are rarely frightened by qualitative methods. The main aim of this book is to help the reader to get to grips with, or perhaps refresh their understanding of, quantitative methods.

Lastly, I should explain the choice of studies discussed here. Apart from those cited in Chapter 2, these are not classic studies in psychology. It is unlikely that you will have encountered them before. The studies I have chosen are all from the twenty-first century and all highlight the diversity of the subject matter within the discipline; they illustrate its intriguing variety. They were chosen from a large number of possible studies, many of which could easily have been substituted here, and would have illustrated the principles of research as effectively as those chosen. The studies described here are indicative of the wide range of research conducted in psychology, and I hope that they represent some of the features that first drew you to the study of psychology.

Ethics

'Science cannot resolve moral conflicts, but it can help to more accurately frame the debates about those conflicts.' (Heinz Rudolf Pagels, physicist, 1939–88)

How Obedient Are You?

In the 1960s, Stanley Milgram conducted an **experiment** into obedience which became one of the most famous studies in psychology (Milgram, 1963). His first interest, in the light of the horrific events of the Second World War, was to find a way of measuring different societies' obedience to authority. He wanted to discover how, or maybe why, people would commit horrible acts at the direction of an authority figure. This is a laudable question to ask, and an answer could help us understand many an ethical dilemma. A lesser scientist might have set off on this quest straight away, maybe visiting the countries in question, conducting a **survey**. Or it is possible that they might have devised an experiment intended to measure obedience and then set about comparing different countries' responses. (For an example of **cross-cultural** study see Chapter 19.) Luckily for posterity, Milgram was more cautious than this. He wanted an **experimental method**, that is, he wanted to manipulate one variable (the **independent variable**) then measure another (the **dependent variable**). Remember, only with experiments is it possible to establish causal relationships, and this was Milgram's goal. He is a thorough scientist so he began what was intended to be a series of studies. The idea was to develop the **apparatus** first. Once he was happy that this would work, he needed to test the experimental design. He was then planning to recruit **participants** in different countries to allow a cross-cultural comparison. As it turned out it was these preparatory stages that ensured Milgram's place in the history books.

His experimental design was quite straightforward. For each trial there would be two individuals, a Teacher and a Learner. The Learner's task was to learn a list of words. The Teacher's task was to test the Learner's knowledge. The Teacher read part of a previously rehearsed list of words to the Learner, whose job was to supply the missing word from memory. If the Learner failed on his task, the Teacher was required to punish the Learner by giving him an electric shock. (The use of 'he/him' throughout this section is necessary as all the participants in the first study were male.) The machine for administering these shocks was a large box, standard size for electrical equipment in those pre-digital days. The voltage was marked on the box, starting at 15 volts and increasing by 15 volts at each step up to the final 450 volts, which was marked 'Danger XXXX'. With each mistake the Learner made, the Teacher was to increase the voltage of the punishment to the next level.

The participants in this study were a **self-selected sample** in that Milgram placed an advertisement in the local paper seeking volunteers. On arrival at the laboratory, each volunteer found himself paired with another, and the two of them drew lots to see which would be Teacher and which Learner. Unbeknown to the volunteers the lots were fixed, and each volunteer always became the Teacher. The person assigned to the role of Learner was not a volunteer but a confederate of the Experimenter, an actor paid for his role in the experiment. Not only was this process of drawing lots faked, so also was the equipment. The machine was only an artifice and provided no electric shocks, nor was it in any way connected to the Learner. But of course the Teacher did not know any of this at the time. As far as he was concerned he and another volunteer had been assigned to these two different roles, and his role incorporated giving electrical shocks to the other guy.

When the experiment began, the Learner was led away to another room and could only communicate with the Teacher through an intercom. From the start the 'Experimenter', a man in a white coat, supervised the Teacher to make sure that he followed the experimental **protocol**. Each time the Learner made a mistake in this memory task the Teacher was to apply an electric shock. As the experiment began, the Learner would complain at first mildly and then with increasing vehemence as the level of shock rose. At one point the Learner would claim a heart condition and ask to be released from the experiment. At a later stage he would cry out demanding to be released. Towards the highest voltages, however, after some loud howls of protest, the Learner would go silent, apparently unconscious. Throughout this whole planned process the real subject of the experiment, the Teacher, would be required to continue to administer electric shocks. When the Teacher complained and queried the advisability of continuing, the Experimenter would reiterate that the experiment must go on, that the Teacher must continue. No physical pressure was applied to the Teacher; he was bound only by the words of the Experimenter, the man in the white coat, the authority figure.

After the end of the experiment the Teacher was **debriefed** and the real nature of the experiment explained. When The Teacher was once more introduced to the Learner, he invariably expressed immense relief to see that this mild mannered middle-aged man had not come to any real harm.

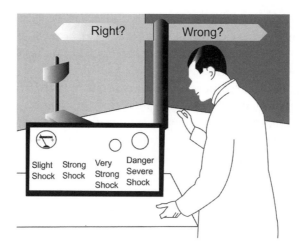

Results

Of the 40 people who played Teacher in this first experiment 26 of them went through to the end, seemingly administering shocks up to the Danger XXXX level. This figure shocked both Milgram and the scientific community when he published his results. He was at pains to stress that none of the Teachers enjoyed what they were doing; they all protested that it was not right to carry on and expressed concern about the state of the Learner. Some even laughed as the shock level rose inexorably, but Milgram argues that it was not mirth that triggered this but rather a release of mounting tension and disquiet. Nevertheless, they carried on to the end. They seemed to be locked into their relationship with the Experimenter; his authority seemed to override their humanitarian concerns about what they were doing to another human being.

After this first experiment Milgram repeated this study in differing formats, 19 experiments in total. Detractors of the first work said that the effect was only evident because the study took place in Yale. Therefore, the argument went, the credibility of this famous university meant that people felt that it must 'be all right' somehow. So they moved the equipment to a less salubrious address in a downtown office, and although the total obedience rate fell, still over 40 per cent of the volunteers took the shocks up to the maximum. He varied the proximity of the Experimenter; the nearer he was the greater the obedience. He also varied the proximity of the Learner; the nearer he was the less the obedience. He tried running the experiment with women as volunteers and the obedience rate remained much the same, although the women showed more stress while taking part. (You can find more details of Milgram's study in any good general or social psychology textbook.)

Can the End Justify the Means?

These days psychologists are bound by a code of professional conduct in research that would preclude running an experiment like Milgram's. For example, the British

Psychological Society has a Code of Conduct, Ethical Principles and Guidelines (2005), which includes Ethical Principles for Conducting Research with Human Participants (see p. 268 below), and Guidelines for Psychologists Working with Animals (see Chapter 7). Apart from these professional codes, most researchers need to seek approval from at least one ethics committee before they can begin any research involving human participants. Ethics committees can be found in universities and hospitals, as well as in research institutes. It is their job to look at, or scrutinise, research proposals to ensure that planned studies are ethical and that, where appropriate, adequate safeguards are in place. No ethics committee would allow a study like Milgram's today. But there were no ethics committees and therefore no ethical scrutiny in the 1960s – it was a different climate altogether.

Judging from this series of experiments, Milgram had stumbled on a very robust effect. His work is still cited today to explain inhuman acts, such as suicide bombers or the systematic abuse of prisoners. However, it has also caused a good deal of fury and indignation about the use of deception in experiments and about the rights of volunteers. Is it acceptable to put volunteers through stressful experiences if it is in a good cause? Is pushing back the frontiers of science an adequate reason to cause distress to another human being? If, in the end, it helps us understand more about the human condition can it be justified? Does this particular outcome justify the means of achieving it? And this leads us to the central question: how are ethical judgements made?

One way we might seek to find an answer is to look at the theories underpinning the study of ethics. One theory, called Consequentialism, says that we ought to do whatever maximises good consequences. Sometimes this is referred to as the end justifying the means, but this is an oversimplification of the theory. Within Consequentialism not all means can be justified by all ends; rather, it is a matter of weighing up both the positive and negative aspects of an action and its consequences in order to decide whether or not it is ethical. Actions then can be judged by the extent to which they contribute to the common good while taking account of the suffering they may cause – a balancing act. An alternative theory is Deontology, from the Greek 'deon' meaning duty. The deontologist would argue that ethical analysis should be based on deciding what the right course of action is in a given set of circumstances, that is, by identifying one's duty. The ethical decision is based entirely on the rightness or wrongness of the act rather than its consequences.

While the approaches of these two theories might seem to be contradictory, in the end each may come to the same conclusion in any given situation. The reason for this is that theory in philosophy does not have the empirical role that it has in science. In this example, the consequentialist could argue in favour of Milgram's work, because its contribution (understanding of how social roles can trap us into behaving against our conscience) outweighs the apparently transient discomfort of the volunteers. Deontologists could argue that the experiment was justified because the researcher was doing his duty in exploring a moral dilemma. Conversely, each theory could allow these positions to be stood on their heads to provide arguments against doing the study.

Theories may provide a framework in which judgements can be made, but they do not provide hard and fast answers. The nature of the decision is far from **objective**. How do we decide what is right and what is wrong? Whether we are looking at consequences or actions, in the end it is a **subjective** judgement. (To learn more about ethical theory, Beauchamp and Childress 1994 is a detailed but accessible read.) Theories provide a means of analysing a situation from an ethical point of view. But there seems to be a long jump from engaging with the theoretical positions to making judgements in individual cases. How can we evaluate the rights and wrongs of conducting an experiment from such a framework?

What Alternatives Are There to Theories?

Theories may be a good starting point, but we tend to need something a little more concrete to make decisions. Decisions cannot be made in a vacuum. Actions and decisions are justified by rules, and those rules should be based on principles that in themselves are derived from theories. So what principles can we derive from the theories outlined above? There are four underlying principles, which are commonly used to help make ethical judgements.

- *Autonomy* means respecting the decision-making capacities of autonomous persons; enabling individuals to make reasoned, informed choices – that is, allowing individuals to make their own decisions about what they experience.
- *Non-maleficence* means avoiding doing any harm.
- *Beneficence* means considering the balance of risks and costs. The overall effect should be beneficial for the individual.
- *Justice* means distributing benefits, risks and costs fairly; for example, ensuring that all in similar positions are treated in a similar manner.

Using these basic principles it is possible to identify rules on which ethical decisions may be based. The first two relate to what the researcher must safeguard for the participants. *Privacy* requires the researcher to have respect for limited access to individuals. A vital part of privacy is the issue of **informed consent**. Respecting a person's autonomy and privacy means that before involving them in research they must first be told what involvement will mean and then agree to it. (This has particular repercussions for observational research; see the Box 2.1.) Agreeing to take part in a programme of research does not necessarily mean that the individual forgoes their right to privacy; there will be many aspects of themselves that they do not wish to share with the researcher. **Confidentiality**, the second rule, means that information about a given individual gained through research should not be available to anyone other than the researcher.

The remaining two rules relate to the nature of the relationship between the researcher and the participant. The basis for the first rule here is *fidelity*, which means that the researcher can be taken at his or her word and when an undertaking

Confidentiality and Anonymity

It is often the case that confidentiality and anonymity are confused. While they are both concerned with respecting the individual they are in fact quite different. Confidentiality means the prevention of disclosure, to other than authorised individuals, of a participant's identity. In contrast, anonymity is the protection of the participant in a study so that even the researchers cannot link the subject with the information provided. Therefore if John Doe takes part in your study, confidentiality requires that you do not tell other people that he has participated. Anonymity would mean that you, as the researcher, would not know which set of **data** belonged to John. You might not even know that the name of the guy who took part was John Doe. Confidentiality may be easier to ensure and manage than anonymity.

of any sort is made to the individual then it will be respected. And last, but not least, is *veracity*, that is telling the truth. This includes imparting information in a comprehensive and objective way. There may be a methodological reason for limited disclosure but this must be carefully justified.

It is evident that veracity and informed consent are clearly linked. Therefore, if research involves deviating from the truth, then how can it be possible to obtain informed consent? And without informed consent, can a study ever be considered ethical? The view of the British Psychological Society is that generally deception should be avoided, although there are occasions when it may be acceptable provided that participants would not experience disquiet or would not object once the deception was known, (see the BPS Ethical Principles for Conducting Research with Human Participants on p. 268).

How Does Milgram's Study Shape Up against These Principles?

Starting with the non-maleficence, did Milgram do his participants any harm? One way to decide that is to ask them, and that is exactly what Milgram did. He revisited his participants later and asked them how they felt about taking part in the study: 84 per cent stated that they were glad to have taken part, 15 per cent were neutral and only just over 1 per cent regretted taking part. Moreover, 74 per cent said they had learned something of personal value and 80 per cent said there should be more research of this nature. So it would seem that not only did they consider that no harm had been done, but they actually reported benefits from taking part, which seems to address the beneficence principle as well. As for justice, none of the criticisms levelled at Milgram has suggested that he did not treat his subjects equally. So this leaves us autonomy, and that seems to be a problem. Can a person be autonomous if they are not fully aware of a situation? Arguably it is not possible to be truly autonomous (namely to have the right or power of self-government without outside control) if the facts of the situation are withheld.

As for the rules, there is no suggestion that Milgram did not maintain confidentiality of his participants, nor that he invaded their privacy or reneged on his fidelity. This leaves veracity, and we know that he deceived his subjects. By doing this he infringed their autonomy, as they were no longer truly self-governing if they were not aware of the facts of the situation. We can see now how veracity is a rule that is needed in order to ensure autonomy. But his participants lacked autonomy because of the deception. They thought they drew lots, they thought there was a learner, they thought there were electric shocks. They thought they were doing one thing and really they were doing something else. They were making decisions about their own actions based on faulty and misleading information.

If the central principle is the reaction of the participants when the deception is revealed, then the Milgram study should be all right; they were all very relieved when the deception was revealed! But it would still not get past ethical approval today. The focus of an ethics committee's reservations would be the undue stress that the participant experiences while being the Teacher and potentially the longer-term stress of knowing what they were prepared to do under duress. We all like to think that we would stand up for what we believe to be right, and that we could not be made to hurt another human being, especially when the pressure applied was only verbal, and in a non-contractual situation at that. The participants here had to live with the fact that they were prepared to administer electric shocks to another person, even while the other protested, and even after they appeared to lose consciousness. This is not a nice discovery to make about oneself.

But Milgram's participants in the follow-up study said that they were glad they had taken part. We should perhaps recall that this series of studies occurred in a less litigious time than now, when suing was not always the first recourse of the offended. But an ethics panel today would construe the experience of taking part as being too negative to permit the study to go ahead – despite what Milgram's participants said after the event.

So how central is the role of deception when it comes to making ethical decisions? Here are a couple of contrasting studies to help you decide.

Zimbardo's Prison Experiment

It has been suggested that one way that Milgram might have overcome the ethical dilemma inherent in his study would have been to brief the participants fully but ask them to role-play – that is, take the role of someone who does not know that the electric shocks are fake. This was a tactic adopted in another iconic study, Zimbardo's prison experiment, conducted in 1971 (see the up-to-date information on his website – Zimbardo, 1999–2005). He recruited volunteers for this study, and they were randomly allocated to be either a prisoner or a guard. Zimbardo's interest was in the interpersonal dynamics in a prison. (Some have called this a **field experiment** but this is not the case. The study was conducted in a mocked-up prison in the psychology department of Stanford University. A field experiment should be conducted in the natural setting in which the behaviour would occur – see the discussion of Piliavin *et al.* (1969) below. This was, rather, a **quasi-experiment** as there was no **control**). The programme was to run for two weeks but had to be stopped after only five days because the situation had deteriorated and gone out of control. The guards were becoming increasingly punitive and repressive and the prisoners were, by turns, hostile and distressed. For the welfare of all involved, the study was abandoned. It was a salutary lesson for all concerned, but there had been no deception, everyone knew what their role was in the study and everyone was fully informed when they agreed to take part. There have been criticisms of the ethics of this study, and Zimbardo himself has expressed concern about his own role in it. However, irrespective of the criticisms, there was at least no deception. (You can find more details of Zimbardo's study in any good general or social psychology textbook.)

Good Samaritanism: An Underground Phenomenon

Piliavin *et al.*, 1969

This study was designed to explore what factors affect the likelihood of a stranger coming to the rescue of someone apparently taken ill on the underground. One of the Experimenters would stage a silent collapse in the middle of a crowded tube train, while another monitored how long it took anyone to step forward to help – if indeed anyone did. As this took place in a real-world setting this is a classic example of a field experiment. It is an experiment and not an observational study because the researchers were manipulating the independent variable by staging the collapse. The study identified a number of factors that appeared to affect the response of other passengers. People responded more quickly if the person who collapsed appeared ill rather than drunk. The race of the collapsed person did not affect the race of the person who came to their aid unless they appeared to have collapsed through drink. The longer the period before someone came to this person's aid, the more likely it was that someone else would leave the immediate vicinity of the 'emergency'. The number of people in the carriage seemed to have no effect on response times.

Can you think of any method other than a field experiment which would produce this information?

This study involved deceit, but was it ethical? Did it put undue stress on those in the surrounding carriage? Thinking about the two studies, in which would you have preferred to take part? Would you prefer to be a prison guard and discover how cruel you can be? Or would you rather be a prisoner, with a clear conscience about your own behaviour but suffering at the hands of others? Or would you prefer to be travelling on the London underground and unwittingly be part of a study when some psychologist feigns a collapse? If you were, and you went to their help, you would probably never know that you had taken part in an experiment – the ultimate deceit – but would that have done you any harm? If you did not go to help the slumped figure, how would you feel later? Would you worry that you should have done? Would you vow to help another time? Or would you forswear travelling on the underground in order to avoid a repeat? In an underground train, there is no escape from a situation until the next stop. After all, if someone falls unconscious in the street you can always walk on pretending you have not seen!

This matter of deceit is not straightforward! Right and wrong are not that easy to ascertain.

What if we could find a way of replicating Milgram without using deceit? One way to remove deceit would be to run the study as Milgram did but to tell participants that they were not administering electric shocks. This would mean no cries or protests from the Learner. What would the results tell us? Probably not very much, as the situation would be so obviously artificial. What if we told everyone that it was a mock-up and used role play instead? I think we have seen the dangers of this clearly enough with Zimbardo's prison experiment. So how else could we repeat Milgram's work but stay within today's much more cautious and stringent ethical code? A group of researchers found a way to do this using twenty-first-century technology.

A Virtual Reprise of the Stanley Milgram Obedience Experiments

Slater, M., Antley, A., Davison, A., Swapp, D., Guger C., Barker, C., Pistrang, N. & Sanches-Vives, M.V. (2006) http://www.plosone.org/article/info:doi/10.1371/journal.pone.0000039

Slater *et al.* (2006) conducted what they termed a virtual reprise of Milgram's experiment. This involved using computer graphics projected onto a screen such that the Learner (a female) appeared to be on the other side of a partition and seen through a window. The participant, as Teacher, sat with the electric shock machine in front of him or her, and an Experimenter to the right. The task was the same as Milgram's. As the number of mistakes made by the 'Learner' over the 20 trials of the study increased, so the shock level given by the Teacher also had to rise. As in the original study the 'Learner' began to complain about the shocks, then protested that she had never agreed to this, then eventually slumped motionless, and did not respond to the final shock at all. Of course the crucial difference was that the participants knew that the 'Learner' was a computer-generated graphic, and that clearly neither she nor the shocks were real. In spite of this six of the 23 participants did not complete the trial and a further half-dozen said afterwards that they had wanted to withdraw. As well as monitoring the early withdrawal rates of the Teachers, the authors also took subjective (rating scales) and objective data from (physiological) measures of emotional arousal.

The authors point to the interesting dilemma that the Teachers experienced. They had agreed to take part in this study and indeed were paid for it, but they were faced with a virtual person who wanted the study to stop. The Teachers knew that they could withdraw at any time but, as the authors say, the 'objections to continuing were not from anyone real so why stop?' (2006, p.2).

This could, of course, suggest that human beings do not like to give electric shocks – even to a fictitious person. Alternatively it could mean that people do not like to be *seen* to be giving electrical shocks. Fortunately the research design addressed this issue directly by having a **control**. A further 11 participants took part in a study with the same requirements except that the 'Learner' was only visible for a brief introductory period. After the experiment began she was neither seen nor heard. All three measures, behavioural, subjective and objective, were compared between the Teachers in the two conditions and all three were **significant**ly different, with none of the participants in the control condition withdrawing early. Thus, without seeing the 'Learner' the Teachers did not seem to suffer the same emotional response.

The authors argue that they have shown that they have identified a method that allows for the continuation of Milgram's work (amongst that of others) because it does not raise the same ethical dilemmas. Interacting with the virtual person produces a similar type of emotional response as interacting with a human. They also argue that their 'Learner' was the most lifelike they could produce given the resources available to them, but that she was still obviously a computer-generated graphic. In time, it may be possible to make a virtual person that is truly indistinguishable from the real thing, but of course, as they point out, this takes us back to our original ethical problem with Milgram – because we must not forget that in both the original and the virtual study no one was actually hurt.

The ethical concerns focus on the participants' experience of administering shocks and what that experience does to them. And herein lies the crucial difference between the two experiments and the crux of the concern. For in both experiments the participants experienced discomfort and stress, as shown in behavioural and self-report measures. In the virtual version, physiological evidence is also available. But from an ethical perspective, the participants did not learn anything damaging about themselves. They may have learned that they had difficulty being cruel to a fictitious person. This does not have the same potential threat to their well-being and self-esteem as the discovery that they could obey an instruction to administer a lethal dose of electricity to another human being.

Conclusion

Identifying whether or not a study is ethically sound is a tricky business. Different types of study have different ethical dilemmas, but some issues may be common to all. To identify areas of potential problems it is a good idea to think through the study design. Are there going to be problems surrounding recruitment? Are there inclusion or exclusion criteria that might create a difficulty? Once recruited, will the experience of taking part present problems for the participants? Might your study be raising expectations which you are unable to meet? Will it put the researcher at risk? Do your participants need debriefing? If so, will telling them contaminate possible future participants? What about the data – how will they be stored, and for how long? Have you dealt with maintaining anonymity or confidentiality?

These days, studies are subject to scrutiny by ethics committees, which normally comprise researchers, professionals and lay people. Their task is no easy task, and they need always to be mindful of potentially the most risky outcome. They can call on the theories, the principles and the rules for guidance. As I have argued in this chapter, even with all these in your armoury there is no easy solution. If we had had ethical committees in the 1960s, we would not have had the studies of Milgram or Zimbardo. Would we have had the Piliavin *et al.* study?

We tend to think that right and wrong are easy to recognise, a black and white situation. In reality most of the colours seem to be varying shades of grey.

Obsessive Compulsive Disorder (OCD)

Experiment – A Randomised Controlled Trial

'Habit is habit, and not to be flung out of the window by any man, but coaxed downstairs a step at a time.' (Mark Twain, author, 1835–1910)

What Do You Know about Obsessive Compulsive Disorder (OCD)?

Have you ever had to go back up the path to the house to check that you have locked the front door even though you are fairly sure you have? There is just this little niggling worry that will not go away so you have to go back to check. Have you ever sat down to a meal and suddenly doubted whether you washed your hands first? Again you seem to recall doing so, but maybe that was yesterday. So, just in case, you get up and go wash your hands – again. At the airport, waiting for your holiday flight to be called, have you suddenly experienced doubt that you have brought your passport, or the tickets, although you made a particular point of leaving them somewhere that would prevent you forgetting? In which case, you just have to unpack your hand luggage and dig deep until you can grasp the desired objects in your hot little hand and your pulse and breathing return to normal. Doubts like these are commonplace and annoying, but we can resolve them by a trivial action that costs us little.

Do you have a lucky mascot, something you take into exams or clutch tightly while your team is playing a crucial match? Or perhaps you have lucky clothes, a scarf or boots, or even underwear that has always brought you good fortune in the past so you make sure you wear it when you really need that little extra boost of luck. Have you found yourself having to tell a lie but kept your fingers crossed behind your back to make it all right? Maybe there are things that you think are unlucky. Would you fly on Friday 13th? Would you walk under a ladder? Have you ever thrown salt over your shoulder to avert bad luck? Have you ever touched wood for the same reason? We do not really think that knocking on wood will bring us luck, but we do it anyway. It is as though we cannot help ourselves.

Some of us have customary patterns of behaviour that we stick to because it is comfortable to do so. Perhaps you always go to the post office *before* going to the supermarket on a Saturday, not for any particular reason, but just because you always have. Or maybe you always buy a take-away meal on a Friday, or wash the car at the weekend. Do you always listen to the same thing, for example the same radio programme, when you are getting up or going to work? We are certainly all creatures of habit and we often develop routines in our daily lives. Many of these routines are beneficial, they remove uncertainty and doubt and save time that it might take to make a choice. Many of them are neutral in effect, and it really would not matter whether we stuck with them or not. Rarely are they damaging in themselves.

All the above are examples of irrational behaviour; the behaviour is not based on reason or logic. Most of the time we know such behaviour is irrational, but that does not seem to stop us doing it. It is not abnormal in any way when it occurs occasionally. However, for people who suffer from a condition called Obsessive Compulsive Disorder, or OCD, their lives are beset, governed or even, in extreme cases, ruined by these types of thoughts and behaviours. The name of the condition refers to the fact that people with OCD have obsessive and unreasonable thoughts on which they feel compelled to act, often against their wishes. Unwanted thoughts or doubts occur frequently; they cannot be dismissed and the only, temporary, relief from them is to repeat some ritualised behaviour. For example, a very common problem in OCD is an ever-present fear of contamination, either through dirt or illness. When this is the case people will go to elaborate extremes to avoid the perceived risk. Not eating out may be a strategy, as may be repeated washing of cutlery. This can deteriorate into not being able to touch items that other people have touched without first washing them. Someone who has OCD is subject to repeated unwanted thoughts and compulsive routines, all the time underpinned by a sustained raised level of anxiety; they seem to be imprisoned by their condition. OCD belongs to a category of disorders known as anxiety disorders.

What Are the Causes and Cures?

There is some evidence that indicates that OCD can be associated with a traumatic brain injury, which suggests that there is a physiological rather than psychological basis for the condition. However there is also evidence that a stressful event in either one's personal or professional life can trigger it. Therefore its aetiology (its cause or origin) is still unproven. The onset is usually gradual, but the problem is that it tends to become more extreme over time. It seems that the constant process of doubting becomes embedded and in itself reduces confidence, thereby increasing the probability of further doubt. It could be that sufferers have trouble remembering, or have less confidence in their memories, or it may be that they have difficulty distinguishing between memories of real or imagined actions.

People who present to their doctors with OCD may be offered either drug or psychological therapies. A range of psychological therapies has been used in the treatment of OCD to greater or lesser effect, and it is beyond the scope of this chapter to discuss all of these. (The interested reader is referred to any basic psychology text or, for greater detail, a review article such as Math & Janardhan Reddy, 2007.) One type of therapy that has been shown to be effective for this condition is behavioural therapy which is based on training behavioural responses. The premise is that the ritualised behaviours are a learned response to anxiety and doubt, a response which in itself increases the underlying problem. Breaking into this cycle by teaching alternative responses moves the patient towards recovery. One particular type of effective behavioural therapy delights in the snappy name of behavioural exposure therapy with ritual prevention, shortened, thankfully, to ERP. It involves two phases of therapy: preparation and treatment. In preparation the individual is encouraged to identify those triggers that cause her/him problems (e.g. shaking hands or eating out) and to rate how much discomfort each causes. The treatment programme allows the individual to develop their own programme for exposure to these triggers with the goal of overcoming the ritualised response. In short the therapy works by breaking down the larger condition into its components parts, making these into small, manageable challenges and keeping the patient in the driving seat throughout.

This therapy works well because the patient can tailor it to his or her own needs. However the nature of the condition and of the therapy allows a standardised approach, so much so that it has been possible to develop this therapy as a series of computer-based sessions. It may seem a little odd to think of a computer as a therapist; nonetheless, it is effective. This is fortunate, as demand for this type of therapy exceeds the supply of trained therapists. The original computerised version used a keyboard and screen, but now it is possible to access by telephone from the patient's own home. This means that it is available to patients across the UK and not just those living near a clinic that offers the appropriate therapy.

This system is called Behavioural Therapy (BT) Steps, and it allows sufferers to tap into a computerised interview through their own telephone. The aim of BTSteps, like all ERP, is to help people deal with their compulsions and obsessive thoughts. It seems a little unlikely, doesn't it? We have all experienced raised anxiety levels from dealing with computerised telephone systems at one time or another! We know that this particular initiative is effective because it reduces the number of ritual behaviours. In fact, the effects are similar to those achieved through ERP sessions with a trained therapist. How do we know this? Because it has been demonstrated through a method called **randomised controlled trials** (see Box 3.1) which are generally considered the gold standard in research.

In these initial RCTs, to test the efficacy of the telephone systems the new version of the therapy (by telephone) was the experimental condition and the control condition was the standard therapy. This is worth noting, because we might normally expect that participants in the control condition received no intervention. In this area, such a design would be unethical, as it would deliberately refuse treatment to a group of patients. It is not uncommon in RCTs for the control group to experience a treatment. This all hinges on what it is you wish to compare. Do you want to see whether the telephone is better than nothing? In that case the control group would

Randomised Controlled Trials (RCTs)

This method of research was principally developed in **clinical trials**. It is now used to evaluate the effectiveness of any form of treatment or **intervention**. One of the two key features of an RCT is that there is a **control condition** as well as at least one **experimental condition**. The second feature is that **participants** are **random**ly assigned to one of the conditions. RCTs normally have an **unrelated design**, with different people in the different conditions.

There is an inherent problem with RCTs as an assessment as it means assigning some people to a control condition. This has ethical dilemmas, as it would be inappropriate to provide no treatment to one subset of patients. This is can be overcome by using as a control those on a waiting list, then assigning them to the active treatment after the trial is over; this means that they receive the therapy sooner than if they had not taken part.

be offered no support (as identified, this has ethical problems). Or do you want to see if the telephone intervention is as effective as the personal one? It was the latter that Kenwright *et al.* (2005) wished to test.

What Is the BTSteps Programme?

Patients can be given access to this programme from anywhere in the UK. They use a manual and an interactive voice-response computer system, accessed through their telephone. There are nine steps in the programme: the first three concern education and self-assessment; the remaining steps guide the patient through regular daily self-exposure to the particular triggers that prompt their own obsessive compulsive response. After facing a trigger they undertake a set activity that lasts at least one hour until the desire to respond in the ritualised manner fades and becomes manageable. As with a therapist, this programme enables users to identify their own particular triggers for rituals and obsessions, such that each programme then becomes tailored to the individual's needs. Patients also develop, with the aid of the programme, their own 'homework' (exercises designed to reduce their OCD response) which they are to use during their one-hour periods of non-response.

If this computerised telephone intervention is effective what sort of support should be offered along with it? What would maximise its therapeutic value? In earlier studies, patients had visited a clinic on several occasions during the trial. Making the treatment available nationwide made this impractical. The researchers wanted to

know whether it was in fact the best way of providing support. Would a regular schedule of calls enquiring about progress be effective? Or would it be better to allow the patients to decide when to make the calls? This is the question that Kenwright *et al.* (2005) set out to answer.

Brief Scheduled 'Phone Support from a Clinician to Enhance Computer-Aided Self-Help for Obsessive Compulsive Disorder: Randomized Controlled Trial

Kenwright, M., Marks, I., Graham, C., Franses, A. & Mataix-Cols, D. (2005). *Journal of Clinical Psychology, 61*(12), 1499–1508

Method

Kenwright *et al.* used a randomised controlled trial to compare the effect of regular telephone calls with patient-instigated calls. Before the study began, the relevant ethics committees gave their approval for the study design. This is standard practice now for all research involving humans or animals. Patients were initially referred to this system by a health professional. They then went through a screening procedure over the phone to assess their suitability for this trial. All 44 suitable patients were given 17 weeks' unlimited access to the BTSteps programme. They could call this programme at any time of any day, without incurring call charges. They were **randomly** assigned to one of two conditions; the authors refer to these two conditions as Scheduled and Requested. In Scheduled, patients received a series of nine therapist-initiated phone calls during office hours, at regular and scheduled intervals throughout the trial. In Requested, patients were allowed to call the therapist when they wanted at any point in the trial, also during office hours; they could make as many phone calls as they wished. The therapist was the same individual in both conditions.

Therefore, this RCT used a **between groups** design to compare two conditions. Because it was between groups, this was an unrelated or **independent groups** design. In an unrelated design such as this it is common for the two groups to a have slightly different number of participants. The **independent variable** (**IV**) was the type of phone call. The **dependent variable** (**DV**) was the therapeutic outcome, which was **operationalised** using two **outcome variables**: by programme completion rates, and by **psychometric** measures designed to assess the extent of their disorder.

Results

Of the 44 who started the trial, 26 completed all stages of the programme. However, the telling point is where the drop-outs occurred: three were from the Scheduled condition, while 13 were from the Requested. A **Fisher's exact probability** test showed that this difference in **drop-out rates** was **significant**. From the psychometric tests it was evident that both groups showed a reduction on the Compulsions scale, but the Scheduled group, unlike the Requested group, also showed a reduction on the Obsessions scale. To test whether this was significant they used an **ANOVA**, which is an **inferential statistic** that can examine the effect of more than one variable at a time. In this instance the ANOVA was used to assess how the measures differed over time and between the groups. It confirmed that the Scheduled group alone also showed a significant reduction on the Obsessions scale. These findings indicate that the Scheduled calls were a better method for keeping people in the therapy and also made the therapy more effective.

■ How Safe Is This Conclusion?

On the face of it, this seems like a straightforward study; all patients had access to the same therapy. The only difference between the groups was the independent variable: the type of telephone support they received. Therefore it seems reasonable to argue that a difference in outcome between the groups is attributable to the independent variable, unless, of course, the two groups were in some way different at the start of the study. The participants were randomly assigned, which is generally taken to reduce such pre-existing group differences. It does not, however, offer a guarantee of this. It merely ensures that any such characteristics are distributed by chance rather than producing a **systematic** or **confounding error**. Even by chance, it is still possible that the two groups were different, which could have produced a **Type I error**. The study design took account of this possibility; all the participants completed the psychometric measures at the start as well as at the end of the **trial**, meaning that the outcome measure was change over time. This controls for any chance group differences.

What Else Could Have Caused This Change?

As the authors point out, the mechanism behind this effect is unclear. We cannot tell whether it was the *content* of the scheduled calls that made the difference, or their *regularity*. A regular schedule provides a framework for the participants. This is much the same principle as lies behind groups such as weight-watchers: the regular weekly weigh-in provides an incentive to keep members on track. We have noted that the only difference between the groups was the type of phone call, but a phone call between two human beings is not itself standardised. Think about the last two calls you made to friends – did you say the same thing each time? Probably not, and likewise the content of the calls in this study must have differed too. In the first place, you might expect that the number of phone calls between the two groups would differ, and indeed they did. The duration of the average call was not very different between the groups, 13 minutes for Scheduled and 11 for Requested. The difference lay in the average number of calls made, which was 7.5 for Scheduled compared with only 1.5 for Requested. This meant that the participants in the Scheduled group received on average a total of 76 minutes of telephone support compared to the Requested, who received 16. Could this have made the difference? It is certainly possible that the extra time on the telephone would have contributed to the difference in outcome. But the amount of time was itself a function of the design. There are two possible underlying mechanisms that might be responsible:

Regular calls > change
Regular calls > more talk > change

Can you think how you might design a study to determine which mechanism makes the difference?

The important thing to recall here is that the greater amount of telephone time lay with the group who did not initiate the phone calls. It might have been expected that those who were free to call as often as they wanted would have used more of the service than their counterparts. As it turns out, the reverse was the case.

We noted also that the completion rate was higher amongst the Scheduled group than the Requested. We would expect that someone who completes a course of therapy would benefit more than someone who drops out. So could this be a mediating variable? Could regular calls keep people in the trial? If this were the case then again we can see two possible mechanisms to effect the change:

Regular calls > change
Regular calls > tendency to complete > change

Whatever the mechanism, it is the schedule that has triggered the difference, either directly or indirectly.

● How Effective Is the Experimental Design?

Although psychological disorders are complex problems, this was a straightforward study. It was a randomised controlled trial of a new intervention, scheduled telephone calls. In order to limit the impact of individual variation participants were randomly assigned to conditions. Even with a **randomisation protocol**, it may not be all plain sailing. It cannot guarantee that the two groups are comparable. Theoretically they should be. The randomisation process should mean that individual differences are distributed across the two groups. It is a matter of **probability** (see Key Topics). There is a high probability that the two groups will be comparable. But there is always the possibility that they might not be.

This study did not rely on the randomisation process alone. For one thing, the researchers also took a **baseline measurement**. This means that the outcome variable was not just how bad the OCD was at the end of the trial, but how much it had changed since the start. A second precaution was to reduce the potential amount of individual variation at the start. It is difficult to show an effect with a very diverse set of participants – i.e. there could have been a **Type II error**. For example, there could be one or two individuals whose condition was either more complex or less severe than the rest. This would mean greater individual variability in outcome, which could obscure the treatment difference. Therefore, it is wise to ensure that the participants are comparable at the start. For this study, there were clear **inclusion criteria**. To become part of the trial, participants had had a diagnosis of OCD for at least two years. (Doctors and psychologists make this diagnosis using the definition in the standard text on disorders: the *Diagnostic and Statistical Manual of Mental Disorders*.) Patients also had to be free from other mental disorders, as this could have confounded results. Moreover only patients who were not involved in alcohol or drug abuse were able to enter the trial. Patients already taking medication for their condition continued on a stable dose throughout the trial. Therefore, all the patients were in an equivalent or at least comparable state at the start of the study. It is best to avoid words such as 'equal' or 'the same', as we really cannot be sure.

We have noted that completion of the trial is associated with successful outcome. Could it be that the people in the Scheduled group were somehow more inclined to persevere than those in the other group? While this is theoretically possible, it is relatively improbable because of the randomisation process.

How Do You Randomise?

As we can see, quite a lot hinges on this randomisation process, but how is it done? There are a number of recognised ways to randomise participants to groups or conditions. It is possible to use a computer program to allocate people to groups, but an older and simpler way is to use a table of random numbers. These can be found in many statistical textbooks. Or random numbers can be generated using a computer spreadsheet program (e.g. Excel). If there are only two groups or conditions, then the simplest way is to allocate all even numbers to one condition, and all odd numbers to the other.

An alternative to randomisation is to use a systematic allocation, for example alternating between one group and another. This is not quite as effective, because the regularity of the process may allow a small bias to creep in, although this is unlikely. Both methods, however, are considerably better than the alternatives. For example assigning the first half of the sample to one group means that the groups might differ as later recruits might have different characteristics. Letting the decision be made by the researcher is open to all sorts of unintentional biases. Allowing participants to choose their group is inviting disaster, as the very characteristic that affects their choice will affect the outcome!

Kenwright and his colleagues used a table of random numbers to assign patient numbers in the trial. Before the trial began, they put each number into an envelope, sealed it and then shuffled the envelopes. As each new participant entered the trial, they opened the envelope at the front to read to which group s/he was allocated. This means that allocation of patient number to condition was made before the study began. It also means that the researchers did not know the order until each new person was recruited.

▲ How Appropriate Was the Research Method?

As has been noted, we tend to think of RCTs as the gold standard of research. The aim of the study was to compare **between conditions**, but the design employed **independent subjects** and the researchers randomly assigned patients to one of the two trial conditions. (You might like to contrast this with the between conditions comparison that is discussed in Chapter 5.) But were there any viable alternatives? Certainly an unrelated design without randomisation would not have been advisable, as we have seen. Is there a related design that would work?

Repeated measures design would not have made sense in this context. The intervention that is the therapy is designed to help reduce the abnormal behaviours and thoughts associated with OCD. Repeated measures designs need **counterbalancing**, otherwise there are going to be problems with **order effects**. This means that some people have Treatment A first and others have Treatment B and then this is reversed. If their first treatment is effective, why would anyone go through a second treatment? And if they are all better at the end of the trial was it Treatment A or Treatment B that did the trick? Or a combination of the two? Or just time itself? It is very hard to unpick the possible cause and effect here, so repeated measures are rarely suitable for studies involving therapies. (See Chapter 5 for details of a repeated measures design.)

A **matched pairs design** might have been a possibility here. The advantage of a matched pairs design is that it reduces individual variability. Variability is always a problem in research with humans and can mask true effects causing a Type II error. The problem with a matched pairs design is identifying the variables on which we should make the match. It is possible that we could match by symptoms, by severity, by duration or by type. The difficulty then is finding matched pairs of people with this disorder, which would be time-consuming and would make recruitment very challenging. It might also involve rejecting patients the researchers are unable to match. (See Chapter 4 for an example of a matched pairs design.)

Would a **single group design** have worked here? The problem with a single group is that all you can compare it with is the baseline measure. A true single group design would mean you could only test the effect of one of these types of treatment at a time and that would clearly not be very satisfactory. If your single group experiences both types of treatment then the design is no longer single group but repeated measures. However, there are some occasions where a single group design is satisfactory. (For an example, see Chapter 6.)

In this study, a treatment effect was evident even with this independent subjects or unrelated design. It would seem therefore that this RCT was the most appropriate experimental method for this study.

What about other ways of exploring this problem? There are two other broad **empirical methods**: **surveys** and **observation**. Surveys include **questionnaires, interviews** and psychometric assessments. Questionnaires or interviews could have been used to ask patients what sort of telephone support they would like to go with the BTSteps programme. This would provide useful data on stated preferences. As with all such self-report measures, the data these measures provide reflect the beliefs and responses of the individuals. Applied to the BTSteps programme, people might think that they prefer open access to a therapist for support. Alternatively they may believe that a scheduled course of phone calls would be better. Survey methods tell us what people think, what people believe. They can tell us more about the experience of OCD. For example, Wu and Carter (2008) have tested the psychometric properties of a questionnaire designed to assess the symptomatic beliefs of people with this disorder.

However, this study was designed to find out what works as treatment. The researchers wanted to know which type of telephone call was the most effective. Efficacy and preferences are two different things! To evaluate a treatment, survey methods alone will not tell us much. In this study, of course, they did use a psychometric tool to measure the level of obsessions and compulsions. In that way, survey methods were deployed as part of the outcome variable. The dependent variable, psychological health, was operationalised as scores on the Obsessive and Compulsive Scale (as well as completion of treatment programme). Using a survey method to measure a dependent variable does not turn an experiment into a survey.

Finally, could we find a way to use observation for this type of study? **Case studies** can be useful in this context, for example Patel *et al.* (2007). They report the case of an individual with OCD who refused both medication and this type of behavioural therapy but responded well to another psychological therapy, a cognitive therapy to help manage stress. The use of **structured observation** is, perhaps, harder to see in this context. It might allow us to see how patients with OCD behave, probably only in a clinical setting rather than in their own homes. We could observe how they cope with a treatment that it routinely provided. This will be of relatively limited usefulness as we would have nothing with which to compare it. This would mean that we could not really evaluate its effectiveness in comparison with other treatments, or even just over time. Some conditions are self-limiting and improve over time without intervention. Of course, we could make a comparison if we observed two different types of treatment. There are problems here though. If we observe the two treatments in different clinics, there are far too many other variables that will differ between the clinics and which might affect outcome. If we use just one therapist in one clinic and get him or her to alternate the treatment, then our observations might tell us something useful. But what has happened to the study then? It is no longer an observational study but an experiment because we have persuaded our therapist to manipulate the independent variable for us!

It could be argued that the other outcome measure from this study used observation, as the authors observed how many of the participants completed the treatment programme. As with the psychometric tools, using a technique for data collection does not alter the design of the study.

This was clearly an experiment as there was an independent variable that was manipulated between conditions. You will usually find that the only useful and practical way to test the efficacy of a treatment is through experimentation.

Conclusion

This is what we may consider a standard piece of psychological research. The subject matter is psychological disorders, and many think that this is what constitutes the subject matter of psychology as a whole. However, this is not the case. Psychology has a very diverse subject matter and is mostly concerned with understanding people and behaviour in everyday settings. The branch of psychology to do with disorders has a variety of names: psychopathology, abnormal psychology, clinical psychology. A relatively small number of psychologists work within this field. Even amongst chartered psychologists in the UK,[1] only 37 per cent are clinical.

What makes the study a standard piece of research is its design. There is one IV that we wish to test, (type of phone support) and there are just two conditions in that IV (Scheduled and Requested). We randomly assign our participants to one of these two conditions. We measure them before we start the intervention, then again when it is finished. We have a clear outcome measure and we want to see whether the two groups respond differently to the IV. Because no prediction was made prior to the study to state which condition would be preferable, the researchers were testing a **two-tailed** or **non-directional hypothesis**, i.e. seeing which of the two, if either, is more effective. If they had predicted that the scheduled calls would have worked better, it would have been a **one-tailed** or **directional hypothesis**.

The design chosen by Kenwright and colleagues allows us to see a marked difference between the groups. The authors compare their findings with those from previous studies and demonstrate that for the Scheduled group the intervention was as effective as being seen by a trained therapist.

The approach enabled patients in remote areas to access effective help by phone, help that they would probably have otherwise forgone (Kenwright *et al.*, 2005, p.1507).

Note

1   The title Chartered Psychologist is legally recognised, and before admission to the Register individuals must:

- have a recognised first degree in psychology;
- have recognised postgraduate qualifications, or have undergone approved postgraduate training and supervision;
- have been judged 'fit to practise' independently; and
- have agreed to follow a strict Code of Conduct and be answerable to a disciplinary system, in which non-psychologists form the majority.

This is very much a practitioner role. Many professional psychologists are academics who are not required to be chartered.

Summary Points	
Design	Experiment – randomised controlled trial (unrelated, between conditions)
Aim	To compare two conditions
IV	Type of telephone support
DV	Psychological health (improvement in OCD symptoms). Operationalised as scores on obsessive – compulsive scale and completion of the course of therapy.
Sample	44 GP-referred patients with OCD
Analysis	Between groups, changes from baseline

Music and Stress

Experiment – A Matched Pairs Design

'When I hear music, I fear no danger. I am invulnerable. I see no foe. I am related to the earliest times, and to the latest.' (Henry David Thoreau, essayist, poet and philosopher, 1817–62)

When Are You Stressed?

Stress is said to be part of modern living. We become stressed at many different types of events. We get stressed sitting in traffic jams, we get stressed by bills, and we get stressed by work. Some people get stressed listening to party political broadcasts. We say we are stressed when we worry about our relationships; we may even claim to be stressed by not having the right clothes to wear for a night out. These are typical of the stressors of our modern lives. Stress is always an unpleasant experience but it is also a natural one. The stress response is one that we have acquired through the evolutionary process as a positive and helpful survival mechanism. Maybe your experience of stress is neither positive nor helpful – but without this handy little human reaction, none of us would be around!

The stress response produces physiological changes in the body. What happens is that our bodies concentrate on vital life signs and shut down on non-essential systems. This means that our heart rate goes up, our blood pressure goes up and our respiratory rate increases. Meanwhile, processes that can be delayed without detriment, such as digestion, are effectively put on hold. This concentration of effort means that blood flow to the limbs is increased and the body is primed for either a fight or a flight. With increased oxygen flowing around in our circulation we are better able to take on an adversary, or to run like crazy to escape one. When our ancestors came face to face with a sabre-toothed tiger, what they needed was to make a speedy exit. The stress response provided them with a burst of maximum speed. Thus the stress response has proven very useful for the human species – convinced yet?

The trouble with our 'stressful modern lives' is that we tend to invoke the stress response for events other than escaping ferocious animals. The potential 'stressors' listed in the opening paragraph are for the most part neutral events; that means they do not cause us actual harm. Furthermore, fight or flight is not really a useful response. We may wish to flee from the electricity bill, but those of us who have tried this have found that it is not a useful survival strategy. So when we complain about our stress levels, it is much more to do with our perception of events than the events themselves. It is only our particular response to them that makes them stressors. In these cases, stress, like beauty, is in the mind of the beholder. This can be a useful thing to remember when you are stuck in a traffic jam on your way to an important meeting. There is nothing you can do to change the fact that you are going to be late; clinging to the steering wheel, drumming your fingers, muttering 'come on, you idiots' through gritted teeth (let alone leaning on the horn), does not change the situation that you are in one bit – but it does distress your body. You have no control over the traffic, but you can control your response to it. You may as well sit back, turn the radio to something that interests you, and accept that being late is not the end of the world and is, in fact, whole heaps better than being eaten by a sabre-toothed tiger.

Incidentally, another key aspect of the stress response is that its evolutionary function meant that it was a designed to be temporary, to enable an immediate but short-lived state. If we allow ourselves to live a life of sustained stress, it puts a prolonged strain on our bodies, which are not designed to cope with this level of central activity – hence the proliferation of stress-related health problems in contemporary industrialised culture.

The stimuli in the environment that we perceive as stressors can be many and varied. We worry about events that have happened, events that are happening and also events that have yet to occur. For example, worrying about examinations: some people feel a lurch of the stomach at the sound of the word 'exam'. Some of us get stressed about going to the dentist, taking driving tests, making a speech. Many brides and grooms view their forthcoming wedding as a stressor, an occasion which should, by all accounts, be a cause for celebration. Some of us even get stressed about going on holiday: will I be ready to go? Will I have made adequate provision for my absence? What will the journey be like? What will the destination be like? Because of the diversity of human nature, for the most part, different people find different things stressful.

There is one thing that is commonly perceived as a stressor by nearly everyone, and that is going into hospital. While many might enjoy a spell away from home, a change from the routine and the humdrum, somehow a hospital stay does not qualify for pleasurable anticipation in quite the same way as a fortnight in the sun or a trip to a snowy ski resort. We tend not to like this particular change for many reasons. To start with we are in an unfamiliar environment, a stressor in itself. We lose some of our autonomy and independence; we can no longer behave as we wish, doing what we want when we want. There are limitations over whom we see and when. There can be an awful lot of waiting around, waiting for others do to things. We have to wear garments that we would not wish anyone to see us wear. The facilities in hospital may not provide the same level of comfort as home – and let's not even think about the food. As if all these indignities were not bad enough, we tend to be ill as well. A hospital stay is therefore rarely seen as a highlight and is generally seen to be stressful.

If a spell in hospital were not stressful enough, sometimes hospitalisation includes surgery, an unpleasant necessity and very much an added stressor. Waiting to be collected from the ward to be taken down to the operating theatre can be very stressful. This stress or anxiety may be fuelled by the passive nature of our role in the coming event, by the visualisation of what is going to be done to us. We may also be concerned about the outcome: will the surgery be successful? Some may even worry about the possibility of awareness under anaesthesia too. Anxiety seems to peak as the patient is taken to the preoperative holding area, a sterile and impersonal environment. In fact, if you are looking for situations that are likely to induce the stress response, look no further than this! It makes other potential stressors, examinations, making speeches, visits to the dentist, whatever, pale into insignificance.

Unfortunately there is an added problem here. The bodily effects of the stress response are not optimal for surgery, and may even have a detrimental effect on the outcome. People who experience high levels of preoperative stress have a slower recovery rate after surgery. This is one of the reasons that patients are often given 'premedication', a sedative drug designed to relax them. This is not just to reduce the anxiety, but is intended to minimise the physiological stress response too. While premeds are useful, the number of anaesthetic drugs now available means that caution needs to be exercised in the use of premedications to ensure inter-drug compatibility. What if there was another way that we could reduce the level of preoperative anxiety in patients, a way that did not involve an addition to the cocktail of drugs used during surgical procedures? It seems that there may be another way, less invasive and intuitively appealing: music.

The sedative effect of music used preoperatively has already been seen in studies dating back to the 1980s. The justification for more research is sound, based on two reasons. The first is that many previous studies had methodological flaws (a commonly cited rationale for further investigation), in particular, in this case, relating to the sample. In some instances all the patients had been experiencing the same type of surgery, which means that **generalising** from the findings is problematic. The ability to generalise findings across differing situations is a keystone of all good **positivist** research. For example, if music relieves anxiety in patients awaiting hand surgery, will it also work for patients awaiting foot surgery? In other instances, where patients from more than one surgical speciality were included, there was no clear matching of the two groups, experimental (i.e. with music) and control (i.e. no music). This is an instance where a **matched pairs design** is indicated (see Box 4.1).

The second reason for undertaking further research was cultural. In the following study, the researchers are based in Hong Kong and all the participants are Chinese. They argue that musical tastes are culturally determined and that therefore evidence about Western responses may not apply equally to a Chinese population (as discussed

Matched Pairs Design

This design means that for each individual entered into one condition in the study there is an equivalent identified individual entered into the other condition. The notion of equivalence here is central to the matched pairs design. What constitutes equivalence has to be determined by the experimental question. The task is to identify relevant **variables** that are likely to have an impact on the behaviour under study. For example in a study involving reading ability in 5-year-olds, the variables that might need to be matched could be: sex, age in months, socio-economic class and family position. If a study was exploring response to high-calorie foods, as well as being matched on **demographic variables**, **participant**s might also be matched on body mass index.

The more variables that are included in the match, the better the match and the more similar are the paired individuals. However, as you can probably envisage, when the number of variables used in the matching process increases, the complexity of the design likewise increases. This, in turn, has an effect on recruitment. If we want to match by sex, age and domicile, for instance, then for every 20-year-old female from Hampshire we recruit into one condition, we need another for her matched pair in the second condition. How much flexibility would be acceptable here? For example would a 21-year-old from Sussex be a good enough match? These types of issues need to be resolved before the study begins; the matching criteria must be clearly stipulated. For this reason, the matched pairs design is often a difficult study design to put into practice and is not as commonly used as **repeated measures** or **randomised controlled trials** (RCTs).

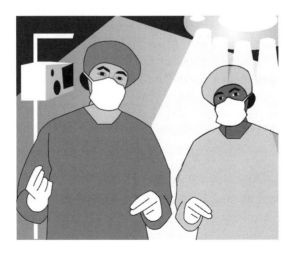

in Chapter 7). For a more detailed consideration of **cross-cultural** issues see Chapter 19. The **aim** of this study by Yung, Kam, Lau and Chan (2003) was to test the efficacy of music as a preoperative stress-reduction technique in a Chinese sample in a controlled **trial**.

The Effect of Music in Managing Preoperative Stress for Chinese Surgical Patients in the Operating Room Holding Area: A Controlled Trial

Yung, P.M.B., Kam, S.C., Lau, B.W.K. & Chan, T.M.F. (2003). *International Journal of Stress Management, 10*(1), 64–74

Method

Yung and colleagues used a matched pairs design where the key variable on which all participants were matched was the type of surgery they were to undergo. There were five types of abdominal surgery: hernia repair, gall bladder removal, prostate resection and two different types of operation on the bladder. Inclusion criteria for this study stipulated no cardiac or respiratory problems, no auditory impairments, no preoperative sedation and the ability to understand written and spoken instructions. There were 82 patients assessed to take part in this study, of whom 66 met the entry criteria; all of these took part in the study.

Stress was to be measured by taking blood pressure and monitoring the heartbeat and rate of respiration (breathing), and by the completion of an anxiety scale. A **psychometric** instrument was designed for this purpose. On arriving in the holding area adjacent to theatre, each patient's physiological measurements were taken and each completed the anxiety scale; this first measure is known as **T1** (Time 1). Between these measures, patients in the experimental condition listened to music through earphones. These participants had an element of choice about the music they would hear, but it was not an entirely free choice. A totally free choice might have been impractical to offer, and there was always the possibility that some might select music to change their mood in another way than to relax them. Three options were available to them, based on selections made by panel of three music instructors. All of the music was slow with minimal rhythmic characteristics, and was intended to relax. As there are cultural differences in music, one option was a Chinese instrumental, one a Western instrumental and the third a mixture of songs in Chinese and English. The songs were the most popular choice, being selected by 80 per cent of the sample; the remaining participants were evenly divided between the two instrumentals. After 20 minutes, still prior to surgery, all four measures were taken again (**T2**, or time 2).

As this was a matched pairs study, it means it was a **related design**, that is, for each person in one condition there was an identified individual in the other condition as an equivalent. Therefore in this type of design the two groups will always be the same size. The **independent variable** (**IV**) in this study is the presence of music: one group with, the other without. The **dependent variable** (**DV**) in this study is the level of anxiety, and this was **operationalised** using four **outcome variables**: three physiological measures (blood pressure, heart rate and respiration rate) and one psychometric measure.

Results

The authors reported **descriptive statistics** including the **means** and **standard deviations** for each group. **Means** (averages) tell us something about the midpoint of a data set and are known as a measurement of **central tendency**. Standard deviations tell us how much those data are spread around that midpoint and are a measurement of **dispersion**. From means we can see general trends within a group.

On all four measures the means for the music group showed drops from the **baseline measurement**, while none of the measures for the control group showed this drop. (The authors do not report whether the type of music chosen affected responses; as two of the three options were selected by only 20 per cent of the sample, the numbers in these groups would have made analysis impractical.) Statistical analysis using **analysis of covariance** showed that there was evidence of a significant reduction in three of the four measures for the experimental group compared to the control. Only respiration rates were not significantly different between the two groups. Therefore the study provides ample evidence that music can produce a relaxing effect in Chinese patients; the effect is not restricted to Western cultures. The authors suggest that the use of music should be considered for stress reduction throughout the perioperative period, although they acknowledge that there are times when this will be impractical.

■ How Safe Is This Conclusion?

The authors selected their design as a result of perceived inadequacies in past research, so does their research stand up to scrutiny? The design is robust, the matched pairs with a **pre-/post-design** provides a firm foundation for hypothesis testing. Note the difference here between this and a repeated measures design. You may think: but they took the measures twice, why isn't that repeated measures? However, the difference between pre-/post-design and repeated measures is crucial. In a pre-/post-design like this the first measure is the baseline, i.e. *before* the experiment starts, *before* the manipulation of the IV. In contrast a repeated measures design means that a measure is taken from each person in each condition, i.e. each measure occurs once the experiment is under way (see Box 5.1). We need a pre-/post-design to see whether our IV produces any change. We can only recognise change if we know how things were before, so we need a baseline measure. This is because human beings are so variable. In this instance, for example, not everyone would have been experiencing the same amount of stress before the music was played. It is reasonable to assume that they were all stressed to some extent given that they were waiting for surgery, but the extent of stress will have varied across the sample. Providing that the participants have been **random**ly assigned to condition then there should be no **systematic error** or **bias** in the data. Random assignment means that any differences found in baseline measures would have occurred just by chance.

What Else Could Explain the Group Difference?

There is one other possible interpretation of the authors' findings, and that has to do with control. It has been established since Glass and Singer (1972) that the experience of stress is heightened by lack of control over the situation. Remember, they were played the music they had chosen. It could well be that those participants who were assigned to the music group felt that they had some element of control over their environment. It may have been this perception of control that reduced the stress, especially in contrast to the others, who presumably knew that they might be played the music of their choice, but then found they were not. This in itself could have contributed to sustained levels of anxiety. The authors point out that their lack of a 'placebo' group is a weakness in the study design. We have to acknowledge therefore that the music itself may not have been the sole cause of the detected relaxation. But does that matter? It can be argued that it is not that important. The authors have found a way of reducing the stress levels in patients prior to surgery. Whether that is the effect of being played music or of being played music that you have chosen is of less practical importance than significance.

From a theoretical point of view, the true cause and effect could be untangled by a series of further studies. It would be possible to compare the effects of compulsory music with optional music. If it is the music that makes a difference then providing it for all should reduce stress for every patient. If it is the element of control, then the options offered could be changed, for example slow songs, an audio book of a short story, or silence. It is remotely possible that being given earphones alone was in some way effective, by simply masking the ears; it would certainly be easy to tease this out in another study. This is evidently a rich area for future research projects.

The authors note that their participants are all volunteers – as would be expected from an ethical perspective. However, it is possible that those most likely to be prepared to sign up for such a study would be those who might like to listen to music anyway. Therefore would such an **intervention** be as effective if offered across the board to all preoperative patients? They also note that amongst the limitations of their study is the fact that it occurred in a single hospital, and clearly needs further investigation in a wider number of establishments. If this study is replicated with a placebo group who are not consulted about musical choice, then they have found a cost-effective way of reducing anxiety without drugs at a critical time in the patient career.

How Comparable Are the Matched Pairs?

This may seem like an odd question given that it was a matched pairs design which is intended to match the groups on an individual-by-individual basis. However, the only variable in this study that was used for matching was the type of surgery.

Are there other variables that could or should have been included in the matching process? There are other variables that are likely to affect the outcome – for example, sex, age, previous experience of surgery – yet these were not matched. Does this mean that we should be cautious about the findings? It is actually exceedingly difficult to match a sample accurately on a variety of different criteria. It would mean that for example every time you recruit a 49-year-old who is having his gall bladder removed and has no previous experience of surgery you need to find another exact match for the other group. A 49-year-old male with surgical experience will not do, nor will a 49-year-old female with no experience. Participant recruitment can therefore be unrealistically slow, extending the study over so long a period that it is impractical to complete. Furthermore other relevant factors may change in the surrounding environment (e.g. changes in personnel, technology or even decor), any of which may act as **confounding variables**.

If matching on all critical variables is impractical there is an alternative, and that is to control for them, which is what the authors did. All their participants were male, thereby eliminating one potential source of variability. Of course, this also has implications for generalising from the results. There is no reason to assume that females would respond to music differently from males. Nonetheless it would be wise to exercise caution in interpretation until such time as the study is repeated with a female sample. Moreover recruitment was restricted to men who had at least one prior experience of surgery, thus reducing another potential element of variation in the sample. The authors did not attempt to control for the number or recency of past surgical experiences, but again this might have been impractical. As for age, recruitment was restricted to men between the ages of 50 and 80, although that in itself is quite a wide band. The mean ages of the participants are given in the paper, broken down by surgery type. Although there appears to be one very young participant in the control group, the overall mean ages are very similar, less than five months apart. The age restrictions and the past surgical experience both indicate that the study should be replicated but with a wider age group and with people new to surgery.

We can conclude that, by controlling for some variables and accounting for others, it would seem that the two groups were reasonably, if not perfectly, comparable.

Can you think of a viable and practical way of improving the comparability of the two groups?

● How Effective Is This Experimental Design?

Given the way that the authors have tackled these basic sources of variability, this is a straightforward repeated measures design. We must not overlook the matter of how each pair was allocated to conditions, which is not reported in the paper. It is customary to allocate on a random basis in an attempt to avoid any systematic bias creeping into the design. This can be easily done with a computer-generated list of numbers – odds go to one condition, and evens to the other (see also Chapter 3). **Random allocation** does not remove the possibility of a between-group difference at the start of the study, but it does reduce the chances of it occurring and is better than a **systematic allocation**, e.g. alternating the allocation of participants to groups.

Even with all these precautions it is still possible that there may have been differences between the groups prior to the experimental intervention, and this could complicate interpretation of the results. In this case, the authors checked this in their data by comparing the baseline measures of the two groups. If there are differences in baseline measures then a simple measurement of change from baseline is hard to interpret. If my respiratory rate is higher than yours to begin with and then mine slows down to the same as yours, is this a product of the experimental manipulation or not? This was exactly the dilemma that Yung *et al.* encountered as their two groups had quite varied measures at baseline. This will happen in many types of study. Although the group with music had significant reductions on all four measures, the evidence of differences at baseline between groups could have presented a problem. The use of analysis of covariance overcame this potential difficulty. This tests the difference between groups in their respective change from their own baseline.

Consider for a moment that you and I complete two reaction-time tasks. After the first trial my average time is 47 milliseconds and yours is 45. We are both then allowed to practise in order to improve our reactions times. After this, in the second trial my average has dropped to 41 milliseconds and yours to 40. If you just look at the second measure, you would say that I am slower than you. However, if what you want to know is how practice affects our reaction times, then you need to look at the changes in our respective scores from our individual baselines. When you do that with these data you can see that in fact practice has had a greater effect on me than it has on you. We would not have been able to determine this if we did not take the baseline measures into consideration. This is the principle of an analysis of covariance.

How Reliable Are their Measures?

One consideration is how the dependent variable was measured. The authors were looking at stress, and the way in which this manifests will vary from person to person. If the focus of the study had been on any one indicator of stress, the authors could be accused of putting all their eggs in one basket. As we have seen, only two of the three physiological measures showed a significant change from baseline. If the authors had chosen only the wrong one of those three they would not have found a discernible change. This would have been a **Type II error** because, as we have seen, there was in fact a change to be detected. Sometimes too many outcome measures can be problematic and possibly indicative of rather woolly thinking. In this instance, however, the selection of four standard measures of stress is justified. All four are clearly seen to be different aspects of a single emotional and physiological state, that of being stressed.

The authors detail the equipment used to take two of the physiological measurements and cite previous studies in which the reliability of the machinery has been established. The third measure, respiratory rate, was taken by simply counting the number of chest movements of the patient. This latter has a potential for an element of **subjectivity** to creep in. However, as was noted, this is the one measurement where no significant differences were found once the baseline rate was taken into consideration. Therefore the reliability of this measure does not affect the overall findings.

The authors also used an anxiety scale as a self-report measure of anxiety. This was not some rough-and-ready questionnaire put together for the purpose of this study. The scale in question was Speilberger's State Trait Anxiety Inventory (STAI), a well-respected psychometric measure that has been in common research use for over 30 years. Its **psychometric properties** have been identified, and its **reliability** and **validity** established. (For a fuller discussion of psychometrics see Chapter 16.) However, the STAI was developed in English, and this sample was Chinese. Luckily, the authors did not have to rely on translating the instrument themselves, as a translation was already in the public domain. When an instrument like this is translated it is foolhardy to assume that its psychometric properties remain unchanged. There is always more than one way to translate any sentence, and subtle nuances and interpretations can easily be lost in the process. Additionally, there may be cultural differences in response to stimuli; therefore translation is only the first step in preparing such an instrument for a different culture. Luckily in this instance the translation had already been tested for its own **factor structure** and reliability, which meant that the Chinese version could be used with as much confidence as the English original.

The authors have been laudably thorough in their choice of measures.

▲ How Appropriate Was the Research Method?

Related designs (matched pairs, repeated measures) reduce the variability in the data that may occur in an unrelated designs. The authors' choice of a matched pairs design is not the only related design, but it is the only possible related design for this study. The other related design, repeated measures, would not have been practical. It would require the same individuals to be having the same surgical procedure twice. In this instance, this would be unethical if it required patients to present for surgery twice, once unnecessarily. Or it would mean a horrendously slow recruitment rate as only patients experiencing two operations in a short period of time could be recruited!

On the other hand an **unrelated design** could be considered. If that were the case then a simple design using two independent groups would not work, because of the inherent variability that we have already noted and also the variation in surgery type. Therefore, it would be necessary to run a randomised controlled trial, often seen as the 'gold standard' in research (see Chapter 3). The rationale behind randomisation is that, by ensuring that allocation to condition is made through a random, unbiased process, differences between the two sets of people are reduced to those that occur purely by chance. This is designed to reduce, but *not eliminate*, constant or **confounding error**.

The nature of this particular study meant that a matched pairs design was preferable because the surgery was varied and there was also a good deal of variation in the numbers presenting for the different types of surgery: prostate and hernia repairs comprised 22 patients each, while the other three procedures each comprised eight or fewer patients. Thus a randomisation process here might have resulted in one of the procedures being over-represented in one condition thereby skewing the results. As has been noted, previous researchers in this area had settled for the easier option of controlling the type of surgery by restricting their sample to those undergoing one specified procedure. This study is an example of when a matched pairs procedure is ideal, when there is one single variable (in this case the type of surgical procedure) that is so crucial to the dependent variable that its occurrence needs controlling across the sample. Controlling by matching by type, as here, tells us more than controlling by simply restricting to one type, as previously.

You might have considered that a **single group design** might work here because anxiety could be measured at two points, after a period of silence in the perioperative room and then again after an equivalent period of music. The danger with this approach is that people might calm down after a prolonged wait and become more relaxed as they get used to their surroundings. A possible solution to this would be **counterbalancing**: half the sample have music followed by silence, the other half, silence followed by music. This may seem like potentially a good idea but there are two inherent problems. The first is that if patients relax with time anyway, then all patients will be more relaxed at the end of the experimental period than at the beginning. This might well bring us back to our old friend, the Type II error: the relaxing over time process would drown out the relaxing effect of the music. The second problem is that those who have music first may be relaxed by this process, and the effect of that relaxation could carry on through the period of silence. It is essentially the same problem noted in this section for Chapter 3. You can't counterbalance a treatment of a problem because if the treatment works, the problem is gone. That may be good news for the patient but it is definitely bad news for the researcher! Furthermore even if you could counterbalance, you are no longer looking at a single group design but repeated measures.

It would seem that the design used here is optimal. However, single group designs can be useful in a parallel context. For example, Spitzer *et al.* (2005) showed music to be therapeutic for depressive patients. This design was appropriate because depression is a chronic and sustained state, unlike preoperative anxiety, reducing the risk of spontaneous improvement over the period of the study as a confounding variable. Similarly Thompson *et al.* (2005) used a repeated measures design to explore the effect of music on the cognitive state of people with dementia. Again, repeated measures design was effective here as the participants' condition was long-term, and there was no surgical procedure involved.

It would be possible to use any of the three main research tools to address this question. For example, we could use **survey methods**, like Choi (2008), who conducted a survey of music therapists which asked about the way they use music to help people with learning disabilities, physical, emotional and psychological disorders and sensory impairments. We could similarly use a survey to gain anaesthetists' views on using music preoperatively. Alternatively we could use surveys to gain patients' views on whether or not they would like to be played music at such a time. We could do this at any point during their hospital career, on the ward, after the premedication (if they are not too drowsy) or postoperatively. Patients' views would be an interesting and legitimate target for research. However, they would be just that, views. They might say whether or not they liked the idea of music, they might say whether or not they thought it would help them relax. But, as with all surveys, what we are looking at here is reported behaviour, which is not the same thing as behaviour itself. If you want to know how something affects behaviour, then it is the behaviour you need to study.

The effect of music on experimentally produced anxiety has been studied in laboratory settings, for example Walworth (2003). In contrast, this study by Yung *et al.* is a specialised area, because of the nature of the problem. There is pretty much nothing else like waiting to be taken into the operating theatre.

Could we try **observation** for this issue? If you want to study how patients respond, you need to use observation in a **naturalistic** setting. That way the study would have **ecological validity**. It might strike you that there is nothing very naturalistic about a twenty-first-century operating theatre. Maybe when you think of what is naturalistic you think of things that are naturally occurring, in which case, the high-tech specification of theatres is very far removed from nature. However, in research 'naturalistic' has a specific meaning which is the situation in which the **target behaviour** naturally occurs. It does not matter how artificial the environment itself may be. If we want to study how astronauts behave prior to take-off we need to observe them in the naturalistic setting of the spacecraft. Similarly, if we want to study preoperative behaviour, we need to do it in the operating theatre.

We could, therefore, conduct an observational study of patient behaviour in the theatre. However, if we want to know the effects of music we would need to observe one set of patients in a hospital that plays music preoperatively and one that does not. This would lead to further complications. To what extent would two such samples be equivalent? What about the hospital staff, the drugs used, the architecture of the building, the lighting, the personality of the surgeons, or the anaesthetists? Any or all of these might have an effect on the patients. All these **extraneous variables** would at best produce a good deal of random error into the study, and potentially confounding error too. Could we therefore just do the study in the one hospital that does play music? We could observe the patients to see if they are relaxed. This would enable us to describe how relaxed patients seem to be if they are played music, but would not provide us with a comparison. If we do not have a

comparator, it is impossible to be certain how to interpret our observations. This is why research designs use a **control** group or condition.

You may think that one way around this is to do the study in one hospital and then introduce music; this way we have our comparator. But, this is not an observational study. Once the research design requires an intervention, then it is no longer observation, it is an **experiment**. We may be using observation as our measuring technique, but the research is an experiment nonetheless. This is indeed the nature of an experiment: where the researcher manipulates the independent variable in order to measure the dependent variable. Indeed this is exactly what Yung and his colleagues did.

Conclusion

This study was an experiment using a matched pairs pre-/post-design. However, within that experimental paradigm, the authors used observation methods (the physiological measures) and survey methodology (the STAI). It is often the case that the overall design may call upon techniques from more than one field of research. Indeed, Cooke *et al.* (2005) used a very similar design and method in an American study which showed that music reduced anxiety amongst day surgery patients. Moreover, a **systematic review** of the literature by a British team, Gillen *et al.* (2008), confirmed the consistency of this finding across similar studies.

Technically speaking this was a **field experiment**, although it was hardly typical of its genre. It would classify as such because it was conducted in the setting in which the target behaviour would normally occur. Unlike most field experiments, here the authors had considerable control over events 'in the field' because they had control over the operating theatres.

Other types of design would not really have been suitable in this instance. It is often suggested that situations can be tested using role-play. Here it is unlikely that this would have been very effective. Ultimately the success of role-play depends on the participants' ability to empathise with their given role. Such ability will vary enormously across samples. In contrast, the anxiety people experience prior to surgery may be universal.

Thus Yung *et al.* have identified what appears to be a clear and useful effect. If replicated this could at little cost be implemented successfully across health authorities world-wide. This is a specialist study in a highly applied area of psychology. As the authors note:

> Research on music to reduce stress for surgical patients has practical implications not only for preoperative care but also throughout the perioperative period. (2003, p.72)

Summary Points	
Design	Field experiment – matched pairs (related, between conditions)
Aim	To compare two conditions
IV	Presence of music
DV	Stress Operationalised as blood pressure, heart rate, respiration rate, State Trait Anxiety Inventory.
Sample	66 patients, 50–80 years, male
Analysis	Between conditions, changes from baseline measurement

Competitive Anxiety

Experiment – A Repeated Measures Design

'When cerebral processes enter into sports, you start screwing up. It's like the Constitution, which says separate church and state. You have to separate mind and body.' (Bill Lee, baseball player, b. 1946)

Do You Play Golf?

Do you take part in any sport, for that matter? Football, tennis, cycling, aerobics? Whether it is sport for fun, for exercise, or for serious competition, a large number of people do. If you do not personally then chances are that you know someone who does. For those who take their sport seriously, the goal is always to improve on the last performance. This applies for those playing competitive sport and for those who are merely stretching themselves to improve their own level of fitness. There are many different things that can affect performance, both between individuals (e.g. build, skill, ability) and within an individual over time. Those who take their sport seriously, be they professional or amateur, strive to improve, or in some cases maintain, their own performance level. This requires long-term commitment to work on fitness levels (e.g. healthy diet, regular exercise) and on proficiency (polishing their skill). Is such tenacity always rewarded? Does it guarantee optimum performance?

There is some evidence that for many athletes, in all forms of sports, performance may be adversely affected when it is needed most: in competitions. An athlete can practice over a prolonged period of time, slowly improving their performance through their dedication and commitment. Then comes the chance to show this to others, to prove to everyone just how competent they have become. In the event, the pressure of this being the 'one big chance' adversely affects performance. This means that the months of practice and improvement seem to be for nothing and the athlete performs at lower level than their capability or 'under par'. Sports psychologists refer to this phenomenon as 'choking under pressure' 'Choking' here means that performance is impaired. 'Pressure' in this context refers to when events combine to make it more important than usual to do your best. Competition is an obvious example of this type of pressure: the bigger the competition, the greater the pressure. Or it may be that a particular coach, talent scout or sponsor has to come to watch. Or even just someone you want to impress at a personal level: partner, rival, parent. Any one of these could add that extra pressure that would make it important for you to do your best and, so unfairly, at the same time make it less likely that you will.

One of the **theories** that attempt to explain why this happens is called the self-focus model. This suggests we are paying too much attention to our own performance when we are anxious; we are not using our learned performance, which has become automatic. Instead we have broken it down into its component parts; we have lost the learned automaticity of the polished performance. The mechanisms that might underlie this effect are unclear, and two possibilities have been suggested. It could be that pressure produces *conscious processing* such that anxious performers revert to attempting to control every aspect of their movement. The anxiety has made them focus on the individual components of performance. An alternative hypothesis suggests that it is to do with limits on *attention*. The theory is that stress and coaching instructions combined cause too heavy a demand on our limited capacity, and this overload interferes with the automaticity we have learned, which, in turn, produces a decrement in performance. Each of these theories has an intuitive appeal and each has been tested **empirically**. The findings have been ambivalent, with support for each theory emerging from research.

How can a researcher attempt to work out which of these mechanisms is responsible for choking under pressure? Any study is going to require its **participants** to perform under pressure, but how can we tell what is happening inside? If people do less well under pressure, how do we know what the mechanisms are? This is where the **hypothetico-deductive method** is required (see Box 7.1).

In the experiment discussed in this chapter, hypothetico-deductive reasoning was used by Gucciardi and Dimmock (2008) to test which of these two mechanisms explained choking under pressure. The **aim** of the study was to compare the conscious processing **hypothesis** with the attention limit hypotheses as explanations.

Choking under Pressure in Sensorimotor Skills: Conscious Processing or Depleted Attentional Resources?

Gucciardi, D.F. & Dimmock, J.A. (2008). *Psychology of Sport and Exercise, 9*, 45–59

Method

Gucciardi and Dimmock used a repeated measures design to examine this (see Box 5.1).

Twenty experienced golfers were recruited to this study, which used a putting task as the skilled performance under examination. To unravel the mechanisms there were three different types of task for the golfers, each of which directed their thinking while putting. The three tasks were that they were required:

1. to think about the *individual component* movements of putting;
2. to think *irrelevant thoughts*; these irrelevant thoughts were to focus either on three different colours or three different animals – each of which was completely unconnected with golf;
3. to think about a single word to describe their *overall* putting technique.

Box 5.1

When Are Repeated Measures Not Repeated Measures?

Repeated measures design means that each participant takes part in each condition of a study. It should logically be called a repeated conditions design; that would certainly make it easier to recognise. Unfortunately, it is saddled with the somewhat more confusing term of repeated measures.

The confusion is likely to arise because many studies use what is called a **pre-/post-design** (see for example Chapter 3). A pre-/post-design is required if the aim is to measure changes in the participants either over time or as a result of the manipulation of the **independent variable** (**IV**). Under these circumstances, measures of the **dependent variable** (**DV**) are taken at the start as a **baseline measurement** and then again after the manipulation of the IV. For example if you wanted to see whether sleep deprivation affected memory, you would need to measure memory first, perhaps by asking people to read and recall a list of objects. Then you ensure that your participants miss a night's sleep, and then they take a second memory test. This repeated testing is necessary because people are so variable – if everyone had the same memory capacity it would not be necessary to take the first measurement. Taking two measures can seem as if you are using a repeated measures design, but in fact this is not necessarily the case. Strictly speaking, 'repeated measures' means that each person has taken part and has been measured in each condition.

Table 5.1. Schematic representation of possible outcome by theory

Theory:	Task type:		
	Individual movements	Irrelevant thoughts	Overall thought
Conscious processing	Decrement	–	–
Attentional limits	Decrement	Decrement	–

How is this going to provide us with answers? It goes like this. If anxiety produces *conscious processing* then performance should be most affected when the golfers are required to think about their individual movements (task 1 above). This is because this task would encourage conscious processing. If, on the other hand, it is to do with *attentional* limits, then performance should be affected in the two tasks with greater attention demands: individual components (task 1) and irrelevant thoughts (task 2). The third task is a **control** condition which should neither place too great a demand on attention nor encourage concentrating on components. So this seemingly complicated design all hinges on whether one or both of the tasks hampers performance.

For each task the golfers completed 10 putts without anxiety as a baseline measure. They then had to repeat the task, this time with the additional pressure of being in a competition with cash prizes. Therefore each golfer had to go through the exercise six times.

This repeated measures study was a **related design** because each participant took part in each of the different conditions. By definition therefore the number of people in each condition will be the same. There were two independent variables. One IV was the task the golfers were required to do while putting, and there were *three* types of task. The other IV was the manipulation of anxiety, which had just *two* levels: with or without. **T1** (Time 1) was without anxiety, but **T2** included the pressure of being in a competition intended to raise anxiety levels. So in total we have six conditions (2×3), hence the golfers had to repeat the trial six times. The dependent variable (DV) was the performance, **operationalised** by the **outcome variable**: distance from the hole. This provides a clear, objective measurement of performance.

Results

Statistical analysis using **analysis of variance** (**ANOVA**) showed that the effect of anxiety differed across the three conditions. In fact the only condition where the performance had deteriorated at T2 was in the component actions task (task 1). This is in line with the prediction from the conscious processing hypothesis. The data also showed that the golfers performed significantly better in the single description condition (task 3), both with and without anxiety, than in either of the other conditions. As Gucciardi and Dimmock argue, their findings show no support for the hypothesis that decrements in performance, or choking, are caused by attentional limits. It is not that anxiety so limits attention that we cannot perform accomplished behaviours. It is rather that anxiety can make us focus on the small actions that together make up the total performance, and it is this that produces choking.

■ How Safe Is This Conclusion?

This is a neat finding as the design of the study allowed for the findings to support one of two conflicting hypotheses. Can we be sure, as a result of this, that thinking about performance has a detrimental effect? No; the study in fact shows that some forms of thinking about performance are actually beneficial. When the golfers were thinking about their overall style of performance, where they focused on such words as 'smooth' and 'easy', they appeared to perform better, even when anxious, than in either of the other conditions even when they were without anxiety. However, the combination of anxiety and being encouraged to think about individual components of their putting seemed to have a detrimental effect. Is there any likelihood that there was any **systematic error** which could lead to a **confounding variable**?

What Else Could Have Caused the Changes?

This was a repeated measures task, six repeats in total, so what about practice effects? Surely doing the task so often would have meant that they were bound to improve over time? This is one of the inherent problems with repeated measures. The authors addressed this in three ways.

Simple practice effects are a problem with any skilled task. Psychology, in particular cognitive psychology, uses many different types of tasks for participants to complete during experimentation. For example they may involve measures of reaction time, mental rotation, hand–eye coordination, reading and critical thinking, amongst others. Researchers must always be mindful of simple practice effects, and take measures to deal with them. One standard technique to do so is to ensure that participants practise prior to baseline so that they reach a learning plateau. From this any further improvement should be minimal and unlikely to create a confounding variable. It is, however, a time-consuming process, and many of the computerised measurements of cognitive behaviour require extensive practice to overcome the initial learning curve. In this case, however, there were no computers; the measures were not so much psychological as relating to physical performance. (This can often be the case in what are termed applied settings, where psychology is applied to ordinary behaviour.) This gave the study the advantage. The authors did not recruit people who had to learn the skill but rather 20 highly skilled experienced golfers. Their experience of the sport ranged from three to 20 years; their handicaps ranged from 0 to 12. Their **inclusion criteria** (relating to experience and handicap) were tight and designed to produce a relatively homogeneous sample. They had in effect already done the practising for the researchers! It is therefore highly improbable that with so much experience behind them there would be any improvement in putting during the 60 putts of this study.

Repeated measures practice effects for IV 1, anxiety. In all cases the golfers performed in the same sequence, without anxiety first. This means that whatever the task they were given to do while putting they would be better at it the second time around. This was necessary from a pragmatic point of view because anxiety is not the sort of independent variable that you can be certain that you have removed. It is not a problem in this particular study as the second condition is the one in which we expect a deterioration. If we were looking for an improvement at the second point then practice effects could be a confounding variable and might well produce a **Type I error**. But if we are expecting deterioration then the worst that can happen is the practice effects might mask a true effect, **Type II error**. That is to say that they could improve in performance through practice but deteriorate through the manipulation which effects would cancel each other out. There is some possibility that this might have happened, as for two of the conditions there was no evidence of deterioration in the anxiety condition from baseline. The authors note that in fact there appeared, at face value, to be an improvement from baseline in both the irrelevant task and the single description condition; however, this was not a **significant** change from baseline.

The important thing to bear in mind here is that the researchers were not looking to see the difference between low and high anxiety *per se*, but were comparing the differences between the three conditions. Thus an overall practice effect would not have been a problem.

Repeated measures practice effects for IV 2, task type. If the crux of the study is the comparison between the groups then practice effects between conditions could present a real threat. In order to avoid this, the study used **counterbalancing**. The golfers were randomly assigned to the order in which they experienced the task type. This means that any practice effects were spread across the tasks so should neither have masked nor produced a change in outcome measure.

The fact that only the component action task produced a decrement in performance is convincing evidence that this conscious processing is responsible for choking under pressure.

● How Effective Is the Experimental Design?

This is a straightforward repeated measures design. Data are collected from each participant, in each condition. The order of task type was randomised for each participant, but for the anxiety condition, low anxiety always came first.

In the first part of the study where anxiety was low, each golfer was only concerned with performing as well as s/he could in isolation and without reference to others. Once there was an element of competition, it was a matter of upping the stakes. This was designed to produce an element of anxiety, an increase in the pressure to perform well. To what extent did this succeed? If the experimental design did not raise anxiety levels then the study would be profoundly flawed. Gucciardi and Dimmock did not leave this essential aspect to chance. They checked anxiety using a published **psychometric measure** for which validity had already been established. This showed a significant increase in anxiety from immediately prior to the first round to immediately prior to the second. Thus it would seem that the manipulation was successful.

Experimental studies usually have a control condition, and we tend to think of this as meaning that in one condition nothing happens. In this study there were experimental conditions requiring participants to focus on an irrelevant task, component actions or a single description describing their putt. Does this mean that there was no control? Far from it: the control condition was the single description task. If you look back at Table 5.1, you will see that neither hypothesised mechanism predicted deterioration in this condition. The other two conditions were in effect being compared with this one. You may wonder why it would not be better to have a condition with no task, as this might feel like a true control. The problem is that this would not be a true control. If there was a condition without a task the researchers would not know what the golfers were thinking about while putting. It is likely that experienced golfers will have developed their own techniques or mental tasks to optimise their performance. Therefore, if the control had been to leave them free of any specific task they would have the added advantage of doing what they would normally do. In this case, any decrement in performance in the other two groups would be partially due to their doing a task while playing. Gucciardi and Dimmock did not want this; they wanted to measure the decrement produced by different types of task. This is why the control condition had to include a task, but not one that either hypothesis predicted would impair performance. Because it encouraged the golfer to think holistically about her/his performance it did not promote breaking down actions into their component parts (conscious processing hypothesis). Because it was a single word it did not produce the same amount of overload on attention as would concentrating on three non-golfing words (attentional limit hypothesis). Although the popular view of a control condition is one where nothing happens, this is an oversimplified version of the truth. A control condition is where the variables of interest are *controlled*.

▲ How Appropriate Was the Research Method?

This repeated measures design has all 20 participants completing all six conditions. Why use this method?

Using an **unrelated design** would mean that they would have been comparing **between conditions** but with **independent subjects**, in which case they would need to take careful account of how they produced the different groups. It would certainly have been necessary to use a **randomised control trial** (**RCT**) in order to have data that were amenable to analysis (as outlined in Chapter 3). How many groups do you think they would have had? If they had chosen to have six groups, one for each condition, they would have found so much individual variation that it would be difficult to show any effect. There would be so much noise in the data that a Type II error would have been highly likely. This would mean they would either have needed two groups (one to experience all three conditions without anxiety, the other to experience all three with anxiety), or three groups (one to each condition experienced with and without anxiety).

What would be the pros and cons of these two designs?

An alternative to an RCT would be a **matched pairs design**. You could argue that matching by years of golfing experience and handicap would produce two reasonably comparable groups. It would take a good deal of time finding matching couples. Even with the strict inclusion criteria used here, the range of golfing experience was 17 years and the range of handicap 13. If the first golfer you recruit has been playing for say eight years and has a handicap of 7, how long before you find a match? It would be possible to do approximate matching: look for someone with experience of between six and 10 years and a handicap of 6–8 for example. This increases the chances of finding a match, but also reduces the accuracy of the match. One is a trade-off against the other. Matched pairs is usually quite a challenging design to use, and is not in common use these days for these very reasons. However, there are times, as explained in Chapter 4, when matched pairs is the optimal design.

You might think that this study used a **single group design**. There was after all only one group. Nevertheless this does not count as a single group design because each participant took part in all the different conditions. This is why it is a repeated measures design. A true single group design, where all the participants undergo just one trial, would not have been suitable for making these complex, between-task comparisons. This study, in using a repeated measures design, with counterbalancing, has taken advantage of each golfer acting as her/his own control. Counterbalancing has taken account of order effects, while using experienced golfers overcomes the difficulty of practice effects in skilled tasks. As the behaviour under study was a practised performance, and as the condition was a type of simultaneous cognitive task, this topic, unlike the therapeutic studies outlined in Chapters 3 and 4, was ripe for a repeated measures design.

Would either of the other two areas of research have worked to explore this area?

Survey methods might have been employed as, for example, Beaudoin (2006), who explored competitive style and motivation amongst female footballers. Jones *et al.* (2001) tested the **psychometric properties** of a new scale designed to measure athletes' attitudes to performance. Fradkin *et al.* (2007) used a survey to link lack of warm-up activities with subsequent injury among women golfers. Survey methods are clearly useful within sports psychology. A survey would have allowed us to ask golfers what types of strategies they use. This would tell us what they think they do. It would not tell us how each approach actually affects performance. It might tell us what they *think* works best. As a species, humans are not really very good at judging or evaluating their own performance. Quite often, cognitive distortions sneak into our account of our performance. It is not that we are lying, but rather that our recall of our experience can be selective. Surveys can tell us about opinions and memories of events, but would not provide objective evidence of task and performance.

Observation has also been used within sports psychology. Neumann and Thomas (2008) have developed equipment that assesses putting accuracy more effectively than simply measuring the distance between the ball and the hole. This might be a useful observational tool in future studies of golfing performance. Observation would be useful, and certainly most experienced golfers are used to being watched; golfing is a public behaviour. The presence of an observer would not be as disruptive here as in many other scenarios. Observation alone would not tell us what they were thinking or how they were trying to control their performance under pressure. It is possible that we could use a combination of observation and survey methods: observe the golfers as they putt while going around the course and, directly after each successful putt, ask them what they were thinking about. This might give us the information we want, although with repeated questioning mid-game the golfers' patience might wear thin. This in turn could lead to unreliable answers as the golfer tries to escape the questioning. It could also produce a high **attrition rate** in the study as golfers withdrew their consent to being watched. It might also lead to the researcher getting her/his head bitten off by resentful golfers!

Another form of observation, **case studies**, has been used to explore individual instances. For example, Bell and Thompson (2007) reported the success of a guided imaging therapy to reduce neurological problems that were affecting the golfing performance of a 40-year-old golfer.

Considering these options, it seems that a repeated measures experiment was much the best way to answer this particular question about performance anxiety. That is not to suggest that other methods could not be used successfully in this area, but perhaps not in order to answer this particular question.

Conclusion

This is a neat example of the hypothetico-deductive method of research. The design of the study meant that the findings could support one of two possible explanatory mechanisms for the phenomenon known to athletes as choking under pressure. In the event the findings provided support for the conscious processing hypothesis. The fact that the control group, focusing on a single-word description of their performance, did so well is interesting in itself, but it is not possible to infer that this is a good strategy *per se*. It may be that the golfers would have performed even better in the anxiety condition if left to their own devices. This would be an interesting further study, comparing single word condition with no instruction.

The authors themselves conclude that:

> The type and amount of conscious processing may influence the anxiety-performance relationship, and that higher-levels of conscious processing may be beneficial for skill execution. (p.57)

Summary Points	
Design	Experiment – repeated measures (related, between conditions)
Aim	To compare three conditions
IV	Type of cognitive tasks
DV	Performance Operationalised as putting error, distance from hole in cm
Sample	20 experienced golfers
Analysis	Between conditions

Change Blindness
Experiment – A Single Sample Design

'We don't see things as they are, we see them as we are.' (Anaïs Nin, author, 1903–77)

Do You Notice Change?

Do you notice when things change? If you take your ordinary route home from class or work and one of the houses you pass has painted its front door a new colour, do you think you would spot this? Maybe you would; maybe you would not. What if the whole of the front of a house had been repainted a completely different colour? Some of us might notice this and maybe others would not. Suppose that there was a new street sign placed directly in your path? You would probably expect to notice this, in order to avoid walking into it. Is it possible that you might just walk around it without noticing that it was new? What if when you got home your own home had been painted a new colour? Unless you have a visual impairment, you would probably anticipate noticing this.

What about people: do you notice when they change? We are familiar with the stereotypical picture of the woman with a new hairdo asking her partner whether he notices anything new. Do you notice new clothes or hairstyles or spectacles or whatever on people with whom you are familiar? Some of us are more observant than others; some of us are more likely to notice these types of changes to familiar items. What if the lecturer in your class suddenly changes her/his appearance apparently in front of you: where once he was wearing a hat, it has suddenly disappeared; her blue cardigan has become a yellow jumper; he is suddenly sporting a moustache or she a ponytail? If this change happened right in front of your eyes, would you notice? If you witnessed them changing their personal appearance, taking off one top and putting on another, you would be fairly certain that you would notice. What if they were obscured from a view for a few seconds and then emerged with the change effected, would you still expect to notice this? And certainly if they actually changed into a different person, you would be bound to notice that, wouldn't you? If at one point your male lecturer has straight brown hair and is clean-shaven but at the next he has curly blond hair and a moustache, there is no way that this change would escape you – or would it?

It seems that, in fact, in certain circumstance we have a tendency to be 'change blind', and we can fail to notice quite substantial changes. It depends on the context in which a change occurs. In the example of the lecturer, if you already knew her/him, then you would be very likely to notice the swap. However, in a different setting, say for example someone serving you in a shop, someone new to you, it would seem that there is a good chance that you might not notice a substitution. Picture this: you walk into a supermarket to do your weekly shop and discover that the particular brand of cereal that you wanted to purchase is not on the shelf. You find an assistant on a neighbouring aisle and ask whether there is a further supply of said cereal in the storeroom at the back. The shop worker in question leaves promising to make enquiries. Two minutes later the assistant returns laden with a supply of your desired item. If the person you approached was fair and wore a blue shirt and white cap and yet the one who provides you with your cereal is dark, wearing a white shirt and a blue cap you would notice, wouldn't you? Well, under these circumstances apparently some of us would not notice such a change. This is an example of where psychological research produces answers that are entirely counter-intuitive.

The main body of research in this area began to be published in the last decade of the twentieth century. Most studies followed a simple formula of presenting participants with a picture of some sort; this picture is the **stimulus** in the **experiment**. The picture then changed in some way, this being the manipulation of the **independent variable** (**IV**). Then participants were asked if they had noticed any change, their perception of the picture being the **dependent variable** (**DV**). If they said they had noticed a change they were asked to describe what had changed. In each instance a surprising number did not notice anything. Over repeated series of experiments, researchers employed increasingly audacious **experimental manipulations** by introducing ever greater and more complex changes. And yet still many people failed to be aware of any change at all. Early studies indicated that we are poor in detecting a change in a simple array of objects, such as a row of letters or digits. It became apparent that we are equally poor in detecting a change in landscape, if for example a building appears or disappears in a cityscape while we watch!

These laboratory studies were then extended to explore changes in what is normally referred to as a 'real-world' setting. Instead of using a laboratory and artificial stimuli, researchers started to explore more **ecologically valid** settings. This means those we encounter in our daily lives. An early step in this research involved showing a short video clip of an office worker. He rises from his desk to answer a telephone in the corridor. The protagonist was played by two different men, the change being made as the camera angle changed. Yet the substitution went largely unnoticed by the audience. The next step was to explore the same phenomenon in live, interpersonal exchanges, in a **field experiment**. This allowed researchers to push the limits of what we know about change detection and also to explore the underlying mechanisms.

What Could Be the Underlying Mechanisms?

There is an interesting contradiction between the large amount of visual information that we are able to process and the small amount of information that we are apparently capable of retaining. This discrepancy is often attributed to the role of attention. Cognitive psychology has shown that attention is a major determinant of memory. When we attend to an item, the process of attention helps us record that item in our memory. On the whole we do not attend to most of the stimuli we encounter. On a trip to a supermarket, you may see hundreds of people and thousands of products, millions of items, but how many will you recall later? If you have had a conversation with a person, or inspected a particular product, then you are more likely to recall them. This is because you had been paying attention to them. Without paying attention, it is unlikely you would remember them nor be able to recall them later. (If we do pay attention and therefore remember something, the duration of that memory depends on a number of variables which are tangential to this chapter. The interested reader is referred to the work of Baddeley, 2007, for a comprehensive text). However, the striking thing about change blindness is that it can occur even when we appear to have attended.

Theory would suggest that failure to detect change may be caused by a breakdown in one of three cognitive processes: encoding the stimulus initially, retrieving it, or comparing the first and second stimuli. In terms of the example of seeking a specific cereal in a supermarket, the first possibility may be an inability to commit to memory the appearance of the shop assistant (the first stimulus). The second option may be that although we remember their appearance we just cannot access (retrieve) that memory later. We have all experienced that sensation, often referred to as the 'tip of the tongue' phenomenon, when we know, for example, a name but just cannot seem to recall it when we wish to do so. It could be that we do not organise our internal images well enough to find the one we need and it is this that produces the failure. If we do not have access to the internal image of the initial stimulus then we have nothing with which to compare the current stimulus to see if it differs. Both these two explanations focus on the mental representation of the first stimulus, in its formation or its retrieval. The third possibility has a different focus, as it suggests that there is a failure to make a comparison between the recorded memory of the first assistant and the appearance of the assistant carrying the cereal (the second stimulus). In this explanation the nature and accessibility of the memory of the first face is not the issue; rather, it is the process of making the comparison that is faulty or flawed or that simply fails to occur. The question for researchers is how to determine which of these three possibilities most satisfactorily explains our inability to detect change?

How Can We Locate the Failure?

This question takes us to the crux of good **positivist** experimental research: deriving **hypotheses** from **theory**. For more information on this approach to research, see

Box 7.1. The three possible theoretical explanations of the phenomenon cited above can be used to form possible hypotheses.

The link between theory and hypothesis can be described as 'If A then B'. Hypotheses are not drawn from thin air but rather are statements of the logical consequences if the theory in question is true. To take an example from the physical sciences: you could start with the theory that fire needs air in order to burn. Drawing on this, a logical **experimental hypothesis** would be: a flame deprived of air will cease burning. The **null hypothesis** in this case would be: a flame deprived of air will continue to burn. To test this hypothesis, you can light a candle (fire) and then put a transparent covering over it, such as an upturned fireproof glass. If fire needs air then once it has burned all the air in the glass the candle flame will be extinguished, thereby supporting the theory. If this happens, we can reject the null hypothesis, as clearly the flame did not continue to burn. However, if the candle continues to burn then the null hypothesis cannot be rejected and there is no support for the theory. The logic of hypothesis testing is considered below.

The Logic of Hypothesis Testing

The logic of hypothesis testing can take a bit of getting used to. It works like this. Suppose that my theory is that Fred Bloggs lives in that house over the road, so I test this by knocking on the door. My hypothesis is that, if I knock on the door, Fred will answer. My null hypothesis (H_0) is that, if I knock on the door, he won't answer. If I knock on the door and Fred answers, all I can say for certain is that Fred is in the house at the present time. I can therefore reject the null hypothesis (if I knock, he won't answer the door) as no longer being valid because he did answer the door. In spite of this, I still have not proven my theory. I cannot take the much bigger step and say that because he answered the door he lives there. If, on the other hand, I had knocked and he had not answered, then I would have no evidence that he lives there, but equally no evidence that he does not.

You have probably spotted that, in fact, both outcomes have alternative explanations. He may answer the door but not live there; he could be visiting, or working there. He may not answer the door, even though he does live there; he could be out, sick, or just not inclined to answer the door. With this example the possible alternative explanations for events are easy to see; it is a relatively familiar experience. With research, however, by definition the material we are dealing with is new and therefore not familiar, which means that alternative explanations may not be obvious. Nonetheless there may always be alternative explanations for phenomena that we encounter, so we must always be cautious in our interpretation of findings. This is the logic of hypothesis testing.

Science is always cautious; we might be able to reject the null hypothesis but that is not the same thing as substantiating, let alone proving, the theory. In research we try to avoid saying that anything is proven. Proof, or the P word, is best avoided. The last thing any researcher wants to be saddled with is a **Type I error**: thinking you have a significant effect when in fact no such effect exists.

In the case of change blindness, the three possible causes outlined previously are the three theoretical explanations for the established phenomenon. The first step, then, is to test whether the memory has been stored. Looking just at this possible theoretical explanation we can say that *if* no memory of the first stimulus has been formed *then* that stimulus will not itself be recognised. Conversely if the stimulus is later recognised then it must originally have been formed, in which case, the fault will lie somewhere in the other two processes: retrieval and comparison. It was this first theory that prompted a series of studies by Levin *et al.* (2002). Their hypothesis was that those who experience change blindness will have a poor memory of the initial stimulus. To test this, they used a field experiment, that is, they ran the experiment in a real-world setting where the type of behaviour might occur naturally and where **participant**s might normally be found (like, for example Piliavin *et al.* in Chapter 2).

Memory for Centrally Attended Changing Objects in an Incidental Real-World Change Detection Paradigm

Levin, D.T., Simons, D.J., Angelone, B.L. & Chabris, C.F. (2002).
British Journal of Psychology, 93, 289–302

Method

This was a single sample **quasi-experiment**. It is a quasi-experiment rather than a true experiment because the researchers used a **convenience sample** rather than **probability sampling**.

The study took place on a university campus, and Levin *et al.* used an established procedure in order to effect the change. The first experimenter, carrying a campus map, approached each prospective participant in turn. The experimenter asked the way to a building that was across campus and not visible from where they stood. In the middle of the conversation, two men carrying a door rather rudely walked between the experimenter and participant, thereby causing a short (one-second) disruption to the conversation. As the door passed between the first experimenter and the participant, the second experimenter, who was one of the men carrying the door, swapped places with the first experimenter. Door-carrier became enquirer and enquirer became door-carrier. The switch took place behind the door, a smooth operation (presumably requiring a good deal of practice first!). Therefore the change itself was not visible or otherwise detectable to the participant, who could only be aware that it had happened if they perceived that their conversational partner had changed.

After the experiment the participant was **debriefed** and interviewed to find out whether they had noticed the swap. Each participant was then presented with a line-up that included the first experimenter and three other people (**distracters**), and asked to identify the person who had initially approached them.

The independent variable was the change in the enquirer. The two male experimenters who doubled as enquirers and door-carriers in this exchange wore similar but clearly different clothes. One had a green shirt, light brown cap and no jewellery, while the other wore a blue shirt, white cap and an ornamental chain around his neck.

The **aim** of the study was to see whether change blindness is associated with a lack of recognition of the first stimulus, i.e. the first enquirer.

Results

Of the 39 participants who took part in this study, 15 (38 per cent) failed to notice the change. This means that the researchers used a **categorical variable**, grouping their sample into categories: 'noticed change' and 'did not notice change'. Categorical variables like this are also called **nominal data**. When you have data like this you can count how many cases you have in each category, which provides frequency counts. Two of those who were classed as noticing the change initially said that they had seen nothing unusual take place, but when asked directly whether they had spotted the change they said that they had. Of those who spontaneously reported noticing the swap, about two-thirds were able to identify the first experimenter in the line-up, compared with only a third of those who did not notice the change. In the statistical analysis they used an **independent chi square test** which showed that this was a **significant** difference between the two groups (**p<.005**). This means that there was only a 1 in 200 likelihood of getting such a big difference between the groups by chance alone if it was not a real difference in memory storage between the groups. (See Key Topics: **probability**.)

You might be thinking that each person had a 1 in 4 chance of selecting the correct target from the three distracters by chance alone. Although it would be difficult to explain why one group should be luckier in their selection than the other, the researchers did measure the 'hit' rate of each group against chance. Those who had spotted the swap had a rate that was significantly higher than chance, while those who had been change blind did not.

It would seem therefore that a considerable proportion of the participants failed to notice that the person to whom they were talking had changed! The majority did notice, so this study is not suggesting that no one notices such things, but given that the change was not only a change of person but also a person in different clothing, you might have expected everyone to notice the swap. The fact that most of those who did not notice were unable to pick the first experimenter from the line-up supports the hypothesis that change blindness is associated with an impoverished memory of the first stimulus.

These data would seem to be indicating a clear link between memory of the first stimulus and the ability to detect change. The two groups, those who spotted the change and those who were change blind, differed in their ability to recognise the original experimenter. What does this tell us about the three possible theories to explain change blindness? It would appear to provide support for the first explanation, namely that the problem lies in remembering the first stimulus. As the task in this study was to recognise the original target, this should overcome any difficulties with retrieving memories that might have been experienced. When recalling a target seems impossible, it is usually feasible to recognise it. For example, if you were asked to recall the name of an actor from a particular film, you might find it more difficult than if you were given a list of names from which to recognise it. Problems with retrieval of information from memory can be reduced by using a recognition task rather than a recall task, providing that information is in conscious memory. (Any data stored in subconscious memory are notoriously difficult to retrieve reliably, and equally difficult to study. What we can argue is that there is little practical difference between an image that may have been stored in subconscious memory but cannot be retrieved and one that was not stored in the first place.) Therefore, we can say that these data establish a link between poor storage in conscious memory and change blindness.

■ How Safe Is This Conclusion?

Does that mean that we have evidence for the first theory, that the image was not properly stored in the first place? Or is there room for error in this study? As there appears to be an effect here there is little possibility of serious random error. **Random error** can mask an existing effect by swamping the data with 'noise', unwanted and irrelevant changes in the dependent variable. It can mask a real effect and lead to a **Type II error**, but it is hard to see how it could produce an effect where none exists – unlike a **systematic error**, which can act as a **confounding variable**. What about systematic error – is there an alternative explanation for this finding? Was there anything about the design of this study that could produce what appears to be an effect but which is actually part of the design?

There is a possible confounding explanation. It could be that, rather than those who experienced change blindness failing to commit the initial stimulus to memory as originally suggested, the second stimulus could instead have acted as 'interference' and resulted in the original memory being eroded by the new stimulus. There are many instances when new information has been shown to overwrite existing data such that the original is lost. This could be an alternative explanation for this finding. Those who failed to detect change may indeed have stored the initial image in their memories only for that memory to have deteriorated or become corrupted by the appearance of the second image. This is a classic example of realising that there is an alternative explanation for a finding – just as we noted above that Fred Bloggs could have answered the door without living in the house.

While this could have been a serious problem for this research, the authors were aware of it and set about addressing it.

Poor Storage or Interference?

In this development, Levin *et al.* again exemplify the type of thinking that is required for appropriate hypothesis testing (see Box 7.1). They argue that there are two possible explanations for their finding in the study reported above: either the image of the first experimenter was not encoded in participants' memories in the first place, or it was but was then overwritten by the image of the second experimenter. Therefore, in their next study they used a similar experimental paradigm, but in the subsequent identification phase there were two recognition tasks: to select the first and the second experimenter. The rationale for this is that if failure to detect change is associated with poor encoding then neither experimenter will be recognised. If, on the other hand, the failure to detect change is a result of interference with an encoded memory, then the second experimenter (i.e. the interference in question) will be recognised but not the first. In this second study, the experimenters were both female, and they both left the scene prior to the interview at the end of each trial, which was conducted by a third member of the research team.

Of the 67 people who took part in this study 19 failed to detect the change. Of these, 7 correctly identified the first person from the line-up and 6 the second, approximately a third of the group in each case. In contrast, of the 48 who did notice the change, 40 correctly identified the first and 36 the second, which is a success rate of approximately three-quarters. As might be expected, the difference between the two groups was significant. Like the last experiment, this one shows that failure to detect change is associated with lack of recognition of the stimuli. However, now we can say that, as both stimuli were similarly affected, it is unlikely to be interference that caused the problem but rather poor initial storage of the stimulus.

These two studies show very similar findings, which suggests that these data are likely to be **reliable**. It is interesting that the incidence of failure to detect change fell from the first study (38 per cent) to the second (28 per cent). The authors suggest that it could be something to do with the stimuli in the later study being women: perhaps we tend to individuate women more than we do men. (You may have come across the old adage that when attending a formal dinner, each man wants to look the same as all the other men, while each woman wants to look different!) It is true that in Western society there are more attributes of female than of male appearance that tend to be varied: dress, make-up and hairstyle are obvious examples. As this happens routinely, we may be accustomed to paying more attention to these details with women than we are with men.

It is worth recalling that not everyone in these two studies was change blind – in fact in each case it was a minority. You may be thinking: if it only affects a minority why the interest? That is one of the aspects of psychology – a phenomenon does not have to affect everyone in order to be worth studying. It is true that most people do detect change, but what makes this area interesting is that you would expect, by intuition, that *everyone* would notice when their conversational partner changes. The fact that some people do not notice such an evident change is surprising and therefore worthy of further investigation.

Going back to the Fred Bloggs analogy in Box 6.1, it would seem that twice Levin *et al.* had knocked on his door, and that twice he had answered. But is this actually evidence that he lives there? Finding the same effect twice, with the same design, still means that the researchers need to consider the possibility of alternative explanations. To do this they need to examine their experimental routine in detail. Could they actually be inducing change blindness rather than just detecting it? This is always a possibility in psychological research, and one that needs checking all the time.

Was the Enquiry Demanding Too Much Attention?

The authors wondered whether the task requested of the participants was too demanding and prevented them from paying adequate attention to the enquirer. Could this be why people were failing to notice the substitution? The initial request to the participant was for directions to a building on campus that was out of sight from where the conversation took place. We are told that the route to the destination was complex, which means that people would have had to visualise the route in order to describe it. It is possible that such a task would take up a good deal of cognitive capacity and prevent participants from focusing on or absorbing details of their conversational partner. The change occurred while the participant was in the middle of this complex task of providing directions across campus. Potentially the experimental design was actually distracting the participants from the feature that would change. In order to explore this possibility, Levin *et al.* tried an alternative approach. Instead of asking for directions the enquirer asked each participant to take a photograph of him- or herself on the campus and provided them with a disposable camera in order to do this. The neatness of this development is that now the participant is being actively encouraged to look at the experimenter in order to set up and take the photograph.

Why do we need to know that the camera was disposable? Partly because when reporting any study we should provide enough information for someone else to replicate, but in this case also because the disposable camera was simple and had only a shutter mechanism and no other switches or dials. The task was therefore very simple, and focused, literally, on the stimulus (the experimenter). And the results? A larger proportion (53 per cent) of participants failed to detect the change in this version than in the door version (38 per cent).

Having thereby satisfied themselves that it was not a matter of attentional overload, the researchers turned their attention to the mechanism that they were using to effect the change.

Did Disruption Cause the Effect?

In the studies described so far, the substitution of one person for another was managed by using the door-carrying technique. Clearly it was necessary to find a way of effecting these changes out of sight of the participants. In live conversation, as opposed to a situation where the change takes place in a filmed sequence, some sort of screening of the moment of change is necessary. Carrying a door had provided the perfect screen. This had meant that the conversation between enquirer and participant had been interrupted. Two people carrying a door through a seemingly naturally occurring dialogue was a rather brutal and unnatural disruption. It is just possible that the startling rudeness of the door-carriers might have disrupted the conversation to such an extent that the participant's focus was destroyed, which would help explain the failure to detect change.

They explored this possibility by using an alternative paradigm. In this there were two experimenters, both dressed in similar clothing this time, but their hairstyle and colour were markedly different, as were their faces and voices. Instead of a brusque interruption this time, the change was effected behind a counter. Prospective participants were invited to take part in a short study for which they would be given some sweets. Those who agreed were directed upstairs to a desk over which hung a sign 'Experiment Here'. From behind the desk, researcher A provided the participant with some consent forms. Once the forms were signed, researcher A, on the pretext of getting some information for the participant, bent down, out of sight, and researcher B stood up in the same place with the papers. In this phase 15 of the 20 participants failed to notice the change. As here the change was effected by a seemingly natural hiatus in a conversation, we can be confident that the effect observed in the earlier experiment was not a product of the abrupt nature of the door-carrying interruption.

When Is Change Detected?

The authors had spotted something about their results which had not been part of the original study question. The participants who noticed the change were all students in their twenties, which happened to be the same age as the experimenters, whereas those who failed to detect the change were all older (35 to 65). There are two possible theoretical explanations for this phenomenon. Change blindness could be more likely with increasing age or the alternative, more interesting, theory was that the phenomenon was a result of 'in-group'/'out-group' distinction. When we meet people who are part of our own in-group, we tend to notice their individual features, the things that distinguish them from other members of our group. However, when meeting members of other groups, our own out-groups, we tend not to notice these individual features but rather to focus on the attributes that are characteristic of the group in question. We tend to see our own in-group as heterogeneous whereas we see out-groups as homogeneous. It seemed reasonable therefore to suggest that this in-group/out-group distinction could explain change blindness. The authors chose to test this possibility and repeated the experiment, but this time with the two of them dressed as construction workers. In this phase of the study all the participants were students in the younger age group. This meant that if the detection rate remained high it would support the first theory that younger people are just better at detecting change. In contrast, if the detection rate dropped, then the out-group theory would be supported. It turned out that the detection rate did indeed drop, and further support for this theory was gathered from the individual comments of participants: once they had noticed they were talking to a construction worker, they stopped looking for individual features. It would seem therefore that in-group/out-group distinctions go some way to explaining some forms of change blindness.

● How Effective Is This Experimental Design?

The design used in these two studies was actually a replication from an earlier study by the two lead authors (Simons & Levin, 1998). In this they had acted as the two stimuli and used the passing-door technique as a means of effecting a change in personnel. Just under half their participants had failed to notice the change in that setting. This means that they already had evidence that this particular paradigm worked. Therefore these studies were actually **replications**, which is an effective way of testing the reliability of findings.

Crucial to this experimental paradigm is that the stimuli, in this case the experimenters, should be manifestly different. Across this series of studies the extent of the differences between the changing characters varied, as we have seen, but the effect was always present to a greater or lesser extent. It could have been that the first experimenter was in some way just plain nondescript, and no one paid any attention to the way he looked. This is an unsound suggestion, partly because more than one pair of experimenters was used in this set of studies. More importantly, this possibility occurred to the researchers and therefore their experimental design included the manipulation of which one went first. Thus, in each study, for half of the trials researcher A was replaced by researcher B, and in the other half the order was reversed.

To test recognition of the experimenters they used line-ups with three distracters on each occasion. This is a standard way of testing recognition. If we simply showed participants the original stimulus and asked 'Do you recognise this?' we would have difficulty being confident about the answers. The question itself has **demand characteristics**, and it would be very easy for the participant to claim they recognised the person because they felt they should. They would not have to be deceitful to make such a claim; they might genuinely believe that they did recognise them.

Using distracters and asking participants to select the one they recognise is used in all sorts of research involving memory: visual (pictures, faces, colours or text, for example) auditory (music, words) and even olfactory or touch memory. It is necessary to be careful in the way in which those distracters are chosen. For example, suppose we are looking at recognising spoken words and the word I would like you to recognise is 'chair'. If I present this stimulus to you embedded in three distracters – astronomy, palpitation and onomatopoeia – the task is rather too easy. If, on the other hand, the distracters are stair, pear, hair, it is a bit more of a challenge. The words in the first set of distracters differ from the stimulus semantically and acoustically, whereas the words in the second set all sound similar to the stimulus and are also all everyday objects. To do the job properly we would also need to take into account word frequency, which is how often a word appears in ordinary speech. For example, 'chair' would have a higher frequency because it is used more than, say, pear. If on the other hand the task involved recognising objects, then the distracters would all need to be everyday furniture, for example, a desk, a sofa and a bed. Likewise with face recognition, just as in a police line-up, it is important the other faces are at least equivalent. If the line-up to pick out the 6-foot-tall, 18-stone bully who took your money includes him and half a dozen small elderly women, the criminal in question would have cause for complaint. Therefore equivalence is all-important in this sort of task.

Levin and Simons took this into consideration when selecting their distracters. They asked seven independent judges to rate the similarity of each potential distracter to the target. In this context judges are not members of the legal profession. They are members of the public asked to help with the research by making judgements about the methods used – a common and necessary practice.

Why do researchers need judges to make these types of decision rather than relying on their own assessment?

They checked that the average similarity rating for each distracter with the target was approximately the same as the rating between distracters and between the targets. So this means that each distracter was as much like the target as they were like the other distracters. The other consideration with a recognition task is that each participant has a 1 in 4 chance of selecting the target by chance alone. However, as we have seen, they checked this statistically and only the change blind performed in the recognition task at chance level.

The other area for potential concern is the way in which the dependent variable was measured. As stated, this was done by interview, but as you have probably guessed it was not simply a matter of asking whether they had noticed that the person had changed, because once more this type of question would be beset with demand characteristics. Instead they used a **structured interview**, in which the questions asked are the same and in same order for each participant. They started by asking whether s/he had noticed anything unusual. If they did not mention the change of partner the questioning about the event continued until eventually the experimenter asked directly whether s/he realised that he was not the person who had originally approached asking for directions. This is a standard **funnelling technique** often used in structured interviews (and **questionnaires**) to provide participants with an opportunity to mention target items spontaneously prior to direct questioning. This allowed them to distinguish those participants who volunteered the information about the change at the start of the interview from those who only acknowledged the change when asked directly. This meant that the researchers could run the analysis twice: first comparing those who reported noticing change at any stage during the interview with those who never made such a report; secondly comparing those who volunteered the information at the start with those who did not. The authors admit that it is theoretically possible that participants were aware of the change but that the social demands of the situation prevented them from reporting it. However, this state of affairs is relatively unlikely as the process described above allowed some people to report noticing only in response to the direct question. As Simons and Levin argue in their 1998 paper, the demands of the situation were more likely to produce over- rather than under-reporting of awareness.

Finally, you may be thinking that these people must have been particularly naive not to notice such a change. However, in the study deploying the change behind the counter, nine of the 20 participants had seen a video or read about change blindness. Moreover, six of them were inadvertently recruited into the study directly after attending a lecture that included a description of the original 1998 study! Clearly awareness of the effect does not provide immunity. One of these reportedly said: 'I thought I would notice something like that. But I didn't. Curious' (Levin *et al.*, 2002, p.293).

It would seem, therefore, that age is not a factor in change detection, but in-group/out-group distinctions may be; that the effect is apparent even when the participants are encouraged to look at the stimulus that will change and even when it occurs in different settings and is not dependent on a crude and unnatural interruption in the dialogue. We can say that the effect is robust as it has now been demonstrated over different formats with different participants and different stimuli. The replication of these studies and the consistency of these findings show that the experimental paradigm was effective.

▲ How Appropriate Was the Research Method?

In this series of studies the researchers used a **single sample design**. It is true that the standard practice was to change the order of presentation of the two interchangeable individuals, but this does not mean that there were two conditions. The analysis did not identify whether the order of the researchers made a difference. The swap-over was designed to **control** for any specific effect of researcher A going first or second. It is relatively unusual to use a single sample design. Most experiments require a control condition for comparison in order to interpret the findings. Can you think of a suitable control for this study? In the experimental condition the enquirer changed, so logically in a control condition no such change would take place. What would be the point of such a condition? To see whether these participants noticed change when in fact none occurred? It does not really make sense when you consider it. If there is no need for a control condition, then the issue of related or unrelated designs becomes redundant. The dependent variable here was participants' response to the exchange. This was **operationalised** as the responses to the structured interview. If the dependent variable had been different, then a **control condition** might have been appropriate. If the aim had been to see whether the exchange had any effect on subsequent behaviour for example, then a control condition would have been necessary. The decision to use a single sample in this instance seems appropriate.

Although it was a single sample study, the researchers used a *post hoc* analysis. This means that, although there was only one sample that took part in the study, the sample could subsequently be divided by participants' responses to the change. Recall that Levin *et al.* compared those who did detect change with those who did not. Davies and Hine (1998) used a similar approach but with a filmed sequence to examine the role of change blindness in eyewitness testimony, and found that over 60 per cent of participants did not notice an identity change.

Much research in change blindness has used field experiments, for example Varakin *et al.* (2007), who also attempted to unravel the thorny issue of where the failure lies, in encoding or comparison of stimuli, but had to conclude that both are implicated. Other experimental paradigms have been used to explore change blindness. Smilek *et al.* (2008) compared laboratory with field experiments and argued that psychological findings really need to be taken from real-world rather than laboratory studies. However, some forms of laboratory experiment can help unravel the mechanisms that underlie change blindness. For instance, Symes *et al.* (2008) used a computer presentation of material to compare how different types of preparation can reduce the occurrence of change blindness.

Was experimentation the only possibility? An **observational study** was not really an option as it would present some difficulties. First, in observation the researcher has no control over the presentation of the stimulus, so change of stimulus here would have to occur naturally. In most settings, waiting around for one person to be replaced by another would probably be a waste of a researcher's time. It might be a possibility if the change was going to be predictable rather than unexpected, for example a change of workers when one shift ends and another begins. Another problem for this type of study is the issue of attention. As we have seen in their series of experiments Levin *et al.* varied the amount of attention that the participant would have to pay to the stimulus by varying the task (approaching a counter, giving directions, taking photographs). In a purely observational study, this would not be possible and therefore the amount that participants attended to the stimulus person would vary enormously and cause a good deal of 'noise' in the data, that is to say random error. A third problem for an observational study in this setting would be knowing whether or not a change had been detected. As we see from the Simons and Levin (1998) study, people carried on talking as though they had not noticed the swap even when they had.

It might be possible to use observation as a technique within an experiment to watch how people respond to the change. It would be possible to film their faces and perhaps analyse the film afterwards. Maybe it would be possible to get observers who were **blind** to the timing of the change to see if they could detect it by simply viewing the participant's face. This would not be an observational study; with the researchers manipulating the change it would still be an experiment.

Would it be possible to use **survey methods** alone? In this way we could ask people whether they think they would notice change, but survey methods only provide information on self-reported behaviour. It might well be worth doing and would give us a second strand of information on change detection related to self-awareness, which of itself would be useful. An alternative use of survey methods in this context would be if there was a suitable **psychometric test** which required the participant to notice or comment on change presented through words or possibly pictures. However, any such response would tell us only about how they responded to the test, which may not necessarily be the same as the way people would respond to a 'real-life' change. Again, such an approach may itself be valid and, used in conjunction with an experiment such as those undertaken by Levin and colleagues, would tell us more about the topic as a whole. As is so often the case, we can see how using more than one method can help build up a body of knowledge about a topic.

Conclusion

This series of experiments is an example of how theories and hypotheses can be developed over time and explored and tested through experimentation. A brief summary of the findings is that people may not notice quite substantial changes in the characteristics of a conversational partner; this phenomenon is apparent not only in laboratory studies but in real-world settings, and is not seriously affected by the way in which these changes are implemented (abrupt or natural), nor by the amount of concentration required to complete the interchange (from giving directions, through taking photographs, to awaiting information). Change blindness appears to be more likely if the conversational partner is part of an out-group, and if the two substitutes are male rather than female. As for the underlying mechanism, it would seem that the failure to notice change lies not in an inability to retrieve the memory, nor in the interference of the first stimulus by the second, but rather in the failure to store the image of either first or second stimulus.

Each individual only took part in the study once, and although several different studies were completed, each with different samples, in each case these were single sample studies. The participants were not in groups nor were they allocated to groups. You might think that the study that tested recall was a **between groups** design because the data from those who noticed the swap were compared with data from those who did not. However, this is not really a between groups experiment as the groups were only distinguished by the data they produced and not by the initial design of the experiment. Likewise you might think that it is a **between conditions** design because sometimes experimenter A was replaced by experimenter B, and sometimes vice versa. However this does not constitute a between conditions design as it was merely part of the **counterbalancing** necessary to control for the individual characteristics of the two people.

Experiments require the manipulation of one variable, the independent variable, and the measurement of the other, dependent, variable. In these experiments the independent variable was the change in conversational partner, and this was manipulated throughout the course of the experiment. The dependent variable was the participants' response. Once again we see that this manipulation of IV and measurement of DV along with control of **extraneous variables** is the essence of experimental research.

Summary Points	
Design	Field experiments – single sample
Aim	To monitor the effect of change
IV	Change of conversational partner
DV	Change detection Operationalised as responses to structured interview
Sample	Convenience sample: people on campus, N=39
Analysis	*Post hoc* comparison

Acoustic Preferences

Programme of Experiments – Animal Studies

'In antiquity there was only silence. In the nineteenth century, with the invention of the machine, Noise was born. Today, Noise triumphs and reigns supreme over the sensibility of men.' (Luigi Russolo, Futurist painter and composer, 1885–1947)

Do You Like Music?

The most likely answer to this question is: it depends. For many people it depends on the type of music. Some like classical music; the famous composers of the nineteenth century such as Beethoven or Brahms retain their appeal into the twenty-first century. Monteverdi's works from the sixteenth century remain regular features at opera houses and concert halls. We have just celebrated the 250th anniversary of the birth of Mozart, arguably the most popular of the classical composers, such is the enduring appeal of his music. More recent composers, also classed as classical – Stravinsky, Stockhausen or Glass – have their followers too, although their musical styles are very different from those of the earlier composers. Maybe you prefer popular music: rock, pop, rap, hip-hop, garage or house? These days there are many different streams in popular music, some derivative, some original. There is also 'world music', music drawn from different cultures across the world now accessible to all through the growth in global travel. In fact, it would seem that somewhere there is the right sort of music for everyone, that there is something for all tastes. This very diversity in types of music shows how many different musical tastes there are.

It is unclear how we, as a species, developed a taste for music. It is part of all known cultures but it serves no discernible function. There are many activities that span cultures, that can be found from simple societies to complex, or from ancient to modern, but the common factor in each case is that they serve a clear purpose for the continuation, protection or organisation of the society. Music, however, seems to have no direct adaptive function. Its evolution is therefore a legitimate focus of research in psychology.

If we break music down into its component parts, however, then we find that there are some consistent patterns in taste. Some individual sounds are more pleasing to the ear than others. For example, notes that are precisely one octave apart played together sound pleasing, at least to Western ears, and we call that *consonant*, whereas some other combinations of sounds, known as *dissonant*, are less pleasing, or discordant. Our preferences for these individual components are known to be consistent across different types of people with different types of musical taste. Moreover, it is not just some musical combinations that we all perceive as unpleasant noise; sounds made by other means can produce a similar universal disapproval, for example the screeching noise made by running fingernails down a blackboard!

Therefore some musical tastes, those concerned with simple sound elements, are common across individuals, while there is individual variation of tastes concerning more complex structures, or compositions.

Where Do Tastes Come From?

So you like some styles of music but not others. How can we explain this? There is a tendency to say that we like the good stuff and that what we do not like is trash. However, this is not a very satisfactory explanation as it is evident that other people do like the music that we dislike; we cannot merely dismiss them as 'wrong'. This area of taste, or aesthetics (the study of 'the nature of beauty, art, and taste and with the creation and appreciation of beauty', according to the *Merriam Webster Dictionary*) was originally the province of the philosopher, but it has become part of psychological research too.

We know that tastes change over time; what was considered beautiful in one century may not be cherished now. Indeed it does not take a hundred years to effect such changes in taste. Victorian fireplaces were removed from older houses in the middle of the twentieth century; now they are reinstated. Frizzy perms were all the rage in the 1970s but are rarely seen today! Equally with music, different styles dominate the record industry at different times. So tastes vary across individuals and over time.

One possible explanation for taste comes from evolutionary psychology. This **theory** suggests that such aesthetic preferences developed as part of the evolutionary process. It is possible to argue that individual tastes developed as means of distributing scarce resources. If people like different things, this will allow a greater number of the species to survive. Diversity can be seen to have a good ecological basis. At the same level, commonalities of taste may be explained in similar evolutionary terms; they may serve a purpose that helps perpetuate the survival of the species as a whole. It could be that these unpopular sounds are reminiscent of those heard by our ancestors as warning signals when danger was detected.

It is widely accepted that the ability to discriminate between pleasant and unpleasant sounds is a function of part of our auditory system which is similar in many respects to that of many other species including our nearest relatives, the primates. If there is an evolutionary explanation for the origin of tastes, then we could reasonably expect to find evidence of taste preference amongst our near relatives the primates; this seems a plausible **deduction**. Do primates have similar auditory tastes to ours? This was the question that McDermott and Hauser (2004) set out to answer in not one but a series of experiments. They reported four, neatly constructed, **true experiments** to tease out the issue of primate auditory preferences. This series is a beautiful example of hypothetico-deductive method (see Box 7.1) at its best. At every step the researchers have considered all possible explanations rather than settling for the interpretation that substantiates their original hypothesis.

McDermott and Hauser's **participants** were male and female adult monkeys, and a group of undergraduates. The monkeys were a species called cotton-top tamarins, found in the wild only in northern Columbia.

Hypothetico-Deductive Method

This requires us to use logic to think through and test theories; 'If this is so, then that must be so.' If I need oxygen to breathe then without it I shall die. If a car needs fuel in order to work, then without fuel it will not work. These are simple conditional statements.

The hypothetico-deductive method can be seen as a series of logical steps. Step 1, we observe facts in our environment. Step 2, using a process called **induction** from these observed facts, we make generalisations or theories to explain what we have observed. Step 3, using deduction we develop a **hypothesis** to test the theory. Deduction is the process of working out what must be so if the theory is correct. Step 4, we test the hypothesis and gather new facts, which may mean that we need to modify our theory.

For example, in Step 1 we observe that the death rate from heart attacks is lower in Mediterranean countries than in Britain or America. Step 2, induction, suggests that this may be something to do with diet. Our theory becomes that Mediterranean diets guard against heart disease. Step 3, our hypothesis, is that by altering the diet of a group of Britons we can reduce the risk of heart disease. Step 4 is a **randomised controlled trial** to test this hypothesis. If the rate of heart disease in the experimental group is lower than that in the control group, then we have evidence to support our hypothesis, which in turn lends credence to our theory.

If we want to test hypotheses we need to think through this logical process and identify 'If then' statements that we can set about testing.

The maximum number of tamarins used in any one experiment throughout this series was six, and the human sample was even smaller, peaking at five. This seems a very small **sample** and may seem to run counter to the general rule that the larger the sample the better. Sometimes with a well-designed and controlled experiment a large sample is not necessary. Incidentally we should not confuse sample size with quantity of data, as we shall see.

Are Consonant Intervals Music to their Ears? Spontaneous Acoustic Preferences in a Non-Human Primate

McDermott, J. & Hauser, M. (2004) *Cognition, 94,* B11–B21

Method

McDermott and Hauser tackled the puzzle of measuring acoustic preferences in primates in an ingenious way, although the principle of this design, a 'maze' in a laboratory, has been used in many human and non-human studies. We normally think of a maze as being a puzzle through which a way has to be found, but that was not the case with this one. The **apparatus** used in these experiments comprised two short passages in a simple V-shape connected by an entrance box. There was a hidden speaker at the far end of each of these passages, and these two speakers were set to play different sounds. For each **trial** in the animal experiments, a tamarin was placed in the entrance box and then the experimenter would leave the room in order to reduce the possibility of **experimenter effects**. Once outside, the experimenter would pull a lever which opened both sides of the entrance box revealing both maze passages. When the tamarin moved into one of these passages, the speaker in that passage would begin to play a sound repeatedly and this would continue for the time that the tamarin stayed in that passage. However, once the animal left that passage the speaker would stop. In this way, the animal's movements within the maze directly influenced which sound it heard. For each trial, the animal was left in the maze for five minutes and its behaviour filmed; each tamarin completed multiple trials in every experiment, and thereby this small sample produced many **data sets**.

The **dependent variable (DV)** was the animal's acoustic preference, and this needed **operationalising**. The preferences were to be identified by *measuring* the time spent with each type of sound, and *defining* preference as which of those two measurements was the longer.

The **aim** was to test whether these animals had a preference for one type of musical chord over another. To do this, the authors paired a set of consonant (pleasant) two-note cords with a set of dissonant (unpleasant) notes. These sounds were set to play for 1.5 seconds at a time on a continuous loop with only short intervals between chords.

Results

When analysing the data, to eliminate one potential source of **bias** the film was viewed with the sound turned off. The meant that those recording the behaviour did not know which sound was paired with which wing. Members of the research team independently noted the time when the animal entered or left a wing of the maze. They used the time shown on the recording, which was accurate to one second. This allowed the total time the animal spent in each wing of the maze to be calculated.

Statistical analysis using a **paired t-test** showed there was no **significant** difference (**p>.05**) between the amount of time spent in each wing. These data showed that the tamarins exhibited no preference as defined by the experimenters. They spent approximately half the time in each wing of the maze. The authors concluded that the animals did not demonstrate a spontaneous preference for consonance over dissonance.

■ How Safe Is This Conclusion?

Research can be a tricky business, and concluding cause and effect is never straightforward, especially with living beings. It is therefore worth considering where there was scope for error and what the experimenters did to address this. They needed to consider possible **systematic errors** which could lead to faulty or erroneous conclusions, as well as **random errors**, which might just mask any real effect.

How Objective Is the Outcome Measure?

The conclusion was based on the amount of time the animal spent in each wing of the maze, as recorded by experimenters viewing the videotapes. If their apparatus had been more elaborate it might have been possible to make objective timings. If they had access to some form of electronic or mechanical means of detecting the primates' presence in either wing, maybe a device that detected either weight or movement in either wing would have been useful. But their apparatus had no such equipment so a judgement had to be made about what constituted entering or exiting either wing. The problem is that human judgement can be very **subjective**. We know that the authors addressed the possibility of systematic error by turning off the volume in the recording; so that those measuring the time were **blind** to the experimental conditions for the trial they were viewing. This meant that they were not going to be subconsciously influenced by their own expectations of what the experiment would show. After all, the observers might reasonably have felt that any creature would prefer to be away from the dissonant chord.

Having addressed the potential for a systematic error in their recording technique, what about the possibility of random error? As human judgement is subjective, what if someone else had watched the recordings: would they have produced different times? Clearly it was necessary for the experimenters to produce very clear definitions or criteria for this judgement – that is, what exactly constituted leaving or entering a wing. But even with stringent criteria it is all too easy for humans inadvertently to introduce an element of variation. If different recorders develop marginally different interpretations of exactly when the animal enters the wing, then the data could become meaningless. For that matter, any one observer could drift in their interpretation over time, which would also have the same effect. This untoward variation in recordings would be an example of what is called 'noise' in the data, a classic random error that could easily mask any real effect.

The authors used a standard statistical technique to check for such effects, namely a test of **inter-observer reliability**. This produces a **correlation coefficient** and in this case this showed a near-**perfect correlation**, that is to say that each of a pair of observers had recorded the same time on just about every occasion. You may think that this was only checking for variation between observers, which leaves the possibility of changes over time. However, the test requires using multiple measurements from each observer and is therefore likely to detect any changes over time. If one or other had begun to drift in their interpretation of the criteria it would have affected the results. If both had begun to drift, it is unlikely that they would have drifted in exactly the same manner over the same period of time. Therefore this test is also checking consistency over time. And with a result as high as was achieved in this case, it means that we can have a good deal of confidence in the consistency of the observations.

How Appropriate Were their Independent Variables?

The independent variable in this study was the sound played to the tamarins, and the basis of this experiment was that dissonant chords are less pleasing than chords that are consonant. Some combinations of notes are clearly dissonant, that is discordant, jarring or inharmonious and very unpleasant, at least to Western ears. Conversely some combinations are clearly harmonious and therefore are usually considered more appealing. The question then becomes; how well did the researchers tap into these two different types of sound? If they did not succeed in doing this with their experimental apparatus then the results would be seriously flawed.

Remember the undergraduate participants? This is where they come in. The researchers also ran this experiment with humans. Now, they did not put them in maze but rather constructed what they termed an analogue of their primate experiment. The humans were tested in a room which was divided into two by a tape on the floor, and they were free to move as they chose. The only instruction given to them was that they should stay in the room for the five-minute period of the experiment. There were speakers on each side of the room, each of which played one of the chords used in the tamarin experiment when the person was in that half of the room. Unlike the tamarins, the humans only did one trial each as this was considered adequate to detect any preference.

The results from this experiment were indeed conclusive: data from four humans were analysed and they spent approximately 90 per cent of their time in the consonant side of the room, thereby demonstrating a clear preference for consonance over dissonance.

You may recall that there were five humans in this study but the data were only analysed from four; data for one person were discarded. You might be thinking this may have been some form of bias on the part of the experimenters; maybe they did not like this man's data, maybe it ran counter to their hypothesis? Certainly all researchers must be very meticulous in the way in which they treat their data. We cannot just select those that suit our story! In this case, however, this man did not move at all during the entire experiment and that is the reason why his data were 'thrown out' (McDermott & Hauser, 2004, p. B17). The terminology the authors use may indicate their exasperation. Other than this phrase, the authors make no further comment on this individual. It may be that this was a case of **demand characteristics** – that this individual decided he would behave in a way that was counter to expectations, possibly even hazarding a guess at what the experimenters were exploring. He may have wanted to deliberately confirm or possibly refute what he thought to be their hypothesis. Or it may have been a case of **evaluation apprehension**, that is the individual did not want the researchers making judgements about him based on how he responded to the noise, and therefore chose not to respond.

This one pesky individual aside, this study shows that the chords chosen had the desired effect on humans so we can have confidence in the effectiveness of the sound recordings.

● How Effective Is This Experimental Design?

Cotton-top tamarins live in wet tropical forests, moist forest in the Andes, and dry thorn forest savannah on the northern coastal plane of their native Columbia, and yet these authors expected to be able to interpret their behaviour in a maze in a laboratory in Massachusetts. Put that way it seems most unlikely that we could learn anything about the species from the way it behaves in such an artificial setting – even if these particular animals were bred in captivity. You could suggest that once put into the maze the creatures were more concerned with getting out than listening to music. In that event, their behaviour through the two wings would be fairly **random** and that in itself could easily produce the equal distribution of time spent in the two wings. If this were the case it would be another example of random error, the noise in the data here being caused by the animals' response to the maze rather to the chords. How can we be certain this is not the case?

The answer can be found in an experiment conducted by McDermott and Hauser prior to the one using musical chords. In this, they used exactly the same experimental method, but instead of music the speakers played recordings of tamarin calls. One of these calls is called a 'food chirp' and is the noise that the animal makes during feeding; this one is predicted to have positive associations for the animal. The second call was the distress scream, predicted to have negative associations.

(It is easy, at this point, to get concerned over the welfare of the animals, and wonder what they did to make the tamarins distressed. The authors provide reassurance on this point. The calls were recorded when the animals were held by veterinary staff for routine check-ups. Evidently the animals did not enjoy being so held, but it was part of maintaining their health and welfare and therefore not, itself, unethical. For the British Psychological Society's position on animal experimentation see the BPS Code of Conduct guidelines for psychologists working with animals.)

Recordings were made of the chirps and the screams in order to produce the necessary stimuli. Two recordings of each noise were taken from three different animals who did not take part in the experiment. In each case, on the chirp and scream tapes, the noises were separated by intervals between one and one and a half seconds long. As in the music study, each animal took part in multiple trials. The results showed that the animals displayed a preference for the chirps over the screams, they spent approximately 60 per cent of their time in the wing playing that tape, compared to only 40 per cent in the other wing.

Therefore this study shows that the experimental method was indeed effective in detecting sound preferences amongst the tamarins, at least with their own calls.

Will Tamarins Respond to Artificial Sounds?

The study described above shows that tamarins demonstrate an apparent preference when given two alternative calls from their own species. Such calls are sounds with which the species would be familiar both in its native habitat and in the laboratory and could therefore be said to have some **ecological validity**. Musical chords, however, are a product of human invention and other animals do not make music in the way that we do. So the lack of a clear preference for consonant chords could indicate that tamarins only respond to sounds that are species-specific. If that is the case, the conclusions drawn from the study would again be spurious.

Once again, McDermott and Hauser have addressed this issue. In an earlier study, indeed the first in this set of experiments, they used exactly the same method as described above, but this time the speakers played two different volumes of 'white noise'. 'White noise' is an acoustic or electrical noise which can be used to mask other noises and sounds, a bit like the hiss from an untuned radio.[1] In one condition the white noise was played at a volume of 60 decibels as measured at the entrance junction of the maze. This is roughly equivalent to the volume of noise made by a dishwasher or one of the louder electric toothbrushes, and is equivalent to the volume of an ordinary conversation. The second recording played at 90 decibels, as measured in the same place, which is approximately the same volume as the noise made by a lorry, a tractor or a shouted conversation.

(Again if you are concerned about the animal's welfare at being subjected to noises of this level it might help to bear in mind that noises at this level are not considered harmful unless experienced for prolonged periods. It also might help to consider that the average rock concert is 110–120 decibels; 90 decibels therefore may be considered unpleasant, but not harmful.)

In this experiment, then, the quieter sound was expected to be preferred over the louder sound, and the tamarins would therefore spend more time in the quiet wing. And indeed this is what was found. The animals spent a total of 70 per cent of the time in the quieter wing of the maze. In a further refinement of this study, they repeated the experiment but with a smaller gap between volumes (75 and 85 decibels) and yet the same pattern of behaviour was seen, with the animals spending 68 per cent of the time in the quieter wing. You will note that, in this study, the time spent in the wing with the intended negative **stimulus** was less than that found in the study using species-specific cries.

Therefore we can have confidence that this experimental paradigm with tamarins works for manufactured as well as natural sounds.

Could They Have a Preference for One Wing Over the Other?

The premise of this whole **experimental paradigm** is that the animals are responding to the sound transmitted through the speakers. What if instead they simply have a preference for moving to the left, or to the right? This would surely make it impossible to draw firm conclusions from the data.

In order to prevent this being a problem, McDermott and Hauser changed which sound was paired with which wing in a very thorough way. This is best explained with reference to the study using white noise, where each animal underwent four trials. The initial pairing of sound and wing for each animal was determined at random, and this pairing was repeated at the second trial, which occurred at least a day later. This means that not all animals had the same initial pairing of sound and wing, and that is important in case the experience of the first trial in a novel environment had an undue influence on subsequent trials. If the first trial did have such an influence, then this could become a source of systematic error, a **confounding variable**, if all animals had the same initial pairing.

For the third and fourth trials, also on separate days, the pairing was reversed. A similar procedure was used to determine sound pairing and wing in the other experiments although the number of trials was higher. This means that each experiment was **counterbalanced**, as the arrangement of the pairing of sound and wing

Table 7.1. Time spent in each wing (white noise experiment)

	Trial 1	Trial 2	Trial 3	Trial 4	Total
Quiet side	78%	88%	47%	68%	70%
Loud side	22%	12%	53%	32%	30%

balanced any possible effect of wing direction across the two conditions. This does not mean that the experimenters eliminated any effect of wing direction, but it does control for it. Without this, any inherent preference for one direction over another would act as a source of random error, masking any real preference for one sound over another. Therefore if there were a preference for one wing it should affect both conditions equally, which means that any difference observed over and above this can really only be attributed to the sound played.

Given that in two experiments, white noise and species vocalisations, a difference was demonstrated, we can be confident that the preference was for the sound and not the direction.

Could the Monkeys Have Lost Interest?

We know that these monkeys ran repeated trials in each experiment; furthermore McDermott and Hauser used many of the same animals throughout the series of experiments. To what extent would the repeated exposure to this experimental set-up affect the primates' behaviour? In spite of the careful experimental design described so far, could there be any **carry-over effects**? Could the experience of having done the trial once have any untoward knock-on effects on subsequent trials? We need only to check for this within the tamarin experiments, as the humans each only underwent one trial, and we need only consider one experiment as the only changes in design between experiments were changes in the stimuli presented. This possibility was explored by the authors in two ways.

McDermott and Hauser examined the individual trial data from the white noise experiment and their results are indicated in Table 7.1. Recall that the pairing of sound and wing was changed after the second trial.

The preference for the quiet side is evident in the first trial and more pronounced in the second. Then, in Trial 3, after the pairing of sound and wing had swapped over, there appears to be no real preference between the two options, but by the fourth trial the preference is once again evident. The **inferential statistics** (paired t-tests) that the authors used showed that there were significant differences in all but Trial 3. Interestingly, their data also show that there is little variation between individual animals on the first two trials and considerable variation on the third, reducing again on the fourth (not indicated in this table). This tells us that the change of pairing did cause some confusion: the tamarins seem to have learned to associate one wing with the preferred noise. However, taking all the trials together it is evident that there was a clear preference for the quieter sound.

The second check was to see if there were carry-over effects between the experiments. How closely spaced in terms of time were each of these experiences for the primates? The authors indicate only that one experiment, that using the tamarin vocalisation, took place three months after the other experiments had finished, and it is not clear how long a tamarin would need to forget the experience, if indeed it ever would. It is a moot point whether when an animal does repeated trials, or in this case repeated experiments, its second and subsequent attempts are influenced by that first **naive** trial. In this particular instance we know that the musical chord experiment occurred after that using white noise. We also know that with white noise a clear preference was shown, but that later with the musical chords there was no such finding. Perhaps by then the tamarins were bored with the whole set-up, had become blasé about the whole thing, that is, had become **habituated** to the experimental paradigm.

If you thought that this might explain the findings in your own study, what could be done to see whether it was the case? If the lack of effect in the second experiment might not be due to the change in stimulus but rather a change in your subjects – how could you check? The answer is to try the first stimulus again to see if it still has an effect, and that is exactly what McDermott and Hauser did. They repeated the white noise version of the study for just one trial for all five animals in the musical chord study and all five showed a distinct preference for the quieter sound, spending a total of 70 per cent of their time in that wing.

Therefore the tamarins were not habituated; taken together the findings mean that, while these primates prefer quieter sounds, they have no preference when it comes to harmony.

Is Indifference Limited to Music?

We have already noted that the construction of music is unique to the human species, (although many birds have musical calls) so perhaps music just has little meaning for tamarins. In the wild they live on fruit, insects and tree sap. Maybe expecting a tamarin to distinguish harmonious music from discordant sound is equivalent to expecting you or me to be able to identify which beetle is the more delicious. It is beyond our experience and understanding of the world and therefore we cannot make such distinctions. To test whether this indifference to a noise that we consider aversive was limited purely to music, McDermott and Hauser tried their experimental paradigm with one further stimulus, this time with both tamarins and humans.

Consider again for a moment the noise that fingernails make when scraped down a blackboard – not a pleasant experience. This was the starting point for the new stimulus, although the sound they recorded was in fact a metal-pronged instrument scraped down a pane of glass, a screech which had been described as a chilling sound in past research. As the authors comment, 'informal tests showed this stimulus produced the desired response in humans'. Having identified their aversive sound they needed to match it with a noise of equivalent volume and duration again, and they chose white noise. All other aspects of the study were the same as for the musical chord experiment, except that the five adult tamarins were new and, unsurprisingly, only four of the original humans were used this time.

The data from the humans showed exactly the effect that had been expected, with them spending approximately three-quarters of their time with the white noise rather than with the screech. However, this was not so for the tamarins, who spent only just marginally over half their time with white noise, and the difference between the times spent in these two conditions was confirmed as not significant using inferential statistics. But these were new tamarins and maybe they would not show the same reaction to aversive stimuli as the original ones had demonstrated. Again the thoroughness of the research team precluded this possibility. Before running these new tamarins with the new stimuli (the screech), they repeated the white noise experiment used in the earlier study and produced very similar findings.

So we can be confident that it is not just music where the monkeys showed no preference; mechanical sounds that humans find aversive did not seem to have the same effect on the primates.

How Safe Was That Operational Definition?

We can accept that the authors have established several **orderly relationships** in their data. Tamarins avoid worrying calls from their fellows, and loud mechanical noises, but do not attempt to avoid dissonant sounds either musical or mechanical, both of which, by contrast, are avoided by humans. How safe is the authors' interpretation of these data that the tamarins show no preference for dissonant sounds? This rests on the **operational definition** used. If you want to establish preferences with humans you can either can ask them or give them a choice of two different options. These options can be presented explicitly or implicitly, as was done in this study, where no options were actually stipulated but the humans were simply free to wander to discover them for themselves. With primates, asking and explicit choices are not options; the only way to determine preferences is to leave two choices available and assume that whichever is taken up is the preferred choice of the primate. In this instance, as the animal was free to move from one side of the maze to the other it was assumed that the amount of time spent in either wing of the maze would indicate a preference for the sound played in that wing.

How valid is that assumption? There are two factors that are relevant in deciding this. The first is the established fact that all animals will avoid aversive stimuli when they can. This can be explained in evolutionary terms: the ability to avoid aversive stimuli is part of the process of natural selection. It keeps animals away from predators or toxins that might endanger them. Therefore if, as in this study, an animal elects consistently to spend more time with stimulus A than stimulus B it is safe to assume that stimulus B is in some way aversive or unpleasant, or at least more so than stimulus A.

The second issue to consider is what we mean by preferences. When we are talking about human preferences, we mean some form of positive emotional response. A preference means a partiality, a predilection for or inclination towards a specific item. I may prefer pears to apples, meaning that perhaps I like both but I like pears more. If faced, however, with two unpleasant stimuli it has harder to use the word 'preference'. If I am to be stung by a wasp or a stinging nettle, I might choose the latter if I perceive it to be less painful and to heal quicker. It would seem odd to say that I have a preference for stinging nettles, however.

With the cotton-top tamarins, McDermott and Hauser have successfully demonstrated what types of sound are avoided, and they have used the word 'preference' as a shorthand to explain this behaviour. Preference here is not a long-standing partiality, but rather a preferred choice of two available options. In fact, it could be argued that this series of experiments was not investigating primate preferences so much as their aversions.

Can you think of a way in which you might truly be able to test primate preferences rather than aversions?

What About This 'Western Ears' Bit?

You may have noticed that in the early part of this chapter reference was made to preferences for consonant music being established in Western cultures. It is well known that the musical scale used in Oriental countries differs from that established in the Western hemisphere. Many Western listeners at first find some forms of Eastern music discordant. In McDermott and Hauser's study the humans used were all studying at an American university, and although no information is given about their ethnicity it is statistically probable that they were Westerners. Herein lies a potential problem with the study. If the sound preference detected in the humans for harmonious musical chords was only a product of their being Westerners, then it would not be universal to humans, let alone primates. However, the screech noise was one that had been used in previous experiments by other authors and has been identified as a noise repellent to all humans, and not culturally specific.

Therefore it is safe to conclude that noises that humans find intrinsically unpleasant do not have the same effect on our primate cousins.

▲ How Appropriate Was the Research Method?

The authors used a series of repeated measures designs in this set of studies, which means they had **related data** for each individual within each trial. This means that each individual (tamarin or undergraduate) experienced both conditions. Is it possible to envisage an unrelated design? They could have done a **randomised controlled trial (RCT)** (see Chapter 3). Each individual would have been randomly assigned to experience only one condition. In theory this is fine. In this instance it presents practical problems. Remember the dependent variable: time spent in each location. If they are only experiencing one condition, this needs rethinking. We could have one wing silent and the other wing with noise. But this would tell us whether they preferred silence to noise. It would be difficult to argue whether they preferred one noise to another. An alternative would be to give them no choice, to subject them to just one noise and watch their behaviour. This would have the same inherent difficulties of the noise/silence design, along with additional ethical concerns. If the animals found a noise unpleasant, they would have no means of avoiding it. The neat simplicity of the repeated measures design is that it shows relative *preferences*. Other designs would only tell us whether or not something was liked, leaving interpretation of preference to the researcher. Indeed, the researchers used the same paradigm later to test tempo preference in primates, (McDermott & Hauser, 2007). They found that, unlike humans, primates prefer slow tempi to fast, and silence to slow-tempo music.

As identified in previous chapters, the main tools of our research armoury are experiments, **observation** and **surveys**, and the latter are clearly inappropriate with primates. However, we could find about musical preferences in humans using survey methods. For example, Rentfrow *et al.* (2003) examined the relationship between personality characteristics and musical preferences. They concluded that their data suggest that personality, self-esteem and cognitive abilities all influence preferences.

Observation is a possibility with primates, but a purely observational study would not be practical as it seems improbable, when observing primates in their own environment, that musical notes or nails on a blackboard would occur naturally. Of course, as the researcher you could bring your own sounds with you, but at that point it stops being true observation and becomes a **field experiment**. Observation as a method is where the behaviour of research subjects is watched and recorded *without* any direct contact or intervention. If we chose to do a field experiment, we could observe a group of primates, then introduce the required sound or sounds and watch for any changes in the behaviour that this sound effects. This might tell us something about primates and auditory preferences. It is likely, though, that there would be problems as the researcher would have little control over the conditions in which the **target behaviour** occurred, i.e. it would be subject to **extraneous variables**. Tropical forests are not the most controlled environments. However, field experiments with primates on other issues have been successful and informative. For example, Garber *et al.* (2008) looked at hand-preference among capuchin monkeys. They found that there seemed to be evidence of hand preference within tasks, but not across tasks.

One type of extraneous variable that might affect our study is the possibility of a confounding variable. For instance, the animals might react equally to all noises as they would be alien to them in that environment. This might lead to the conclusion that they have no preference when in reality it is the novelty and unpredictability of the situation that is causing their response. We could try to overcome the problem of novelty by repeating the sound until the primates were used to it. The problem is they might get used to the pleasant and unpleasant noise at the same rate once they realised that neither was followed by danger, and then we would have no effect. Or, if the noise caused flight, it would be difficult for the animals to become accustomed to it as they would not be around long enough. There might also be problems of group behaviour: is primate A responding to the noise or just responding to primate

B's response? Problems such as these might produce a systematic effect on the data and could lead us to draw flawed conclusions from our study.

Another difficulty when introducing a novel stimulus, in this case a noise, in a natural environment is that the researcher cannot control other events spontaneously occurring at the same time. For example, there could be squabbles amongst members of the group, the arrival of the alpha male, or the prospect of a predator appearing on the horizon. This would be an example of random error and make interpretation of the subsequent behaviour very difficult.

Having noted these difficulties with field experiments, the sense in using a true experiment seems obvious for this particular research question. However, observation of these animals in their natural habitat would also be useful to see how they respond to naturally occurring sounds. This would be a legitimate research question, but quite different from that reported here.

Conclusion

This elegant series of experiments by McDermott and Hauser provides clear evidence of what attributes of a sound a tamarin finds aversive. A brief summary of the findings is that these primates will take evasive action based on the volume of a manufactured sound but not on its quality. The authors conclude that 'if humans and nonhuman primates share acoustic preferences for sounds, this capacity evolved more recently than the divergence with the New World monkeys such as the cotton-top tamarin (i.e. some 40 million years ago)'.

Each individual had a choice of paired sounds throughout the study and therefore the experimental design used throughout was **within subjects** or **related design**, that each individual effectively worked as their own **control**. If some animals had been assigned to one condition (e.g. dissonance) and others to the alternative (e.g. consonance) the design would have used **independent subjects**, which in this particular case would have been hard to interpret. You might think that this study was a **between groups design** as the response of the humans as well as primates was noted, but this would be mistaken interpretation. The humans and the tamarins were separate experiments, and the humans were used as a validation of the features of experiment, in the 'analogue' of the primate study. If an experimenter wishes to do a between groups study, then the two groups take part in one experiment, with the same apparatus and **procedure**.

One feature that makes it possible to determine cause and effect in an experiment is that the researcher has control over the relevant variables. Part of the structure of experiments requires the manipulation of one variable, the **independent variable** (**IV**), and the measurement of the other, dependent, variable. In these experiments the independent variable was the sound played on the speakers. This was manipulated both for each trial and for each experiment. The dependent variable was the behaviour of the subjects, more explicitly, which sound they avoided. This manipulation of IV and measurement of DV along with control of extraneous variables is the essence of experimental research.

Note

1   In physics, the formal definition of white noise 'the noise that has constant magnitude of
    power over frequency'.

Summary Points	
Design	Laboratory experiment – repeated measures
Aim	To compare two conditions
IV	Type of noise
DV	Preference Operationalised as time spent in each wing of maze
Sample	Cotton-top tamarins (N=5)
Analysis	Between conditions

Appendix: Research with Animals

For some people, any research involving animals is wrong; for others it is acceptable
providing appropriate welfare standards are maintained. As with most matters of
conscience, this is not an easy issue to resolve. The interested reader is referred to the
British Psychological Society's guidelines for psychologists working with animals, in
the BPS Code of Conduct, Ethical Principles and Guidelines (British Psychological
Society, 2005), from which the following extracts are taken:

> Psychologists work with animals for a variety of reasons. The most obvious use is in
> research, and it is this that has commanded most attention in the general media.…
> Many psychological studies are non-invasive and involve only observation of the ani-
> mals, but some research questions cannot be answered adequately without the manip-
> ulation of animals; and all studies of captive animals necessarily involve keeping
> animals in confinement.…
>
>   The researcher is … required to demonstrate that consideration has been given to
> *r*eplacing animals with non-sentient alternatives whenever possible, *r*educing the
> number of animals used, and *r*efining procedures to minimise suffering (The three R's:
> Russell & Burch, 1959). Psychologists who work with animals should, therefore, keep
> abreast of new developments in animal welfare, with new ways of reducing the num-
> bers of animals required for the procedures, and with refining the procedures so as to
> enhance the welfare of the animals concerned.

Cognitive Costs of Racial Prejudice

Experiment – Unrelated Three-Factor Design, Between Groups and Between Conditions

'Prejudices, it is well known, are most difficult to eradicate from the heart whose soil has never been loosened or fertilized by education; they grow there, firm as weeds among rocks.' (Charlotte Brontë, author, 1816–55)

Are You Affected by Prejudice?

Prejudice can be defined as an adverse judgement or opinion formed beforehand, without knowledge or examination of the facts. With this definition there are few of us who can claim to be entirely without prejudice. Do you think that tabloid papers print the truth? Do you believe that all television channels are equally good? Some people think that all tabloid papers print only nonsense. Others believe that certain television channels transmit nothing but rubbish. What about politicians: do you think that they are generally well motivated, or truthful? Many people apparently do not think so. If we think that all politicians are self-serving, we have made an adverse judgement without knowing the facts about each individual concerned. Journalists, estate agents, advertising executives, city bankers: do you truly judge each one entirely on her or his own merits? Or are you inclined to believe that one or other of these groups is untrustworthy? Do you have a predisposition to mistrust them? Such a predisposition is in itself a prejudice. These types of prejudice are fairly commonplace in society, and while they are rarely positive forces, the harm done is pretty diffuse. If you have been able to answer honestly that you do not have such a prejudice regarding any of the above parties, and that you know of no groups, institutions or corporations about whom you have preconceived ideas, then indeed you may be one of the few people who truly are without prejudice.

An alternative and more austere definition is an irrational suspicion or hatred of a particular group, race or religion. Sadly, history and societies across the globe are littered with this type of prejudice. The targets or victims of prejudice comprise nearly all identifiable groups within society at one time or another. Just think of the history of the UK. How did the indigenous Britons feel about the invading Romans or vice versa? Or the Celts and the Angles? The Saxons and the Normans? More recently our societies have seen nationwide prejudice against Jews, black people and Muslims, amongst others. Victims of prejudice find themselves disadvantaged, with restricted access to society's resources. Accounts of any society where prejudice is sanctioned by the state provide harrowing stories of how the out-groups struggle to survive. The twentieth century saw some very ugly examples of what happens when prejudice is not only tolerated within a society but actively encouraged. While prejudice is by definition in the mind of the individual, once it affects the way that individual behaves it becomes discrimination. Where prejudice is allowed to flourish, state-sanctioned or not, it will result in discrimination and its victims will endure hardship and suffering. We have seen what happens when a society is structured around such discrimination in, for example, South Africa for much of the latter part of the twentieth century, or more recently in Zimbabwe. We have seen racial discrimination become outlawed in some countries in response to civil rights movements. The type of racial segregation commonplace in much of the United States until the 1960s is now unthinkable. Regrettably legislation can only address discrimination, the manifestation of prejudice, not prejudice itself. Only education and enlightenment can achieve the latter.

The costs of racial prejudice for its victims are well documented, as are the more subtle costs for its perpetrators. What about third parties, those who only witness racial prejudice? Is there also a cost for them in terms of its effect? This is the question that Salvatore and Sheldon (2007) set out to address. They argued that while blatant discrimination these days is against the law in most Western countries, prejudiced individuals will resort to more ambiguous forms of racial discrimination. It is no longer socially acceptable to exclude someone from opportunities because of their skin colour. But the truly prejudiced individual will find another way to exclude him or her, to find another reason behind which they can hide the unacceptable face of prejudice.

Salvatore and Sheldon wanted to explore the costs of witnessing both types of prejudice, blatant and ambiguous. They argued that the experience of racial prejudice is specific to each racial group. In the United States, whites, as a group, have no experience of being the victims of prejudice, unlike blacks. For this reason the researchers proposed that black participants would be more sensitive to ambiguous prejudice than white participants. Moreover, some past research had suggested that victims of prejudice develop strategies for dealing with it in order to reduce the detrimental emotional effects of repeatedly encountering such negativity. For this reason Salvatore and Sheldon predicted that whites would be more affected than blacks by witnessing blatant prejudice.

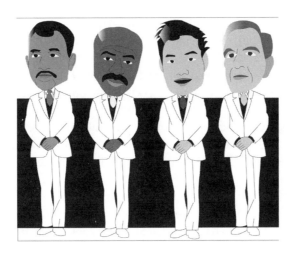

Cognitive Costs of Exposure to Racial Prejudice

Salvatore, J. & Shelton, J.N. (2007). *Psychological Science, 18*(9), 810–815

Method

Salvatore and Shelton designed an elaborate and neat **experiment** to measure the cognitive effects of being exposed to racial prejudice. They did this by inviting their participants, 250 college students, to take part in what were ostensibly two unrelated studies. The first study was described as helping a company decide whether it should change its employment procedures. **Participants** were told that the **aim** was to compare two processes, one where the decision about applicants was made by a single individual and one where it was made by a team. To do this they were to evaluate a series of recent decisions. They were also told that they would be randomly assigned to look at one of these processes, individual or team, but in fact all were assigned to cases where the decision was apparently made by a single individual. At this stage they were provided with a dossier of information about recent hiring decisions and asked to read through it, after which they would be asked to complete a questionnaire about these decisions. Some participants were given a dossier containing decisions that were blatantly racially prejudiced; others received documents where the racial prejudice was more ambiguous, and a third group received dossiers without any evidence of racial prejudice.

Once the participants had read through their dossier, the researcher apologised for not having the questionnaire ready, and participants were invited to take part in the second and apparently entirely separate study while the location of the missing questionnaire was discovered. Thus each participant read through the materials prior to completing the cognitive task. The real aim of the study was to see whether the experience of reading these materials had an effect on the cognitive performance of participants.

The second study was computer-based and required participants to complete a cognitive task, a computerised version of the Stroop task. The original hard-copy version of this task was developed in the 1930s and has subsequently become a classic in cognitive psychological experimentation. A set of single stimuli, e.g. 'xxxx', is presented to the participant, with each 'xxxx' printed in a different colour, the task each time being simply to identify the colour of the print. This may seem like a ridiculously easy task and hardly challenging. However, the trick is that while this set of stimuli is neutral, another set of stimuli is presented consisting of the names of colours, and here each name is in a different colour from the colour in which it is printed. For example, the word may be 'blue' but the ink colour is red, the next word is 'green' but the ink is blue, the third word is 'red' but the ink is green. This then becomes quite a difficult task as it requires you to use what is called selective attention. In order to do this, you have to ignore the word and attend instead solely to the colour of the ink. In fact you have to concentrate on not reading! The difference between the time taken to identify the colour of the row of 'xxxx', the **control** (easy) condition, and the time taken working out the difficult, conflicting or incongruent, condition is therefore taken as a measurement of high-level cognitive function. The second condition is nearly always found to be more difficult: this is a robust effect that has been well established in the literature. For the original hard-copy version of the task, the response required was to name the colour. With the computerised version participants need only identify the correct colour name by pressing a key. The advantage of the computerised version is the accuracy of computer-recorded timing on each **trial**. In Salvatore and Shelton's study, participants completed 92 trials.

From the contrast between these two apparently separate studies it is easy to see that participants would accept that they were unrelated. The aim was to compare the cognitive effects of encountering prejudice on black and white participants.

Results

The **dependent variable (DV)**, cognitive performance, was operationalised as the Stroop score. This was calculated by subtracting the **mean** time to respond to the neutral control **stimuli** from the mean time to respond to the incongruent stimuli. This final Stroop score was then compared between the levels of the **independent variable (IV)**, namely with and without racial prejudice. An **analysis of variance (ANOVA)** showed that exposure to racial prejudice had a **significant** detrimental effect on cognitive performance. To be specific, it showed that this effect was different for the two groups. As predicted, black participants showed a decrement after exposure to ambiguous racial prejudice while white participants' decrement was worse after exposure to blatant racial prejudice. This finding is particularly pertinent as it shows that not only does witnessing racial prejudice result in a cognitive cost but also that different ethnic groups respond differently to different forms of prejudice.

The results of the analysis of variance also showed that there was an **interaction** between the race of the participant and that of the victim of prejudice. While black participants showed a greater effect if the prejudice was displayed by a white manager against a black applicant, white participants showed a greater effect if the victim was white and the manager was black. Thus the cost of prejudice for both groups was highest when they were the same race as the victim and a different race from the perpetrator.

■ How Safe Is This Conclusion?

This is potentially an important finding with considerable implications for society. But how safe is it? In order to assess this we need to look in more detail at the method. The aim, you may recall, was to compare black participants with white. This is a between groups comparison, but clearly participants were not randomly assigned to these groups. Ethnicity makes pre-existing groups; nonetheless, this is a between groups comparison with an unrelated design.

What about the hypothetical character displaying the prejudice: what race should s/he be? And what about the victim of the prejudice: what race that should that person be? In order to understand the dynamics of the effects of racial prejudice it is necessary to control for each of these variables in turn, and to do that requires a neat but quite complex experimental design. How this was achieved can be explained by examination of those dossiers.

The dossiers contained information allegedly about decisions made by a human resources manager relating to the selection of candidates, including: the details of the job, details of four male applicants, and the manager's decision along with its rationale. Each of these factors needed to be manipulated in turn in order to achieve the appropriate **counterbalance**.

What Was the Design of the Study?

As the race of the person making the selection decision would affect the perception of prejudice, this needed to be **controlled** for across the two groups of participants. This component of the design is an example of a **group difference** study. Therefore, for some of each group the information about the manager indicated that he was black, and for the remainder of each group it indicated that he was white. Of the four applicants, two were plausible but unremarkable candidates for the job in question. The third applicant had poor qualifications which did not meet the specification in the job description. The fourth, in contrast, was very well qualified as well as being a graduate of the prestigious Yale University and was designed to be clearly the best applicant for the job. Therefore the best choice of candidate was always number 4 and the least qualified was number 3. Across all the dossiers, the race of the manager was the same as the race of the poorly qualified candidate, and different from the race of the highly qualified applicant. Half of each ethnic group of participants received a dossier where the manager was black; for the other half, the manager was white.

There were three versions of the document relating to the decision about the candidate, and it was through these that the type of racial prejudice was manipulated.

Table 8.1. Study design and numbers of participants

Race of participant N			Black 119					White 127			
Race of manager and weak candidate N	Black 41			White 78			Black 75			White 52		
Type of prejudice: **B**latant, **A**mbiguous or **N**one N	B 13	A 13	N 15	B 20	A 38	N 20	B 20	A 37	N 18	B 17	A 18	N 17

Was it necessary to do this? Could they have just given each participant the version where the victim was the same race as the participant, given that is where the most striking effects were found?

In the no prejudice condition, number 4 was the selected candidate and the accompanying notes did not mention anything to do with race. In the blatant prejudice condition, the recommendation was to hire the least-qualified candidate with notes indicating that bias about the race of the well-qualified candidate had led to his being excluded. For the ambiguous prejudice condition, there was nothing in the rationale relating to race but still the least-qualified candidate was selected. These three conditions were spread across the sample. This complex bit of planning is summarised in the table above. It means that the race of the manager and the type of prejudice were each controlled for across the two sample groups.

This is a complex **unrelated study design**. There are two independent variables: race of manager and type of prejudice. On top of this there was a between groups comparison (black or white participants), but this cannot strictly be called an IV because it was not manipulated by the experimenters.

Each participant appears in only one of the 12 cells at the bottom of Table 8.1. Their race meant that they were only eligible to be assigned to any one of six. There were three **factors**: race of participant (two **levels**: black and white); race of manager and weak candidate (two levels: black and white); and type of prejudice (three levels: blatant, ambiguous and none). There were therefore six versions of the dossier, meaning six conditions to which participants were assigned by **random allocation**. As is often the case with true random allocation, the final numbers in each condition varied.

How was the Independent Variable Distributed?

If you are particularly quick at mental arithmetic you may have noticed that the total number of participants adds up to 246 rather than the 250 recruited (the reasons for this can be found in the manipulation checks below). Without completing that necessary addition, we can see at a glance how the numbers pan out across conditions. There are almost even numbers on both groups, so near as to make little difference. For both groups a greater proportion of the participants had the condition with the manager being of a different race. As for the numbers in each of the twelve subgroups, the variation here is nearly to a factor of 3. Does it matter?

Contrary to popular belief, this type of variation in group size across conditions is not really a problem. Indeed, with true random allocation group sizes are very rarely equal. Providing that each of the individual subgroups or 'cells' has a large enough sample to enable analysis, we do not need to worry about this type of variation. Most **inferential statistics** can deal with and account for groups or cells of different sizes. The only time that it might matter is if one of the cells showed considerably more variability in the scores than the others. This would tend to suggest that maybe the **sample** was not necessarily representative of the **population** from which it was drawn. For this reason, Salvatore and Shelton included with the **descriptive statistics** on their **data** the **standard error of the mean** (**SEM**) (see Box 8.1) to show the comparability of the different groups.

Box 8.1   Standard Error of the Mean (SEM)

Think of it like this. If you randomly selected a sample of say 20 9-year-olds from a city and measured their height you would probably find that the variation across those 20 was not very great, and that the majority would fall within a band of about 15 cm from each other, with only a few being noticeably above or below that band. Therefore you could feel reasonably confident that the mean height of your sample was pretty close to the mean height for 9-year-olds across the city, including all those who were not included in your sample. In fact, the smaller the range of heights in your sample, the more confident you would be that you had a representative sample of the population of 9-year-olds in the city.

If by way of contrast you selected a random sample of 20 children under 18 from that same city, you would find a considerably greater variation in height. Some of those children might be small babies and no more than 40 cm tall (or long) while others might be strapping 17-year-olds towering up towards 200 cm. You would then feel much less confident that the mean height of your sample accurately reflected the mean height of the population of children as whole. So it is all to do with variability. For this reason researchers often use a measurement of variability called the standard error of the mean (SEM). This is a standard way of measuring how likely it is that the mean of the sample reflects the mean of the population: the smaller the SEM the closer the sample mean is likely to be to the population mean.

With race and prejudice type carefully controlled across the sample and as sample size is not a problem where else might we need to check the detail in this study in order to set any store by its conclusions? What about the all-important **outcome measure**, the dependent variable?

How Was the Dependent Variable Measured?

As already explained, the Stroop test is a classic in experimental cognitive psychology; its effects are known to be robust. If you ever tried to do this test yourself you are probably inclined to believe this. You may recall that this version was computerised: is it safe to rely on this? After all some people are much more used to using computers than others. Some of us work with them on a daily basis and are very accustomed to the keyboard. For others it still presents a bit of challenge. Finding the key you want is not always as simple as it should be – sometimes the one really needed seems to hide from the persistent novice in a deliberately playful way. This should not have been too much of a problem here as only four keys were required for the task and they were colour-coded. Nevertheless, some people are just ill at ease with computers, so could a variation in computer skills be a problem here?

Luckily this does not present a problem here for two reasons, one to do with the task and one to do with the experimental design. The experimental design randomly allocated participants to conditions. This means that each participant had an equal chance of being assigned to each of the six conditions for their race. This is considered a reasonable way to account for individual variation in a sample. It is not as effective as controlling for identifiable variables, as was done with the race of the manager in this study. It usually is quite difficult to control for all the potential individual features that might affect results. When control is not an option, then random allocation is the next best thing. It is certainly considerably better than either allowing people to choose their condition, or assigning the first half of the sample to one condition and the second half to the other. The danger of that type of allocation to condition is the possibility of **systematic error** creeping into the sampling process. For example, the first participants might be the keenest, or the researcher might be fresher early on, or less practised, and any one of these factors could have a bearing on the results and produce a **confounding variable**, every researcher's nightmare. Therefore, in this study if there were some people who were less used to computers than others they should, theoretically at least, have been evenly distributed across the conditions. Thus random allocation is a handy technique to minimise the impact of individual variation. **Systematic allocation** is the next best option. For example, this might involve alternating between conditions, each for each participant, or for every batch of five or similar. This should mean that individual differences are spread across groups. Unlike random allocation however, systematic allocation is predictable, and it is all too easy for subtle **experimenter effects** to sneak their way into the study.

Secondly, the task takes account of differential experience of computers. You will recall that the experiment requires participants to do two different types of task, the easy, control version ('xxxx') and the challenging, incongruent version (with non-matching colour names). These are randomly ordered throughout the pro-gramme so the participant does not know whether to expect an easy or a difficult task for each trial. The measure or score that is used for Stroop is the time taken to do the difficult task minus the time taken to do the easy task. This measure takes account of the different response times of individuals. If those who are not used to computers take a little longer to press the key than others it does not affect the final outcome as this hesitancy will affect both tasks, thereby maintaining the differential between the two. The difference in response times across the tasks is a measurement of how much harder the incongruent task is. It is a measure of selective attention, requiring you to filter out the conflicting information from the colour names in order to attend to the colour of the lettering.

It is not an easy task to complete, nor is it an easy task to explain in the first place. In order to ensure that all participants received the same standard instructions, with the same amount of support, the computer program provides the explanation for what to do. It is, of course, possible that some participants may have come across the Stroop task before, while for others it is a new and bewildering experience. This should not affect the results, for the same reason as that given above regarding differential computer experience. But how do we know that people have understood the instruc-tions given them by the computer? There are no interpersonal cues that a human instructor might notice to signal that their explanation has not been fully grasped. This is compensated for by the program, which provides a practice session of eight attempts first, enabling the researcher to check that the task has been understood. In fact a cou-ple of sets of data, over and above the 250, had to be discarded for this reason.

This Stroop task, then, is a quite a useful device for experimental psychology. You may have noticed that the number of trials for each participant was quite high at 92. Even with eight of these as practice, this still means completing 84 trials on the trot. This might seem a little awesome, and indeed you might expect people's concentra-tion or vigilance to fail after while. This could in itself have an effect on variability in the times, making the results difficult to interpret. The researchers were careful to control for this and for any misunderstanding of the Stroop task itself. They did not use all the scores in their analysis. This might sound alarming – did they just select the scores they liked the look of?! Needless to say, that was not the case. They needed to be sure that their data were uncontaminated. How they did this is reported in full in their paper, making it clear how some scores were discarded.

First, they discounted any times taken from trials where the wrong answer was given. This means that if participants stopped trying to do the task correctly, or just guessed at the correct response, those trials were likely to have been discarded. The second data-trimming technique they used to was to discard any **outliers** or extreme scores. This was done on a person-by-person basis. For each type of task for each participant they took the mean or average time and worked out a statistic called a **standard deviation**. This is a measure of how much a set of data varies around the mean. They used this measure to calculate, for each person in turn, what constituted an outlier for them for that particular task and discounted any such scores. This means they discounted any inadvertent lapses of attention which led to unduly long response times or any anticipatory response which led to unduly short reaction times. In each case this was only classified as an outlier for the participant concerned. This produced an individualised and therefore sensitive trimming of the data. Once these data had been discarded the mean score was calculated afresh for each participant for each type of task, and the overall Stroop score could then be calculated as the difference between the two.

Therefore the Stroop task and its data were subjected to a rigorous research process which enables us to have confidence in these data.

● How Effective Is This Experimental Design?

The whole study is based on the assumption that two things are being measured in one outcome measure: cognitive function and response to prejudice. We may accept that Stroop measures cognitive function as it is an established test that has been used in many experiments over the last 70 years and has been shown to detect changes in cognitive function. The response to racial prejudice is equally central to this study, and the materials were designed expressly for it. How do we know they are **valid**? The whole premise of this study is based on how participants will perceive those quite extensive dossiers. The researchers tried to ensure that participants would read through their own dossiers and assimilate the material by saying that they were going to be asked to complete a questionnaire about it at a later stage. So there was every incentive for the participants to read it. Is that enough? Do we know they read it? Do we know that they perceived the judgements in it as prejudiced when it was intended that they should?

Salvatore and Sheldon did not leave this to chance. Their study included what are termed **manipulation checks**. These are checks to see that the experimental manipulation has worked as intended. First, they checked the participants' ratings of the four candidates. Participants were asked to express their level of agreement with two statements about each of them, one saying that the candidate was suitably qualified and one that they personally would hire that candidate for that job. These scores were analysed and confirmed that: (a) candidate 3 was seen as unsuitable; (b) candidate 4 was seen as suitable; and (c) the race of the candidate did not affect these responses. There were just four participants who did not rate candidate 4 as the more suitably qualified, so their data were excluded from the subsequent analysis (hence there being only 246 participants in Table 8.1). These checks and precautions meant that the authors could be confident that the candidates had been evaluated by the participants as the authors had intended, and that the participants were not themselves exhibiting prejudice.

They also checked the extent to which the HR manager's selection and rationale were perceived as being racially motivated. Participants' ratings of this were analysed and showed that he was seen as most prejudiced in the blatant prejudice condition, and least prejudiced in the no prejudice condition. Therefore, we can be fairly confident that the participants in two of these three conditions believed that they had just witnessed prejudice. The authors note that the ratings of prejudice were much higher when the HR manager was white and candidate 4 was black than when it was the other way around. They suggest that this is in line with a dominant stereotype of where prejudice may occur in Western society.

▲ How Appropriate Was the Research Method?

As we have seen, this complex study used an unrelated design. What would the alternatives be? A repeated measures design would have involved each participant in making more than one judgement. The moment that occurs, the point of the study is going to become apparent to the participants. Recall that the researchers successfully disguised their study aim. They even disguised the fact that the 'two studies' were related. If participants had had to read two dossiers (one with a black manager and one with a white one), it is likely they would have guessed the aim. It is even more likely if they had been asked to read three dossiers, one with blatant prejudice, one ambiguous and the third with no prejudice. The prospect of them reading all six versions is absurd; there is no way that in that case they could have failed to guess the aim. The moment that participants' attention is drawn to the aim of a study it will affect their responses. The neat thing about the way in which this study was conducted is how well their attention was directed away from the aim. Each participant who had a dossier with prejudice in it must have felt that they had stumbled on corrupt practice in an existing company. They remained shocked by this even when their attention was drawn to an apparently unrelated computerised task. This really had to be an unrelated design in order to work so well.

Observational studies could be used to explore some responses to prejudice, but it would be impossible to measure cognitive performance objectively through observation. Remember, for a study to be observational there can be no manipulation of the independent variable, so it would be necessary to observe prejudice where it is occurring, which would make it a difficult task to do logistically. It might be possible to use observation as a technique, if not as an overall design. For example, a field experiment would mean that the IV could be manipulated in a real-life setting and participants' responses observed. There would, obviously, be ethical difficulties if the prejudice was too blatant. If it was too subtle, it would be difficult to be certain that everyone had noticed it. Manipulation checks would be harder to organise, too.

Observation has been used to look at other issues arising from racial prejudice. Analysis of pre-existing or **secondary data** also counts as observation, and this technique was used by Johnson (2008), for example, who looked at data from the 2001 Race, Crime and Public Opinion Study. He found that racial prejudice and perceived racial bias account for racial differences in attitudes to criminal justice systems. How racial prejudice permeates those criminal justice systems has also been shown using another sort of secondary data, **archival data**; analyses of such public records examined racial differences in conviction rates. One example is the work of Tomic and Jahn (2008), who showed that differences in the dismissal rate of cases suggested that there had been more aggressive policing of black people in some situations.

Survey methods could be used to seek people's opinions on the issue of prejudice. Scales have been developed for this purpose, for example the Scale of Anti-Asian American Stereotypes (Lin *et al.*, 2005). Alternatively, surveys could be used to find out about people's experience of prejudice. This would be useful information and would tell us about important factors in our society.

As always, a mixture of different methods allows us to build up a bigger and better picture of the phenomenon under study. Neither surveys nor observation would be able to tap into the striking effect noted in this study: the consequence of encountering prejudice.

Conclusion

The simple conclusion from Salvatore and Shelton's work is that experiencing racial prejudice has a disruptive effect on higher cognitive functions. The simplicity of this conclusion belies the complexity of the study needed to demonstrate it. Controlling for race across the conditions was a necessity in order to understand the dynamics. A simpler study looking at just the race of the participant, the race of the manager, or the type of prejudice might have been easier to run but would have fallen short of identifying racial differences in response to prejudice. Furthermore, the finding that the two races respond differently to different types of prejudice would have been difficult to establish unequivocally if the investigation was conducted over separate studies. It is sometimes possible to repeat an experiment with a second, different, sample group, but if you are looking for group differences then conclusions drawn across two separate studies are unsafe. You could not be certain whether a different result from the second group reflected real intrinsic group differences or was brought about by subtle and unintended changes in the running of the experiment.

As the aim was to compare the different responses of blacks and whites, no design other than a between groups comparison would have worked. The complexity of the experimental design meant that there were in effect 12 groups, (as shown in Table 8.1). Why was this necessary? Why could there not have been just the two groups? If they had not also manipulated the race of the manager then they would not have found that the effect is greater when the participant is the same race as the victim but a different race from the perpetrator. If they had not had two types of prejudice, they would not have discovered that the different races are affected by the different conditions. If there had been no blatant prejudice condition, they might have concluded that only blacks are affected. Conversely, if there had been no ambiguous prejudice condition, the conclusion might have been that only whites are affected. The third, control, condition was necessary to identify what the Stroop scores would be without experiencing prejudice. Therefore, there was no way that this study could have been simpler in design without the loss of valuable information.

The beauty of Salvatore and Sheldon's design is that there appeared to be no obvious connection between the two halves of the study. Those undertaking the Stroop task did not know that it was to measure their responses to the first task. This makes it a great deal easier to infer effect. Had the participants been told that the aim was to measure their cognitive abilities after being exposed to prejudice it is likely that they would have become self-conscious about their own responses, and this would have contaminated the results.

This draws our attention to the fact that the participants were deceived about the nature of the experiment. Is this ethical? (For a fuller discussion of ethical issues see Chapter 2.) According to the guidelines issued by the British Psychological Society (see p. **268**), deception in research can sometimes be acceptable if (a) it is justified and (b) the participants are not being asked to consent to something that a reasonable person would refuse to do if they knew the truth. In this instance, it would seem that the study fulfils both these criteria.

This carefully designed and complex study, therefore, allows us to draw quite robust conclusions about the detrimental effect of encountering racial prejudice. The potential ramifications of these findings are alarming. As the authors cautiously state, simply encountering racial prejudice is

> likely to disrupt cognitive functioning for blacks and whites … leading to suboptimal performance on tasks that require the online deployment of attention. (2007, p.815)

Summary Points	
Design	True experiment, unrelated, three-factor comparison
Aim	To compare the effect of two IVs on two groups
2 IVs	Race of victim and type of prejudice
DV	Cognitive performance Operationalised as scores from Stroop test (time for incongruent task minus time for neutral task)
Sample	University undergraduates N=250, (black N=122, white N=128)
Analysis	2 (between subjects factor; race) × 2 (race of victim) × 3 (type of prejudice)

Mate-Selection Strategies

Experiment – A Mixed Two-Factor Design, Within and Between Groups

'Sex appeal is fifty percent what you've got and fifty percent what people think you've got.' (Sophia Loren, actress, b. 1934)

What Makes Someone Attractive?

There are many different things about individuals that influence how attractive we find them. You need only glance through the personal advertisements in any newspaper to see what it is that we seek in a potential mate. It may be that we think their eyes are important, or their figure, perhaps their hair. Maybe having a good sense of humour is the single most quoted requirement. Certainly while the physical characteristics people seek through advertisements vary considerably, this one requirement seems ubiquitous. There are not many advertisements where the seeker is looking for someone with a poor sense of humour!

If you stop to think about what you would expect to find attractive, you might think of some aspect of physical appearance. Or would you focus instead on a personal attribute such as personality, interests, or even material wealth? It would seem that, for women at least, one thing that influences how attractive they find some people is what other women appear to think of them. It is tempting for a woman to respond to this suggestion with the forceful claim that she is quite capable of making up her own mind, thank you! It seems somewhat trivial to suggest that other women's perceived views might affect such a personal matter of choice, but there is some evidence that this is so.

In the animal world this phenomenon has been known for some time, and is referred to as 'mate-choice copying'. It has been suggested that copying another female's choice of mate has a good evolutionary basis as it can save the female costs in terms of time and effort in seeking a suitable mate. A male that has already attracted and possibly retained other females has proved himself acceptable as a mate. Furthermore, as mate-selection can be a tricky but vital business, copying others' selections could be one way to learn. You might think that the way the male behaves with his existing female mates is what attracts new females. An alternative suggestion would be that the new female wants to join the group of existing females. Apparently neither of these is the case. Females have been shown to find new males attractive if they have similar characteristics to the target male. This suggests that, in the animal kingdom, at least, it is not the presence of other females that makes the male desirable, but rather their endorsement of his characteristics.

Mate-choice copying has been noted in birds (e.g. Japanese quail), fish (e.g. guppies) and arthropods (e.g. wolf spiders). It has been more of a problem trying to find evidence of it amongst mammals. The trouble is that mammals are not as easy to study. Mammalian behaviour is considerably influenced by the context in which it occurs. This makes laboratory experimentation problematic. Laboratory studies are useful for studying specific responses (see for example the experiment using cotton-top tamarins discussed in Chapter 7). As a research method, laboratory work allows the researcher to have control and therefore reduce the number of **extraneous variables**. But if you want to know about the normal, naturally occurring behaviour of animals then it is usually better to study them in their own habitat. To do this you can use either **observational studies** or **field experimentation**.

The trouble is the lack of control inherent in both observational studies and field experiments. Once outside the laboratory the research will be affected by **variables** other than those of interest. This lack of control means that cause and effect are difficult, often impossible, to establish. If a female mammal selects a male that already has a partner, is that mate-choice copying or simple conformity? Are they merely doing what all the other females in their group do? To date, this has been the problem in studies of mate-choice copying amongst mammals in the wild; the results are open to more than one interpretation and therefore inconclusive.

It is difficult to explore with other mammals, what about us humans? How could we explore that? Perhaps go along to a club and watch how people pair up for the evening. If we observe a female approach a male who already has a girlfriend in tow, would that be evidence of mate-choice copying? We would find it difficult to argue that this is the only explanation for the observed behaviour. She might have arranged to meet him there; they might be old friends, she may be a friend of the girlfriend, or an old flame who wants him back. You can probably think of another half-dozen plausible explanations, none of which would have anything to do with mate-choice copying.

This was the problem that Jones *et al.* (2006) chose to tackle, and they found an effective way of studying mate-choice copying among humans. Instead of using observational studies or field experiments, they chose a laboratory-style setting where they had more control. But, as with other mammals, human behaviour is affected by the context in which it occurs, so how can we encourage mate-choosing in a laboratory – of all unromantic places? Should we fill the place up with teaming masses of twenty-somethings and wait to see what happens? Perhaps not. In fact, what Jones *et al.* did was a classic example of **hypothetico-deductive** reasoning. In this instance it goes something like this. Choosing a mate must begin with seeing and then selecting

an individual. To make the selection, the female must find the male attractive. Mate-choice copying means females find males with mates more attractive. If other females have chosen a male as a mate they must have a positive regard for him. Seeing another female smile at a male is an indication of positive regard. Therefore, if mate-choice copying occurs amongst human it follows that a female will find a male more attractive when there is evidence that another female already likes him.

This type of analytic reasoning begins to break down the possible processes involved in mate-choice copying into their component parts, making it amenable to investigation. It is no longer necessary to look at the whole process of mate selection, which is fortunate as this would be difficult to do as experimentation! In fact, we no longer need to look at relationships at all, but just this first simple step: attractiveness. If somebody else finds that guy attractive, does this make him seem more attractive to others? In fact, what we are looking at here is the first step in the process of mate choice: attraction. In this study, attraction was measured purely as a response to individual faces. The **aim** of the study was to look for evidence that preference for faces can be socially transmitted. The **hypothesis** was that

> women's preferences for men's faces are influenced by facial cues of other women's attitudes to those men. (2006, p.2)

Social Transmission of Face Preferences among Humans

Jones, B.C., DeBruine, L.M., Little, A.C., Burriss, R.P. & Feinberg, D.R. (2006). *Proceedings of the Royal Society* (doi:10/1098/rspb.2006.0205)

Method

Jones *et al.* (2006) chose a primarily **within subjects** experimental design to explore this. The researchers presented their 28 young female **participants** with eight pairs of colour photographs of male faces, facing directly to camera, and asked them to rate the relative attractiveness of each face in the pair. This represents the **baseline measurement** or **T1** (the first time of testing).

The **dependent variable** (**DV**) was preference for men's faces as measured by an eight-point rating scale:

A is 'much more attractive' than B
A is 'more attractive' than B
A is 'somewhat more attractive' than B
A is 'slightly more attractive' than B
B is 'slightly more attractive' than A
B is 'somewhat more attractive' than A
B is 'more attractive' than A
B is 'much more attractive' than A

Note that this means that, in each case, participants were asked to make *relative* judgements of attractiveness between the two faces within each pair.

Then came what could be termed the **intervention**, the manipulation of the **independent variable** (**IV**). This consisted of the participants being shown the same pairs of faces again, but inserted between the two faces in each pair was a female face in profile. Because it was in profile it looked *as though* the female was facing one of the pair, but the three photographs were clearly separate. In four of the eight pairs of male faces, the female face was smiling, while in the remaining four the female face was neutral. Eight different female profiles were used, one for each of the pairs of male faces, and none of the faces appeared in more than one trio.

If preference can be socially transmitted then the smiling female profile should augment the attractiveness of the male face. To test this, the next step, **T2** (second time of testing) was to show the original pairs of faces again exactly as at T1 (that is: without the female profile). The participants were again asked to rate the relative attractiveness of each pair of faces. If the experimental manipulation had been effective, then the second rating of the face towards which the female had been smiling should show an improvement on the first. The experimental procedure involved the participants seeing each of these eight sets of faces three times: T1 (baseline rating); as part of the procedure (with the female face); and finally at T2 (second rating).

In this study the DV is the preference for men's faces as measured or **operationalised** by the scale to rate relative attractiveness. There are two IVs, the direction of the female gaze and the female facial expression, smiling or neutral. The manipulation of the IV meant alternating the direction and expression of the female profile. Did the IV affect the DV? Did the female's facial expression affect the rating?

Results

The **outcome measure** was calculated by subtracting the baseline rating of attractiveness from the second rating; this means that a positive score indicated an increase in reported relative preference. This was primarily a **related**, **repeated measures design**. Each participant saw 16 male faces, four being smiled at, four being looked at neutrally, four with the female smiling away from the face, and four with the female looking neutrally away from the face.

Statistical analysis using **ANOVA** (**analysis of variance**) showed that there had indeed been a **significant** increase in the rating of attractiveness after participants had seen the target male being smiled at by the female. Moreover, there was a decrease in the ratings for those targets that had been in the neutral expression condition. Therefore, there was evidence to support the prediction that female humans are influenced by other women's approbation of a male. To put it another way, this suggests that the preference for faces has been transmitted as a social process; seeing a woman smile at a man makes him seem more attractive to other women. This, in turn, could be taken to suggest that something akin to mate-choice copying might occur in humans.

■ How Safe Is This Conclusion?

This seems like quite a striking finding. As we have a significant change in the attractiveness rating then we have to assume some sort of change has taken place. The manipulation of the IV seems to have been effective. But is the conclusion safe? And is it really evidence of mate-choice copying? Let's look at these two questions separately. We need to explore the notion of cause and effect first: is it possible that there could have been a **confounding variable** that might have produced a **systematic error?**

What Else Could Have Caused This Change?

Maybe it was nothing to do with the female face; perhaps it was just that the faces were no longer novel. The participants, after all, had seen the face several times when they made their final rating; perhaps they had just become used to it and were even growing to like it. This seems plausible and there is some evidence from other areas of psychological research that we like best those things with which we are familiar (see, for example, Zajonc's work on mere exposure, 1968). Or could it just have been having the female there? Was it in some way the presence of a female in amongst the male faces that produced the rise in ratings of attractiveness?

Neither of these possibilities explains the findings. If either familiarity or the presence of a female had been the deciding factor, then both faces would become more attractive to the participants. Because each male face was presented in a paired set, the rating of attractiveness was always relative – that is how attractive the target was in comparison with his paired image. Mere exposure or the presence of a woman might produce an increase in the ratings for each face but would presumably leave the relative preference unchanged. However, the significant increases were found from T1 to T2 in the rating of attractiveness of the target face only. The one that became more attractive was always the man towards whom the female appeared to be looking. Therefore, we have to conclude that it was the direction of the female gaze that affected the significant increase in attractiveness.

The female was shown in profile, so she was always looking at one of the men. Could it be just the fact that she was looking at the target man that caused the rating change? Perhaps the fact that he was the object of female attention was enough to produce the effect. Or alternatively maybe it was that the effect of the direction of her gaze that made the difference. Often when we see someone looking in a particular direction, we follow their gaze and look there too. So perhaps the female's gaze directed the participant's gaze to the target man over and above the other man in the pair and that affected the judgement of attractiveness, perhaps through the familiarity mechanism outlined above.

However, the design of the study controlled for both these possibilities. On half the occasions the woman was smiling, for the rest her expression was neutral. This is why there are two IVs in this study: the introduction of a female profile and the facial expression. The **inferential statistics** showed that the significant increase was restricted to only those faces at which the female appeared to smile. There was no such effect when the female face was neutral. If it was just a matter of being the object of female attention then the increased rating would have been found in each pair, irrespective of the woman's expression. Equally, if it was something to do with the direction of the gaze, again the effect would have been found in each pair.

Is This Evidence of Mate-Choice Copying in Humans?

Once we have accepted that it was the smiling that made the difference and produced this effect, who says that this has anything to do with mate-choice copying? Perhaps this is a general positive effect of seeing one person being smiled at and nothing to do with mate selection. The study by Jones *et al.* shows that this effect was at some level related to the mating game because they used this paradigm with 28 young males as well. They predicted that the smiling female would lower the rating used by the males, that it would have the reverse effect on the males compared to females. These two predictions were based on the same theory about mate-choice copying. If there are good evolutionary reasons why women might be drawn to males who have already proven themselves as mates, then it follows that men would find such a male a threat. The findings confirmed both predictions, with men raising their ratings for males in the neutral condition, and lowering them for those in the smiling condition. Taken together, with the findings from the women, this sex difference in responses suggests that at least the underlying reasons for this effect may be founded in human mate-selection strategies.

Therefore, by carefully controlling for different and conflicting explanations, it would seem that this study shows us that the presence of a woman smiling at a male face increases how attractive that male appears to other women. It also produces a decrease in positive responses in men. The effect cannot be explained by increasing familiarity alone nor by the direction of the female's gaze, but seems to be a function of her smiling in apparent approval at the male face. This suggests that there was no confounding variable producing a systematic error. Were there other extraneous variables that could have produced **random** noise in the **data**? Uncontrolled, these might have masked a real effect (**Type II error**) so what might they have been and how did the researchers control for them? The first issue is in the nature of the **materials** used.

Were the Faces Comparable?

The materials in this study were photographs of faces – what about those faces themselves – is it possible that the ones that came to be seen as more attractive were in some way qualitatively different from their pairs? If some were generally more attractive than others it could have produced a Type II error. Equally such an imbalance could produce an effect that did not really exist (**Type I error**). A lack of equivalence here could pose a serious threat to the **validity** of the data. So we need to be sure that the faces are at least reasonably equivalent in attractiveness.

Just exactly how can we do that? I might think that Brad Pitt and Keanu Reeves are equally attractive – but do you? How about Keira Knightley and Natalie Portman? Remember the old saying: beauty is in the eye of the beholder. This is a **hypothetical construct** and a **subjective** judgement which makes it a real challenge for measuring. If we want to compare the height or weight of two people we can use an **objective** measuring method. If two men are both 196 cm high then we can say that for all intents and purposes they are the same height. A similar assumption can be made about their weight if each weighs 75 kg. But as for the attractiveness of their faces: how can we go about ensuring the equivalence of that? Objective **measures**, jaw length, distance between the eyes, length of nose are of very little use and are not going to give us any real help. Attractiveness is entirely subjective, so how are we going to check comparability? This is a big and very tricky issue so the authors had to tackle it in two ways: first they endeavoured to pair faces of comparable attractiveness, but secondly, just in case, they had a failsafe design.

The selection of the faces was the starting point. The first selection was 30 male faces taken from an existing database. All were young white European adults, as keeping race and age group constant reduced two sources of variation. These were then rated by a group of 40 young female participants, of a similar age to the sample for the main study. The rating scale here was a simple seven-point scale from 1 (very unattractive) to 7 (very attractive). Taking the average of these 40 ratings for each face produced for each a general measure of attractiveness. Based on these, pairs of faces with similar ratings could be identified, and eight of these pairs were chosen for the main study. Thus, the two faces in each of these pairs had had been rated as similarly attractive before the main study began.

Jones and colleagues took account of another issue in their selection of pairs of faces based on these ratings. They took only those faces where the average of the 40 ratings was neither at the top nor the bottom of the range. They needed to make sure that these ratings were in the middle. Extremes at either end would have created problems. If the faces had been seen as very attractive prior to the **experimental manipulation**, then it would have been difficult to produce an increase in the attractiveness. Conversely, if the faces had been very unattractive, it might have been difficult to increase the attractiveness. Therefore by taking only the middle-range faces, the authors avoided the danger of **floor** or **ceiling effects**.

● How Effective Is This Experimental Design?

This question leads us to the second check used by the researchers to control for individual differences in the faces used. They alternated which male in each pair was the target face. This is a technique called **counterbalancing**. The principle of counterbalancing means that the distribution of any potentially confounding variable in an experimental design is spread out across the participants in such a way as to minimise its effect. In this study, counterbalancing needed to take account of which male the female profile faced. If we call one pair John and Fred, then in one condition the female faced John, and in the other condition her profile was turned towards Fred. This means that if the two faces in each pair were not equivalent despite the careful measures used for face selection then the effect would be balanced out and should not jeopardise the testing of the hypothesis.

Thinking about equivalence of faces, what about the females? What if the smiling females were somehow more appealing, more attractive than the neutral faces? This could have presented a problem. But again it was addressed through counterbalancing. In each set of three faces, the female was smiling in one condition but not in another.

If you have followed the logic of this, then you may have spotted a potential problem. In one condition she faced John; in the other condition she faced Fred. In one condition she smiled, in one her expression was neutral. So does this mean that she always smiled at John and was always neutral when facing Fred? This would have been a problem, and could have produced a potential **bias** in the findings, as John would always have had the added advantage of the smile and Fred never would have done. However, Jones *et al.* used a fully counterbalanced design, which means that their counterbalancing took both of these possible problems into account. Therefore, participants in their study were assigned to one of four groups, as in Table 9.1, which shows the pattern for one pair of faces. Remember, there were eight pairs, so for each group there were four pairs with a smiling female profile and four with a neutral one.

This table shows us the two variables that are being manipulated. The female's facial expression is important because it is part of the hypothesis testing. But the second one, alternating which of the two male faces is the target, is equally important for this design, just in case one face is preferred to the other. It is part of the checks and balances needed in this study – hence the term 'counterbalancing'.

Each participant is randomly assigned to one of the four conditions. Each sees the same eight pairs of male faces. In the experimental manipulation half the pairs have a smiling woman inserted between them and the remaining half have a woman with a neutral expression inserted between them. This leads us to the one final area where there could have been a problem in the design: which way was she looking? If the target face and therefore the direction of her gaze were always to the right, or always to the left, there could have been some form of bias in the responses. We know that there can be side biases in the way in which we look at images and also in the way in

Table 9.1. Demonstration of counterbalancing (N=28)

Group	A	B	C	D
N	7	7	7	7
Target Face	Female smiles at 'X'	Female smiles at 'Y'	Female looking neutrally at 'X'	Female looking neutrally at 'Y'

Table 9.2. Summary of experimental design

Variable	How managed	
Sex	Between subjects	Two groups of participants
Direction of gaze IV	Within subjects, repeated measures	Each participant sees 16 male faces, eight of which are object of gaze
Facial expression IV	Within subjects, repeated measures	Each participant sees 16 male faces, eight of which are being smiled at
Individual differences within pair	Counterbalanced across four groups of participants	Each face is object of gaze in half groups.
Differences between pairs	Counterbalanced across four groups of participants	Each pair has smiling profile in half the groups.
Side	Controlled across all	Each set of three presented twice for each participant, one with female facing left

which we look at facial expressions, so this was another variable that the researchers needed to **control**. They could have elected to have half their photographs with the female facing one way, and the rest with her facing the other way. But this would have meant that they were adding to the counterbalancing plan indicated above. As it would be necessary to counterbalance side with both target face and facial expression, there would have been eight conditions – making the analysis even more complex. Instead they took a simpler and better step: they showed each picture twice. The experimental manipulation therefore involved the participants looking at 16 sets of pictures, eight with female profile and the target face to the left, and eight with them to the right. In this way they controlled for any possible bias in the order in which information was processed without having to counterbalance.

How Do You Analyse Such a Complex Design?

The design of this study meant that the DV was assessed by measuring the change in ratings from T1 to T2. Because the researchers were comparing male and female response (between subjects) to the two different types of photos (within subjects) this was a mixed design. There were six variables identified by the researchers (see Table 9.2). One of these was an existing group difference (sex) and then there were the two independent variables, gaze and expression. These were the comparisons of interest. As well as these, the design counterbalanced two further variables. In total, then, the analysis needed to take in account these five variables or factors,(see Box 9.1). This sixth variable (side: left or right) was controlled for and it therefore did not require analysing.

The researchers' predictions meant that they needed to test whether the facial expression had an effect, whether female and male participants responded differently and whether their counterbalancing design had worked. If the counterbalancing design worked, then there should be no differences between the four groups indicated in Table 9.1. In this instance the ANOVA was used to assess how each of these factors affected the change in ratings from T1 to T2. It showed that the responses of the female and male participants were significantly different: while the women showed an increase in their ratings where the female profile was smiling, the men showed a decrease in exactly the same conditions. This is called an **interaction**; it means that the two categories

Box 9.1

Independent Variables and Factors

Sometimes these two terms are used almost interchangeably but they do have distinct meanings. IVs are part of an experimental design. The researcher manipulates the IV and measures the DV. The hypothesis makes a prediction about whether or how the IV might affect the DV. Hypotheses state cause and effect – which the experiment sets out to test. Factors, by contrast, are any variables that might affect the DV, including the IV. There may be a pre-existing grouping variable which strictly speaking cannot be called an IV as the experimenters are unable to manipulate it. In this chapter, sex is such a grouping variable; in Chapter 8 it was race. These variables are certainly factors but not really independent variables.

Other variables that might affect the results are also potential factors. In this case, there are three possibilities: differences in the individual faces, differences in the pairs, and the side of presentation. In the event, the last of these has been controlled so it does not need to be treated as a factor. Analysis of variance (ANOVA) tests to see how much of the overall variance in the data is caused by each of the factors in turn. ANOVA is an inferential statistic that can examine the effect of more than one factor at a time. The hope is always that the IVs and any deliberate group selections will show a significant effect, but that the counterbalanced factors will have no effect. If counterbalancing works properly then this would be the outcome.

In some cases the only factors in a study may be the independent variables. In others, as we have seen here, there are more factors than IVs. While all IVs can be called factors, not all factors are IVs.

NB. The term 'factor' is used in a slightly different way in a statistical method called **factor analysis** – see Box 18.1.

Table 9.3. Demonstration of attractiveness ratings

Participant	T1		T2	
	Face A	Face B	Face A	Face B
Me	5	4	**6**	4
You	3	6	**4**	6
MEAN	4	5	**5**	5

of one variable (men and women) reacted differently to the two conditions (smiling and neutral). The ANOVA also tested the effect of varying which face in each pair was the target face and which pairs had smiling and which neutral female profiles. Neither of these was significant, which means that the counterbalancing worked. Any effect of the individual faces was balanced out across the experimental design.

Why Take a Baseline?

This experiment took a baseline measure at T1, prior to the experimental manipulation, then repeated the measure at T2. This was very effective for this study, and it is unlikely that any alternative design would have worked as well. It certainly would not have been as effective with this relatively small sample size. As we have already noted, individual judgements about attractiveness are widely varied. The rationale for a baseline measure is that it takes account of this initial variation. What is being measured here is *change* in ratings. Think about a small example. Using a simple seven-point rating scale for attractiveness, I might think person A slightly more attractive than person B and rate A as 5 and B as 4. In contrast, you might think person B is the more attractive so you rate A as 3 and B as 6. The experimental manipulation is intended to produce a positive change in our ratings for A, while our ratings for B remain unchanged (see Table 9.3).

If all we have is the post-manipulation measures then we will have person A scoring 6 and 4, **mean** rating 5, compared to person B scoring 4 and 6, mean rating 5 – no difference! In contrast a repeated measures design shows that the experimental manipulation has produced increases in both our ratings for A while our ratings for B have remained constant – thus we have a demonstrable effect. Without that initial baseline measure the effect would be lost. In the study discussed in this chapter, the DV is calculated as a change from baseline, which is essential.

▲ How Appropriate Was the Research Method?

We have seen how this mixed design worked. Were there any viable alternatives? Given that one comparison was between the sexes, it is impossible to envisage how this could have been done through a related design. That aside, the IV was the female's facial expression, and this was a within subjects comparison. Each participant experienced both conditions. What were the alternatives?

This was, in part at least, a repeated measures design. It does not perhaps feel like it because it all happened in one go. The usual format for repeated measures is for each participant to experience each condition in turn, counterbalanced, of course. But this had the key feature of a repeated measures design, which is that as that each participant experienced each condition.

One other **related design** is a **matched pairs design**. This would have meant ensuring that each participant in one condition was matched with a participant in the other condition. What would we use for the matching? We are asking them to make very subjective assessments of attractiveness. In such conditions it is unlikely that any pre-existing variable (age, social class, etc.) would be effective for matching here. A psychometric assessment of personality is equally unlikely to account for this type of individual difference. For example, do all extroverts find the same type of face attractive? The only meaningful match would have been to match them on their first assessment of the faces. If we could do this successfully then a matched pairs design might work. But just think of the logistics! There are eight pairs of faces and for each there are eight possible scores. You could be recruiting from now till eternity before you found enough people to match on all eight pairs. If you only roughly match, then the pairing is also 'rough', which is not a good idea.

An **unrelated design** would be prone to extensive individual variation likely to mask any effect (Type II error). The only way to cope with this would be **randomisation**, which, in theory at least, spreads the variation across the conditions. This worked well in the study discussed in Chapter 8, but the extent to which it would work in this context is debatable. The scope for different responses to the pairs of pictures is great. While a **randomised controlled trial** could work, you are likely to need a much larger sample to show an effect.

It would seem then that the design chosen by Jones and colleagues was the optimal design for the circumstances.

As discussed earlier in this chapter, it is hard to envisage how **observation** would work for this topic for humans. It is possible that an analysis of published data (which would count as observation of **secondary data**) might tell us something about divorce and remarriage rates. High remarriage rates of divorcees might be indicative of a range of other issues: maybe they like being married; maybe they are more attractive or possibly more dependent, or maybe more settled generally. This could never be used for evidence of mate-choice copying. Other types of secondary observation can tell us about mate selection, for example, Smahel and Subrahmanyam (2007) analysed teenage internet 'chat rooms' and found partner selection to be a major activity therein. (For another example of this type of study see Chapter 13). There are many observational studies published exploring mate-selection in the animal world and covering all sorts of exotic species. Studies of dung beetles (Le Roux *et al.*, 2008), Formosan underground termites (Husseneder & Simms, 2008) and savanna baboons (Berkovitch, 1991) give an indication of the variety evident in the literature.

Survey methods seem equally unpromising for this particular topic. If you ask people whether they find members of the opposite sex more attractive if they appear to have a partner already, the answers you get are not likely to be helpful! However, it is possible to use such methods to explore aspects of mate selection: for example Cobb *et al.* (2003) explored the psychometric properties of an appropriate scale: the Attitudes About Romance and Mate Selection Scale (ARMSS).

Conclusion

This study used a necessarily complex but elegant design to explore social transmission of face preference among humans. By carefully controlling for variables that may have obscured the effect, it demonstrated that seeing a woman apparently smile at a man makes that man more attractive to other women but produces a negative response in other men. In contrast, seeing a woman looking neutrally at a man decreases his rating for other women, but increases it for men.

This latter finding needs further consideration. The original plan for the study was that the neutral face was the **control condition**. It means that any difference noted was purely the result of the smile, rather than a response to the presence of the woman or her gaze. A control is normally intended to produce no change in the DV, but here we saw a change that was the polar opposite of that for the **experimental condition**. There are a couple of possible reasons for this. It may be a direct result of the experimental effect. If the manipulation has produced a change in response to those targets in the smiling condition, the mere lack of a smile may have had a detrimental effect on the other targets. Alternatively, it could be the nature of the neutral condition itself. A person who is not smiling is more than just not conveying a positive emotion. To look at someone neutrally usually means keeping a serious face. A serious face is tantamount to disapproval. From this study here we cannot tell whether either of these explanations accounts for the change found amongst males and females in the neutral condition.

Can you think how you might design a study to tease out these two possible explanations?

It is worth noting that the materials in this study were individual photos. Although the female face is said to be 'looking at' the target face, this is really shorthand for describing the direction of the profile. The three faces were always obviously separate photographs. At no point were the images presented as a scene with three people interacting. This makes the effect more profound. Had it been a single scene, participants may have been responding to the dynamics of the people depicted. That three separate pictures could produce this effect suggests that this response is hardwired into our systems. The artificiality of the **stimulus** may be indicative of the strength of the response.

We have seen a clearly demonstrable effect that has a different manifestation in each sex. Is this relevant to mate choice? The women in this study were not actively selecting a mate, but rather judging a photograph, a fairly artificial experimental task. This is a long way from choosing a mate, let alone a parent for future offspring or a lifelong partner. That an effect was demonstrated is useful and interesting. The ratings changed as a result of the experimental manipulation. The ratings are taken to reflect the participants' response to the stimuli, the faces. It is reasonable to assume that the manipulation changed the way that people felt about the photographs. It does not tell us any more than that, and it certainly does not tell us why this change occurred. One plausible explanation for this is the evolutionary explanation indicated earlier. But that interpretation has not been demonstrated. These results could be taken to corroborate that theory, but should not be considered conclusive. Conversely, if the results had been negative and no such effect had been demonstrated that would not have disproved the existence of mate-choice copying in humans. It is always a big step from supporting a hypothesis to establishing a theory, and it is important not to get carried away too quickly.

This study took a theory from which it developed two complementary hypotheses which were then tested. It did this by operationalising the variables into something that could be measured. This process of breaking things down into manageable sized pieces is the essence of research. The study demonstrates that face preference can be socially transmitted even in artificial contexts. This may accord with a theory of mate-choice copying, but does not in itself confirm its occurrence amongst humans. The authors neatly sum up the relationship between their study and the bigger picture:

> Nonetheless, in so far as attractiveness ratings of opposite sex faces reflect mate preferences, our findings are … consistent with the suggestion that social transmission may influence women's mate preferences. (2006, p.4)

Note the caution in the inference – a hallmark of good research. Human behaviour is a highly complex process; breaking it down into its component parts makes it amenable to analysis. Piecing those parts together afterwards, extrapolating from findings to theory in order to understand even one small aspect of human behaviour, is no easy matter.

Summary Points	
Design	True experiment – mixed two-factor comparison: within and between
Aim	To compare effect of two IVs on two groups
2 IVs	Female gaze and female facial expression
DV	Preference for face Operationalised as mean relative preference rating over eight pairs of photographs.
Sample	Women (N=28); men (N=28)
Analysis	2 (between subjects factor: sex) × 2 (within subjects factor: direction of female gaze) × 2 (within subject factor: female facial expression) – changes from baseline measurement

The Autistic Spectrum

Structured Observation

Autism itself is not the enemy … the barriers to development that are included with autism are the enemy. The retardation that springs from a lack of development is the enemy. The sensory problems that are often themselves the barriers are the enemy. These things are not part of who the child is … they are barriers to who the child is meant to be, according to the developmental blueprint. Work with the child's strengths to overcome the weaknesses, and work within the autism, not against it, to overcome the developmental barriers. (Frank Klein, autism advocate)

Are You Familiar with the Term 'Autistic Spectrum'?

This phrase 'autistic spectrum' is used to describe a range of disorders that affect the individual's ability to interact socially with others. Autism was first identified as recently as the 1940s by Dr Leo Kanner in the United States. It is one of most commonly diagnosed disorders on the autistic spectrum and is detailed in the Diagnostic and Statistical Manual of Mental Disorders (DSM-IV). This is a tome published by the American Psychiatric Association and commonly used to define mental disorders. Autistic spectrum disorders, or ASD, taken as a whole, are one of the four most commonly occurring developmental disorders. Estimates of the incidence of ASD vary, but some suggest it may be as high as 3–4 in 1000 children. The diagnosis may be made as young as 18 months. The child is usually diagnosed by the age of 3. The parents may notice that the child does not interact with them, or with other family members, in the way that might normally be expected. The child may appear to fixate for long periods of time on an everyday object. He or she may prefer staring at this to making eye-contact with his or her mother or father. The National Institute of Mental Health lists the following possible indicators of ASD:

Does not babble, point, or make meaningful gestures by 1 year of age
Does not speak one word by 16 months

Does not combine two words by 2 years
Does not respond to name
Loses language or social skills
Poor eye contact
Doesn't seem to know how to play with toys
Excessively lines up toys or other objects
Is attached to one particular toy or object
Doesn't smile
At times seems to be hearing-impaired

These indicators show how the disorder typically affects the social behaviours of the child. Adults with ASD may find it difficult to make social relationships, and may experience limitations on social imagination and creativity. They may also lack flexibility and resist change, preferring to repeat familiar experiences. Verbal and non-verbal communication can present difficulties. Some will also experience different types of sensitivity to sights and sounds from the rest of us. In some instances they may be more sensitive than other people. In other ways they may experience a relative lack of sensitivity, especially in interpersonal situations.

At approximately the same time as Kanner identified autism in Germany, Dr Hans Asperger identified a similar but milder disorder now known as Asperger's syndrome. There has been a good deal of debate about the extent to which Asperger's syndrome is part of ASD, or whether it is in fact a discrete condition. This lack of consensus amongst researchers and professionals alike has led to problems in both the diagnosis of and the estimated prognosis for these disorders. If they are evidently separate entities then presumably differential **interventions** are required. If, alternatively, they are effectively different levels of the same condition then it is probable that a more standardised approach to support or intervention may be appropriate. Certainly the lack of clarity on this issue has suggested that the diagnostic classification system may lack validity. This is clearly an issue that needs resolution.

However, how can such a dilemma be solved? Studies have compared the cognitive function of individuals with high-level functioning autism with those who have been diagnosed as having Asperger's. These focus on their neuropsychological profiles, speech, motor skills, or developmental histories. However, for a variety of reasons none of these measures has been conclusive. The indicators for these conditions are behavioural, and largely social behaviour at that. Therefore, it would seem that behaviours rather than abilities might be amenable to a classification system. This was the topic chosen by Macintosh and Dissanayake (2006) for their observational study. They chose to observe three groups of children: one group had been diagnosed as having high-level functioning autism (HFA), one as having Asperger's disorder (AD) and the third group were typically developing children (TD).[1] The focus of this observation was the social behaviour of the children in their own environment. It was hypothesised that both HFA and AD would exhibit significant social impairments compared to the typically developing group. The question of interest was the extent to which these deficits would differ between the two diagnostic classifications.

A Comparative Study of the Spontaneous Social Interactions of Children with High Functioning Autism and Children with Asperger's Disorder

Macintosh, K. & Dissanayake, C. (2006). *Autism, 10*(2), 199–220

Method

The **aim** of Macintosh and Dissanayake's study was to compare the social behaviour of the three different groups.

The **sample** in the study comprised children aged 4–11: 20 with HFA, 19 with AD and 17 TD children. All attended mainstream schooling. The children were observed in their school playground during free periods throughout the school day, with the observer remaining as unobtrusive as possible. The study employed **structured observation**, which meant that the categories of behaviour that were to be coded were developed prior to the beginning of **data** collection. As the plan was to compare social behaviour, the **coding schedule** for the observer was designed to reflect this. The categories of activity included *social play* (involving others and including turn-taking and common goals or focus, with or without rules) *conversation, unoccupied* (purposeless or self-stimulatory) and *other purposeful* (non-social, nonplay activity). Macintosh and Dissanayake also reported who initiated any interaction and how many partners were involved in each. Verbal interactions were distinguished from non-verbal, and the quality of the interactions of both the target child and partners were recorded as either positive (prosocial or neutral) or aggressive.

Results

Data from the observation schedules meant that the amount of time children spent in each activity could be calculated. The data were analysed using **analysis**

Table 10.1. Behaviour frequency by group

	Most fcommon amongst		Least common amongst
Social play	TD	AD	HFA
Conversation	AD	TD	HFA
Unoccupied	HFA	AD	TD
Other purposeful, non-social non-play activity	HFA	AD	TD

of variance, i.e. **ANOVA** or **Kruskal–Wallis** as appropriate. Kruskal–Wallis, like ANOVA, allows you to compare two or more conditions in one go. It is used when the data are not eligible for ANOVA (see **parametric statistics** in the Glossary). The analyses showed a pattern of **significant** results. The children in HFA group spent the majority of the time unoccupied, and indeed both HFA and AD children spent more time unoccupied than did the TD children. The AD children spent the majority of their time in conversation, more than the HFA children. Conversely the TD children spent the majority of their time in simple social play, and significantly more than the HFA children. Unlike the TD children, HFA and AD children spent a similar amount of time in purposeful non-play, non-social activity. The TD children were also involved in group activity, (involving three or more individuals) more often than either of the other categories of children. This complex pattern of comparisons is summarised in Table 10.1.

The main difference between children with AD and those with HFA was that they were more frequently involved in verbal interactions with others and in initiating interaction. This is reflected in previous research suggesting that children with Asperger's have better language skills and are more socially motivated than children with autism. There were no other substantive differences between the two diagnostic groups in their playground behaviour. In contrast, both HFA and AD children differed from the TD children by having much less social interaction, less play, fewer sustained interactions and less group play. However, as the authors note, this is not to suggest that either of the diagnosed groups refrained from social play altogether; they just spent less time in this type of activity than the TD children. Interestingly, all three groups engaged in structured, rule-driven play, suggesting that in this type of play neither of the two diagnosed conditions presents an insurmountable barrier. The rules governing such activity may enable children to join in more readily than other types of play, where AD and HFA children are uncertain how to behave or interact.

There were three very positive findings from this study. There were no significant differences between the groups in the quality of the interactions, nor in the number of social invitations or bids received by their members. Moreover negative or aggressive behaviour was a rare occurrence in all three groups.

Given the commonality in behaviours between HFA and AD and the lack of evidence of a deficit or social skill that is unique to either group, the authors argue that this presents evidence that the two conditions are similar in nature, differing only in degree, with AD being the milder. The authors acknowledge that the diagnostic classification dilemma cannot be solved by an observational study alone, but argue that their findings 'are most compatible with the notion that Asperger's disorder is not a unique syndrome but rather lies on a continuum with autism' (2006, p.216).

■ How Safe Is This Conclusion?

This was an observational study with behaviour taking place in its natural setting, and the researchers had no control over events – which is, of course, characteristic of observation. This gives this method one of its main strengths, its **ecological validity**. Ultimately the behaviour is recorded by one human being watching another – can this be reliable? The problems surrounding eyewitness testimony constitute a major area of endeavour in psychology; Chapter 6, on **field experiments**, has demonstrated what poor observers we human beings can be. It is reasonable to take a close look at how this observation was done and what safeguards were put in place to ensure both the **reliability** and the **validity** of the data. In order to check reliability, we need to know more about the observations; to be sure of validity, we need details of the target behaviour, the children and the diagnosed disorders.

How Reliable Are the Observations?

The paper details the **protocol** followed by the observer for collecting the data. The period of observation was broken down into smaller time periods, and for each of these a note was made as to whether or not the particular target behaviour occurred. The target children were identified prior to the observation, thereby removing a potential source of bias. An observer free to select which children they wish to observe may be influenced by factors such as the level of animation or the attractiveness of the children into unwittingly collecting data on an unrepresentative sample of children. However, even with a pre-selected target, an observer may see and/or record the behaviour that they are expecting to find. This is not to suggest that researchers are naturally crooked or devious, but rather that, as humans, we are unconsciously drawn to see or notice specific behaviours and are rarely as dispassionate as we would like to believe. (If you have ever been party to a decision to buy a car in which the colour of that car was discussed, you may have observed this phenomenon at first hand. Once the decision is made about the car – for example that the car to be purchased is green – you will notice over the next few days that there are an astonishing number of green cars on the road. It will begin to feel like everyone has followed your example and gone out and bought a green car, or possibly resprayed their existing car with your chosen colour. In reality, of course, the number of green cars on the road has remained constant; what has changed is your awareness of them. As a species we

Box 10.1

Observation and Field Experiments Compared

It can be easy to muddle up these two types of study because both are undertaken outside the laboratory; both are concerned with behaviour in its natural setting. In observation, you do not attempt to manipulate the behaviour observed in any way but simply watch what naturally occurs. For this to be a successful method we need to make sure that the presence of the researcher is not affecting the behaviour. The researcher needs either to be hidden or to seem to be a natural part of the environment – which can be easy in a public place, as part of the crowd.

With animal studies it is a different matter. Usually the researcher needs to have spent so long near the animals that they are habituated to her/him. (See for example the work of Jane Goodall (1986), who has spent much of her working life living with chimpanzees that came to accept her as part of their environment.)

In contrast, once the researcher wants to change or manipulate the behaviour under study, the study becomes a field experiment. Remember, the term 'field experiment' does not necessarily mean that the research occurs in a pastoral setting. The study of helping behaviour outlined in Chapter 2 was a field experiment, but it is hard to think of a more urban environment than an underground train carriage! In a **field study**, a researcher may use observation as the means of data collection, which can add to the seeming confusion. But the golden rule is this: if the research involves manipulating something, then it is some form of experiment. If this something occurs in a natural setting, then it is likely to be a field experiment. If observation occurs without manipulation then it is an observational study.

are really prone to these types of bias in our perception of the environment. It may be irritating when you are choosing a car, but it could be calamity for a research project.)

The first precaution employed in this study was that the observer was **blind** to the diagnostic category of the child being observed; they did not know to which of the three groups (HFA, AD or TD) any given child belonged. This precaution should reduce the chance of **observer bias** in the reported behaviour. It is unlikely that it can remove that bias altogether as the observer, despite her/his best intentions, may have come to a conclusion about the diagnostic status of the target child during the observation. To reduce the likelihood of this, however, the observation protocol required that the researcher to use a **time-sampling technique**. This meant that s/he was to observe the child for a limited period, in this instance 30 seconds.

A longer period of observation per target might increase the likelihood of the child engaging in stereotypical behaviours, thereby revealing its diagnostic category. One alternative to time-sampling is **point-sampling**, where the observer watches each target in turn and records their behaviour at that point. This can be an effective means of sampling observed behaviour, especially in animals, or behaviour that occurs in isolation from others. However, with social behaviour, which is subject to the vagaries of people other than the target, such a technique may lead to the recording of behaviour that may not be fully representative of the individual. In this study, Macintosh (the observer) recorded the behaviours that occurred during the 30-second period and then coded each according to the dominant activity observed. A second alternative sampling strategy is **event-sampling**, where the observers are counting the number of target events observed, for instance, in this context it could have been group play. The observer would then record the information leading up to, during and after the event. This type of sampling usually requires that a recording technique such as film or video is used in order to observe the details of the several different people involved. In this study, however, event-sampling was not appropriate as in each case specific individuals were under observation.

Having chosen time-sampling as the optimum technique, Macintosh and Dissanayake took two further precautions to ensure the reliability of the data. The first of these was that each individual was observed on two separate occasions, less than a fortnight apart. This meant that they could be more certain about the representative nature of the data. This is the observational equivalent of **test-retest reliability**. The other precaution was to have a second observer sample 20 per cent of the observations, and then the two sets of coded behaviours were compared. This 20 per cent sample was evenly drawn from all three diagnostic categories. A **correlation coefficient** was calculated to see to what extent the codes coincided between first and second observer. This type of correlation coefficient can range from 0 to 1, the nearer 1 the figure the greater the degree of agreement between observers. The coefficients for the comparisons reported here ranged from .69 (moderate level of agreement) to .99 (very high level of agreement). This provides a measure of **inter-observer reliability** (this method was also used in the study described in Chapter 7).

Taken together, these precautions mean that we can have a good deal of confidence in the reliability of these data.

● How Effective Is the Study Design?

Data being reliable is only half the battle. If they are not also valid, then the reliability counts for little. For data to be valid they must represent the variable of interest. For example, if I observed facial expressions of students reading in the library and counted the number of times people furrowed their forehead, I could well produce very reliable data. If you observed the same people independently of me, it is likely that you would come up with pretty much the same data, and this inter-observer check would test the reliability of the data very neatly. However, supposing that the target behaviour I am trying to observe is concentration: would I have successfully

operationalised the behaviour (variable) of interest? It is doubtful, partly because some people can concentrate without furrowing their brow and partly because it is not just concentration that causes people to furrow their brow; they may be worried or cross, or maybe the print is just very small! Therefore the validity of my data would be very much in doubt.

How Was the Coding Schedule Devised?

Macintosh and Dissanayake were careful in their selection of target behaviours. They deployed a structured observation technique, where the types of behaviour were clearly identified before the data collection began. They did not rely on their own hunches about the types of target behaviour, nor did they leave it to 'common sense' – a pitfall which too many have failed to avoid. Instead, they identified and defined, i.e. they operationalised, their target behaviours based on recent past research on the social interaction of children on the autistic spectrum. They also provided detailed information about these definitions in the appendix to their paper so that readers could scrutinise these at their leisure without being diverted from the story of the findings in the main body of the paper.

How Safe Were the Diagnostic Categories?

The one remaining area where errors could be found is in the children themselves. The first potential problem would be in the categorisation of the children into the three diagnosed groups. If this is not carefully done, then subsequent comparisons would be meaningless. The diagnoses of the two clinical groups were completed by experienced psychiatrists and clinical psychologists using the diagnostic criteria from the *DSM*-IV. Not content with this alone, clinical and developmental histories of all the children were also examined to confirm these diagnoses. Therefore thorough criteria were applied to identify the two clinical groups.

All the children were aged between 4 and 11, and when the ages of the children within each of the three groups were compared, there was no significant difference; thus on this aspect all three groups were comparable. All the children also undertook an IQ test, and only children whose IQ was above 70 were included in the sample. The IQ test provided information on their overall mental age and their verbal mental age. There was no difference between the groups on their mental age but there was a difference on the verbal mental age; the TD average score was the highest, and the HFA the lowest. Now you might think that this would put a question mark against their findings. After all, if the groups had different levels of communication, how could a comparison of their verbal interactions be meaningful? Luckily this is less of a problem than it might at first appear. The statistical analysis used by Macintosh and Dissanayake took this discrepancy into account. Every analysis they ran to see whether there was a significant difference between groups also tested whether this differential verbal ability had any effect on the outcome. In only one case did it impact, and that was on the initiation of the exchange. This is perhaps not surprising, as having more language would make it easier to initiate communication. It would seem probable, then, that the differences in language ability were not the cause of the overall differences in behaviour. It is more likely that both of these are **correlated** with an underlying motivation towards being a social creature.

The other area where potentially there could be **confounding variables** is the environment. For example, if the children from the clinical groups attended specialist schools, they might be accustomed to a different level of interaction from the TD children. However, in this study all 56 children attended mainstream schooling, so this was not a difficulty. Finally, social interaction does not happen in a vacuum, but is affected by others. As these children were all playing in their own school environment it is possible that the other children might have differing expectations of them: if, for example, an HFA child was generally less social than other children in their class, then their classmates may have, in time, become less inclined to attempt to involve them in play. However, there was no evidence that this was the case, with children in all three groups being subject to a similar number of initiations from their fellow pupils.

▲ How Appropriate Was the Research Method?

This observational study had all the advantages of the naturalistic setting providing a familiar environment and routine activities for the children involved. While maintaining this minimal interference for the children's daily behaviour, the level of care and control that went into the study design show what structured observation can achieve. This type of observation, where behaviour is coded according to a preexisting schedule, is nearly always **non-participant observation**. In practice, being a participant observer does not normally allow time for the type of rigorous coding required.

There are some wonderful classic participant observational studies, to which the interested reader is referred in the references to this chapter. Generally speaking participant observers, whether disclosed as in Whyte's study (1945) or undisclosed as in Rosenhan's (1973), take notes or record information as events unfold and then later write the study presenting **qualitative** rather than **quantitative** data. The qualitative data may comprise descriptions of events from the observer's point of view, the observer's reactions to those events and direct quotes from the participants. Undisclosed observational studies are rare these days, as the lack of **informed consent** gives rise to ethical issues. The advantage of truly observational studies is that the behaviour under scrutiny is naturally occurring behaviour and not the product of the research design. In this way observation avoids many of the pitfalls that can beset experimental work.

Observational studies give rise to a consideration of ethical issues. In Macintosh and Dissanayake's study the authors report that the observer remained as unobtrusive as possible. This is different from being an undisclosed observer. The school, the teachers and probably the parents/carers would have given consent for this observation to take place. Playing in a school yard is essentially public behaviour, and as such observation does not present the ethical difficulties associated with observing private behaviour. The observer needs to remain unobtrusive so that her/his presence does not affect the way the children interact.

One other form of observational study that can be helpful in this area is the **case study**. One such instance is Levy and Fowler (2005), who reported a case where an autistic adolescent's ability to tell a story coherently improved markedly if he was offered practice with help from adults. By the end of the study he could recount the story as well as an unimpaired, although younger, child. They suggest that with the right type of input some HFA children can be taught the skills to pull elements of information into a coherent whole.

Is there any other way in which data such as those provided by Macintosh and Dissanayake could have been gathered? It is possible that safe and ethically sound experiments can be devised to compare the different responses of these three groups of children. For example, Roseman *et al.* (2001) conducted a **double-blind crossover trial** of a drug called secretin, which had been shown to produce some improvement in autistic behaviour. They used observational measures of behaviour as their **dependent variable** (**DV**). Although there was evidence of improvement in some of the individual children, the data for the whole sample showed that that secretin was not significantly different from a **placebo**. This approach could be adapted to compare the responses of children with different levels of autism. However, any such approach does not examine normal social behaviour but only differences in responses to stimuli (in this last case, the new **stimulus** was the treatment). As such, laboratory work might be more suited to exploring differences in ability rather than daily social interaction. Experimental work could incorporate a **time series study**, where multiple measures are taken over a period of time, with and without the presence of an independent variable. A study by Hoeppner *et al.* (2007) used this design to monitor the heart rate of children with autism when exposed to stressful events. They argue that time series analysis enables an **idiographic approach** to exploring intraindividual variation.

A field experiment would, by its nature, have introduced at least one new variable into children's environment which would have changed the dynamics of the situation. Not only would this have reduced the ecological validity of the study but, for the clinical groups in particular, it could have presented further problems; children on the autistic spectrum can be averse to novelty and change, turning a new stimulus into a confounding variable.

Survey methods might have produced some interesting results if the researchers had sought the opinions of teachers, parents or carers. Surveys for children of this age group are unlikely to be useful unless they are very carefully designed, and it would be impractical to consider a detailed survey asking children about their social behaviour. However, useful information could be obtained using survey methods from adults, either family/carers or professionals. For example, Williams *et al.* (2006) conducted a survey of parents of children with autism to find what they considered to be useful strategies for encouraging their child to sleep at bedtime. These sorts of data would tell us how such children are viewed, or provide an insight into living with different categories of child. A **cross-sectional study**, for example, could compare the responses of carers of children with higher-functioning autism with those whose children had Asperger's. Even then, the results would need to be interpreted with caution. They would not tell us how the children behave but how the adults see their behaviour – a fine distinction which it is all too easy to lose.

Conclusions

This is a neat observational study, which provides insights into the classification of childhood disorders. The authors do not claim that their study should settle the issue of diagnosis for these two types of disorder. They acknowledge that the problematic distinction between higher-functioning autism and Asperger's will only be decided with a good deal of painstaking **empirical** evidence. As is always the case, building a body of research evidence to address any real-world dilemma is a slow process, involving many researchers and more publications. This is one piece in that jigsaw.

Note

1   It is often useful to abbreviate the names of groups when describing a study in order to avoid repetition of lengthy phrases or names. However, it is always advisable to make sure that any such acronym is meaningful and therefore easy to remember. While most readers can quickly learn to recognise, for example, HFA as higher-functioning autism, it is considerably more difficult to follow when letter names are chosen arbitrarily, such as 'groups A, B and C'.

Summary Points	
Design	Structured observation
Aim	To compare behaviour of three groups
Sampling frame	Children diagnosed with higher-functioning autism or Asperger's and in mainstream schooling
Sample	Children, aged 4–11: N=20 with higher-functioning autism; N=19 with Asperger's; and N=17 typically developing
Sampling technique	Time-sampling: recording behaviour that predominated during specified interval
Materials	Coding schedule
Analysis	Between groups comparison using verbal mental age as covariate

Cognitive Maps

Clinical/Laboratory Observation

'The intellectual takes as a starting point his self and relates the world to his own sensibilities; the scientist accepts an existing field of knowledge and seeks to map out the unexplored terrain.' (Daniel Bell, sociologist, b. 1919)

Do You Know Where You Are?

The answer to this may seem obvious: you can no doubt say what room you are in, what building and what geographical location. Taking a slightly larger picture, however, do you know whereabouts you are in relation to other identifiable places? Can you, for example, from where you are currently sitting, point to the direction of your nearest town centre? Or your nearest library? Maybe you can see the town centre or the library from where you are, so try something more challenging: can you, without using a compass, point to the direction in which you would find London, New York or Rome? To do this you need to know the relative position of your current location and the target city. This piece of knowledge may have two components: one about where you are and one about the target. Do you know how the compass maps on to your current position? Which way is due north for example? Sometimes we already know this information, and sometimes we can work it out, for example in relation to where the sun rises or sets. Sometimes we have no idea. Some people are very attuned to this; others are not. The second thing we need for this task is knowledge of geography, which we can only get from maps. If we do not know where the target city is located on the planet, we cannot be expected to know in what direction it lies. For some people, these two skills seem to be relatively easy; others find either or both of them challenging. Some people find map-reading easy; others do not. Some people can speedily learn their way around a new building, campus or town; for others this process takes longer and for some seems nearly impossible. Try this for yourself by asking people in your social group to point to some fixed distant and unseen point (a known building, a location or even a compass point). You don't even have to know the correct direction yourself. Just see how many of them accept the challenge and point without hesitation and how many are unsure. For those who do point, see how many different directions they select.

Why should this be? Why are some people better able to locate themselves and navigate spatially? This area of study is sometimes termed 'environmental perception', and refers to the way in which we develop an understanding of our spatial location. One explanation for this variability among humans has been based on the idea of cognitive maps. This is a term that was originally coined by Tolman in the 1940s. He ran a series of experiments exploring the maze-learning abilities of rats, and reviewed these findings with reference to human spatial learning abilities. Cognitive maps have been studied by many different disciplines, not just psychology (e.g. anthropology, archaeology, planning). Comparative psychologists have been interested in exploring the cognitive mapping ability of animals, in particular their homing ability. Cognitive maps have been suggested as an explanation for the extraordinary migration patterns of some bird species. Every spring, swallows find their way from South Africa, flying north over the African continent, taking the western route along the coast, the eastern route up the Nile or the central route across the Sahara. They cross the Mediterranean and travel north along the eastern coast of Spain, over the Pyrenees, northwards through France and across the Channel to return to the area of the UK whence they came. This epic journey of 6000 miles (nearly 10,000 kilometres) they undertake twice each year, returning to the warmth of Africa every autumn to avoid the British winter. It is an arduous journey, and many of them do not survive it; but enough succeed to maintain stable levels of the population (other environmental threats permitting). It is an extraordinary achievement, one that most humans would find impossible. We would need the aid of maps, compasses or conversational enquiries to do it just once, never mind twice a year.

The differential in cognitive mapping abilities among humans has also been the subject of scientific scrutiny. Until recently this type of study was limited to seeking differences between groups or **correlational** research to discover what abilities may relate to such spatial abilities. There has been some evidence to suggest that there are sex differences in spatial abilities, with males having the advantage. More recently, research has identified concentrations of the male sex hormone, testosterone, *in utero*. This would suggest that our spatial abilities are determined at birth depending on the amount of testosterone in the mother's womb.

Where Can We Find These 'Cognitive Maps'?

Cognitive maps are an example of **hypothetical constructs** (see Box 11.1), and as such measuring is not easy.

With animal research it is sometimes a different matter. On occasions, and when ethically appropriate, either vivisection or *post mortem* examination may allow the scientist to examine the animal's brain and note any specific structures, changes or

Box 11.1

Hypothetical Constructs and Measurement

The problem is that the subject matter of psychology is notoriously difficult to access and measure accurately. We can only observe the way people or animals behave and then make inferences about the systems or the mechanisms that underlie that behaviour. This is why it has been necessary to develop hypothetical constructs. A formal definition would be that hypothetical constructs are theoretical objects or processes that are invoked in order to interpret observed phenomena. Put more simply, it is one way of explaining the way that things work. We assume that people have memories because we are able to recall things. We assume that people have personalities because we all seem to behave slightly differently. We assume that there is such a thing as intelligence because it explains some types of individual difference. Each of these is an abstract concept. We do not know that it exists; we have not seen it. We know that people have two hands because we can see them. We know that people have brains because these can be seen (by surgeons for example, although most of us have not seen a real brain). With hypothetical constructs we do not have this same level of firm evidence.

With memories, for example, we know that meanings, episodes and views are somehow stored in our brains, and we call the system that does this a memory. But we have yet to observe a person's memory directly. We can measure its capacity by experimental testing, but this is a very different type of measurement from the type we use to measure someone's height, weight or body temperature. Scales, rulers and thermometers are no use here. We can use recently developed scanning technology to see what part of the brain is activated when responding to a recall task, but this falls short of identifying that part of the brain as the memory. We can use **psychometric assessments** to measure particular types of capacity, but we are still inferring from our results, rather than measuring directly. (See Chapter 16 on psychometrics.)

abnormalities which may be associated with particular phenomena or behaviour. With humans this has only been possible in rare case studies, and then always *post mortem*. Much of what we have learned about the structure of the brain has been discovered in this manner. Evidence from *post mortem* examination or, very occasionally, from surgery, has helped tell us what parts of the brain are used for what function.

Largely as a result of this type of work it has been hypothesised that the area of the brain responsible for spatial awareness, for cognitive maps, is an area called the hippocampus. This is part of the structure of the brain found in both humans and animals, and is therefore considered an 'old' part of the brain as we have it in common with other species. (In contrast the frontal lobes are considered to be what sets humans apart from other species.) The brain is normally described as a bilateral organ, which means it comprises two more or less equal halves or hemispheres, each of which has a hippocampus. The word itself comes from the genus of the sea horse, because the anatomical shape of this structure in the brain similar to that of the animal. The hippocampus is known to be responsible for both memory and spatial awareness, which explains its importance in our understanding of cognitive maps.

That we know the role of the hippocampus in this activity is a splendid example of how different research activities can combine to increase our understanding. Four strands of activity were woven together to produce this. The animal laboratory studies of Tolman and others involving maze-learning formed one strand. This was combined with the work of comparative psychologists exploring migration and homing instincts in different species. The third strand came from clinical work with human beings, which allowed us to see how different types of injury or damage to the brain affected behaviour and performance. This form of data collection is at best sporadic and invariably opportunist, awaiting a suitable and consenting case. This makes systematic collection of such information painstakingly slow. The fourth strand is developing technologies. The area was greatly aided by the introduction of electroencephalographic recordings, or EEG, developed in the early part of the twentieth century, which allowed observers to trace electrical activity in the brains of mammals or humans. These four different strands of research activity were woven together in an integrated study by O'Keefe and Nadel (1978), a classic in cognitive neuroscience, which spelt out the role of the hippocampus in cognitive maps.

How Can We Explore Cognitive Mapping in Humans?

Identifying the hippocampus as the physiological basis of cognitive maps was a major step, but it raises many further questions. We all have hippocampi; why, then, do some people have better cognitive maps than others? Can we acquire good cognitive mapping skills? Is this type of spatial awareness something that can be learned? Do you need to have a particularly well-developed hippocampus in order to have good mapping abilities? Or will practising your skills have a direct impact on your hippocampus? This was addressed by Maguire *et al.* (2000) in a study using MRI scanning.

The arrival of magnetic resonance imaging, or MRI, scanning has meant that it is now possible to look at the anatomy inside people's heads while they are alive and awake and without causing them any harm. It is a method of neuroimaging and is non-invasive, allowing us to see the shape and structures of the brain. It is also possible to use this technology to monitor and pinpoint activity, namely thought processes, cognitions, as they happen. This is known as fMRI, functional magnetic resonance imaging. MRI scanning has provided opportunities for medicine and for research. MRI provides better-quality information than we could ever have gained from EEGs. EEGs were a great advance in their time because the technology allowed us to measure some form of output from within the human cranium, previously an impenetrable 'black box' for science. It is particularly useful in monitoring changes, as it responds immediately to changes in activity, so its temporal resolution is very good. It measures overall electrical activity but does not provide any spatial mapping onto the cortex to identify where the activity occurs. MRI scanning can produce a 3-D picture of the brain and allows for a more detailed exploration of what is happening and where. This picture of the brain is more than just an image: it can itself be subjected to **quantitative analysis**, as we shall see.

It was this technology that allowed Maguire and her colleagues to investigate hippocampal activity and cognitive mapping. They wanted to understand the relationship between acquiring spatial knowledge and the hippocampus. In particular they were interested in whether increased experience of spatial navigation resulted in structural changes to the human hippocampus. Research had already established that for mammals and birds repeated behaviour needing spatial memory, such as food storing, resulted in increased hippocampal volume. It was also clear that this volume could change across the seasons depending on the need for this type of spatial memory, i.e. in the autumn/winter when retrieving stored food. Differences had also been established between groups of humans, for example males and females, musicians and non-musicians. What remained unclear was the thorny issue of cause and effect. Are such differences in the structure of the brain always determined at birth, as in the case of being male or female, or can they equally be produced by subsequent activity? For example, is the successful study of music predetermined by the structure of the brain? Or is it that prolonged involvement with music changes the brain's structure? The authors decided to explore this latter possibility by comparing the brain structure of those with and those without extensive experience of spatial navigation.

The **sampling frame** for this study was London taxi-drivers. This is a neat example of how sampling frames differ from **populations**. The population under study here is, potentially, humankind – the researchers were investigating attributes of the human brain. For this they needed to select a sample of humans. However, for this study the data needed to be collected from one particular group of humans who had a specific characteristic. That characteristic would provide a group that was relatively homogeneous in terms of the attribute under study (in this instance, the hippocampus). Therefore the study chose to recruit a sample from the sampling frame of London taxi-drivers. Please note that the sampling frame here was not all taxi-drivers, as this would not have provided the same uniformity. Taxi-drivers in different locations have different training requirements. Therefore, in this study, the population was humans, the sampling frame was London taxi-drivers, and the **sample** was the group of 16 cabbies who took part in the study.

Navigation Related Structural Changes in the Hippocampi of Taxi Drivers

Maguire, E.A., Gadian, D.G., Johnsrude, I.S., Good, C.D., Ashburner, J., Frackowiak, R.S.J. & Frith, C.D. (2000). *Proceedings of the National Academy of Sciences of the United States of America, 97*(8), 4398–4403

Method

Maguire *et al.* used MRI scanning to examine the brain structure of 16 male London taxi-drivers, specifically recruited for this study. London taxi-drivers were selected because of the training required for the job. While taxi-drivers should always demonstrate a good knowledge of the location in which they work, in London would-be taxi-drivers have to undergo a period of extensive training, which is colloquially known as 'the knowledge'. They have to be able to find their way between thousands of different city landmarks, and they need to be able to find the shortest or most direct route. It normally takes at least two years to learn this (it can take four), and there are stringent tests at the end of the training to make sure that the applicant really can find and describe their way around London. Thus, the job and its requisite training make these people the ideal subject for this study.

Examining the MRI scans of the brains of London taxi-drivers would not alone provide us with the data needed. For these data to be useful the researchers needed to be able to compare them with scans taken from people who are not taxi-drivers. This provides a **comparator** which would enable the researchers to decide whether the hippocampi of taxi-drivers differ from the brains of others. As it turned out, it was not necessary to recruit a second, comparator, sample; instead 50 scans were selected from an existing bank of scans of healthy people who were not taxi-drivers.

It is noteworthy that the number of cases in these two groups differed substantially, the control having more than three times the number of members. Despite what some people think, this is not in itself a problem. The larger the number of scans in the control group the better, as this should produce data that are closer to the population mean (see Box 8.1 for further information). The rule of thumb for sampling is that the greater the number, the more likely it is that the data will be representative of the population.

The **aim** of this study was to determine whether there were structural differences in the brain between those with and those without extensive experience of spatial navigation.

Results

Two types of analysis were used to explore the scans.

The first measurement is called voxel-based morphometry, or VBM, which is an automated technique that measures the density of the grey matter in different regions of a scan. (It might help to think of this almost as though that part of the brain was being weighed.) The VBM showed that there was a statistically **significant** greater density of grey matter in the brains of the taxi-drivers compared to those of the control sample, but this greater density was confined to one small part of the brain, the posterior (or back) of the right hippocampus. Initially, it seemed that there might also be less grey matter in the anterior measure for the taxi-drivers than for the control, but once more stringent statistical measures were taken this apparent difference was no longer significant.

The second analysis used the scanning procedure to take virtual 'slices' of the brain. These slices were taken from the coronal plane (from in front of the cranium) and were slightly tilted forward at the top in order to optimise the view of the hippocampus. For each subject there were at least 26 images, each covering an area 1.5 mm thick, thereby representing the full length of the hippocampus, approximately 4 cm. The hippocampus was then measured counting the pixels in each of these slices. These images were divided into three regions of the hippocampus: the posterior, the body and the anterior. For each of these an average or **mean** figure was calculated to represent the overall volume of both the left and right hippocampus as measured in the images. The pixel count showed that there was no overall difference in hippocampus size, nor in the body (or mid-section). There were two significant differences: the anterior (or front) of the right hippocampus was significantly smaller amongst taxi-drivers than among the controls while the posterior was significantly bigger. These findings, of course, confirm those of the VBM.

Finally the authors looked at the relationship between amount of time spent working as a taxi-driver and these structural changes. They found a significant correlation in each analysis, for the VBM and for the pixel-counting data. There was a **positive correlation** with the changes in the posterior section, which means that as the number of years of driving increased so the two measures of density also increased. There was a **negative correlation** in the anterior section, which means that as the number of years of driving increased so the density decreased.

This means that long-term service as a taxi-driver is associated with increased volume in the back of the hippocampus and decreased volume in the front. This suggests that:

> the professional dependence on navigational skills in licensed London taxi drivers is associated with a relative redistribution of grey matter in the hippocampus. (2000, p.4402)

■ How Safe Is This Conclusion?

One of the original questions underlying this study was to determine cause and effect. Is it possible that, rather than structural changes occurring as a result of being a cabbie, it is in fact the other way around? Maybe it is the very structure of the anatomy of the brain that draws particular people into this type of employment. From the first part of the study, comparing the two groups, it is not possible to identify cause and effect. It is the results of the second analysis, the correlation, that provides convincing evidence here. If it was simply the structure of the brain that led people to be good at navigation, then you would not expect changes over time. Although correlation cannot establish cause and effect, these data suggest that the longer you work as a cabbie the more profound these changes are.

How could you set about conclusively determining cause and effect in this instance?

The authors note that for this correlational analysis they had to exclude the data from one of the subjects as he had been working as a cabbie for 42 years, and the next nearest to him had been working for 28 years. This one extreme case was considered to be too much of an **outlier** to be included in the results. It may have occurred to you that this could have been a rather neat way to 'cook the books'. What if this one **participant** had not shown these changes: would the overall effect of a correlation still have been evident? After all, dropping one out of 16 is losing over 6 per cent of your data! However, the study provides us with this individual's data, which show that his changes were the most extreme of the sample. Therefore we can conclude that the authors were not selecting data to make their argument but, rather, merely being cautious in their analysis.

Despite the advanced technology used for this study, one of the **dependent variables (DV)** was operationalised by counting the number of pixels in the scan. This is not fully described in the paper; it is only noted that the individual who did the counting was experienced in the technique. Is it possible that we could have some form of **experimenter effect** here? The authors must have known what they were looking for. Could this have influenced the person who was expected to do the tedious business of pixel-counting? Furthermore, the VBM analysis was conducted first, and the findings from the pixel count supported it. Could it be that the VBM findings produced a **bias** in the judgement of the individual responsible for the count? It would not have to be a deliberate effect, but could they have inadvertently encouraged this person to err on the expected side when a difficult judgement call had to be made? This is particularly important as the differences in the anterior were only statistically significant with the pixel-counting and not with VBM. You might think that there would be a particular pressure to find an effect here. The authors ensured that there was no danger of this as the technician doing the counting was **blind** to the identity of the individual scans; when counting pixels s/he did not know whether the scan in question came from a taxi-driver. The person was also blind to the overall results of the VBM process; thus the two analyses were conducted independently and yet both told a similar story.

● How Effective Is the Observational Design?

The scans from the taxi-drivers were compared with 50 from 'normals', which in this instance means people who do not drive a taxi for a living. These were not recruited just for this study but were drawn from an existing database of scans. All the scans had been taken at the same unit using the same equipment so they should be comparable in definition and detail. The normals here comprised males and were of a corresponding age to the taxi-drivers in order to control for any age-related changes. We know that handedness is a function of hemispheric dominance (right-handed people have a dominant left hemisphere in their brain, and vice versa) Therefore, this potential source of error was also controlled, as all participants from both groups in this study were right-handed. There were more scans in the comparator group than in the study group, but this is not in itself a problem. The data from all 50 were used in the VBM comparison, but in the pixel-counting exercise only 16 were selected. Each of these was exactly age-matched with one of the taxi-drivers, making this part of the study a **matched pairs design**. As this was a legitimate criterion for selecting a reduced sample size it presents no problems.

We are not provided with much information about the control group other than that they were not taxi-drivers. But taxi-drivers are not the only people to rely on spatial knowledge to make a living. What about bus-drivers, lorry-drivers, naval captains, pilots? They also routinely navigate their way between complex spatial positions. What about cartographers for that matter? Or even weekend ramblers? I am sure there are many more types of occupational or hobby groups that could be cited here. How do we know that they were not included in the control group? Have the researchers been rather lax in not checking this? The answer is no – because it does not matter in the slightest if one or more of the control group have advanced spatial knowledge. The finding here showed that the taxi-drivers had changes in the brain that were not seen in the brains of non-taxi-drivers. If that control group included any spatial specialists, it would mean that the difference between taxi-drivers and another control group would be all the more extreme.

It would seem therefore that the comparator group was a suitable **control**.

It is useful to consider the differences and common points between this observational study and that described in the previous chapter on autism. Both studies have identified a group of people to observe to tell them more about the population of interest. Macintosh and Dissanayake observed behaviour in order to shed light on diagnostic categories. Maguire and colleagues observed the effects of behaviour on the human brain. Macintosh and Dissanayake observed naturally occurring behaviour; Maguire *et al.* used advanced technology in order to see physiological structures hidden inside the human skull. These two studies may seem at first to have little in common, but it would be wrong to focus only on their differences. Both are purely observational studies, albeit using contrasting techniques for data collection; both simply observe things that exist independent of the research programme (children's behaviour or anatomical structures); neither instigates or manipulates the object under study, and both provide information on naturally occurring phenomena.

▲ How Appropriate Was the Research Method?

This study is purely observational. It is clearly **non-participant observation**, as it is indeed a clinical study with the participants being drawn into a clinical environment in order to make these observations. There was no element of a **survey** here – for once, the taxi-drivers' views were not sought! It is true that the researchers must have asked them questions to find out their age, duration in post and length of training, but gathering background information of this sort does not constitute a survey. Because a good deal of equipment is used to collect data it may be tempting to resort to the language of experimentation. You may have noticed that the authors refer to a *control* group. But this was no **experiment**. There was no experimental manipulation of an **independent variable** (**IV**); all the researchers did was to observe existing aspects of the world around them. This may not be the archetypal observational study commonly found in social or developmental psychology (see Chapter 10) and even in ethology and sociology. Admittedly very high-tech equipment was needed in order to do the study, but that makes no difference; an **observation** it remains.

Would **survey methods** have been useful? A survey could tell us whether people say that they can easily find their way around a new town. They might report being able to read a map, cross a city, or know which way is north. We might find **between groups** differences here, but they will be differences in self-reports. The development of a psychometric measurement of cognitive maps could provide useful information about people's ability; this was the aim of Kearney and Kaplan (1997) when they began the development of such a tool. However, without the MRI scan it would not provide us with detailed information about the anatomical structure of the brain. We could have surveyed brain surgeons or similar to see if in their experience people with particular types of damage to the head experience particular types of navigational problems. Without **objective** data their responses would be only subjective impressions, which themselves are subject to all the biases and selectivity that we know humans to experience. If a neurologist, or similar, did note what appeared

Table 11.1. Schematic representation of study design

	Topographical	Not topographical
Sequencing	route	plot
Not sequencing	landmark	frame

to be a systematic trend in her/his patients, s/he would need at that point to start collecting objective data to explore the issue further. An alternative for such an individual would be to write an account of a particular patient of interest, which would then be considered a **case study** (see Chapter 14). Case studies often provide useful insights, although it is not possible to generalise across a population based on the evidence from a single case.

Would experiments be possible in this area? There has been much work looking at cognitive maps in animals. Recent examples include the work of Wray *et al.* (2008), who examined the concept of cognitive mapping in honey bees. Singer *et al.* (2006) used an experimental maze procedure to look at cognitive mapping in rats. Is experimentation also possible with humans? Indeed, yes, as it turns out, Maguire and colleagues had previously published details of just such an experiment.

Experimental Findings

In 1997 Maguire *et al.* ran an experimental study to explore brain activity and cognitive maps. They used a different sort of imaging technique, positron emission tomography, or PET scanning. This allowed them to watch functional changes in the brain in response to different stimuli. This time, instead of looking at the anatomical structure of the brain the authors wanted to see how it responded to different types of task. Once again their sampling frame was London taxi-drivers, the rationale for the selection being the same. In this study 11 taxi-drivers took part in four different tasks while undergoing PET scanning. This enabled the researchers to identify which parts of the brain were involved for different types of tasks.

There were two independent variables in this study: sequencing and memory type. Sequencing means that the information that the subjects are required to produce for a task has to be presented in a specific order. In this study two tasks involved sequencing and two did not. Memory type was either for topographical (spatial) information, or non-topographical information, which required providing descriptions from memory but did not involve the recall of spatial information. There were four experimental tasks: describing a route (sequential and topographic), describing a landmark (topographic but not sequential), describing a film plot (sequential but not topographic) and describing a single frame from a film (neither sequential or topographic); see Table 11.1.

The findings from this experiment showed that the topographical tasks activated different areas of the brain from the activity produced by the film-based tasks. This allowed the researchers to compare the effects of sequencing in each type of task. Their findings are detailed and beyond the scope of this chapter, except to say that the only task that appeared to activate the hippocampus was that which required both sequencing and topographical information, namely describing a route. The findings of this experiment will have influenced the research team to undertake the second observation study. If thinking about routes uniquely activates the hippocampus, what then would the effect on the hippocampus of repeated activation? How better to find out than ask a cabbie for help? This is a neat example of the **hypothetico-deductive method** at its best.

Conclusion

Maguire and colleagues have shown us that repeated activation over time does alter the structure of the brain, at least in the case of the hippocampus. They have shown that it is this part of the brain that it is activated by recall of route information, and that the longer a person has been using the facility, in this instance the longer they have been a cab-driver, the greater the changes. They suggest that it is the right posterior hippocampus that is used in the storage of spatial information. They propose that the process of becoming a taxi-driver, of 'doing the knowledge', lays out the basic route map of London in storage in the brain and then over the years of his/her career, the driver learns more details and short-cuts and accommodates new traffic routing, and thereby fine-tunes that image, thus further activating that part of the brain. They further suggest, using the law of **parsimony**, that their findings

> reflect an overall internal reorganisation of hippocampal circuitry … in response to a need to store an increasingly detailed spatial representation where changes in one hippocampal region are likely to affect others. (2000, p.4402)

They have reached this conclusion through a series of studies drawing on more than one research design, including the clinical observation reported here. They have identified two clear groups in their sampling process, one of which is characterised by a repeated need to draw on stored spatial information, and the other not. The comparison of the data between this group and the control group has made it possible to draw inferences from the data and to suggest causal mechanisms for the differences in the observations. They have run a between groups comparison using **inferential statistics**. They have also used a correlational analysis to explore the effect of long-term exposure on the observed phenomenon. They started with unequal numbers in their two groups, but this was not a problem. They have excluded the data from an outlier, not in order to prevent it spoiling their story, but rather because it would have positively distorted their findings, making them more extreme than they already were. The apparatus required for this study was beyond the means of many departments and only likely to be found in hospitals.

This study may not have represented a classical observational design – there was certainly no clipboard involved in the data collection! However, it is representative of a new form of research, one made possible by technological advances. Innovations in technology are enabling all scientists to explore areas that were previously not available for scrutiny. The human head was the traditional 'black box' that behaviourists chose to ignore as it was not amenable to scientific analysis, only conjecture. Twenty-first-century scanning techniques are effectively allowing us to observe what is going on inside that box.

Summary Points	
Design	Clinical observation
Aim	To compare physiology of two groups
Population	Humans
Sampling frame	London taxi-drivers
Sample	Taxi-drivers (N=16) and scans of non-taxi-drivers (N=50); all male, all right-handed, taken from an MRI database
Apparatus	Magnetic resonance imaging scanner
Analysis	Between groups comparison

Eating Disorders and the Media

Observation – Quantitative Content Analysis

'A newspaper is a device for making the ignorant more ignorant and the crazy crazier.' (H.L. Mencken, journalist and critic, 1880–1956)

Are You Happy with Your Weight?

This is a question to which many of us in the West are inclined to say 'No'. Some of us would like to gain weight, but many more wish to lose it. For some people, weight loss is a medical recommendation as obesity is a real problem associated with a range of serious and chronic illnesses. However, in our society many people who are not defined as obese[1] still wish to lose weight, to be thinner, and this is more common amongst women than amongst men. If there is no clinical reason for it, why is this desire widespread?

Our society promotes slimness as attractive, although it is worth bearing in mind that this has not always been the case. Social historians tell us that in times of plenty a society is more likely to value thinness, whereas in subsistence societies plumpness is appreciated more. Our relationship with food in the West is troubled, not by a lack of supply, which our ancestors experienced, but by the extraordinary diversity of foods available to us. When there were routinely only one or two foodstuffs available, our ancestors were not tempted to consume more calories than they needed. If food is boring and monotonous, we only eat what we need. But if food is plentiful and diverse we are tempted to eat when we are not hungry. We are tempted to carry on eating after we are satiated. With a table laden either literally or figuratively with many different and complex foods, we find it difficult to stop. Suppose that the only thing to eat for, say, nine days out of 10, was potatoes – no salt, no butter, no flavourings of any sort, just plain boiled potatoes. How many do you think you would eat? It is the wide variation of food available to us that encourages us to overeat and overeating in turn creates a climate where slenderness is prized.

Being slim has, therefore, a social or cultural rather than an intrinsic value, and it is undoubtedly valued in our society. Values like these may arise from social pressures within society and are then promulgated by the media. Some would go further and argue that the media initiate them in the first place – but this argument is difficult to defend as the media exist within, and are part of, our society. The people who make the decisions about what appears in the media are also part of our society and subject to its influences. There may be commercial decisions taken about what type of image will sell, but these decisions are not taken in a void, and are subject to prevailing social values. The extent to which the media shape or reflect our social values is a long-standing debate. What is beyond dispute is that, in an industrialised society, the media play a major role in influencing and promulgating social values.

We can see this through the use of slender models in the media: film, television, music videos, newspapers and magazines. If you consider the celebrities of our times they are nearly all very slender, and this is a relatively recent trend. Marilyn Monroe, an iconic image from the 1950s, was said to be a size 14; she was certainly a more curvaceous shape than most film stars today. These days, a size zero is considered desirable. There was considerable alarm in the mid 1990s about what the media dubbed 'heroin chic'. This referred to catwalk and photographic models who were not only thin enough to be described as emaciated, but who were also characterized by pale skin, dark circles underneath the eyes, and jutting bones. There has been a reaction against this look, but the models we see everywhere in the media are still complying with the idealised slender shape.

The pursuit of thinness is equally apparent through the number of products available designed to promote weight loss: so-called 'diet' books, programmes, self-help groups, foodstuffs. These products are promoted through advertising in the media, another way in which the media become involved in promoting social values for body shapes. In fact this all-pervading ethos has even distorted the word 'diet'. It used to mean a pattern of eating and drinking, and had no prescriptive value; now being 'on a diet' means a programme of restricted food intake. Different diets come in and out of fashion – the F-plan diet, the Atkins diet, the Hay Diet, etc. – this is a multimillion-pound industry and evidence of a real social pressure to be thin.

One of the many unfortunate effects of this pressure is a growth in the incidence of eating disorders. As a rough definition, eating disorders are characterised by an abnormal obsession with food and/or weight. What words come into your head when you think of 'eating disorders'? For many the phrase is synonymous with anorexia nervosa, although in fact this is only one of several eating disorders. Anorexia, characterised by weight loss and body image distortion, is now widely recognised as a mental illness, although this was not always the case. It is known that approximately 40 per cent of the sufferers will be teenage girls; that the incidence is thought to be below 0.5 per cent and that between 10 per cent and 20 per cent of suffers will eventually die as a result of the disease. So it is a serious and potentially fatal disease, but it is not the most common eating disorder. Bulimia nervosa (binge eating followed by purging) is estimated to be three times more prevalent than anorexia. Both disorders are based on an unhealthy relationship with food, which is now commonplace within Western society.

What the Papers Say

There has been a good deal of media hysteria about eating disorders. Newspapers thrive on lurid stories of celebrities' lives spiralling out of control. Such stories sell papers and, more particularly, magazines. Ironically, the magazines that print such stories are the same magazines that carry images of stick-thin models in order to sell consumer products. It was for this reason that Inch and Merali (2006) chose to investigate media reporting of eating disorders. They noted that popular magazines sell self-improvement designed to encourage striving towards some ideal of beauty. The same type of magazines also tend to present case histories about issues of concern as part of their features. Eating disorders is one of the more frequently selected topics.

Investigating newspapers may seem a roundabout way of looking at eating disorders, but there are good clinical grounds for this approach. First, these articles tend to provide details on the amount of weight lost, or the lowest weight 'achieved'. This is known to be a source of risk for those already inclined towards or suffering from eating disorders. Such patients have a tendency to compare themselves unfavourably with others. The focus on weight can act as a spur to competition, a most unhealthy consequence of the media preoccupation.

You may be thinking that most people tend not to believe what they find in magazines, so it does not really matter what is said. That old maxim about not believing what you read in newspapers is well recognised. We know that people are more likely to believe information that is pertinent or salient to them. If someone who wants to lose weight reads that so-and-so reduced to a mere 84 lb by consuming non-food items to reduce hunger pains, they may identify this as a potentially useful strategy for their own weight loss. They may choose to do this irrespective of whether or not they believe that so-and-so did it. This type of copy-cat behaviour has been demonstrated amongst eating-disordered patients in earlier studies.

A Content Analysis of Popular Magazine Articles on Eating Disorders

Inch, R. & Merali, N. (2006). *Eating Disorders, 14,* 109–120

Method

Inch and Merali chose to examine popular women's magazines in order to test two **hypotheses**. The first was that anorexia would be featured in more articles than bulimia. The second was that the articles would focus more on the disordered behaviours associated with the eating disorder than on the physical consequences of having such a disorder. They selected nine magazines based on two criteria. The first criterion was that the magazines selected should be concerned primarily with image, the second that their target audience should be the age group most at risk from eating disorders. They searched all editions of these magazines over a five-year period. Luckily this did not involve a trip to the newsagent with a wheelbarrow as they were able to use an electronic database. This identified all articles about eating disorders published in these editions. The definition they used for article selection was any article where the words 'anorexia' or 'bulimia' were mentioned at least three times. The **population** in this study is not people but magazines. The **sampling frame** is the nine magazines, and the **sample** comprises the articles they identified.

The next step was to record the celebrity status, gender, race and age of anyone cited in the articles as suffering from an eating disorder. They also recorded details of the illness and the types of behaviour mentioned.

Results

Inch and Merali found ample support for their first hypothesis: approximately 76 per cent of the cases detailed in the articles had anorexia, with only 8 per cent suffering from bulimia. The remaining 16 per cent had a dual diagnosis – that is to say, they were diagnosed as suffering from both illnesses. Having turned the qualitative material into numbers, they used a **chi square goodness of fit** test, which showed that the greater preponderance of anorexic cases in the articles was statistically **significant** ($p<.01$). This **probability** value means that the chances of getting this particular uneven distribution if the magazines did not really have a bias towards articles on anorexia was less than 1 in 100. (Probability is explained in more depth in Key Topics). Their second hypothesis was also supported: the average number of disordered behaviours mentioned was 8.50 per article (range 0–36), whereas the average number of physical consequences of the illness was 5 (range 0–37). This time they used a **paired t-test**, which showed that the difference was statistically significant. Again the probability was $<.01$, which means that the likelihood was less than 1 in 100 of getting this big a difference purely by chance.

It would therefore seem that magazines focus on anorexia more than bulimia, even though the latter is the more common disorder, and that magazines also focus on the disordered behaviours associated with the condition more than its adverse health consequences. The authors argue that there are inherent dangers in both these two tendencies. The focus on anorexia as an eating disorder can lead people to think that only those who are seriously underweight have an eating disorder. Thus bulimic women reading these magazines may consider they do not really have a problem because they are not underweight. This in turn would perpetuate such behaviour while also making it less likely that the sufferers would seek help. The focus on strategies for augmenting weight loss and the relative neglect of the negative consequences of such behaviour are also sending all the wrong messages. There is evidence that some young women are influenced by others' accounts of weight loss to such an extent that they are inspired to experiment with those strategies themselves.

When magazines did present information on the adverse health effects of anorexia or bulimia, they highlighted predominantly minor and transient symptoms. Fatigue, for example, was mentioned in 12 articles (slightly over a quarter), while cardiac problems were cited in only 7, kidney damage, in 4 and unstable blood pressure in 3. Only half the articles mentioned that such disorders are potentially fatal. However, most articles noted that the disease was long-standing. The authors argue that this mismatch between the information on adverse effects but recognition of long duration can give the impression that the long-term effects of such an illness are relatively minimal.

■ How Safe Is This Conclusion?

There were some interesting findings from this analysis, but how do we know that these findings are useful? How do you go about doing a study like this? Take a look at the magazines next time you are in a doctor's or dentist's surgery – should we include all of them? Perhaps we could go to the local newsagents and buy one copy of everything on display? Would these strategies provide us with appropriate information for such a study? Either of these would work if the task was to try out **content analysis**, but whether the findings from such a sampling strategy would be generalisable is debatable.

Luckily Inch and Merali were considerably more stringent in their approach to identifying a sampling frame, a means of delimiting the potential **target population** in a way that allows access to every case. After all there are a very large number of magazines published, even if the target population is restricted to English-language publications. They identified two criteria on which to base their sampling frame. The first criterion was for the publications to be 'image-focused', a classification system identified by previous researchers. The second criterion was that the magazine's target audience should have the same demographic characteristics as the section of the population known to be most at risk of developing eating disorders. This process led them to identify the nine publications for inclusion in their sample. The next step was to select a time frame for the publications, and they selected a five-year period (1998–2003). The last methodical step in their selection involved searching an internet database of popular magazine articles for all articles in the selected magazines, using the search terms 'anorexia', 'bulimia' and 'eating disorder'. Finally, for an article to be included in the sample the words 'anorexia' or 'bulimia' had to appear at least three times. This was to ensure that the only articles included were those that focused on an eating disorder rather than mentioning it in passing.

These four steps allowed the authors to start with a vast population (all English-language magazines) and to reduce it to a manageable size (42 articles) in a manner that was systematic and objective.

Once they had made their selection of raw material, can we be certain that their analysis of the content of the publications was also objective? We know that individuals respond differently to different **stimuli**; just because you find a book gripping does not mean that all your friends will too. So how personal or idiosyncratic was this analysis of the articles used in this study?

The authors detail the categories they used to code the material and the options available in each category. These are set out for public scrutiny so that readers can judge for themselves whether or not the coding seems appropriate. Furthermore, the two authors completed this process on the material separately and without discussion and then compared their categorisations to see whether they had independently come to the same conclusion. This process is referred to as **inter-judge reliability**, and uses statistical procedures to measure the extent to which independent classifications agree. The authors used a **correlation coefficient** (Pearson's) to measure the extent to which their codings agreed. The coefficient was .97, which is very near the top of the range for this statistical method and represents a very high **correlation** between the two coders. Inch and Merali argue that this attests 'to the objective and factual nature of the information' (2006, p.113) provided in the articles. Had the information been more subjective it is likely that there would have been greater variability in the codings.

Whenever **reliability** is tested in any research study, the aim is to see how reliable the measurements are. If a study is reliable it means that if it were conducted again in exactly the same manner it would produce the same results. In this instance it is clear that the authors' ratings were reliable because they matched so closely. This sort of reliability can be threatened if the categorisation process is not transparent or if the categories are not mutually exclusive. It is not as easy as it might seem sorting out useful categories.

Next time you are watching a commercial television channel, try to find categories for the products being advertised. You could start with some simple ones like financial products, cars, household and beauty. See how many you can do before you start having to generate extra categories or revisit and redefine the ones with which you started.

It is evident from the high correlation figure (.97 is pretty close to 1.0, the highest possible coefficient representing a **perfect correlation**) that these two authors had a clear and effective categorisation process which worked well and produced some hard and **objective data**.

● How Effective Is the Observational Design?

You may be thinking that the design of this study contains an inherent paradox. The data in this study were qualitative, and qualitative psychology does not claim to be objective but, rather, embraces subjectivity (see Box 16.1). We need to distinguish here between **qualitative data** and **qualitative approaches**. By taking as their sample the text of magazine articles, Inch and Merali were using qualitative data. Words, accounts, articles and texts – these are all clearly within the category of data that can only be described as qualitative. Quantitative data, on the other hand, might include biological measurements, scores from attitude or rating scales, or frequency counts of behaviours or cases; in fact they involve numbers. The qualitative data in this study may have included a few numbers in amongst the text (e.g. weight in pounds or kilograms, or number of calories consumed), but these numbers were only isolated cases set within a backdrop of many words.

But what did the authors do with these qualitative data? They coded them, using, as we have seen, a rigorously objective process. Once they had categorised them, they counted the number of occurrences of each category. They did this in two ways. They identified first the types of disordered behaviour described and recorded the presence or absence of each of these (**nominal data**). Second, they recorded for each article how frequently each behaviour was mentioned (**ratio data**). This is a standard **quantitative approach** to dealing with qualitative data. The data may start out being qualitative but through the coding process they are reduced to numbers, which are much easier to manipulate and can be analysed using statistical procedures. So the data here are qualitative but the methodological approach is quite clearly quantitative. A qualitative approach, by contrast, would have focused on the words themselves and explored the possible meanings of words and phrases used throughout the articles (see Chapter 13). Depending on the theoretical framework of the authors, the qualitative researcher would have looked to identify themes in the data or built a theory from the basic building blocks of the words and phrases used in the texts, which is called **grounded theory**.

So we need to distinguish qualitative data from qualitative research. It may be worth noting that, while quantitative researchers can take qualitative data and use quantitative methods of analysis, the reverse, qualitative researchers taking a qualitative approach to quantitative data, is not a possibility. Quantitative researchers can impose structure at several points in the research process, as considered in Box 12.1.

▲ How Appropriate Was the Research Method?

As the media are known to be major purveyors of social values, analysing their content is one objective way of identifying the detail, extent and slant of the information that they sell. Any form of media can therefore be a legitimate target for social research (see for example the study described in Chapter 19, where television and newspaper reporting were analysed). Inch and Merali used quantitative content

Box 12.1

Structure in the Analysis of Qualitative Data

The use of structure in observational research can be seen as a continuum. At one extreme we have **structured observation**, where the categories to be coded are operationalised before the research begins. There is an example of this in Chapter 10, where the observers had clear categories of behaviour to record for the children they observed. These categories were fully operationalised, providing the observer with clear guidelines for recognising and distinguishing between behaviours. Inch and Merali used a similarly structured approach for their content analysis. The identified the variables (categories) relevant to their study prior to data analysis. They, too, operationalised their codes before beginning the analysis. These are **quantitative** methods for **qualitative data.**

Compare this to that the method described in Chapter 13, which is a form of conversation analysis, where the target information is identified in advance, but not defined. The target in that case is the membership of groups, and so all information that provides insight into this is included and reviewed using a qualitative analysis. A similar approach is used in the study described in Chapter 19, where observers were given instructions about what to look for but were required to identify the relevant themes from the data. Unlike the study described in Chapter 13, however, this approach then produced quantitative data, as themes were counted and compared.

Further along the continuum, structure is not imposed but built from the responses. There is an example of this in the study described in Chapter 17, where interview transcripts (qualitative data) are analysed. Here the researcher seeks meaning in what is said by respondents and builds a picture of themes from the narrative.

At the other extreme is the entirely **unstructured observation**, where the authors are providing an account of a phenomenon they have observed. This can often be used, for example, in case studies, and indeed there is some evidence of this in the study described in Chapter 14, although the researchers in that case also report a good deal of quantitative data.

analysis of a particular type of magazine, but are there alternative research methods that are suitable for this particular topic? What other methods could we use to examine this area? Let's look at the three main types of research method.

Survey methods might be an option. It would be possible to survey the people responsible for the production of such magazines, and explore their views, or their understanding of their company's policy on the reasons for publishing articles on eating disorders. It would be possible to do this through **semi-structured interviews**, or maybe using **questionnaires**. Interviews would allow you to explore new issues as they arise from respondents' answers, so are the more flexible method of the two. With questionnaires, you can have **open questions** (e.g. How would you describe your policy on … ?). The drawbacks here are that different respondents may respond to this in different ways, or their answer in itself may require further probing (e.g. 'Better than it used to be.' What was it like before? How has it changed it? Why did it change?). Either way the problem is the same, namely the researcher has lost control over the discourse. An alternative method might be to use a **rating** or **attitude scale** of some sort. There are problems inherent in the appropriate development of such scales (as outlined in Chapter 16), but once these are overcome scales can produce data that are very easy to handle, although not always as easy to interpret. Ahern *et al.* (2008) used such a scale to look at the relationship between young women's views of fashion models and their attitudes to weight. They found that those women who view underweight models positively also tend to have a 'drive towards thinness' themselves. This was particularly evident amongst those who reported that the media were a useful source of information about appearance.

There are psychometric scales that are used to screen for eating disorders in clinical and non-clinical populations. Mond *et al.* (2008) compared two of these: the 22-item Eating Disorder Examination Questionnaire and the five-item SCOFF questionnaire. (The latter acquired its name because it asks about making yourself Sick, losing Control, losing more than One stone, worrying about being Fat and feeling life is dominated by Food.) The data suggested that either assessment method could act as an effective screening tool, although SCOFF was slightly less sensitive. Screening for such disorders is a different approach from that of Inch and Merali; it takes no account of the role of the media.

If we are looking at people's opinions of the media's role, we can use, at one extreme, interviews that provide rich qualitative data, or, at the other extreme, scales that produce numerical scores. Depending on the focus of our questions, they may elicit opinions or information on self-reported behaviour. These would be legitimate targets for research, and would tell us something about this sector of the publishing industry. Likewise each of these methods could be used to gain the views and self-reported behaviour of the potential purchasers of the magazines. It might even be possible to involve people who have had eating disorders in some form of survey and ask them about the role that magazines played in the onset of their problem. Retrospective views like these would be interesting but not necessarily very reliable. More effective is an approach such as that used by Moriarty and Harrison (2008), a **longitudinal study** using a survey. They found that the number of hours spent watching television influenced the likelihood of the development of eating disorders amongst girls, but not boys.

Another possibility would be to try some form of **experiment**. For example, you could use two different articles on eating disorders, one focused on the type of undesirable information listed above, the other on the more useful facts that are currently under-used in reporting (e.g. adverse outcomes). With these as the

Why would it be necessary to have two groups rather than one group reading and responding to both articles? Why a **between subjects** design rather than a **within subjects** design?

stimulus material, two groups of respondents could be asked to read the articles, and their responses to those articles could be measured.

Ethical principles would require the use of healthy respondents, as such an experiment with people already suffering from eating disorders would be dangerous for the reasons already outlined. There are other dilemmas that would need to be resolved. How would you measure your sample's responses? Are you interested in an emotional reaction, or swaying opinion, or providing health education? Or to put it another way: the **independent variable** is the content of the article (because this is what you are manipulating), so what would be your **dependent variable** (outcome measure)?

These are issues that you would need to think through, but they are not insurmountable. Let us assume that you run an experiment to see whether the type of text read affects people's views of eating disorders. Suppose it does, and suppose that these two sample texts produce completely different responses from the two groups: what would this tell us? It would tell us just that people respond differently to the articles, which in itself would be interesting. The question is, can we transfer this information directly to the real world? There would be limitations to this because this study would lack **ecological validity**. The way that respondents react to a piece of text that has been provided to them for experimental purposes may be quite different from the way that they might respond to an article in a magazine purchased from their corner shop. Clearly a difference between two conditions would mean a real difference, but we would know little about how they might respond in the real world. The trouble with humans as respondents is that they tend to seek meaning from every situation, and then respond to that situation based on the meaning they have identified. This is an example of **demand characteristics**.

What about **observation**? In fact that is exactly what Inch and Merali did, but it was a different form of observation from that described in the previous two chapters. Theirs was **indirect observation** because they did not observe behaviour but rather pre-existing material, in this instance printed magazines. There was no primary data collection here – and we would not count purchasing the magazines. An alternative approach to these qualitative data would be to continue to use a qualitative approach, rather than their quantitative approach. In this case, the data would not be reduced to numbers but rather the meaning of the words and the themes behind them would be studied and interpreted (see Chapter 13). This would still be content analysis, and as such it would be indirect observation.

Is there a way in which you could use direct observation for this topic? It would be possible, but it would have its limitations. It would be hard to see which pages of a magazine someone was reading without leaning over their shoulder, which would hardly be unobtrusive! Nor could we know, through observation alone, how or whether they were affected by what they read. Perhaps the way around this would be to join a relevant social group (e.g. a slimming club) and then use **participant observation** to see to what extent magazines, their articles, or celebrity gossip are discussed within the group. Alternatively, we could use **non-participant observation** and observe purchasing behaviour, and indeed we could set up a coding system of purchasers so that we recorded their sex, approximate age, build and what other purchases they made at the same time. This way we might have a profile of the types of people who purchase the magazines in question – although some of this information may well be available from market research databases of the publishing companies concerned.

We could use any of the three major types of research method for this area, but each would be providing very different data from those reported in the article. We could discover the views or self-reported behaviours; we could see how people respond to different types of article; and we could observe who buys the papers in question. All of these are viable methods of collecting information on the same topic as the one that Inch and Merali chose. It is not that one method is better than another, but that each method provides a different aspect of the same picture. If researchers use all these methods, then together they can build up a complete picture of who buys what, what is in each magazine, what response it produces and what motivates the generators of the articles. This is how research is supposed to work, putting the jigsaw together.

Conclusion

This observational study used indirect observation on existing social material. These types of data are sometimes referred to as secondary data, because the authors did not collect them in the way that we have seen in the studies cited in earlier chapters. At the start of the study the data were qualitative. By means of rigorous and objective categorisation, they were turned into quantitative data, making it possible to count the frequency of individual topics. Inch and Merali acknowledge that their study does not show cause and effect, nor did they intend it should. What it does show is how eating disorders are represented in a medium whose target audience is highly at risk of succumbing to such illnesses.

Many of the articles were written as informative, possibly cautionary, tales, yet their content had the potential to do more harm than good. Articles that were less prurient and more factual would provide safer material. Inch and Merali detail recommendations for magazines that would minimise these unwanted effects of the current coverage. They suggest broadening the material to cover eating disorders other than anorexia and including case reports of people of varying sizes. They recommend greater focus on adverse effects and healthy meal and exercise plans and that weight information should cover only pre-illness or recovered weights. They argue that in this way articles really could act as public information on this difficult topic.

Contrast the approach described in this study with that described in the following chapter. Both use content analysis for the subject of eating disorders, but that is where the similarity ends.

Note

1   Obesity is not a **subjective assessment** but has a clinical definition: having a body mass index (BMI) greater than 30. BMI calculation is: weight (kg)/height (m^2). Thus someone who is 1.6 m (5' 3") tall and weighs 64 kg (10 st 1 lb) has a BMI of 25 (64/2.56). For a person of this height to be clinically obese they would need to weigh more than 77 kg (just over 12 st).

Summary Points	
Design	Indirect observation – content analysis
Aim	To analyse existing qualitative material
Sample	Young women's magazine articles (N=42), secondary data
Apparatus	None required
Analysis	Quantitative content analysis

Eating Disorders: The Experience

Observation – Qualitative Content Analysis

'The Internet: absolute communication, absolute isolation.' (Paul Carvel, Belgian writer and editor, b. 1964)

Who Are You?

If someone asks you that question, how do you phrase your response? We often start by providing our name, usually the least interesting piece of information. Our names are just handles for other people to use when they want to talk to or about us. Where do you go after giving your name? We can provide information about what we do (career, jobs, course, studies). This is a common way that we define ourselves. Another way is to identify ourselves by our family relationships (one of three children, mother, husband, etc.). In most cases we give this information without the names of the rest of our family members, unless it is likely that the other person will know them ('I'm Jack's son' 'John's wife', 'Susie's twin'). The third likely option is to explain ourselves by our interests; this is most likely for those who are particularly enthusiastic about their own interest ('I'm a keen tennis player', 'I enjoy travelling', 'I keep goats'). We may offer all four of the above, thereby providing a short biography. It depends on who is asking us, the nature of the occasion, and how we would like the conversation to develop. Whatever we choose to say, we are providing information about our identity. When we tell people about ourselves we are, in one way or another, projecting an image of how we see ourselves or perhaps how we would like to be seen.

We project our identity not merely through self-description but also through what we say and what we do. The notion of identity is quite a complex one. For most of us, our identity is multi-faceted. We may see ourselves differently in different settings. We need to use different aspects of our character, of our identity, depending on the setting. In some formal environments we may make an effort to appear more sophisticated, or more competent or more subdued, for example, than when relaxing with our friends on Saturday night.

One salient aspect of identity is being part of a group. Think of your experiences in school. Each school class has several social groups, and your identity amongst your classmates was partly defined by your group membership. These groups provide support and friendship for their members. Social groups develop in classrooms even though the individuals are compelled to be there. The groups are made up by their members finding like-minded individuals, but the pool from which these can be drawn is limited by the membership of the class. This type of group is very different from ones that are formed by a common interest. Social groups can arise from a shared interest in a sport or in a hobby (e.g. a squash club or bee-keeping association). Classroom groups tend to be more conscious of boundaries than common-interest groups. This is because the latter are well defined and membership is clear and conspicuous; turning up every weekend to join in the activity makes you a member. In the classroom, groups need to work harder to develop boundaries. To the casual observer, these boundaries are not apparent. Thirty people sitting in a classroom can appear to be a fairly homogenous group. Making subgroups within that requires more effort to distinguish one's own group as separate from the other groups in the room.

This is where the nature of identity becomes pertinent. The identity of the group is defined by the nature of its members, and the identity of the members is defined through their membership of that group. The relationship between groups and members is symbiotic. Social scientists talk about in-groups and out-groups. Briefly: in-groups are those to which we belong and out-groups are the rest. (Social psychology has a wealth of literature on this topic, including classic studies by Allport in 1954, Sherif in 1966 and Tajfel & Turner in 1979; see a good social psychology textbook, e.g. Hogg & Vaughan, 2007). Generally speaking the boundary between in-groups and out-groups is most jealously guarded if members of the in-group perceive themselves to be threatened in any way. Threat can arise if members of the group do not feel themselves adequately set apart from the rest, in which case members can work to express the coherence of the group and its separation from the rest. People can express their membership of a group by their behaviour, by their speech or by their appearance. If you consider the history of teenage culture in the West you can see the evolution of different groups or subcultures: from Teddy boys, through mods and rockers, hippies, punks, Rastas, New Romantics, hip-hoppers and rappers. Each of these has emerged as a distinct group, with their own appearance, their own music and if not their own language, then their own colloquialisms. Being a member of one of these groups has provided teenagers with an identity that has set them apart from their parents and other adults.

Groups can be a cohesive force within a society by bringing people together and providing support and friendship. They can also have negative effects. They can be divisive and disruptive (e.g. the British National Party), or domineering and despotic (e.g. the Nazi party), or controlling and corrupt (e.g. the Zanu PF party). Groups can also be damaging if they promote behaviour that is harmful in some way. These days subversive groups, who sanction behaviour that the rest of society finds unacceptable can thrive through technology: the internet has facilitated contact which previously would not have been possible. Finding like-minded individuals for particular activities would have been a difficult and maybe even dangerous pursuit before the arrival of this technology. These days it is easy to search the web to find groups that support all sorts of interests. There are groups where membership appears to encourage behaviour that is damaging, not just to third parties but to its own membership. There are sites that promote suicide or self-harm, and there are also sites that promote eating disorders.

These sites are commonly referred to as Pro-Ana sites and they serve what is called the 'Pro-Ana community'. This terminology has developed and identifies members as Ana, those with anorexia nervosa, or Mia, someone with bulimia. These sites tend to be fairly short-lived because internet service providers or gatekeepers will act to close them down. The sites then often reappear with a different web address and a different name, but many of their original members still seem to find them. The sites seem to be generated and run by (mostly) young women with eating disorders. They may consider themselves self-help sites, but the help is not towards recovery. Instead, they provide support and a sense of belonging for their members. The content of these sites is largely members' contributions. A member will post a question or comment and start a new thread, and other members will reply to or comment on this and so the thread grows. Many of the comments are supportive and empathic. This virtual community of people seems to find in these sites the sustenance that they refuse to accept from nourishment.

These sites were the subject of an **observational study** by Giles (2006), who wanted to explore how they portray identity and membership. Cyber communities differ from other in-groups as they lack physical contact. Because of the nature of the medium, members can convey their identity only through words, and possibly posted images. They are not restricted by their own personal appearance, and nobody really knows what other members look like. When we meet people in real, as

opposed to virtual, communities, we make judgements about them based on how they look, what they are wearing, how they talk and how they behave. (For a fuller discussion of this area, impression formation, again see any good social psychology text.) In a cyber community there are no such restrictions. Membership of the group is established by the content of the messages you post. These are the only way that others in the group can form an impression about you; these are the key to your identity. Giles's analysis of these messages tells us about the in-group identities and out-group perceptions of this community's members.

Constructing Identities in Cyberspace: The Case of Eating Disorders

Giles, D. (2006). *British Journal of Social Psychology, 45*, 463–477

Method

Giles identified 20 websites for his analysis, many of which were no longer in existence by the time he published his study. All the data downloaded came from discussions or message boards. Many of the messages were concerned with typical teenage problems and not directly related to eating disorders, so these were discarded from the analysis. Instead he looked at those threads which were interesting because they focused on either the identity of the disorder or the experience of being a sufferer. His particular selection was any discussion that included an element of argument between contributors. Contributions to threads varied in length from brief comments to lengthier observations. Having downloaded this material, he then printed it in order to read and analyse it. In total 150,000 words were included in the **data set**.

Results

Giles used a process called membership categorisation analysis (MCA) which is one way of looking at qualitative data based on interactions. The process involves looking at the way in which different categories of identity are, in the first instance, suggested and, subsequently, agreed upon and used by contributors to the interchange. The analysis requires the researcher first to identify, from within the data, the main categories that are used throughout the interchange. Once these have been established, the characteristics of each category need to be outlined. Finally, the analysis explores the way in which these characteristics are used by the contributors. Sometimes they may be used to establish in-group membership, or to identify and thereby distance an out-group.

He found several out-groups identified in the data. 'Normals' are anyone who does not have an eating disorder. They are despised for their lack of self-discipline and their lax approach to body fat. 'Haters' are a subgroup of Normals who intrude into the Ana world by posting messages on the site. These messages are considered inflammatory by the community as they often comprise advocacy against continuation of the disorder and dire warnings about the dangerous outcomes. Although Haters constitute a clear out-group, like all out-groups they provide a unifying force for the in-group. Members are united by their dislike and distrust of Haters and so the community gains cohesion in the face of this adversity. The 'Wannabes' were considered more of a nuisance to the community as they were perceived as disingenuous and lacking credibility. Their presence diluted the true purity of the rest of the community. 'Fakers' or 'Wannabes' are seen to tarnish the reputation of the true anorexic.

Interestingly, there was also conflict within the community. There were 'Newbies' who, as the name suggests, were fledgling members of the in-group, whose right to membership had yet to be established. There was also conflict about the relative positions, or even merits, of Ana and Mia. Some appeared to see Ana as a purer form of the condition, and Mia as a less rigorous and more indulgent approach to weight loss. This position was not universally accepted; some took the opposing view. Others confessed to swinging between the two stances.

Giles suggests that the conflicting identities of site members need to be understood as a means of protecting a beleaguered community from attack by intruders. The identities delineated throughout the postings – to which contributors aspire or, alternatively are assigned – provide reinforcement against the 'normal' world. They act as a way of defining and protecting this tormented community.

■ How Safe Is This Conclusion?

Giles's work paints a vivid picture of the experiences of this cyber community. How should we interpret his findings? How can we evaluate this study?

The first point to note is that, unlike those described in all previous chapters, this study takes a purely **qualitative** approach. The previous chapter started with qualitative data, but the analysis used turned this into **quantitative** data. Consider for a minute the commonalities between the two studies. Both are on the topic of eating disorders, both used secondary data and both started with words as their data set. Both used a categorisation system to organise and analyse their data. Inch and Merali had hypotheses, Giles had a research question. While Inch and Merali categorised and *counted*, Giles categorised and *interpreted*. While Inch and Merali retained and claimed objectivity, Giles makes no such claim; rather, he embraces the subjectivity of his approach. These contrasting approaches to research are part of the fabric of psychological research. It is not that one approach is right and the other wrong. Nor is one orthodox and the other subversive. The joy of research in psychology is that these two approaches can live alongside each other, with neither being hailed as definitive. In some studies, the two are used together to provide a fuller picture of the object of the investigation (see Chapter 18). As a result of the different approaches, we must use different criteria for evaluating this study from those we used to evaluate quantitative methods.

One question we ask with quantitative studies is about the representative nature of the sample selected. In Giles's study, we find a starkly different approach to sample selection:

'Threads were chosen largely for their level of interest …'
'The data are not in any particular way intended to be representative of the overall material found on pro-ana sites.' (2006, p.467)

The author acknowledges selectivity in the sampling process. Compare this with the inclusion criteria set out by Inch and Merali (see under 'Method' in Chapter 12). In order to explore the way that identities are constructed in this community, he needed to focus on issues where they were discussed. The only quantitative pieces of information we are given are that there were 20 websites, and the number of words in the final data set. We are not given any details of the websites, for which Giles provides good reasons. We are not told how he reduced the downloaded material to this final data set. We are told what his rationale was for going about this. He selected 'those exchanges that implied a degree of conflict or debate' (2006, p.467). Notice the use of the word 'implied' (quite a **subjective** concept). Contrast this with Inch and Merali, who provided the names of the magazines, gave the dates of publication and selected on the following criterion: 'To be included in this research, an article had to mention anorexia and/or bulimia at least three times within the text of the piece' (Inch & Merali, 2006, p.112).

In short, if we tried to select the material used by Inch and Merali, we have enough information to do so. Any such attempt should finish up with exactly the same articles as they did. If we tried to repeat Giles's study, we would not necessarily find or include the same material as he did, and not just because of the ephemeral nature of the websites.

Does it matter that we cannot replicate his study? Does it matter that his selection of the data set is as subjective as its subsequent interpretation? This qualitative approach does not seek to emulate the stance of the quantitative researchers. It is not just quantitative research without the rigour, it is an entirely different philosophy. The underlying assumption is that humans are not amenable to quantitative analysis, that we are varied and idiosyncratic individuals. For the qualitative researcher, what Inch and Merali have done is to *reduce* rich qualitative data to mere numbers. Qualitative research is about the subjective interpretation of the human experience, not its quantification. There are many different approaches to analysis within this methodology and the interested reader will find many useful texts, for example Smith (2008) and Silverman (2004).

Within this paradigm we need to accept that the researcher is not attempting to be objective. Because the raw data are words, the analysis is based not on number-crunching, but on arguments, debates and themes. A researcher can put together an interpretation of the data as a narrative for others to read and debate. When we ask whether Giles's conclusion is safe, we need to judge it on the merits of the argument presented along with the data. His description of the community makes a compelling read and his interpretation of the discourse is convincing.

● How Effective Is the Observational Design?

This study selected website message boards as its **population**, and the 20 sites in particular as its **sampling frame**. (In qualitative research like this, these words do not have the same connotations as they usually do. These researchers do not use **probability sampling** methods.) The initial interest was in the way that identities are constructed in cyberspace. This is because internet users are free from normal constraints on identity construction. The **target population** here was users of Pro-Ana websites because these are established by and for people with eating disorders. Giles chose discussions where there was conflict, which meant he could identify and describe in-groups and out-groups for this community. These sites are controversial. They offer advice on how to increase weight loss and how to deceive family members about nutritional consumption and, in Giles's phrase, they offer 'a dialogue of resistance against medical and professional construction' (2006, p.464) of eating disorders. They typify a subculture, one whose values and norms are in conflict with society in general. As a subculture, its membership is contentious, and fraudulent intrusion is resented. Therefore, appropriate identity construction becomes a passport to membership. Inappropriate contributions, those that are out of line with the dominant ethos, are rebutted and the contributor regarded with suspicion.

There is another reason for selecting such material for analysis. Message boards provide a real source of interchange. This is a quite different approach from research with primary data. A comparable study collecting primary data would be to set up such a website, making it clear that it was for the purpose of research and seeking contributions from those with eating disorders. This would no doubt provide some interesting responses, but they would be researcher-prompted. If the researcher asks for or provokes data in this manner it does not have the same **ecological validity** as an existing discourse.

It is difficult to collect data on naturally occurring spoken conversations. Recording either electronically or in note form spontaneous conversations between individuals is generally considered an intrusion on their privacy. Once permission is sought to do this, it changes the nature of the conversation as the **participant**s become aware of the researcher's presence. In any conversational analysis there is an inherent tension between the demands of privacy and the **validity** of the discourse. For this reason, analyses of internet message boards or discussion forums are becoming popular with researchers. These provide an opportunity to examine real conversations without breaches of a person's privacy.

There is, as Giles points out, a paradox about the Pro-Ana message boards. The contributors, as we have noted, jealously guard their own territory and fear intrusions from 'Haters', 'Fakers' and 'Wannabes'. As a subculture, they thrive on their separateness from society. They are aware of the dangers of allowing others into their community, where they have all left themselves exposed by the nature of the material they have posted. Yet very few Pro-Ana sites have any real restriction on membership. It is instead up to the members to watch for inappropriate contributions and respond accordingly. In fact they police their own sites, and it is this process which establishes in-groups and out-groups.

These websites offer a particular opportunity to analyse authentic interchange, and Pro-Ana websites are of special interest because of the nature of the illness. Eating disorders belong to a group of illnesses which remain controversial within the medical profession. Others include syndromes such as chronic fatigue, Gulf War syndrome and irritable bowel syndrome. The role of the mind in these illnesses is hotly contested within the medical profession and between physicians and patient groups. Some see all these illnesses as psychosomatic. Eating disorders are generally acknowledged to have psychological causation, but medicine tends to treat the physical consequences of the illness. This fact and the symptoms of the illness contribute to the sufferer's sense of isolation from society. Medical **intervention** is designed to help people with anorexia gain weight, exactly what anorexics fear most. Given this, it is little wonder that anorexics perceive themselves as an embattled community, a counter-culture in direct opposition to mainstream society.

For these reasons there is ample justification for selecting these sites as the object of study. As noted, Giles gives no details of his selected sites, and this is partly because the sites tend to be transient in nature. There are **ethical** reasons for withholding this information too (see Box 13.1). First, it helps protect the anonymity of the contributors whom he quotes in the paper; he is thereby protecting his sources. Furthermore, he argues that he cannot present this information as there is a tendency for vulnerable people to use details from published articles to obtain information and visit Pro-Ana sites; he is thereby also trying to protect his readers. (This is a moot point, as any interested individual can find Pro-Ana sites by using a search engine. But by withholding the names he is at least refraining from 'recommending' a given site.)

He raises another ethical issue about this research. It is suggested by some that taking messages from the web means involving in research people who have not consented so to do. This is an interesting dilemma and one worth considering. The British Psychological Society's *Guidelines for Ethical Practice into Psychological Research Online* (2007) state:

> The Society's general ethical guidelines note that, unless consent has been sought, observation of public behaviour needs to take place only where people would 'reasonably expect to be observed by strangers' (Code of Ethics and Conduct, 2006: 13), essentially vetoing observation in public spaces where people may believe that they are not likely to be observed.

If we accept the premise that behaviour conducted in public is a legitimate target for analysis, then this is a case in point. Posting messages on a website with unrestricted membership means that you are implying consent for anyone with access to

Box 13.1

Ethics and Observation

The central tenet of observational research is to look at naturally occurring events, not those contrived by the researcher. This is true whether the study uses direct **observation** (as in the study described in Chapter 10) or **indirect observation** using **secondary data**, as in this case (and that described in Chapter 12). The question then becomes: when is it all right to observe people's behaviour? In this context, behaviour should be viewed in its broadest definition, including written contributions.

In direct observation, it is usually considered reasonable to observe people in a public place where they would expect to be seen by others. Observing people in the street, in a crowd, is therefore acceptable; peering over the window ledge of their home is not. Attempts at concealing yourself while observing is problematic, but remaining unobtrusive is acceptable. Covert observation generally presents ethical dilemmas. Therefore, electronic observation may also be unethical if it uses technology to see or hear behaviour across distances. Observation in public places from an acceptable distance is one thing, hidden microphones at a restaurant table quite another.

In indirect observation, a similar principle can apply. Speeches that people have made are clearly public property and open to analysis. Rooting through someone's dustbin for their private correspondence is obviously unethical. Reading historical correspondence or diaries may be acceptable depending on the age of the information and the views of the author's descendants. A seventeenth-century diary presents fewer problems than one written in the 1990s. It is often a matter of costs and benefits: costs for the originator and their family, benefits to society or the scientific community. Ethical committees may take differing views on particular instances depending on the composition of their membership.

the web to read your material. Contributors post their messages in the hope that they will be read and responded to by other contributors. Whether there is a real distinction between reading and responding to or reading and analysing such material is a matter for individual interpretation.

If you were a member of an ethics committee and a proposal for this study was submitted, what would you identify as the issues for consideration?

▲ How Appropriate Was the Research Method?

Giles provides good reasons for selecting his chosen research material: a naturally occurring discourse and an interesting community for identity construction. It provides a rich opportunity to look at identity construction and how in-groups are maintained and policed, and also provides information on the experience of eating disorders. It is evidently not the only way that insight into anorexia can be obtained, but it is a rich source of information. In contrast to other, more direct, approaches, we cannot be certain that the contributors are all anorexics. Sadly internet message boards of any sort encourage cranks who enjoy masquerading under a false identity. That said, given that the original sampling frame was 20 websites, it is unlikely that all the contributors are fraudulent. It is apparent from the study that these sites do provide a sense of community for those with the disorder. Many of the messages are supportive of other contributors (providing they are accepted as Ana or at least Mia); their comments are sympathetic and helpful. The fact that they are helping each other to sustain a way of life that has extremely adverse health consequences does not undermine the caring nature of the responses. Rather, it tells us about the distorted and frightening perceptions common among those with eating disorders.

Could such information have been gained using a different research method? We can certainly learn a good deal about disordered populations from another observational method, a **case study** (see Chapter 14). The difference between the two methods is that case studies are written by experts. The frame of reference starts from the point of view of the professional clinician, which is the opposite approach to that used in this study. Herein lies the crux of the difference. The approach used by Giles identifies the concepts and preoccupations of the contributors a bottom-up rather than top-down approach.

It was suggested earlier in the chapter that an alternative approach would be to set up a Pro-Ana website. This should not be done without a declaration that it was a research tool; that would be unethical, effectively luring potential contributors into providing information that they might not otherwise disclose. It would be necessary to make it clear that the website was for research, and that would certainly change the nature of the contributions. People posting messages would be 'talking' to the researcher, rather than to each other. Nonetheless this might well provide useful but different information about anorexics. This would not be observation but rather one form of survey method. Once you are asking questions, however general the prompt, you are into the province of survey methods. Other survey methods can be and have been used to uncover the anorexic experience. For example, Freedman *et al.* (2006) invited their participants to write letters to their disorder, first seeing the disorder as a friend and secondly as an enemy. The results were equally rich and informative about the experience of anorexia, but did not address the issue of the social construction and in-groups and out-groups. Other survey methods that shed light on the topic would include **questionnaires** and **standardised assessments** such as the Eating Disorders Inventory (Garner *et al.*, 1983). Interviews would also be a possibility; they could then be transcribed and subjected to **discourse analysis**.

However, there would be ethical issues too, which may well mean that only a trained psychotherapist could conduct such interviews.

Due to the vulnerable nature of this group it is difficult to envisage an appropriate form of experimentation. Researchers have used **experiments** to look at restricted eating patterns amongst a normal population (for example, Ogden & Greville, 1993), and treatments for eating disorders could be evaluated using **randomised controlled trials**, as we saw in Chapter 3 with a different sort of disorder.

Conclusion

Like the research in the previous chapter, this observational study used indirect observation of existing social material to provide useful insights into our understanding of eating disorders. The focus here was on the experience of people with the disorder, rather than on the images projected in the media. Like the Inch and Merali paper, this study started with a collection of qualitative data. Unlike theirs, however, the analysis used was qualitative and interpretative.

This method of data collection is relatively recent and has only been made possible through the development of the internet. There are other types of websites that promote unhealthy and worrying behaviours, and these are equally amenable to analysis. As Giles concludes:

> By serving as a counterculture to official discourse around health and illness, the web may serve to undermine the professionals so that ... more people find ways of opting out of conventional society ... if they can locate supportive communities on-line. (2006, p.475)

Summary Points	
Design	Indirect observation, content analysis
Aim	To analyse how the community constructs identities
Sample	150,000 words taken from Pro-Ana message boards
Analysis	Qualitative – membership categorisation analysis (MCA)

Face Recognition
Observation – Clinical Case Study

'In the 1940s, in the foyer of a Manchester hotel, I saw a distinguished looking woman whom I believed I knew although I could not remember her name. I paused to talk to her and as I did so, I vaguely recollected that she had a brother. Hoping for a clue I asked her how her brother was and whether he was still in the same job. "O, he's very well thank you," came the reply. "And he is still King."' (attributed to Sir Thomas Beecham, musician and conductor, 1879–1961)

Are You Good at Recognising Faces?

Some people are really good at recognising faces. They can see a face once and then be able to recognise it easily. Have you ever heard anyone say 'I never forget a face'? Some people who say this mean that they are good at recognising faces, but may not be able to place them in context – let alone name them. Some of us, on the other hand, are really bad at recognising faces. Being greeted warmly by someone who knows your name but whom you do not even recognise, let alone know the name of, is quite an embarrassing moment. A common embarrassment is knowing that you recognise the face but cannot recall the name and are not even sure how you know the person or where you met. We often find that meeting someone out of context can be confusing. If you bump into someone you know as the checkout person in your supermarket in a different setting, it can take a while to place them. It is almost as though you do not recognise them without a till. Maybe it is not quite as difficult as the experience quoted above of Thomas Beecham!

One set of faces you probably expect to recognise without any difficulty are those of your nearest and dearest. They can change their hair (colour or style), apply make-up, grow a moustache or whatever and yet we have no difficulty distinguishing our closest relatives. We know that people with dementia have difficulty recognising anyone at all as the disease develops. These sad cases aside, recognising

members of the immediate family is a given – but what about distinguishing between them? That is straightforward too, you would think. It is true that mothers may call their children by each other's names, but it is not because they are failing to recognise them. It is much more a matter of not attending to which name they are using.

A person who confuses family members is somewhat of a novelty and worth investigating. This is what Abe *et al.* (2007) did when such a case presented at their clinic.

Selective Impairment in the Retrieval of Family Relationships in Person Identification: A Case Study of Delusional Misidentification

Abe, N., Ishii, H., Fujii, T., Ueno, A., Lee, E., Ishioka, T. & Mori, E. (2007).
Neuropsychologia, 45, 2902–2909

The patient was a 74-year-old woman who had Alzheimer's disease plus another, more reversible form of dementia, caused by poor absorption of cerebrospinal fluid in the brain. She had been living with her two daughters and she had shown increasing memory loss over the preceding eight years. She began to experience loss of appetite and she subsequently lost weight. She started mistaking her daughter for her neighbour and then for an old school friend. Then she developed an unusual gait and began to have frequent falls, at which point she was referred to the clinic.

In the hospital she was alert and cooperative, and her speech was normal. Just after admission she showed signs of delusional misidentification syndrome (DMS) which means that she began to confuse members of her family. In particular, she would mistake her daughter for her sister. She was quite confident in her conviction, and nothing that the daughter or the medical staff could say would change her mind. DMS is known to occur amongst people with schizophrenia and those with some organic damage in the brain. This case was unusual in that the DMS occurred only with members of her family, that is, people to whom she was emotionally close. It was for this reason that the team of neuroscientists wished to investigate further. Their **aim** was to help reveal the cognitive and neural mechanisms of person identification.

Method

The first step was to take some magnetic resonance imaging (MRI) scans to see what organic damage had occurred. The second step involved using a battery of **psychometric assessments** to identify exactly what the woman could and could not do. They assessed her intelligence with three **standardised assessments**, and her attention with four simple tasks. They used another three standardised assessments to assess her memory, five tests to explore her language ability and a further two tests to assess her visual perception. After these, she completed some tests designed particularly for her memory problems. With an extensive test battery like this, it is just as well that the patient was cooperative!

Results

The scans showed the types of organic change associated with Alzheimer's disease as well as those associated with the more reversible form of dementia. These problems were mostly located in the right hemisphere of the brain. As a result of this diagnosis, a minor surgical procedure was performed which improved her gait and balance and reduced the incidence of DMS, but did not change her general cognitive functions.

As for the psychometric assessments, these showed problems with her intelligence, attention and memory, but her language scores were good. The facial recognition part of the visual perception test showed some interesting results. She performed well when recognising famous faces and with tasks involving novel faces. However, tasks involving recognising photographs of her family presented her with problems and she made many mistakes. She also showed some errors in recalling places she knew. She was unable to recall famous events from the previous 40 years, but she was able to recognise them.

The tests, specifically designed for her, used recent photographs of current family members. When presented with their names and asked to specify her relationship to them, she did well with her sisters, but very poorly with her daughters. Her autobiographical memory was poor and showed no sense of time. She consistently underestimated her own age, believing herself to be in her forties, and those of her daughters, who she thought were in their twenties.

The impairment, identified throughout these tests, showed a specific and unusual pattern. Her problems seemed to be found entirely in recognising her husband and her daughters, and remembering events in her own life. When she misidentified her family members she was always mistaking someone who was currently in her life for

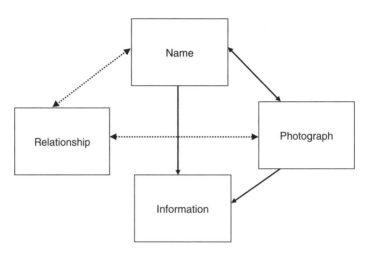

Figure 14.1. Recognition of daughters.

someone from her childhood. She seemed to have difficulty with current information, as though more recent memories were not adequately encoded. The authors
conclude:

> It appears that the retrieval of relationships between oneself and family members may
> require a special cognitive process dissociated from the retrieval of names, faces and
> other person-specific semantic information. (2006, p.2908)

■ How Safe Is This Conclusion?

One of the problems of working with someone who has dementia is ensuring that
they understand the task. If the question you ask them is not properly understood
then you are not going to get the correct answer. Have we any evidence that the
woman in this case study did understand? There is ample evidence provided in
the paper. There were effectively four main variables used in testing her DSM:
faces (photographs), information (person-specific information), names and
relationships.

As illustrated in Figure 14.1, she could name her daughters from their photographs and she could pick the correct photograph in response to a given name. So to
that extent she recognised them. She could also provide person-specific information
about her daughters, from either the photographs or their names, so she knew about
them as people. The impairment was found when she was tested on their relationship to her, and this happened with both names and photographs. She knew they
were close relatives, but mistakenly identified them, usually as her sisters. There was
a similar problem recalling her relationship to her husband from a photograph, but
no difficulty in recalling his name. As she did not show this level of difficulty with

tasks relating to her mother, father or sisters, it was clear that she understood what she was being asked to do. The problem lay with recognising her daughters and husband.

Is it possible that she retained her understanding of some family relationships but had lost her understanding of others? Her results would be explained if she no longer knew what 'daughter' or 'husband' meant. However, she was also tested with famous pairs of related faces and showed no difficulty with daughter or husband concepts there. The impairment was much more specific than that.

● How Effective Is This Observational Design?

As a case study, this offered a good deal of data. In the first place, there was the information presented by the referral process, which provided a history of the patient. Then the researchers collected physiological data using MRI scanning, and then the patient completed a comprehensive test battery. The data from all these three sources were combined in order to build a picture of this particular pathology. From this picture, Abe *et al.* drew inferences about the way that humans encode information.

On the face of it, the conclusion seems to be rather risky. The authors have studied only one patient who, at their own admission, is an unusual case. Yet on the basis of this they are making sweeping statements about the way human memory is encoded in the brain. The argument about samples has always been the larger the better. Bigger numbers and you are more likely to be able to generalise. This study is reporting on a single patient – is it reasonable to offer such a generalised conclusion?

This is rather the point of a case study such as this. This was not just any old **participant**. It was the unusual nature of her case which makes it worth turning into a case study. And it is that uncommonness that makes it possible to offer conclusions. That might seem a little odd at first, especially in comparison to other studies in this book. But there is a logic to it.

Case studies have been a useful source of data for psychologists since the nineteenth century. One famous study was by Pierre Broca, which was published in 1861 and identified the part of the brain that is responsible for speech. Broca identified this *post mortem* in a patient who had had a speech impairment. By examining the man's brain and comparing it with other brains from non-disordered people he could see where the differences lay, which explained the impairment. In those days, of course, there was no technology that allowed physicians to explore the brains of live people; *post mortem* examination was the only option. These were the types of data that gave us the foundation for our current understanding of how the brain works. Just as Broca could compare his patient's brain with other brains and thereby come to a general conclusion, so can Abe and his colleagues. If there is a single case with an unusual functional problem, then comparing that brain to 'normal' brains, provides very good evidence for the organic cause. The difference between Broca and the study reported here is that we no longer have to wait for patients to die. MRI scanning allows us to look inside the cranium of a living patient.

We can see, therefore, that one distinctive case can allow us to offer conclusions about how brains work because the abnormality detected in the scans coincides with a functional abnormality. It is worth noting that this is not the only case study of this particular functional problem. Abe *et al.* cite two other similar case studies that have been published and whose findings conform to theirs. They also cite evidence from previous studies that indicate that this type of memory appears to be formed in the right prefrontal cortex. Taken together, this looks like quite convincing evidence. Although one isolated case might not, in itself, be conclusive, set against a backdrop of a few other distinctive cases, and some more generalised knowledge about what happens where in the brain, it is reasonable to draw a conclusion.

We are told that this patient completed at least 17 different psychometric assessments (of which at least six were standardised) and this was prior to the tests of recall and recognition of her own family members. Some of the standardised assessments (see Box 14.1) are lengthy to administer, for example the Wechsler Adult Intelligence Scale (WAIS), which usually takes one and half hours to complete with a non-disordered sample. In total this was clearly an exhaustive and potentially exhausting battery of tests. It may seem rather an onerous task for a patient to complete so many. Was it really necessary? The problem with testing cognitive function is that there is no one single test that will allow us to identify the existence of impairment. Even if a global measure does suggest an underlying difficulty, it is still necessary to test each system separately to locate it. The paper does not detail how long it took in total to complete the tests, but we have to conclude that this was done over a period of days, probably weeks. Collecting data on all these different types of cognitive function enables us to see how specific the impairment is.

▲ How Appropriate Is This Research Method?

This is a case study and as such it is classified as **observation**. You will have noticed that, in spite of this, the patient was asked to complete a large number of psychometric assessments. You might be wondering why, as she answered questions, this is not classified as a survey rather than an observation. Survey methods, or at least psychometric assessments, have been used here, but the overall design is still observational. Survey methods as an overall design involve a sizeable sample. When just one person is being asked questions it does not count as a survey. Moreover, the psychometric assessments were in some ways equivalent to the MRI scans, because they both use standardised equipment to compare the individual to what would be expected from a healthy person of the same age and sex. Both measures allow us to identify abnormality.

As has been suggested, case studies are common in neuropsychology and have helped to build up our knowledge base. When an unusual case presents, it provides the scientist with the opportunity to improve their understanding. There are other ways that we could collect data to contribute to this topic. Other types of observational study would be possible, for example, by observing patients' behaviour at visiting time in a geriatric ward with dementing patients. Such observation would

Standardised Assessments

When a test is initially developed it needs to be put through a rigorous process of **reliability** and **validity** testing (see Chapter 16) before it can be considered a useful measure. For a test to be amenable to interpretation it requires a process called standardisation. This means that tests are administered to large number of people in the **population** for which they are intended. The data from this are used to establish population **norms**. These take into account some demographic factors, depending on the type of test and what is considered relevant. For example, the WAIS was standardised on several samples of disordered and non-disordered adults and its norms are published in the manuals. Norms can be presented as measures of **central tendency** and **variability**, for example **means** and **standard deviations**, or **medians** and **quartiles**. Alternatively, they can be presented as some form of standardised score, such as **T scores** or **stanine scores**. The standardisation sample for the WAIS comprised 1880 individuals, and these were carefully stratified by sex, race, occupation and educational achievement. The norms are given in the manual broken down into nine age groups.

This process is required if we want to be able to interpret scores from a test appropriately. If you think about an ordinary academic examination 100 per cent is the top mark it is possible to get. How far short of 100 per cent my mark is tells me how far away from top marks I am. With a psychometric test, without norms this type of interpretation is impossible. If I am told I have scored 7 on a subscale, is that good? Or bad? Or mediocre? Unless I know what people of my age usually score I cannot understand or interpret the meaning of 7. IQ tests were standardised to a mean of 100. This means that a score above 100 represents higher intelligence than average, while a score below indicates lower intelligence than average. Without norms, it would be difficult to interpret any scores.

Standardised assessments have two further advantages. First, they can be used in applied settings (educational or clinical, as we see in this chapter) for single individuals. Just as we can use a thermometer because we know what the normal human body temperature should be, once a test is standardised with norms, we can use that assessment because we know what the appropriate score should be. We can therefore interpret individual scores. The second advantage is statistical. If a test is standardised it is usually appropriate for use with **parametric inferential statistics**. With non-standardised assessments it is safer to use **nonparametric** statistics.

allow us to see how people responded to the sight of their family, but it would not tell us very much about face recognition, let alone anything so specialised as the particular impairment described here.

 In a study observing responses of elderly patients seeing their family at visiting time, what other variables might affect the target behaviour? Why would it be difficult to draw inferences about facial recognition from this behaviour?

We could consider using some form of **survey method**. We could ask patients about any difficulties they were having, or we could ask their carers or clinical professionals about their experience of problems with facial recognition. This would provide interesting information about people's reported experiences, but it would not be systematic. As with all survey methods, it is more likely to tell us more about the people we are asking than about the condition. Furthermore, interviewing people with different forms of dementia would present its own problems.

There is, however, a role for **experimentation** here. Some studies have evaluated ways of improving face recognition in patients. Hawley and Cherry (2004) found ways of training people with dementia to recognise new faces. Hochhalter *et al.* (2000) used a **randomised controlled trial** to see the effects of behavioural training on face recognition for people suffering dementia as a result of alcohol abuse. Also relevant are studies that have compared facial recognition in different age groups. Firestone *et al.* (2007) compared the way in which older and young people scanned photographs of faces. They noted that older people tend to use a more selective scanning approach. They also noted that each age group was better at facial recognition when the targets were in their own age group. Rizzo *et al.* (2002) developed a test for measuring facial recognition and set out to establish norms for its performance, using 187 healthy adults with an age range of 21 to 70. They found that age and education showed significant effects on performance, but that sex did not. The test they developed incorporated 50 faces of famous people, an interesting mixture of film stars, politicians and royalty! The test is intended for neuropsychological assessment of patients with brain disease. Unfortunately its use will be limited to its native Italy, as many of the famous faces are part of Italian public life and would not be recognised elsewhere. We can see that many different types of experimentation can help build up a picture of how facial recognition occurs and how it can be measured.

Conclusion

This case study has described in some detail the impairment experienced by one woman with dementia. The thoroughness of the assessments she has undergone has enabled the researchers to pinpoint both her functional impairment and some physiological pathology. The relative rarity of her condition makes these data interesting and the MRI scanning, combined with psychometric assessment, helps to pinpoint activity. This study provides one piece of evidence to help neuroscientists map function onto the human brain.

Summary Points	
Design	Observation, case study
Aim	To identify the cognitive and neural mechanisms of person identification
Sample	One 74-year-old woman
Apparatus	MRI scanner and battery of psychometric assessments of cognitive function
Analysis	Comparison with extant data on normals

Choices and Decisions

Survey Methods – Quantitative Questionnaire

'You and I are essentially infinite choice-makers. In every moment of our existence, we are in that field of all possibilities where we have access to an infinity of choices.' (Deepak Chopra, doctor and writer, b. 1946)

Can You Make Decisions?

When you are faced with an array of possible options, how do you go about making a decision between them? When you stand outside the local multiplex, for example, surveying a list of a dozen different films, does it take you long to decide what you would like to see? If your friends are planning a night out and are considering a choice of activities or venues, how do you go about choosing one option from their list? When you look at a menu in restaurant, how do you decide? Some of us may think through each of the options, in the last case, for example, the dishes that tempt us, and try to envisage what each will be like, to think through its taste, and try to make a decision based on what we actually feel like that particular day. Others may identify one dish that they know they like and select that without further consideration of the alternatives. And these are all fairly frivolous choices. What about more serious ones? How did you decide what course you wanted to study, what university you wanted to attend, where you wanted to live? How will you decide what you want to do when you leave university?

It has been suggested that there are two different strategies that people use when making choices: satisficing and maximising. Satisficing is when you select an option that you believe will be satisfactory, fit for purpose, in contrast to maximising, which is the selection of the best possible option, taking into account all the possible costs and benefits. This distinction, and indeed the term 'satisficing', were originally coined by Herbert Simon, a twentieth-century American political scientist whose innovative thinking was influential in several disciplines: economics, artificial intelligence, organisation theory and decision-making amongst others. Simon argued that because the human brain is limited in its capacity to process, order, categorise and store information, deciding on the best possible option can be complex and time-consuming. Instead we often elect to satisfice, to select an option that appears to meet a given need. If you think about this distinction, you may be able to identify times when you used one of these strategies. In the examples above, satisficing would involve selecting a film, evening out or dish that you know you like without worrying about whether you might enjoy another alternative more. It is likely that you will have encountered occasions when you have wanted to use one of these strategies and been exasperated by a companion's insistence on using the other. If you choose to use a satisficing approach, the meticulous thoroughness of someone considering all the other options can seem like time-wasting. Conversely, if you wish to maximise, a satisficing companion will complete their choice first and may become irritated with your slow deliberations!

In the 50 years since Simon's original thesis, this distinction has been used in cognitive psychology to explore the processes involved in individual choice selection, and in social psychology to explain group decision-making. In recent years, an unexpected corollary has been observed concerning the use of these two strategies, satisficing and maximising. It has been noted that they lead not only to different experiences during the decision-making process but also to different responses to those decisions after they have been made. In order to maximise effectively, individuals need to ensure that they have an exhaustive list of all possible options before selection, and furthermore that they have considered and evaluated all the attributes of those options. As part of this process the individual is also likely to compare their own decision with that of others, both during and after the decision. The reason for all this behaviour is to improve the chance of selecting the best possible option.

The expectation would be, therefore, that maximising would lead to selecting better outcomes. But, paradoxically, it would seem that maximisers are likely to feel less satisfied with the outcome of their final choice than satisficers! There are two possible mechanisms to explain this. One is **subjective**, that having invested so much time and effort in the selection process the expectations of that 'perfect' option are raised to unrealistic levels, thus leading to inevitable disappointment. The alternative is objective, that there really is something wrong with the final choice despite the best endeavours of the maximiser. This might be the case if true maximising, the effective weighing of all the aspects of all possible options, is beyond an individual's cognitive capacity.

To identify which of these mechanisms is responsible for this phenomenon, we need to compare the choosing process and the outcome of both the thorough maximiser and the more pragmatic satisficer. To monitor this in a real-life setting, rather than a laboratory, we need the branch of research that can be subsumed under the heading of **survey methods**, in short, asking people. This was the approach adopted by Iyengar *et al.* (2006).

Doing Better but Feeling Worse: Looking for the Best Job Undermines Job Satisfaction

Iyengar, S.S., Wells, R.E. & Schwartz, B. (2006). *Psychological Science, 17*(2), 143–150

Method

Iyengar and colleagues chose as their **sample** university students who were coming up to graduation from a sample of 11 colleges across the USA. The choice process in question was that of finding a job. As is usually the case in psychology (see Box 11.1) the object of interest in this study, choice strategies, is a **hypothetical construct**, and, by definition, not directly observable. They recruited their **respondents** by enlisting the help of the careers service in each college. Students who were beginning to search for a post-graduation job were directed by their university's careers service to a website for this survey.

A total of 548 respondents completed the initial round of **data** collection at **T1** (**Time 1**) and they were contacted via email to complete a second survey approximately two months later (**T2**) and a third two months after that (**T3**). These three time points were chosen to cover the process of finding a job, from initiating the process, through applications and interview, up to accepting a job offer. The **aim** was to examine the types of choosing strategy (maximising or satisficing) used by respondents, to measure how respondents felt about the process and their subsequent choices (subjective **measures**), and to compare those final choices (**objective data**).

This survey was more than just a **descriptive survey**. Iyengar and colleagues used **questionnaires** and **inferential statistics** to test their predictions or **hypotheses**, so this is an **analytical survey**. It can be difficult to recognise the difference between an analytical survey and a **quasi-experiment** using survey methods; this distinction is considered in Box 15.1.

When Is an Analytical Survey a Quasi-Experiment?

Sometimes researchers set out to test hypotheses by asking people questions. Sometimes they are doing an analytical survey and sometimes it is a quasi-experiment. This can be a bit confusing. But there is a simple way to tell which is which. When the questions are about opinions, experiences or behaviour that exist separately from the research project, then it is an analytical survey. An analytical survey may compare responses from different groups (as in this study), which would be an **independent design**. Or it may compare responses to different types of questions, which would be a **related designed**.

An experiment using survey methods, on the other hand, would be when the researchers ask questions about material they introduce. For it to be a true experiment, they will be manipulating that material (the **independent variable (IV)**).

For example, take a look at the classic study by Luchins (1957), which you should be able to find in an introductory text. His study involved two versions of a story about a fictional character, and he wanted to compare responses to the two. This type of study is called a ***vignette* study** ('vignette' means a short story or brief description of a scene). This was an experimental design, as he manipulated key attributes in the two different versions of the story, thereby manipulating the independent variable. Prior to taking part in the study his respondents held no views about the character, as they had never heard of him. But if I were to ask people's views about a well-known fictional character, for example Bridget Jones of diary fame, it would be a survey, because the expectation is that such views would already exist. If I were to compare men's and women's views, my study would be an analytical survey.

On this subject, see also the discussion in Chapter 19.

How Can You Go About Measuring People's Strategies?

As well as seeking information on **demographic variables**; a first task was to seek data that would allow the authors to distinguish maximisers from satisficers in the sample. For this they drew on an instrument designed to measure maximising tendencies which had been developed in past research by one of the authors, Schwarz and his colleagues in 2002 in an extensive study of nearly 1800 respondents. For this, respondents responded to a series of items such as 'When I am in a car listening to the radio, I often check other stations to see if there is something better playing, even if I am relatively satisfied with what I'm listening to.' They recorded their answers on a nine-point scale where 1 indicated 'strongly agree' and 9 indicated 'strongly dis-agree'. This is one of a number of standard response scales often used in the social sciences. By using this type of numerical rating response, a total maximising score could be calculated for each respondent by adding up the scores for their answers.

The second task was to measure two other aspects of behaviour that the authors predicted would be likely amongst maximisers but unlikely amongst satisficers. The first was to do with attention to alternative options, which they measured at T1 by asking how many jobs respondents anticipated applying for. This was also monitored at T2 and T3 by asking how much respondents thought about options other than those they were currently pursuing. Researchers also measured the extent to which respon-dents reported being subject to external influences. They were asked about whose opinion they sought before starting the search, and to what extent they compared their job-seeking progress with that of their peers. This last question was also repeated at T2.

The third task was to measure how respondents felt about the process of choos-ing, and then about their subsequent choices. The researchers used a rating scale for respondents to record how they felt emotionally at each time point. This scale com-prised seven different negative emotions (e.g. stressed, tired, worried) and the task was to rate their current emotional state on a nine-point scale where 1 meant 'not at all' and 9 'extremely'. To indicate how they felt about their final choice, respondents were asked to report how satisfied they were with it, and how confident they felt that they had made the right choice. This involved another nine-point scale, with 1 again being 'not at all', and 9 'very satisfied'/'very confident'.

The final measurement task was to find a way of objectively comparing across the eventual choices, that is, the jobs that respondents accepted, and for this the researchers used annual salary as means of comparison across the sample.

Results

The first task was to identify which type of choice-making strategy their respondents had used. They did this by dividing the sample into two by their **scores** on the maxi-mising tendency scale. The half with the highest scores were designated Maximisers, and those with the lowest, Satisficers. (Initial capital letters here are justified as the term is now referring to two groups in the sample rather than type of person in the **population**.) As predicted, at both T1 and T2, when compared with the Satisficers, the Maximisers anticipated applying for a higher number of jobs, reported more worries about the size of the job set available to them and were more likely to admit to being reliant on external influences. This indicates that they conformed to the standard profile of a maximiser making a choice. As for how they felt about the process, at each stage they reported more negative feelings (e.g. stressed, tired, over-whelmed, depressed), and although this did decrease over the three time points, overall they were finding the whole process more emotionally costly than did the Satisficers. And once they had chosen? At T3 maximisers reported lower levels of satisfaction and confidence about their accepted job offer. As a whole then, and in line with past research, the Maximisers had a pretty poor time of it.

Was there any advantage to being a Maximiser? Was there any benefit from all that effort and worry? It seems there was. Comparing the annual starting salary of the chosen job, the Maximisers on average had offers that were 20 per cent above those of the Satisficers. So there had been some gain from all the work and worry put in to the job search. Yet in spite of this they were still less happy with the outcome than the more modestly paid Satisficers.

■ How Safe Is This Conclusion?

This study has shown that, objectively, maximisers do appear to do better than satisficers, but in spite of this the level of satisfaction with outcome is lower for maximisers. The authors consider possible mechanisms for explaining this finding. They suggest that it may be that the problem for maximisers is the number of options that they consider, as the effort entailed in this pursuit can result in unrealistically high expectations. Because those expectations are unrealistic, the maximiser is then bound to be dissatisfied with their final choice. The process of maximising has, in itself, led them to overestimate the potential benefits of the 'best' choice. The authors use an apt phrase to describe this:

> Maximising tendencies seem to cast a long shadow on people's evaluations of their decision and search outcomes. (2006, p.148)

The argument that maximising does improve final choice is based on the size of the starting salaries; while this is clearly objective, to what extent is salary a reasonable measure of success in job choice? This issue is tackled by the authors themselves, who point out other aspects of job satisfaction that could be measured if a study was to follow candidates into their new posts (e.g. working conditions, colleagues, etc.). However, we then come full circle, for measuring these variables could not be objective. It could only be done by self-report, which is by its nature subjective. It is reasonable to assume within a capitalist society that starting salary is likely to be a consideration in job-seeking for graduates. It would be unwise to suggest that it is the only criterion or that it is paramount, or even that it is universal. Its objectivity is the key, given that it is likely to have had at least some influence on at least some of the respondents. Whether it has an undue influence on maximisers compared to satisficers could be the task of another study to discover!

Thinking about the subjective experience of dissatisfaction, we note that the authors suggest that it is, in fact, a product of the process of maximising itself. Is there an alternative explanation? There are two possible **mediating variables** that may have occurred to you.

Could maximisers be better job applicants than satisficers? Or, turning that around, is being a maximiser part of being a strong applicant? The authors ensured that they could explore this possibility by looking at other factors that might affect the process of job application. Among the demographic variables collected was the respondents' Grade Point Averages (GPA, a measure of their undergraduate academic marks). Obviously, we could expect that students with better grades might have better job prospects than those with poorer grades. Maybe it was the discipline the maximisers were studying, maybe they study subjects that lead into professions with higher starting salaries? What about the reputation of the university? Graduates from prestigious institutions might also command higher pay. America's 124 universities are ranked by US News World Report annually and the top 15 universities form an elite group, have a highly selective application process and an enviable reputation. In this study, respondents whose universities were ranked in that top 15 were compared with the rest as they could be expected to achieve better job offers on the prestige of the university name alone. All three of these factors, GPA, subject and university, did indeed affect the starting salary. The striking finding is that, even when these effects are taken into account, maximisers still have significantly higher salaries than satisficers. The effect of maximising on starting salary outweighs these other factors.

The second possible mediating variable would be the personality of the maximiser. Are maximisers just inclined to be miserable? Indeed there was some evidence that maximisers were feeling less positive at T1. But, when that was taken into account, lower levels of satisfaction at T2 and T3 were closely associated with the two characteristic behaviours of maximisers: worrying about the size of the available job set, and confidence in their own choice. This finding is in line with the previous study by Schwartz *et al.* (2002), that the effect of maximising on an individual's emotional state is independent of their temperament. Rather, it is these two characteristic behaviours that are integral to the negative aspects associated with maximising.

As neither academic achievement nor negative disposition can explain the finding, it would seem that it is indeed the activity of maximising that affects both initial salary and level of satisfaction.

● How Effective Is This Design?

Iyengar and colleagues' findings are neatly summed up in the title of their paper. They have shown that maximisers may do better from an objective point of view but, in spite of this, feel worse. We have seen that this study identified its respondents as maximisers or satisficers, measured some demographic variables, their choosing behaviours, their emotional state, their confidence and satisfaction – really quite a lot of complex and abstract information – all by just asking questions! It sounds so easy when put like that. As psychologists, we should be able to set out to measure any abstract variable, any hypothetical construct; let's just ask people questions and we'll have all the information we need for measurement and we can push back the frontiers of science! It probably comes as no surprise that it is not quite that easy. Let's take a close look at what these authors did in order to 'measure' these variables and to identify the two groups. We know that they asked their respondents something over 60 questions, and that for many of these they used a nine-point rating scale. How did that work?

Determining the Groups

The instrument used to measure maximising tendencies comprised 11 items taken from a scale that had been developed by one of the authors, Schwarz, in previous published research (Schwarz *et al.*, 2002). When those authors began development of this scale they started with 33 items, and the number of items was reduced through an iterative process of data collection and analysis. By the end of a series of four studies developing and testing this scale the number of items had been reduced to 13, 11 of which were used by Iyengar and colleagues. This means that many of the **psychometric properties** of the instrument had been explored and detailed. (This topic is discussed more fully in Chapter 16.) This is a big step out of the way when using any form of questionnaire or rating scale. It is particularly important in a study such as this one where the responses have been used in a calculation to produce an overall score.

They needed to identify two groups amongst their respondents, maximisers and satisficers. To do this the authors divided the sample into two around the midpoint or **median** of the overall scores on the instrument designed to measure maximising tendencies. This means that those with the highest score in this sample were classed as maximisers while those with scores in the lower half of the sample were classed as satisficers. Therefore for this study, the authors used this **median split** to produce two groups that showed a difference on this particular measure. This was effectively an **operational definition** for this study; this was how they defined and measured maximising. An alternative would have been to use a cut-off point established in past research. This was not a viable option in this study for two reasons. First the scale is relatively new and has not yet been subjected to a process of **standardisation** through the collection of **normative data**. Therefore, there is as yet no clear cut-off point in the scale scores to establish maximising versus satisficing. A second reason relates to the sample in this study; as the authors explain, these scores, *overall*, were higher than those found in previous studies. This was not surprising as it has already been shown that maximising decreases with age. As these respondents were students and had a median age of 21, their average scores could be expected to be higher than those for the population as a whole.

The disadvantage of a median split is that the lowest scores in the top half of the sample are only slightly above the highest scores of the lower half. This can mean that the two halves of your distribution are not as far apart as you might like. In this instance, this did not present a problem.

Why Bother With All This Scaling Business?

Given all these difficulties with dealing with numbers you may be thinking, why bother? Why not just ask people one question, and form your two groups from their answer? Indeed the possible wording of such a question can be found in the Schwartz *et al.* paper that details the development of the study. In the preparatory work for their first study they asked 11 psychology undergraduates to examine the statements that were being compiled to measure maximising tendencies. The task for these 'judges' was to say whether each of these statements tapped into an inclination to 'get the best out of any situation' or 'settle for good enough' (2002, p.1180). You might be thinking, 'Well, why not just ask this question of the respondents and be done with all this scaling business?' It's a good question! Suppose they did use a single question: do you try for the best in any situation or settle for good enough? What do you think the most likely answer would be? What would you answer? I suspect that most of us would hedge our bets and reply 'It depends on the situation.' By using a scale that includes statements relating to specific behaviours (tuning radios, shopping for clothes) the respondents are presented with statements about situations in which they can visualise themselves and estimate their own likely response.

What About the Other Questions on the Questionnaire?

The authors used other scales to collect information to test their predictions. We have already noted that respondents were asked to use nine-point scales to indicate different factors in their job-seeking behaviour, their emotional state and their level of satisfaction with the process. Unlike the maximising scale, these questions were designed specifically for this research, so had not been subjected to the same process of development. But, also unlike the maximising scale, these questions were not designed to measure a single psychological construct, but were rather about self-reported job-seeking behaviours. Instead of reporting how they would typically behave in a given hypothetical situation, respondents were reporting how they were job-seeking and how they were feeling about this process. The authors wisely chose to use the same of type of response scale here, consistency making it easier for respondents, who would have become used to making such judgements.

As noted earlier, information on demographic variables was sought as well, including age, sex, ethnicity and details of their university and their academic performance. Seeking such information was a prerequisite for this particular study as any one of these could have been a **confounding variable** in the study. Many novice researchers are inclined to seek this type of information from their respondents whether or not it is pertinent to the research question. When putting questionnaires together it is a good rule of thumb to go for the minimalist approach and never to seek unnecessary information.

It might seem that asking this type of question was the easy bit. After all, as social beings these are the sorts of questions we might ask of others in a social setting or in any form of interchange. But framing these questions unambiguously in a questionnaire format is not as easy as you might think. When we ask questions in ordinary conversation we can tailor the follow-up question to the response to the first question. With questionnaires this is not usually possible without developing long strings of optional questions, which make the questionnaire very unfriendly. You have probably heard about the case of the guy who responded to the question 'Sex?' in a questionnaire by replying 'Twice a week'. Careful drafting and **piloting** of even the most straightforward questions is essential.

What About the Sampling Technique?

This survey was conducted electronically; you may recall that prospective respondents were referred to the website by their university careers office. Electronic or internet surveys are becoming a common way of collecting data these days, and many researchers are learning to appreciate the convenience of this method in comparison to the older pen-and-paper method. The data are often retained by the software and easily 'migrated' to an alternative package so web surveys save time on data collation, coding and entry into a statistical package. While electronic surveys mean convenience, however, they also present the researcher with problems about recruitment and response rates.

The manner of **recruitment** is known to be instrumental to a study's success. With conventional pen-and-paper methods either the questionnaires are delivered by post or an individual, usually the researcher, approaches people in person. Response rate is likely to be affected, as personal approaches are known to be more effective than remote requests for information. With an internet survey, there is little possibility of a personal approach and prospective respondents are normally emailed or approached through some other medium, usually electronic. In this instance the initial approach was midway between personal and remote because it involved careers officers. As these people were there to help the respondents, at least that invitation to take part came from a personalised source. That source was independent of the research, and by being at one remove may not have had the positive effect on recruitment that can be achieved by a direct personal request from the researcher. Nonetheless, this method of recruitment may be considered more effective than is common for web surveys. To aid recruitment, prospective respondents were offered an inducement to take part, as there were five $200 prizes to be awarded by raffle (an example of a **random** process for distribution).

A good **response rate** is vital for good **quantitative** research because only then can the data be considered to represent the sample. (To what extent the sample represents the population is a different issue; see Chapter 8.) If out of every 100 questionnaires sent out only three are returned then few conclusions can be drawn from the resulting data (other perhaps than that the research needs to be redesigned!). Conversely, if all 100 are returned the researchers can be confident about the data (once they have overcome their initial shock). The question is: what is the cut-off point for acceptability? Do we need an 80 per cent response rate? 50 per cent? 30 per cent? Authors are divided on this. But one thing is certain, and that is the response rate should be quoted in any subsequent report to allow readers to judge for themselves.

This introduces a problem for this study. If a researcher gives or sends out a number of questionnaires they can calculate the response rate by presenting the number of completed returned questions as a percentage of the number sent. (If three out of every 100 are returned, the response rate is 3 per cent, if 80 are returned, then 80 per cent). The method of recruitment used here is not easily amenable to this type of calculation, as the number of people who were referred to the website was not

recorded. The authors knew that some estimation of response rate was necessary, and
to this end collected information from the careers offices about the number of students they saw during the academic year in question. They divided this by four, as the
recruitment only occurred for a three-month period (one-quarter of the year). They
used this to estimate the response rate for each institution in turn. From this they
calculated that it ranged from 17 per cent to 53 per cent; while the former is low, the
latter is more than acceptable for a distance survey. The variability between institutions may have been caused by the way in which individual careers officers recruited
people.

Respondents were followed up at two subsequent time points; this raises another
thorny issue, which is **attrition** or **drop-out rate**. All those who had responded
to the first survey at T1 were emailed by the authors at T2 and then again at T3 to
alert them to each of the follow-up surveys (also web-based). The $200 prize induce-
ments were only awarded amongst those who completed all three surveys, an incentive not just to take part but to complete. Nearly 70 per cent of the T1 respondents
completed the second survey and 56 per cent completed the third. These figures are
relatively high; one might have expected a higher drop-out rate, and possibly this
is the effect of the incentive. The authors provide this information, which allows
the readers to draw their own conclusions about the representative nature of
these data.

If we take a step back here, and put these figures in context we must conclude that
the data are drawn from a sample that represents something between one-sixth and
one-half of the **sampling frame** (the 17 per cent and 53 per cent figures quoted
above). Only just half of these provided a full set of data. Put like that, it is arguable
whether it is representative of the potential sample and highly debatable that it is
representative of the population in question.

So How Important Is a Representative Sample?

Researchers worry about the extent to which their sample is representative of a population of interest. If we want to find out how many students on a psychology course
could be classified as extroverts, we can hand out a questionnaire in a lecture and
wait for the students to complete it (although the question of **ethics** must not be
overlooked). This way the data are collected from each member of the class and
therefore could be called representative of the population of interest, i.e. those students on that course. This is always assuming that most if not all the students on the
course attended that particular lecture. It is likely that some students will have been
absent, through illness, family business, or any one of a variety of personal reasons.
If the group size is 50 and only one is missing, we can be confident of our findings;
it is unlikely that our solitary missing student would change the overall picture presented by the data. If on the other hand we are foolish enough to try to collect the
data in a 9 a.m. lecture the day after the Psychology Society Christmas party, we may
have only 10 in the group, and this would mean that the data are not representative.
In particular, if we are looking at extroversion this could affect things quite seriously

as the most extrovert may have been enjoying the party into the small hours and unable to struggle up in time for a lecture. So the extent to which the data would be representative of the year group would depend on attendance at that lecture.

If, on the other hand, our topic of interest was extroversion amongst psychology undergraduates in the UK, how many would we need to sample to feel that the data provided us with a picture that was representative of this group? Would we do it by university? By county? By region? By country? By university type? How many would we need to feel that we knew what the picture was? What if, instead, we were interested in extroversion in the population of the UK as a whole? These are difficult questions and there are no easy answers. To get this right you would need to be very thorough about **sampling strategies** and **pilot work**.

In the Iyengar *et al.* study, we know that the response rate was something between one-sixth and one-half of the potential respondents. But the potential respondents themselves were restricted to those using the university careers service, and as such represented a **cluster sample**. And they were restricted to only a handful of universities at that. So the sampling frame was a fraction of the population in question. Then, from this already limited pool, the final sample was a **self-selected** or volunteer sample, and these are notoriously unrepresentative.

Can We Rely on These Data at All?

The short answer to this question is, yes, we can. The main reason for this confidence is that the study did not set out to examine the incidence of maximisers (or satisficers) in any given population. Rather, the aim was to compare two groups *within* the sample. You may recall that these two groups were identified by using the median score for maximising as a way of dividing the sample into two groups. As has already been noted, the maximising scores for this sample were higher than scores of the same measure obtained in other studies, the mean being 5.2 compared with 4.8 in an earlier, larger, study cited by Iyengar *et al.* The fact that the current sample had higher scores may have been to do with the demographic: this sample was younger and all university-educated. It could even have been affected by the offer of the inducement. You could argue that maximisers, in their need to seek the best possible option in every situation, would be more susceptible to inducements than satisficers.

Does this mean that the inducement might have biased the sample? It is possible, but it doesn't matter! This may seem like a contradiction in terms. If careful research is designed to avoid bias, why should the possibility of a sample biased for whatever reason not be a problem? The answer is because the crux of this study is the comparison between the two groups. Their respondents may have been more inclined to maximise than most. But even so, the authors found a difference in strategy, satisfaction and outcome between those two groups. That is to say that the satisficers may not have been as inclined towards satisficing as others in the population; nevertheless, they were different enough on this dimension from the rest of the sample for **significant** differences in subsequent behaviour to be evident.

Therefore even when your groups are not representative of the sample from which they are drawn, let alone representative of the population as a whole, you can divide them on one variable and then measure another variable. If this process then shows a significant difference you can be fairly sure that you have a robust finding, that you have found a real difference. The low-scoring group identified by this method may not have been composed of satisficers by the standards of the wider population, but they were more inclined to satisfice than their counterparts who scored above the median. Therefore the authors could compare the responses between the two groups formed by the extent of respondents' tendency to maximise.

This type of situation would suggest that any difference found would, in fact, underestimate the real difference in the population.

▲ How Appropriate Is This Research Method?

This study used survey measures, in particular questionnaires. This type of study used to be called a pen-and-paper measure, but this is no longer suitable, as we have seen, since the introduction of electronic surveys. How else could we research to aid our understanding of this type of individual difference? Observation is difficult to envisage here, but **experimentation** is one possibility. Researchers have used experimentation to identify factors likely to induce a satisficing response. Garst *et al.* (2002) showed that when people were presented with plausible hypotheses as explanations for events, they were more likely to adopt a satisficing strategy. Where they felt the existing hypothesis appropriate, they were less likely to generate many viable alternatives. Reader and Payne (2007) explored the likelihood of respondents using a satisficing strategy when asked to assimilate information about a single topic, the human heart, from four possible sources with a tight time limitation. Satisficing would involve continuing to read a source that seemed good enough, rather than swapping between the four. They discovered that satisficing was reduced if short summaries of the sources were provided, which encouraged full sampling.

These types of study tell us more about satisficing as a response but do not tell us how satisficers and maximisers differ in life choices. This question could be explored through experimentation, perhaps by providing respondents with a selection of hypothetical choices in a series of vignettes, which could first be ranked, using clearly defined objective criteria. If the task were purely hypothetical it is unlikely that the final choice will have real meaning for the individuals taking part and, therefore, may not produce the required level of investment and appraisal that would promote the use of a maximisation strategy. Conversely, if the task is designed to have meaning for the respondents they may bring other values and beliefs to it that might distort their final choice. Either way, an experimental approach here is likely to encounter problems of **ecological validity**. For this to be an effective study, the array of outcomes must have real value and consequences for those taking part.

Conclusion

Iyengar *et al.* have used a well-designed study to explore the differences between maximisers and satisficers. This was an analytical survey because it set out to test some specific predictions (hypotheses), and therefore can be distinguished from descriptive surveys where the task is to find details of a given population. Because the design was a **between groups** comparison, it required an **unrelated** or **independent design**. Because the groups could not be identified until after data collection, they were formed *post hoc*. The questionnaire used in this study was one that had already undergone development, and some of its psychometric properties had been established by previous research. This study has further developed this measurement tool, producing ample evidence that this does indeed measure the extent to which an individual may use a maximising choice-making strategy. They have shown that when it comes to career-seeking, maximisers explore more options, check against external reference points and worry more than satisficers. Furthermore, maximisers appear to benefit from this process if salary is used as an objective measure of success. Nonetheless, they are less happy with their final choice than are satisficers.

The very neat thing about this study is that the researchers have used tangible evidence to address a theoretical conundrum. Prior to this study the research had already suggested that maximisers were less satisfied with the outcome of their decisions than were satisficers, but the mechanisms behind this were unclear. Could maximising just be a very ineffective strategy for making a decision, maximisers thereby finishing up with worse outcomes than satisficers? Or was it that the maximising itself is in some way associated with dissatisfaction? If one accepts the premise that salary is a reasonable measure of outcome then this study provides support for an association between maximising and dissatisfaction. We do not yet know cause and effect. Does maximising make you dissatisfied? Does a level of dissatisfaction lead to maximising? Or possibly there is a third, as yet unrecognised, variable that leads to both! In short we do not yet know what the independent variable might be here.

 Can you think of any way of testing whether there is a third variable?

Postscript

Oddly enough, the word 'satsificing' has come to have an alternative meaning for some social scientists. Ironically, it is used in survey methodology to refer to a way of answering survey research. The argument is that thorough question-answering may involve a good deal of cognitive effort, and some people may therefore take a short-cut through their cognitive processes by satisficing. Satisficing here can either mean incomplete consideration of each of the questions being asked, or presenting answers that are likely to appease the researcher but may not reflect the respondent's opinion. It is suggested that this form of satisficing is when participants are not motivated or when the task appears difficult. This use of the word is more common in the USA than in the UK.

Summary Points	
Design	Survey methods: questionnaire
Aim	To compare two groups
Sample	548 university graduates
Apparatus	Questionnaire – electronic
Analysis	Between groups identified *post hoc* through median split

Measuring Romance

Survey Methods – Scale Development

'How on earth are you ever going to explain in terms of chemistry and physics so important a biological phenomenon as first love?' (Albert Einstein, physicist, 1879–1955)

Have You Ever Been in Love?

Our society places a good deal of emphasis on romantic love. Much of our culture consists of extolling its virtues or dwelling on its agonies. Think of all the music you know, and consider what proportion of it is about love and relationships. The books we read often focus on this too – certainly many of the classic novels are love stories: *Jane Eyre, Wuthering Heights,* or *Pride and Prejudice* for example. Romance plays a big part in the paperback market, whether it is 'chick lit' or Mills & Boon. The image of romantic love seems to permeate our culture. We are encouraged from an early age to seek it; we consider it our right and our expectation. We become depressed and anxious when it eludes us; we fall into the depths of despair when we lose it. They say love makes the world go around; certainly it sometimes seems that the world revolves around it.

If love is such a powerful force in human existence, how on earth would we set about measuring it? This was pretty much the task that Wei *et al.* (2007) set themselves when they decided to measure relationship style. You might think any attempt to measure such a nebulous subject would require an extensive test battery, but the measure they developed consisted of just 12 items. To be strictly accurate, they did not call it 'love' but 'attachment'. Whatever name is used for it, this is yet another **hypothetical construct** (see Box 11.1). It might seem churlish to describe love in this way; ardent lovers would argue forcefully that love is real. As we cannot see it (although we may recognise the symptoms), touch it, smell it or taste it, we have to accept that it is an abstraction. At an **empirical** level, we need to recognize that any abstract concept is hypothetical, a matter of conjecture. Synonyms for *hypothetical* are *theoretical*, *imaginary* and *supposed*. For hard-nosed psychologists, love is not so much 'a many splendored thing' as a supposed explanation for some forms of human behaviour!

In psychology we often find that we need to measure a hypothetical construct. **Qualitative** psychologists prefer to focus on people's descriptions or accounts of experiences, but **quantitative** psychologists like measuring things. It is easy to see how some constructs might be measured. For example, it is easy to measure reaction times; modern technology allows us to do this accurately. We are also familiar with the idea of measuring intelligence, although what exactly is measured by intelligence tests is hotly debated. We can envisage how memory might be measured by requiring people to memorise and recall material. To measure any ability, skill or function requires very specific **operational definitions**. For example, with memory do we want to measure storage or recall? Semantic or episodic? Verbal or spatial? Long-term or short-term? It is necessary to be very specific to do the job properly, but it is relatively easy to visualise how we might set about it. Other constructs are less obviously amenable to measurement, and this is the province of **psychometrics**, from *psycho* 'to do with the mind' and *metric* 'measurement'. Psychometrics usually involve questionnaires or scales, although it can also include other tasks. It usually, although not always, involves some form of scoring. The score can then be interpreted as a measurement of the construct and sometimes allows for a categorisation of the **respondent**.

Psychology by Numbers?

It may seem a little odd to think of measuring these abstractions through survey methods. It is a task not without its challenges. For example, if I wanted to measure attitudes to sport, I might construct an **attitude scale** with 12 items, each referring to a different sporting activity. Suppose I ask you to use a seven-point scale to rate how much you like each of these. In this scale 7 means 'very much' and 1 means, 'not at all'. There might be a couple of sports that you really enjoy (you rate these 6 or 7), a couple you are happy to play (4 and 5), maybe half a dozen that you are lukewarm about (2s and 3s) and a couple you actively dislike (1s).

Having collected these data I can then produce an average score from your responses, which is how scores are often calculated. This particular example will give you an average score of 3.25. The maths here are sound – this is indeed the average of those 12 scores. But what does it mean? What does it tell me about you and your attitude to sport? Virtually nothing – because you are merely responding to the 12 sports I have included in the scale. I cannot use this score to say that it tells me how much you like sport for example, nor does it tell me how much sport you do. It certainly does not tell me anything about you as a person, about your attitudes and your views. As a measurement of any characteristic about you it would be useless, it has no **validity**. Simply asking questions and allowing respondents to answer by numbers does not in itself produce a meaningful score. A good deal of work has to go into a developing a questionnaire or rating scale first, before its authors can claim that it measures anything at all.

In this example, there was a seven-point scale; Iyengar *et al.* (see Chapter 15) used a nine-point scale in a similar way. There is much debate about what is the right number of points for such scales. While there is a lack of consensus, there is general agreement that anything beyond 10 is likely to be difficult for the respondent to use and may invalidate their answers. (However, scales with 100 points are also considered acceptable, see **visual analogue scales**.) Some scales are developed where all the possible responses are expressed in words and later converted to numbers by the researcher. For example, in Spielberger's 1983 State Trait Anxiety Inventory (a well-established **standardised** assessment with **normative data**) the responses for the scale designed to measure trait anxiety are 'almost always', 'often', 'sometimes' and 'almost never'. With a small number of options it is possible to use words or phrases that will allow meaningful responses. With larger scales developing appropriate and consensual wording can be problematic and is usually avoided. In these instances, such as in the example above, labelling the two extremes is considered adequate, allowing the respondent to develop their own interpretation for the graded responses in between.

The suggested scale about sport would be an example of a unipolar or ordinary rating scale, one that measures the presence or absence of a characteristic. This was probably the only appropriate measure for the construct in question. In other instances, in particular, with attitude scales, it is customary to use a **bipolar** set of responses, the most common of which is the **Likert** method. Here the respondent is presented with a set of statements, for each of which they indicate the extent of their agreement with the statement by choosing from 'strongly agree', 'agree', 'neither agree nor disagree' 'disagree' and 'strongly disagree'. Thus it is possible to respond in one of two opposing or bipolar dimensions. One consideration is whether to have an odd or even number of responses. This is more than a matter of aesthetics. With an odd number of responses, the respondent is able to choose the middle option, which is effectively neutral, neither positive or negative. It is also difficult to know what that middle option might mean, and therefore how to interpret it. Many scales overcome this by using a **forced choice** method, where there is an even number of responses (be it two, four, six, eight or ten) thereby forcing the respondent to make a choice between being in favour or against. In Iyengar's study, to measure the presence of maximising tendencies, a simple rating scale was a more appropriate choice than a bipolar scale. It would be difficult to argue that satisficing is the polar opposite of maximising as it appears simply to be a different type of strategy.

When is a unipolar scale more appropriate? The answer is that constructs such as anxiety, intelligence or, as in the previous chapter, maximising tendencies are generally considered as being on a continuum. That is, some people are hardly anxious at all, some are slightly anxious, some are really quite anxious and some are very anxious indeed. Or, in the activity that is the focus Iyengar's study, when job-seeking, some people will maximise all the time, others will maximise some of the time, while the remainder may not maximise at all. It is unlikely that we will have the three neat categories that this description suggests. Within any one of those three groupings there will be a good deal of variability. By using 11 statements each with nine possible options the authors are allowing their respondents to grade themselves on a continuum with a possible 108 points. This produces a finer grading than a single question could ever manage and also takes into account and indeed reflects the variety within the **sample**. The point of scaling methods like this is that the score represents the extent to which that construct is found in the respondent.

There is another reason for this approach as well, and that is to do with the way that people respond to questions. If a single question had been used asking whether you try for the best in any situation or settle for good enough, the most likely answer is 'It depends on the situation.' By using a scale that includes statements relating to specific behaviours (tuning radios, shopping for clothes) the respondents are presented with statements about situations in which they can visualise themselves and estimate their own likely response.

Ensuring a reasonable number of items was the first task for Wei *et al.* when they set out to measure romantic attachment. They were not starting from scratch, because a scale had already been developed by Brennan, Clark and Shaver in 1998 (cited in Wei *et al.*, 2007); it was called the Experiences in Close Relationships (ECR) scale, and it was designed to measure a general pattern of attachment in relationships. Although the title of the scale suggests it is tapping into respondents' past, this is misleading. The aim is really to see how people think they normally behave in a romantic relationship; you could say their style of attachment. The scale had 36 items which were taken from an original collection of 323 items! This large haul came from taking all the items from previous scales measuring adult attachment. In doing this, Brennan and colleagues rather neatly dealt with the issue of **content validity**, which means checking that a scale covers all the aspects that are thought relevant by experts in the field.

It is argued that a 36-item scale can be rather daunting for prospective respondents. You may think that 36 is not many considering the number at the start, but responding to 36 questions is still a relatively lengthy task. Long scales mean that some respondents will not stay focused on the task while completing it. It can also mean **attrition rates** increase as people who start the scale lose interest and fail to finish. It can deter some people from taking part, and so create problems with recruitment. A shorter scale also makes it possible to measure attachment, and – at the same time – combine this with the use of other questionnaires.

The 36-item scale had been subjected to psychometric assessment which had established its validity and **reliability**. It had also been shown that the scale had two **factor**s, two underlying constructs that contributed to the scale. There were therefore two subscales: avoidance and anxiety. Avoidance may be described as a reluctance to commit, a fear of intimacy, and the need to stay independent within any relationship. Anxiety is characterised by a fear of rejection, excessive need of approval and seeking

constant reassurance. High scores on either or both of these factors are seen as indicating an insecure attachment style. Conversely, low levels suggest security.

Given that this much had already been established on the 36-item scale, it may seem like a relatively easy task to trim it down to 12 items. Yet it is not such a simple matter. The only step that this group of researchers did not need to undertake was developing the items in the first place. This meant that **face validity** had already been established – meaning that the scale looked like it was measuring what it set to measure. This had been done by Brennan *et al.* when they took their 323 items from all the then extant scales intended to measure the attachment. In the first instance you need to be careful in deciding which items to drop and which to retain, and once you start doing that, the work to establish the psychometric properties is no longer relevant. You have to start all over again. Once you tamper with a scale you need to be able to show that the final product still measures what you say it does, that it measures something that is consistent over time and that all the items contribute meaningfully to the overall scale score. Wei *et al.* had quite a task on their hands. It required a series of six studies for them to reduce and authenticate the ECR – short form.

The Experiences in Close Relationships Scale (ECR) – Short Form: Reliability, Validity and Factor Structure

Wei, M., Russell, D.W., Mallinckrodt, B. & Vogel, D.L. (2007). *Journal of Personality Assessment, 88*(2), 187–204

The **aims** of study 1 were to identify which of the 36 items to include, to check the **internal reliability** of the short form and to compare the factors with those of the original scale.

Method 1

The sample comprised 851 undergraduate students, nearly equal numbers of each gender, predominantly white with an age range of 18 to 45 years. Only 6 per cent reported being in a romantic relationship at the time of the study. Respondents were awarded course credits[1] for taking part. They completed the original 36-item ECR. This used a seven-point 'partly anchored' response scale. It was partly anchored because the two extremes and the midpoint were labelled 1 'disagree strongly', 4 'neutral/mixed' and 7 'agree strongly'. Nine of the items required reverse scoring. This is because some items were phrased in the opposite manner from the rest. For example, on the avoidance subscale, most of the items suggested avoidance such as *I am nervous when partners get too close to me*. Agreeing with this statement suggests a tendency to try to avoid close relationships. Selecting 'agree strongly' here would be scored as 7. The reverse-scored items on this scale suggested the opposite point of view, for example, *It helps to turn to my romantic partner in times of need*. Agreeing with this statement indicates a readiness to be intimate. Choosing 'agree strongly' here would be scored as 1.

Results 1

To identify which items to include in the short form Wei *et al.* used both statistical methods and common sense. The statistical method they used was called **exploratory factor analysis**, which finds the factors or subscales that underlie responses (see box 18.1 for an example of how factor analysis can be used in psychometric assessment). This was the technique that was used by Brennan *et al.* with the original version through which they identified the two subscales, avoidance and anxiety. Wei *et al.* used it separately on each of these subscales to see if further underlying factors could be identified. They then looked to see which items had the 'highest loadings' on these underlying factors, which means the items that had the strongest relationship with the factors. They identified a total of 21 items that had high loadings on these underlying factors. This was the statistical bit of the selection process.

To reduce it further, they looked at the content of the items in the scales to find close matches of content, and then discarded one of two. For example, *I worry that romantic partners won't care about me as much as I care about them* was deemed to be saying the same thing as *I often wish that my partner's feelings for me were as strong as my feelings for him/her*. In this instance the first was retained and the second discarded.

As well as duplication, another consideration was whether to keep some of the reverse-scoring items. Items that need reverse scoring are recommended for scales because it encourages the respondent to respond to each item in turn rather than develop a **response set** and just tick all the same points for each of the items. By these means, the 12 items for the short form scale were identified.

To check that the new smaller scale had internal reliability, **alpha coefficients** were calculated. This is a measure of how much each of the items relate to each other, also called **item analysis**. Like all correlations, the possible range is 0, meaning no correlation to 1, representing a perfect correlation. The correlations for the anxiety and avoidance subscales were .78 and .84 respectively, which shows an acceptable level of internal consistency or reliability for each subscale. To check that the two subscales were really measuring different factors, scores from these were correlated and that correlation was only .19. This relatively low figure shows that they reflect different dimensions of attachment.

To compare the factors in the new scale with those from the original, Wei *et al.* used **confirmatory factor analysis**. Unlike the exploratory version, this method allows you to test whether your data fit a specified **factor structure**. They selected a structure that comprised the two subscales which were seen as oblique (correlated with, but separate from, each other) plus the effect of the wording of the item (positive or negative) – which took account of any response set that might occur. Through this, they showed a good fit for both the 12-item and the 36-item versions to their hypothesised model. Therefore, they seemed to have produced a statistically sound shorter version of the ECR.

■ How Safe Is This Conclusion?

It is safe as far as it goes, but with all types of factor analysis there is reasonable element of interpretation required from the findings. Once interpretation is involved in a quantitative study, there is room for error. In order to satisfy themselves that their results had not been distorted through error, Wei *et al.* undertook Study 2. The aims of this were to **replicate** reliability and factor structure from Study 1 and to compare the **construct validity** of the 12-item and 36-item versions.

Method 2

The sample consisted of 425 college students, 61 per cent of whom were female and 76 per cent of whom described themselves as single. They completed the ECR-36 and three other scales: two to measure depression, the other to measure excessive reassurance-seeking. The other scales were selected to assess **criterion validity**: this means making a prediction about how the scores in question will relate to the other variables. Wei *et al.* predicted that the anxiety subscale should **correlate** with excessive reassurance-seeking and that both subscales should correlate with depression measures.

Results 2

The alpha coefficients were .78 and .88, very similar to the first study. The correlation between the two subscales was again low, at .28, indicating they are distinct dimensions. The confirmatory factor analysis again confirmed the factor structure. The correlations were **significant** between avoidance and excessive reassurance-seeking and between both subscales and depression. Furthermore, the results from

ECR-12 and ECR-36 were very similar. The replication from Study 1 suggests that those conclusions were safe, and criterion validation suggests that both versions have construct validity.

■ How Safe Is This Conclusion?

It is safer than with only one set of results, but Wei *et al.* decided to replicate the reliability and factor tests again while checking validity against a different set of measures.

Method 3

This sample comprised 229 undergraduates, 65 per cent of whom were female, and half of the sample reported being in a committed relationship. Again the ECR-36 was completed, along with four other measures of emotional states, about which predictions were made as part of the validation.

Results 3

Alpha coefficients were again very similar, .79 and .87; the correlation between the scales was again low, .25; and the fit to the factor structure remained good. Again the predicted correlations between high scores for anxiety and avoidance and scores from the other questionnaires measuring a variety of negative emotional states were significant.

■ How Safe Is This Conclusion Now?

Even the most sceptical would have to admit that with three studies of different samples providing the same type of results, we can be fairly confident about the internal reliability and the factor structure. The later two studies provide good support for construct validity. Wei *et al.* embarked on fourth study to test reliability over time, **test-retest reliability**.

Method 4

This sample of 122 undergraduates, 56 per cent of whom were female and 72 per cent of whom described themselves as single, completed the ECR-36 twice at an interval of one month. If the scale is measuring a stable characteristic then the results from the two assessments should be very similar. For good measure, the researchers also checked the alpha coefficients for a fourth time.

Results 4

Alpha coefficients remained high: .81 and . 88 at **T1**, .81 and .87 at **T2**. The test-retest coefficients for the ECR-12 were anxiety .80 and avoidance .83; for the ECR-36 the figures were .82 and .86. As these correlations are high (near to 1) both subscales were shown to be stable over time for both the 12-item and 36-item versions. As a further check, they looked to see whether there was a change over time on either scale and found no significant changes.

■ Is This Conclusion Safe Yet?

Consistent findings over four studies make a convincing picture for the internal reliability of the short form and Study 4 tells us that there is also consistency over time. Is this enough? Recall that the point of these studies was to develop a new, shorter version of the scale. Have you spotted any way in which the short form was used in Studies 1–4 that has differed from its intended future use? Each time it has been used, respondents had completed the full 36-item version. To date no study has just used the short form. This is for a good reason; Wei *et al.* needed to compare the new version with the old, so needed data from both. But it is just possible that the experience of completing the whole scale in some way influenced the way that people responded to the 12 items in the short form. For this reason, Study 5 used only the ECR-12, and repeated the analyses of earlier studies with the full version.

Method 5

The sample comprised 257 undergraduates; 64 per cent were female, and half of the sample were single. This time respondents completed just the short form, the ECR-12 together with a further eight measures of emotional and psychological well-being for the criterion validity. This test battery meant that in total respondents had to answer 143 questions.

Results 5

The alpha coefficients were similar to all the previous studies (anxiety .77, avoidance .78), and the inter-correlation coefficient remained low at .28. Confirmatory factor analysis once again showed a good fit between the new data and the existing model, thereby confirming the two-factor structure. The correlations between the other psychometric measures were all significant in the predicted directions and thereby supported the new scale's construct validity.

■ Is This Conclusion Safe Now?

You might think that Wei *et al.* must have covered all possible bases with these five studies. However, if you are particularly alert you may have noticed that the test-retest reliability was only run with the 12-item subset from the original 36-item version, and not on its own. Therefore, in their sixth and final study in this series, they set out to check this.

Method 6

There were 65 undergraduates this time who completed the ECR-12 twice at an interval of three weeks. Three-quarters of this group were female and just over half the sample were in a committed relationship.

Results 6

Once again the alpha coefficients were similar to those in previous studies (anxiety .84 and avoidance .85) and the correlations from T1 to T2 were high, as previously (anxiety .82 and avoidance .89). Again the data were tested to see whether there were significant differences on either subscale between T1 and T2, and there were not.

■ Is This Final Conclusion Safe?

Six studies, nearly 2000 respondents and countless inferential statistics: can we now have confidence in their findings? I think we can, although this painstaking and time-consuming study schedule is not a guarantee. What provides us with confidence here is that all the results from all six studies are telling the same story. They are all confirming the same set of findings.

● How Effective Is This Design?

The purpose of this schedule of studies was to establish the psychometric properties of the new short form version of the ECR. A new version needs to have its properties demonstrated in just the same way that is required for a brand-new scale. With this task, the requirement was to ensure that the psychometric properties were not impoverished by the reduction in the number of scale items. As we have seen, this meant that several of the analyses involved testing the new reduced version against its parent scale. If this had been a brand-new scale this would not have been an option, obviously. A new scale would require a similar process, but the testing would have been against theoretical models rather than an earlier version.

Psychometrics, or psychology by numbers, is one way in which psychologists can set about measuring hypothetical constructs. In designing such a measuring tool, be it from scratch or from a longer/earlier version, there are two issues that must be addressed: reliability and validity.

Reliability is about the consistency or repeatability of a set of measurements. We need to make sure that any measuring instrument provides a reliable measurement. If your watch were to go at different speeds on different days it would not be much used to you, and you would probably get quite confused into the bargain. There are two types of reliability: internal and external. Internal reliability means that all the different items in the scale should be tapping into the same construct. There are several ways of doing this. Wei and colleagues used the alpha coefficient, which is a measurement of how all the items in the scale correlated with each other: the higher the correlation, the greater the degree of internal consistency. It is generally considered that an alpha coefficient of .75 or above is high enough to demonstrate reliability. Wei *et al.* found all their alphas to be above this level. An alternative method for demonstrating internal reliability is called the **split-half method**. For this the items in the scale are randomly divided into two subscales and then these are correlated with each other.

External reliability, or **test-re-test reliability** means that you would expect to get the same set of results if measures were taken on more than one occasion, assuming no major changes have occurred in the respondents (see Box 16.1). External reliability can be assessed by asking the respondents to complete the test on two separate occasions. If the construct you are measuring is stable over time, then you would expect to get very similar scores at those two time points. This is exactly what we saw in this study. Once you have those two measures from different time points, there are two things you can do to test consistency. You can look to see whether those two measures are closely related, using a measurement of correlation. Alternatively you can look to see whether the measurements have changed, using a test of difference. In this case Wei and her colleagues used both of these tests to establish the consistency of measurement over time.

Having established reliability, researchers need to address the issue of validity. It is no good having a consistent measuring tool that provides the same answer over time if I am not measuring what I intend to measure. For example, suppose that I am interested in anxiety. It is an established fact that anxiety can cause an increase in heart rate. Measuring heart rate is clearly an objective measurement. I could measure the heart rate of my sample by taking their pulse. I could then identify those with a rapid pulse as being more anxious than whose pulse is slow. Or could I? This would be a largely spurious inference. To begin with, there is quite a wide variation in what is a normal, at-rest pulse in adults. Secondly, not everyone who is anxious will have an increased heart rate. Thirdly, some people may have an increased heart rate for other reasons (e.g. exercise, illness). Monitoring heart rate as measurement of anxiety is therefore invalid.

We need to find a way to demonstrate validity. We can use criterion validity where we can identify a criterion by which our scale can be judged. We can do this by comparing the results of the new scale with an established measure of the same construct, this is **concurrent validity**. In this instance Wei *et al.* compared their results with those of the fuller version, which provides one form of support. A more independent measure would provide firmer evidence. If there is another scale that purports to measure the same construct then we could use that, although the new scale would need to have some clear advantage over the existing scale in order to justify its development in the first place. A second sort of criterion reliability is **predictive validity**. Here the researcher makes predictions about the outcomes from the scale in relation to future events. In this study, checking people's relationship status a few years later would allow us to test its predictive validity – ethical issues permitting. Another form of criterion validity is to use a **known groups** criterion. If you wanted to develop a measurement of political conservatism, you could validate this by

External/Test-Retest Reliability

You may be wondering why two sets of measurements are necessary; surely a second measurement would be expected to be the same as the first. It would be with a truly **objective measure**, but not necessarily with a **subjective measure** such as this one. If I wanted to measure your height, providing you are fully grown adult, and I measured your height twice at an interval of three weeks, I would expect to get exactly the same measurement – the joys of objective measurement. If, on the other hand, I was to ask you how much you like apples using a nine-point scale, where 9 means 'a great deal' and 1 means 'not at all', you would have to make a subjective judgement. Supposing that you do quite enjoy apples (although they are not your absolute favourite) you might respond '6'. If I was to ask you to make the same judgement three weeks later, provided you did not remember what you had said the first time, you would have to make the same judgement again and therefore this time might well say '5', '6' or '7'. If you chose 5 or 7, it is unlikely to mean that your opinion of apples has changed in the intervening three weeks, but rather that your decision on how to report your opinion has shown a small amount of variation. If everyone in my sample, like you, provided answers the second time that were, at most, only one measurement point away from the original response, then I would have a high correlation between the two measuring points. Those who had chosen high the first time still chose high, those with the middle ranges would still be there and those who do not like apples would still be giving low numbers. If I looked to see whether there was a difference between these two time points, I would be unlikely to find anything significant.

If I had only asked you the one question (in this case, about apples) there is a good chance that you would remember what you had said the first time. When there are 12 items on the scale it is much less likely that you will remember what you said for each in turn. Indeed, researchers usually discourage people from trying to recall what they said earlier but rather ask them to base their second response on what they currently believe to reflect the true level.

asking members of the Conservative and Labour parties to complete it. You would predict significantly higher scores from the Conservatives.

There is also the issue of construct validity. This can be demonstrated by testing theoretically driven hypotheses of the construct in question in relation to other measurable constructs. In the study in question, the authors argued that those who scored high on the ECR scale would experience negative emotions so as well as the ECR they administered measures of depression. Their data provided support for their argument: high ECR scores correlated with high depression scores – which is evidence of construct validity. I suggested at the start of this chapter that the study had set out to measure love, or at least relationship style. The authors themselves refer to the notion of 'adult attachment' as being the focus of their interest. Although their scale is labelled *experience* of close relationships it does not ask people whether they have had a specific experience but rather how they expect to behave in a relationship. The instructions given to their respondents were:

> We are interested in how you generally experience relationships, not just in what is happening in a current relationship. (2007, p.188)

The authors argue that high levels of anxiety or avoidance are a sign of having difficulties with adult attachment, and that low scores are indicative of a more secure orientation. This construct will no doubt benefit from further examination and refinement.

The rationale for developing this scale in the first place was to improve response rates and reduce attrition with a more manageable scale. It may seem ironic that they felt the need to reduce a scale from 36 items to 12 and in order to validate this used a test battery which at one point comprised 143 questions! This is not as contradictory as it might appear. Have you noticed what each of the samples from all six studies had in common? They were all undergraduate students. We know that in at least one case course credits were offered as an inducement to take part. It is relatively easy to persuade students to undertake extensive batteries, either through offering an extrinsic reward (course credits) or an intrinsic reward (satisfying their curiosity about psychological research). It is not as easy with other types of respondents, hence the need to reduce the scale. This raises the question of whether these samples are representative of the **population**. They are all students, they are mostly young, and they are predominantly white. The answer is that they are probably not representative, and **generalising** from the sample to the population would be a mistake. The authors refer to an earlier paper where they showed with the ECR-36 that ethnicity moderated some responses.

Oddly enough, this lack of representativeness does not matter. This series of studies aimed to establish the psychometric properties of the instrument. These properties are generally not considered to be unique to one type of respondent. Once this scale is used in research the factor structure can be tested again, as can the reliability and the validity. The findings reported here may be supported by findings from other populations, or maybe they will require modification. Scales are normally developed on relatively captive samples, partly because of the extensive testing required, as we have seen. The point of these studies is to discover whether these scales have the requisite properties in this population. If they did not have them in this population, it is likely that the scale development would be halted or at least reconsidered.

Because of the relatively specialist nature of these respondents, it would not have been wise to try to standardise the assessment on this sample. Usually when standardisation occurs, researchers collect data from several distinct groups so that future users of the test can decide what comparator to use. For example, a test might be standardised on males and female separately, looking at different age groups, and different socio-economic groups. Once a test is standardised, we have normative data – average values for specific subgroups in the population, against which we can compare individual responses. These are usually calculated as ranges rather than absolute scores. For example, when IQ tests were standardised the **median** for the population as a whole was 100 (50 per cent of the population lying above and 50 per cent below). It was calculated that roughly a third of the population would score between 85 and 100, and another third between 100 and 115. This meant that if a person scored above 115 they were in the top 16 per cent of the population. Wei and colleagues have not attempted standardisation with this measure, and it may well be that, given the construct, standardisation would not be useful.

For what types of psychometric assessment do you think that standardisation might be most useful and why?

This research design was therefore effective in that it allowed the authors to demonstrate that they had a useful measure that: was internally and externally reliable; has evidence of construct validity; and has two subscales, each of which contributes meaningfully and separately to the overall construct. They have shown that the reduced version of the ECR is on a par with the original full version.

▲ How Appropriate Is This Research Method?

As discussed above, this approach to establishing psychometric properties of a scale is necessarily a large-scale and extensive project. Given that this was their aim, there was no real alternative in terms of research methods. This is very much a standard **nomothetic approach**, that is, establishing laws that can be applied to the population as a whole. This is not to suggest that the subject of attachment cannot be considered through other types of research approach. Survey methods in general can contribute to our understanding of adult attachment, both its causes and its consequences. For example, Torgersen *et al.* (2007) found that twins tend to have similar attachment styles, and that this is more pronounced in monozygotic (identical) twins than in dizygotic (fraternal) twins, suggesting that hereditary and shared environment contribute to attachment style. Fortuna and Roisman (2008) compared self-report and interview data on adult attachment and found a relationship between attachment problems and self-reported psychiatric symptoms. Doumas *et al.* (2008) found that the pairing of an anxious female with an avoidant male was a risk factor for intimate partner violence from either protagonist.

Observational research can also contribute. Gormley (2004) describes two case studies demonstrating a link between attachment problems and suicidal tendencies. Even **experimental** work can help us understand the role of attachment. Dewitte and de Houwer (2008) showed that high scores for anxiety and avoidance were associated with reduced attention to angry faces, and that those with high avoidance scores tended to look away from happy faces. Quirin *et al.* (2008) showed that attachment anxiety was correlated with the hormonal secretions under unrelated stress conditions, suggesting links between the anatomical development of the hippocampus with the development of the self. As always, all different research methodologies can add to our understanding of the topic.

Conclusion

Developing a scale is not an easy business and requires sustained endeavour to produce a tool that can be useful in psychological research. Wei *et al.* have shown that their new short form of this scale is a reliable and valid measure of adult attachment and is fit for purpose. They have demonstrated that this truncated version has the same psychometric properties as its parent scale. The authors exhort future users to consider using the short form in preference to the 36-item scale. Its potential use can span many areas of psychology, for as the authors say:

> Adult attachment has become a major focus of research in personality, social, clinical, counselling and developmental psychology. (2007, p.187)

Note

1 Course credits are often used on psychology courses to encourage undergraduates to take part in research to help the department and to gain experience of research as a participant. The mechanisms for recording and implementing systems of course credits are diverse.

Summary Points	
Design	Survey methods, scale development
Aim	To test the reliability, validity, and factor structure of a scale
Sample	Undergraduates (N=1949 over six studies)
Materials	Experiences in Close Relationships (ECR) scale plus sundry other psychometric assessments of emotional and psychological well-being
Analysis	Factor analysis, alpha coefficients, correlations and t-tests.

Paranoia

Survey Methods – Interview

'I envy paranoids; they actually feel people are paying attention to them.' (Susan Sontag, essayist, novelist, filmmaker, and activist, 1933–2004)

Ever Thought That You Were Being Watched?

Have you ever walked down a street and felt that there was someone following you? Not just walking behind you but actively following you? Have you ever thought that you were being watched but been unable to see anyone doing so? Sometimes we have experiences like these, and they can be very unsettling. Usually there is a simple explanation which might be apparent to an observer. It may be an acoustic glitch; echoes can sound like some else walking at your pace, for example. It can sound as though it is coming from behind you, and when you stop to see if they catch up they stop too, confirming your suspicions. Sometimes the cause is not so obvious, but such experiences can often be an example of our minds 'playing tricks' on us.

Have you ever said that it seems as though events are conspiring against you? Sometimes when a string of things go wrong, it can feel like that. You are rushing to get to an important meeting and you cannot find a pair of socks that match. The telephone rings as you are leaving the house, requiring you to reopen the door to answer it. The bus is late; you don't have the right change for a ticket. A passing car splashes a puddle over your ankles and shoes, and as you enter the meeting room, panting and sweating, you realise that you have left your handkerchief at home. And you really had wanted to make a good impression! At such moments we tend to believe that this series of adverse events are in some way connected. In reality, they are only connected because of their impact on you, but there is no connection between their causes. It can feel as though there must be because you are feeling so thwarted and persecuted. For most of us, this feeling of persecution is a transient sensation. By the time we are recounting the events of the morning from a distance we can see that it was a combination of being in too much of a hurry, not paying adequate attention and bad luck, all coloured by the pressure of the occasion.

The feeling of being watched or being at the centre of a personalised conspiracy is for some a permanent state of affairs. It is a symptom of paranoia. A definition of paranoia is a tendency towards excessive and irrational suspicion and distrustfulness of other people and their motives. Being paranoid means being suspicious without reason and wrongly believing that someone is trying to cause you harm. People with paranoia are perpetually in fear of the next attack or betrayal. Every time something goes wrong it appears to be evidence that the fear was justified, and so reinforces it. People with paranoia feel isolated because they are unable to trust anyone, and this becomes a vicious circle: paranoia leading to mistrust, to isolation, to increased paranoia. This downward spiral can get out of control, leading to serious mental health problems.

Many psychological problems lie on a continuum. At one end there are minor manifestations amongst a healthy population, at the other extreme conditions requiring treatment. There is evidence that some people experience paranoia in a mild form that does not prevent them functioning normally – maybe as many as one in five of us could be affected. Others have a more extreme form that results in, or is part of, a psychotic condition. Psychologists have suggested that some psychotic conditions are best understood as an exaggerated form of normal functions, and paranoid delusions may be one. Research into non-clinical samples has looked at the incidence of paranoid beliefs amongst healthy individuals, tried to identify the causes or precursors, or evaluated the treatments. There has been a paucity of research into how it feels to have paranoid thoughts until this was investigated by two researchers from the University of Manchester. Their **aim** was to find out about people's experience of paranoia.

The Subjective Experience of Paranoia: Comparing the Experiences of Patients with Psychosis and those with No Psychiatric History

Campbell, M.L.C. & Morrison, A.P. (2007). *Clinical Psychology and Psychotherapy, 14,* 63–77

Method

Campbell and Morrison (2007) recruited two groups of **respondents**. There were six patients who had been diagnosed with schizophrenia; five were contacted through community health teams and the sixth was approached by one of the researchers. The non-patient group also consisted of six people, all of whom were academic staff or students. These had been identified from an earlier study where their responses to a questionnaire on delusions had indicated that they experienced some paranoid thoughts. **Data** were collected by interview with the flexible use of an **interview schedule** using **open questions**. Having a schedule means that the interviewer can cover the same ground with all respondents; open questions means that the respondents are free to respond fully and thoroughly. The interviews took between an hour and an hour and a half each to complete, thereby allowing full discussion of the issues. As they were recorded the flow of the conversation was not interrupted. The recordings were transcribed for analysis.

Results

Campbell and Morrison used a process called Interpretative Phenomenological Analysis (IPA) which is designed to deal with **qualitative** data. The name is a bit of a mouthful but it describes the two key features of the analysis. It is *phenomenological* because it is concerned with the way in which we see things/phenomena, our experience of those phenomena and the meaning we attach to them. (This comes from the word 'phenomenology' which is the study of subjective experiences.) It is *interpretative* because a key feature of the analysis is acknowledging the role that the researcher's own beliefs play in the analysis. IPA uses an **idiographic** approach, which means that it focuses on the individual and her/his personal experience. (Contrast this with the **nomothetic** approach described in Chapter 16.) The basis of IPA is that language is representative of a person's cognitive state (Smith *et al.*, 1999).

The process of the analysis begins with the researcher reading and rereading the interview transcripts until they are fully familiar with the accounts given. The next task is to identify themes and then to establish links between the themes. These links can be horizontal, looking at how the themes interrelate, or vertical, establishing a hierarchy of superordinate and subordinate themes. From the themes identified by Campbell and Morrison, it was possible to see commonalities and differences between the clinical and non-clinical groups. For example, both groups saw potential harm from weak evidence, felt confused because they could not make sense of their experiences, suggested that their paranoia was influenced by negative experiences and saw it as a means of protection, although they reported that paranoia had an adverse effect on the way they viewed themselves. There was inherent and acknowledged conflict between the positive aspects of protection and the negative effect on self-image. Paranoia was seen as a necessary defence from external threats, despite its detrimental internal effects. Both groups talked a good deal about anxiety and its role in their thoughts. Unlike the non-clinical group, the patients described the increasing and unmanageable power of their paranoid thoughts, believed that the thoughts originated outside themselves and beyond their control, acknowledged that the beliefs were strange but did not suggest they were inaccurate. The way that the non-patients described paranoia was much more acceptable in Western society than the way the patients did. However, as the authors point out, this difference may lie more in the way that non-patients perceive social reality and can thereby tailor their discourse accordingly. Non-patients were also able to talk about positive as well as negative beliefs. As the patients focused only on the negative, the authors suggest that a balance of the two may be a component of psychological health.

As a result of these and other themes identified, the authors make three recommendations for the clinical management of paranoia. They suggest therapy should focus on building self-esteem, managing anxiety and helping patients towards a realistic interpretation of negative experiences. They also suggest that future research should examine how patients come to believe that their thoughts are beyond their own control.

■ How Safe Is This Conclusion?

The authors have interviewed only 12 people, six of whom were patients. Is it reasonable to draw conclusions from so small a **sample**? Qualitative data such as these are normally drawn from a small sample. It is a very different approach from that identified in Chapters 15 and 16. They are not concerned with **probability sampling**, but rather prefer to focus on the individual, arguing that the individual voice is a valid and authentic form of data. Therefore **purposive sampling** is appropriate. This is as systematic, in its own way, as random sampling, but it is designed to find specific groups of people who may possess or demonstrate a particular characteristic. In this case we saw that patients who had paranoid thoughts formed one group. The other required people with no psychiatric history who had reported experiencing some paranoid thoughts. They were identified through scores on a questionnaire in an earlier study. A **quantitative** researcher would argue that their sample was representative by outlining the un**bias**ed selection process. The qualitative researcher, by contrast, would argue that their sample was representative of the target population because its members had been carefully selected to have the right characteristics.

Qualitative approaches are philosophically different from quantitative methods. **Generalising** from the sample to the population is not the purpose here. Qualitative researchers do not attempt to say that their data represent all the data that would have been collected if everyone in the specified **population** had been included. Instead, they are saying that the data represent the views of the sample and that this provides us with information about the population (see Box 17.1).

Apart from generalisation, quantitative research stresses the importance of **reliability**. To what extent might the data from this research be considered reliable?

Box 17.1
Representative Samples and Generalisation: Purposive and Random/Systematic Sampling

Suppose our population is a class in a primary school and the aim of the research is to find out about their reading skills. Quantitative researchers want to sample, say, 20 per cent of the class. They can use a **random sampling** method, putting all the children's names in a hat and drawing out the required number. They can use **systematic sampling**, taking every fifth name from the register. Both these techniques provide the requisite number and remove any potential source of bias from the selection process. This does not ensure that the 20 per cent will be entirely representative of the class, but it does demonstrate that the researchers have followed best practice to achieve a representative sample. The selected children may, by chance, still not be representative, but by chance alone rather than any systematic bias. Qualitative researchers, on the other hand, might look at the characteristics of the children in the class and select their respondents accordingly. They may select some children who are confident readers and some who are trailing behind according to the teacher's records.

The objective of the quantitative researcher is to gain information from their sample that can be generalised to the rest of the population. Suppose they are measuring reading age. The reading age of the sample is generalised to describe the reading age of the class. (We can see that the bigger the sample the more confident we can be that its average reading age will be an accurate representation of the whole class.) The objective of the qualitative researcher is to discover how the children feel about learning to read. The data will show how both groups feel about reading. This information will provide insight into how *some* of the children will feel about reading, but this stops short of a generalisation. The research does not claim to have tapped into the feelings of all the children in the class, but shedding light on how some of them feel may help us understand the class as a whole. While the quantitative researcher strives towards generalisation, the qualitative one argues that as this is never certain, and so prefers a more realistic goal.

Some qualitative researchers eschew the idea of reliability, arguing that the centrality of the researcher's role means that others, presented with the same data, might come to different conclusions. This is not the view of all qualitative researchers and is not an invitation to ignore rigour or thoroughness of methodological approach. Some would argue that there are two requirements for qualitative research. The first is to outline the collection and analysis of data so thoroughly that another trained researcher presented with the same data would produce the same types of outcome. Campbell and Morrison provide exactly this level of information in their article. The second is that the outcome should be both a coherent and a plausible description of the phenomena under investigation. Again Campbell and Morrison have achieved this with their description of the **subjective** experience of paranoia. They have also been able to distinguish ways in which patients' and non-clinical respondents' experiences differ.

Nearly always, when the notion of reliability is raised, so is its twin concept, **validity**. How valid are the findings from the current study? In some ways validity is less of a problem for qualitative researchers generally because their approach frees respondents to put their own point of view. Contrast the difference between this method of using open questions at interview with the psychometric approach that requires respondents to complete a questionnaire or scale from which a number or classification is calculated by the researcher. That scale should be theoretically driven, designed and tested before data collection begins. If a person scores 46 on a measure of anxiety, the quantitative researcher may categorise that person as highly anxious, even if the word anxiety did not appear on the scale. In this latter instance respondents frequently do not even know the point of the research until afterwards, and not always then. Validity is, then, an issue as the researcher needs to be able to demonstrate that they have indeed measured anxiety as opposed to, say, introversion, melancholy or even intelligence. The interviewee, by contrast, is told what the interview will be about beforehand and is an active **participant** in the research process. When the researcher reports their findings the themes and the theory emerge from the data.

Nonetheless, in this study Campbell and Morrison used IPA, which does not claim to be objective. The analysis recognises the interpretative role of the researcher. So how do we know that the themes described in the paper come from the respondents rather than from the researchers? IPA uses illustrations from the original transcripts to demonstrate and illustrate themes. Researchers present examples from the interview, in part, as evidence for the existence of the themes. These quotations also illustrate and amplify the themes, allowing the reader to judge for themselves their validity.

Campbell and Morrison went one step further and made clinical recommendations on the basis of their analysis. If that analysis were purely a matter of personal interpretation it would not be safe to make recommendations about future therapeutic practice. Their paper provides many illustrative quotes to support their interpretation of the data. The authors also completed an extra phase in their analysis: **respondent validation**. This means that they consulted the respondents' views on the emergent themes. Some of the themes were subsequently updated in the light of the comments received.

The thoroughness of their approach provides the reader with considerable confidence in the given interpretation of the data.

● How Effective Is This Design?

In this particular study the researchers are interested in what the two groups have in common and how they differ. To what extent are these two groups comparable? Campbell and Morrison draw attention to some inequalities, as the groups were not matched on gender, age or socio-economic status. It is yet to be ascertained whether these factors affect the subjective experience in question. This study was the first to explore this area, and future studies may tell us about the role played by demographic factors.

The flexible use of an interview schedule meant that the respondents were free to express their own views, in their own words. This approach produces very rich idiographic data, which then, as we have seen, require analysis. This can be quite a daunting task. The transcription of an hour's worth of interview is likely to take several hours and possibly produce a dozen pages of script. In this instance there were 12 interviewees; this is a lot of material to analyse. Was there an alternative?

Interview methods can vary from the entirely **unstructured** at one extreme to the **fully structured** at the other. There are several types of unstructured interview. A **non-directive interview** allows the respondent to take the conversation in any direction that they want. In this instance it would have meant inviting each respondent to start up a conversation about themselves. They may or may not mention their paranoid thoughts. Their selection of material is seen as insightful and informative but, as you may imagine, the analysis is even more daunting than that outlined above. Slightly more organised is an **unstructured interview**, where the topic of conversation is specified but the route taken through the material is entirely individual. In this instance the interviewers might have invited people to talk about their paranoid thoughts and experiences but then allowed each interview to develop according to their responses. Alternatively, there may be an agenda for the interview where the overall topic is broken down into component issues, each of which needs to be discussed – although not necessarily in the same order. In this case the topics might have been the beliefs about paranoia, its functions, and their experiences of it, as well as discussion of other life events.

Campbell and Morrison used a **semi-structured interview** where not only were the topics set but the information sought was defined. For example, one of the topics was background information, and this included:

Can you tell me about your current situation?
How do you spend your time?
What are the things you enjoy?
Who is important to you? (2007, p.77)

The authors describe using this schedule 'flexibly', which we assume means that they did not have to ask each of these questions in turn if the information given already provided what was sought or if an alternative order felt more natural. Nor is it essential that the questions were asked using exactly the words given above. Minor relevant digressions are permitted and prompts for further information encouraged.

A fully structured interview means that the interviewer asks exactly the same questions, using the same words and in exactly the same order for each respondent. Digressions are not permitted and prompts should be standardised across all interviews. A fully structured interview might include the latter three questions above, asked in a standardised manner, but would be unlikely to include the first question, which is too broad for this purpose. All the questions used in Campbell and Morrison's interview were open questions. These are designed to encourage the respondent to answer fully and freely. **Closed questions** mean that only a limited number of responses are available. Examples of closed questions to replace those given above might be:

Are you currently in paid employment?
What is your job?
Do you have any hobbies?
Would you say you had a large circle of friends?

For three of these the answers are either 'Yes' or 'No'; the other requires some sort of job title. Sometimes interviews not only use closed questions but provide the interviewer with a range of possible answers from which the respondent must select one. These can be either subject descriptions or estimations of **objective data**:

How large would you say your circle of friends is:
    Very large
    Quite large
    Quite small
    Very small?

How large would you say your circle of friends is:
    More than 50
    15 to 50
    5 to 14
    Fewer than 5?

Sometimes the range of answers is read to the respondent, or else it is presented on a flash card for the respondent to read and select their own. This is most likely to happen if a series of questions is asked where each requires a response from the same set of possible responses. For example:

Please tell me how much you agree with each of the following statements using one of these five options:
    Strongly agree
    Agree

Neither agree nor disagree
Disagree
Strongly disagree

A fully structured interview using only closed questions is really the oral presentation of a questionnaire with the interviewer writing the responses instead of the respondent.

Had Campbell and Morrison used a different type of interview structure they would have gained different information. A looser structure might have produced some rich material but would probably have made a comparison between the two groups impractical. If they were not guided through the same material, then it is harder to assume that any omissions from responses of one group can be interpreted as a genuine group difference. A tighter structure would have meant that the researcher was framing or restricting the possible responses.

We know that respondents' answers were recorded and transcribed in this study. This is the **standardised procedure** when interviews are not fully structured, and sometimes even when they are. With an interview that is fully structured with closed questions there is no need to record, as the interviewer can either tick a box or write a single word or phrase as required. Some interviewers will take notes as they go along in preference to recording and then write up an account of the interchange. It is all too easy for the researcher's own interpretation or recall of events to colour that write-up and perhaps inadvertently distort the responses. For this reason, some would argue that a cross-check using respondent validation is advisable.

IPA is just one of many different ways of analysing qualitative data and qualitative researchers tend to have their own preferences for analyses. The authors describe their analysis as 'quite complex' and 'less than parsimonious' (2007, p.74). This is almost inevitable given that they had two tasks, to describe the subjective experience and to compare between groups. IPA was a good choice because its emphasis is on the relationship between language and internal state. The underlying assumption is that the words we use reflect our internal processes. By familiarising oneself with the way respondents discuss things, we can begin to interpret how they are experiencing and responding to phenomena. In just the same way as psychometrics assumes that answers to a scale give information about characteristics of a sample, so IPA assumes that the language used provides an insight into psychological processes. (For more information on qualitative analyses see Silverman 2006, Cresswell 2007 or Corbin & Strauss 2008.)

Campbell and Morrison could have used questionnaires with these open questions instead of interviews. What effect would that have had on the type of data collected?

▲ How Appropriate Is This Research Method?

Their stated aim was to find out about the subjective experience of paranoia, and we have seen how the semi-structured interview is likely to have been the most appropriate form of interview. Other **survey methods** could be used to provide different types of information. For example, Thewissen *et al.* (2008) used a structured form of diary self-assessment to study fluctuations in self-esteem and in paranoia. They found that low levels of self-esteem meant higher levels of paranoia. Coombs *et al.* (2007) deployed a battery of psychometric assessments on a large non-clinical sample and identified three different subtypes of paranoia. Gracie *et al.* (2007) used a similar approach with a sample of students and identified **correlations** between paranoia and other measures of psychological disturbance. These examples, all of which are quantitative incidentally, show that survey methods are useful in exploring paranoia, but finding its correlates makes a different type of contribution to our understanding. These methods would be unlikely to provide such rich data about the experience.

Observational studies are likely to be restricted to either case studies or observation of secondary data; it is unlikely that direct observation would play a useful role. **Experimentation** might tell us about the way in which paranoia affects performance. An example of this is the study by Shryane *et al.* (2008) who used an experimental task and showed that paranoia was associated with impairment in understanding of another person's point of view. Moritz and Laudan (2007) used a different experimental design to look at how threatening cues affect reaction times. They found that people with paranoia showed faster reactions directly after seeing a picture of a potentially threatening item such as a gun. This effect was not detected in the healthy **controls**. Again this is useful information in our understanding of the condition, but from a completely different perspective to that employed by Campbell and Morrison.

Conclusion

This study has given an insight into the subjective experience of schizophrenia in a way that probably would not have been achieved by different research designs. The authors have provided a detailed account of their method and analysis as well as clear illustrations from the original transcripts. By doing this they have met the criteria required of the qualitative researcher. We must be wary when reading such subjective accounts and not confuse self-report with fact. As with all survey methods, self-report is useful and instructional provided it is seen for what it is: a personal experience. Campbell and Morrison draw our attention to this distinction:

> All participants involved believed that negative life experiences contributed to their experience of paranoia; whilst this does not necessarily indicate that life experiences are causally related to paranoia we can conclude that negative life experiences are central to people's causal model of paranoia. (2007, p.74)

Summary Points	
Design	Survey methods: interview with open-ended questions
Aim	To find out about the subjective experience
Sample	Patients with diagnosis of schizophrenia (N=6) Non-patients with experience of paranoid thoughts (N=6)
Apparatus	Interview schedule, voice recorder, and Peters Delusions Inventory
Analysis	Interpretative Phenomenological Analysis (IPA)

Understanding Heavy Drinking

Survey Methods – Qualitative and Quantitative

'An alcoholic is someone you don't like who drinks as much as you do.'
(Dylan Thomas, poet, 1914–54)

Do You Like a Drink?

Alcohol seems to be part of the fabric of our civilisation. There are cultures within our society that refrain from drinking, but the dominant culture construes alcohol as perfectly acceptable. Alcohol is offered for celebrations and special occasions – we recognise the clink of glasses and the pop of champagne corks as symbolising celebration. It is also proffered at times of crisis and misery too, to help numb the pain of loss or disappointment, or just to help you brace up and carry on. Alcohol is portrayed in the media as a social and often glamorous activity. It is used as a prop, literally and figuratively. Bars that sell alcohol are intended to be social places. The disinhibiting effect of alcohol helps people relax, eases socialisation and is perceived as making a party go with a swing.

Alcohol consumption is not a recent development. Far from it: its history can be traced back as far as 7000 years BC. Archaeologists have found the remains of vessels from that period in China which had been used to ferment a drink made of rice, honey and fruit. Ancient civilisations in Egypt, Greece and Rome all made and consumed alcohol, usually beer or wine, although by 3000 BC Indian civilisation had learned to distil. In medieval Europe and colonial North America, until relatively recently in terms of human history, 'small beer' (a fairly weak beverage by all accounts) was the main drink for people of all ages at all times of the day. It was considerably safer to drink than water, which was polluted and dangerous until the engineering developments of the nineteenth century. Historically, there have been fluctuations in the way that the consumption of alcohol is tolerated. In the UK, there was rising concern in the middle of the eighteenth century about the ready consumption of gin, which was cheap and easily available. Beer was seen as a much safer option, as epitomised by Hogarth's cartoons of Gin Lane, a place of decline and debauchery, and Beer Alley, where the inhabitants are prosperous and content. Parliament finally set limits on the consumption of gin. A similar phenomenon occurred in the United States in 1920, when the manufacture, transportation and sale of alcohol were made illegal. This lasted for just 13 years and was repealed under pressure, as many social problems were attributed to prohibition and its resultant black market.

In the UK in 1979, the Royal College of Psychiatrists set out guidelines for sensible drinking which, at eight units of alcohol a day, are now considered to be generous. In 1992 the government paper *The Health of the Nation* set tighter guidelines: 21 units per week for men and 14 for women. These days there is much media concern about young people's use of alcohol and the problems and dangers of binge-drinking. It would seem that being inebriated is not perceived as a problem in some circles, and indeed for many it is a frequent occurrence. It is not just the young who are drinking more than is recommended; there is concern about other age groups too. According to the Institute of Psychiatry the proportion of males drinking over the recommended limit has remained stable at just under a third, but the proportion of women exceeding their recommended limit has been rising and is now approximately one-fifth of the female population. Health professionals are concerned about the inevitable rise in related health problems that our current drinking patterns will generate. Excessive alcohol consumption can lead to increased risks of some forms of cancer, brain damage, liver problems, heart disease and stroke. These are the main killers in Western society already, and we seem to be encouraging them by our current behaviour. At a societal level, there is evidence of an increasing problem.

The healthy drinking guidelines are given as units of alcohol because different types of alcohol have different strengths, and a unit represents 8 g of ethanol. By developing a standard unit the guidelines can be applied across the board. Some bottles now indicate on their label how many units they contain, but most do not. The problem is that very few people know how to calculate them – the Institute of Psychiatry suggests that the proportion of people who can is as low as 8 per cent. It is evident that health educators are not getting their message across, and this may be one of the reasons. The measurement of alcohol content is little understood by most people, and this means that ideas about what represents acceptable, sensible or even excessive drinking will be varied. Our image of what constitutes drunkenness is pretty well understood by most people, but that is a different issue. What do you think constitutes excessive drinking? The Dylan Thomas quote at the start of the chapter provides us with one sort of definition, but it may be quite an accurate description of how some people define what is excessive, as we shall see.

If measuring alcohol units is a problem for drinkers, measuring people's attitudes to drink is a problem for psychologists. There are quick screening tools designed to help people tell whether they are drinking too much, such as the Alcohol Use Disorders Identification Test (AUDIT) (World Health Organisation, 2001). There are also clinical tools designed to look at alcohol dependence, such as Leeds Dependency

Questionnaire (Raistrick *et al.*, 1994), which was developed to measure exactly that – *dependence*. Alcohol dependence is a clinical concept identified by compulsive use, lack of control and an inability to prioritise other activities. Thus defined, dependency is an extreme state, not necessarily characteristic of all heavy drinkers or all of those who exceed the current guidelines. If we confuse dependency and heavy drinking it will not help us to understand people's approach to alcohol or their own drinking. This was the issue tackled by Hartney *et al.* (2003). They argued that the conceptualisation had been dominated by the clinical field, based on **data** from alcohol-dependent patients. They used a **mixed methods** approach, **quantitative** and **qualitative**, to explore this. There were two novel **aims** to their research: to assess the adequacy of the current models of drinking for a group of heavy but non-clinical drinkers, and to discover how heavy drinkers view dependence.

Untreated Heavy Drinkers: A Qualitative and Quantitative Study of Dependence and Readiness to Change

Hartney, E., Orford, J., Dalton, S., Ferrins-Brown, M., Kerr, C. & Maslin, J. (2003). *Addiction Research & Theory, 11*(5), 317–337

Method

Hartney *et al.* (2003) recruited their **sample** (**N**=500) using advertisements and word of mouth, a combination of **convenience** and **snowball sampling**. To be eligible to be included, **respondents** had to have consumed over twice the recommended guidelines for most weeks in the previous year. All respondents were interviewed by trained researchers, and these interviews were recorded. All respondents completed the Leeds Dependency Questionnaire (LDQ) and also the Readiness to Change

Questionnaire – RCQ (Rollnick *et al.*, 1992). This is a scale that was developed to determine whether a heavy drinker was ready to change his/her drinking habits, and its **validity** had been established (Heather *et al.* 1993). Respondents can be classified as being in one of three stages of change: *precontemplation*, meaning they are not even thinking about changing; *contemplation*, where they are beginning to consider the need for change; or *action*, which means they are making changes to their behaviour. Two subsets, each of 25 people, were identified, and data from these interviews transcribed verbatim and examined; in one subset the focus of the analysis was the subject of dependence and in the other the readiness to change.

Results – Quantitative

The LDQ has a response range of 'nearly always', 'often', 'sometimes' and 'never'. For eight of the 10 items in the scale the **modal** response was 'never' and for the remaining two it was 'sometimes'. This suggests that this scale was not really appropriate for this sample. These people were not dependent in the clinical sense and did not relate to the items in the scale. The RCQ has two methods of scoring, one simple and one complex. This may seem a little odd, but the simple one is for use in the clinical setting, the complex one for research. With this sample, these two scoring systems produced very different answers: the simple method placed 68 per cent in the contemplation stage, but with the complex method this figure was reduced to 39 per cent. This meant that categorisation for this sample was unreliable and unhelpful. The individual responses were examined and showed that about 40 per cent of the sample were reporting responses from more than one of these stages. The authors argue that the RCQ is not suitable for this sample as it assumes the stages of change to be discrete and separate, yet these respondents were evidently selecting items from different stages.

Results – Qualitative

The data were analysed using **grounded theory**, which involves repeated sampling and analysis of data – an iterative process. The object is to develop a theoretical framework based on the responses of the respondents. The data from the interviews about alcohol dependence identified four elements in the respondents' perceptions of dependency. The first was an evaluation of the motives for drinking: are there socially acceptable reasons for having a drink? The implied association is that dependent drinkers have unacceptable reasons for drinking. The second was their opinions of other drinkers, in particular those they perceived as problematic. The third issue related to the idea of taboos about drinking, each of which was cited as indicative of dependence, for example, keeping a hidden supply of alcohol. The final factor concerned physical problems of dependence, such as tremors. These four main elements were used to indicate respondents' implicit ideas about alcohol dependence. Respondents would compare their own behaviour to these in order to demonstrate their own lack of dependence. (This social comparison is familiar theme in psychology. We tend to select our comparators in order to consolidate our own point of view.) It was evident that their social environment was an important aspect of their drinking behaviour.

The data from the interviews on readiness to change also showed respondents comparing their own drinking behaviour with that of others and again reference was made to what was socially acceptable. These interviews also considered prompts to change, including being advised to do so, and reasons based on finances, health and body weight. Change in behaviour was often seen as being linked to other life transitions, for example, pregnancy or moving house, or it might require a change in social relationships. There was an element of tension and contradiction in some of the dialogues, suggesting that the drinkers were aware of the possible need to change and at the same time were able to distance themselves from such thoughts.

Taken together, the quantitative and qualitative data suggested that both models of dependence and stages of change were inappropriate for this sample in that the respondents had quite a distinctive way of viewing dependence and establishing their own distance from it.

■ How Safe Are These Conclusions?

These data paint a picture of how heavy drinkers view dependence and their own drinking behaviour in relation to it. To decide how safe these conclusions are we need to examine this sample in a little more detail.

The sample was recruited through advertising and by word of mouth. This means that the participants were largely **self-selected** as they were volunteering to respond to an invitation. This is clearly not **probability sampling** – is this a problem? Probability sampling here would have involved recruiting a very large number of people and asking all of them for details of their drinking habits, before selecting those who would qualify as heavy drinkers. This would not be very cost-effective, and it might also be problematic in recruitment. Those who were identified as heavy drinkers might not have been willing to discuss their drinking, and this would, thereby, have restricted the numbers who took part. The way that Hartney and colleagues recruited their sample ensured that those who came forward were willing to talk about their drinking, which is a more efficient way of collecting data.

The question then becomes: to what extent were these 500 people representative of other heavy drinkers? This is harder to answer as we cannot know whether our known sample is representative of our unknown **population**. With 500 respondents we can assume that their views are representative of at least a reasonable proportion of heavy drinkers. There is no reason to assume that these 500 would be markedly different from all the rest of the heavy drinkers in the country. So with some reservations about the universal applicability of what they have found, we can be confident that they have identified a real trend.

Hartney *et al.* argued that the **psychometric measures** from past research were unsuitable for this sample. This raises the question of how their respondents differed from those in previous research. If the samples were not comparable, then differences would tell us little. Suppose you tried out a reading test for 6-year-olds on a group of adults: you would hardly be surprised if it did not show much variation in responses. Stating that the test was no good for discriminating amongst adults would not come as a surprise. If the heavy drinkers in this study were plainly different from those in previous research, then this would explain why the scales turned out to be unsuitable.

The authors provide us with details about their sample so that we can decide for ourselves how comparable it is to those used in earlier studies. The age of this sample is compared with that of the alcohol-dependent sample in the study by Raistrick *et al.* (1994) and by those in the study by Heather *et al.* (1993). There are no major differences in any of the other **demographic variables** to suggest that this sample is out of line with that in the other studies. As for self-reported weekly alcohol consumption, that of the sample in the study by Hartney *et al.* is less than that of the dependent sample from Raistrick *et al.*, but more than the nondependent sample from the same study, and also more than that of the excessive drinkers in the study by Heather *et al.* This sample seemed to represent a population that lay between the clinical and community samples in the Raistrick *et al.* study. In comparison to the Heather *et al.* study, this sample was larger and had a greater percentage of women and professional workers. Despite these minor differences, the comparison between the samples seems appropriate.

If we accept this, the next issue to address is whether those selected for interview, the two sets of 25 taken from the sample of 500, were representative of the sample as a whole. For that matter, we need to know how they were selected. Hartney *et al.* tell us the criteria for selection, which were based on the quality of the interview recording and ensuring the representative nature of the subgroups by monitoring sex, age, occupation and alcohol intake. They provide the reader with these details, so that readers can decide for themselves to what extent this **stratified sampling** has been achieved. The percentage figures for the main sample and the two subgroups, for each of these criteria, cannot realistically be expected to be identical. The important feature is that they should be plausibly comparable, which they are.

By providing the reader with detailed information, the authors have given ample evidence about the representative nature of the sample and the subsets. This allows us to have confidence in their conclusions.

● How Effective Is the Research Design?

In some ways this is an unusual study in that in the authors have selected two psychometric measures to use and have then presented data and arguments showing why these measures are unsuitable! In most research studies justification of chosen methods is a more common theme. It was different in this study because the researchers were setting out to see whether the current measures of drinkers' attitudes to alcohol were suitable for this type of respondent. Their data showed this not to be the case.

The quantitative data provided largely negative results; is this, in itself, a cause for concern?

What would you usually conclude if a researcher told you that the measuring scales they used were unsuitable for their sample?

It is not possible to set out to show negative results. It is never appropriate, for example, to have a **null hypothesis** as your **experimental hypothesis**. You cannot decide to show that two groups do not differ. It is a bit like the jury system in some ways: the prosecution has to establish guilt; the defence counsel is not required to establish innocence. (See Box 6.1 for further discussion of the logic of hypothesis testing.) Normally a study that uses inappropriate measurement tools for its sample would stand accused of a poor research design. Think back to the example of the reading tests for 6-year-olds used on adults. There would be no justification for selecting such a measure with such a sample. Why use a measure that is inappropriate?

In this instance, the selection of tools was a reasonable choice as they were validated measures for an apparently comparable group: dependent drinkers. Using them for non-dependent but heavy drinkers is the beginning of trying to under-stand the difference between the two types of drinker. If the responses had simply shown a different pattern of positive responses, this would have allowed these meas-ures to be used for non-clinical drinkers. As we have seen, this was not the case; the data were largely negative as the items did not seem to resonate with the sample. What can be inferred from this? Hartney *et al.* wanted to explore this further, so they compared the **factor structure** of responses from these data with that of earlier research. They used **factor analysis** to find out what might be the underlying factors shaping people's responses (see Box 18.1).

Hartney *et al.* found that the factor structure for the RCQ data was similar to that in the study by Heather *et al.* In contrast, the LDQ had been shown to have a single factor in the study by Raistrick *et al.*, but in this study it clearly had two factors: one which they called 'drinking ideation', which involved planning and thinking about drinking, and the other which they called 'achieving and maintaining intoxication'. By incorporating these assessments, the comparison between the past research and the current study is made clearer. The fact that the two samples produced different factor structures is further evidence that the scale is not working as intended for this population.

The results from the study are not entirely negative, because of the nature of the research design. In combining both quantitative and qualitative data the researchers have not just shown that the existing scales are inadequate for this population, but have given us an indication how this group of drinkers thinks about dependency and readiness to change.

This was a **single sample** study, in spite of the two subgroups. The researchers collected data from 500 people, all of whom fitted the study criterion for what con-stitutes a 'heavy drinker'. You might have expected them to collect data from a

Understanding Factors

Factor analysis is used in many types of research, but perhaps most commonly with psychometric measurements such as those used in the studies in this chapter and in Chapter 16. It is a statistical procedure that looks at relationships within the data and identifies underlying factors. This is not always easy to grasp when first encountered.

Suppose we had a rating scale that was designed to measure attitudes to smoking. If we ran factor analysis on data collected using this scale we might find that it showed there were three underlying factors in people's responses. It would do this by number-crunching and **correlating** the responses. The outcome of this would group items together – in this instance factor analysis would produce three groupings of items. This would suggest that there were three underlying factors that influence people's responses to the scale.

Factor analysis does the maths, but the researcher has to interpret the findings. The only way to do this is by looking at the content of the items in those groupings. Suppose that one of our three groupings included items about the health effects of smoking both for the smoker and for those affected by secondary smoking. We would probably label this factor 'health'. Another grouping of items might include reference to the smell and taste of tobacco and the waste products of smoking (cigarette butts and ash), so we might label this factor 'experiences'. Our third grouping might comprise items about smoking prohibitions, where and when people are allowed to smoke. We might decide to call this one 'restrictions'. One important thing to notice about these groupings is that they might include positively and negatively worded items; for example 'experiences' might include items like 'I enjoy the taste of cigarettes' and 'I dislike the smell of tobacco smoke'. People who experience smoking positively would be expected to agree with the first item but not the second.

If we wanted to check that this factor structure was effective, we would need to collect a second lot of data and undertake **confirmatory factor analysis**. We could also look at the **internal reliability** of each factor. Wei *et al.* (see Chapter 16) did both of these things in the development of their scale.

The idea of the factors here is that they would be three constructs that underlie people's responses to the scale. For example, a man might score negatively on say, health and experiences, but positively on restrictions. This would mean that he considers cigarettes a health threat and does not personally like the smell/taste/residue, but that he is against formal restrictions on people's liberty to smoke. This underlying factor structure helps us understand how people might feel about the topic of smoking.

different sample, perhaps a group clinically identified as dependent, and compared the results from the two. That would have been one way to approach the matter. This was a neater design than that, given the research objectives. They wanted to see whether these scales were useful for this group of drinkers. Their use had already been demonstrated with clinically dependent drinkers, so there was no need to collect further data to establish this. Moreover, the validation studies of these two scales had reported enough detail of their respective samples, and psychometric properties, to enable a comparison. This is one example where we can begin to see the need for, and the benefits of, publishing validity and reliability data. As this comparison with existing data was possible it was the most **parsimonious** approach to answering the research question. In research, a parsimonious approach is usually the best way. Two groups here would not have told us any more than the one group did. Remember **Occam's razor**!

▲ How Appropriate Is This Method?

Given their objectives, it is hard to visualise how else the authors might have been able to set about this task. **Survey methods** seem to be the only option when the research question is about the suitability of survey measures! They could perhaps have incorporated other measures as well as those taken – but until the inadequacy of those two scales had been demonstrated there was no requirement to look at other measures. To do so would not have conformed with the Occam's razor principle. Furthermore the selection of other scales would have been largely guesswork given the lack of information on this particular group. Other researchers have noted problems with our current assessment tools. Keyes and Hasin (2008) used survey methods to examine the relationship between income and alcohol misuse. They suggest that current diagnostic criteria for alcohol abuse require revision. Survey methods have been used extensively in the area of alcohol misuse. For example, Wu *et al.* (2007), using survey methods, found comorbidity of alcohol abuse and depression amongst teenagers.

The issue of alcohol misuse can be explored using other methods, to improve our understanding of the topic as a whole rather than testing scales. For example, **observation** of **secondary data** was used by Augustin-Normand and Consigny (2007), who looked at the data on admissions of teenagers to emergency rooms, over a six-month period, in a French hospital to determine the extent of excessive alcohol consumption amongst the this sample. Hazelton *et al.* (2003) used another observation method by describing a **case study** of an 88-year-old woman with a history of alcohol abuse, amongst other problems, and outlined clinical and ethical considerations for the care of such cases. As with any condition or pathology it is possible to use **randomised controlled trials** to evaluate the efficacy of treatments. Paschall *et al.* (2006) evaluated a web course to educate new undergraduates about alcohol and found it **significantly** improved knowledge about alcohol and increased negative attitudes to alcohol misuse. Markowitz *et al.* (2008) used a similar methodological approach to compare two types of psychological therapy for depressed patients who also had a history of alcohol misuse. The particular sample in the study by Hartney *et al.* might have made a suitable group for **action research**, given their willingness to talk openly about their drinking. This could lead to assessing ways of helping people to reduce their drinking, involving the participants actively in the development of the research process.

Conclusion

Apart from the stated aims of the study, there were two reasons why this work was required. First, this group of non-clinical heavy drinkers is a concern to the health professions but has been somewhat neglected in research, which has had a tendency to focus on clinical samples. Secondly, finding out more about this group of, as yet, non-dependent drinkers may help in understanding the way dependency can develop. The qualitative data from this study provided an insight into the perceptions of this group. Hartney *et al.* (2004) highlighted an equivalence they had found between views in their community sample and those of clinicians:

> An interesting parallel between the untreated heavy drinkers who participated in our study and the professionals who attempt to understand and treat substance use problems described by Raistrick *et al.* (1994), is that both are divided between those who believe dependence to be of crucial importance, and those who consider it to be unimportant or non-existent. (2004, p.191)

Summary Points	
Design	Survey methods: questionnaires and interviews
Aims	To assess the adequacy of the current models of drinking for a group of heavy drinkers To discover how heavy drinkers view dependence
Sample	Heavy drinkers (N=500)
Materials & apparatus	Leeds Dependency Questionnaire (LDQ) and also Readiness to Change Questionnaire – RCQ (Rollnick *et al.*, 1992) and a voice recorder
Analysis	Grounded theory

Attributing Success and Failure

Cross-Cultural Study Using Mixed Methods

'Success and failure. We think of them as opposites, but they're really not. They're companions – the hero and the sidekick.' (Laurence Shames, author, b. 1951)

How Are Our Athletes Doing?

For two weeks every four years the Olympic Games draw the attention of the world. Athletes from nations across the globe come together in a spirit of peaceful but earnest competition, based on universal moral principles. The modern Olympiad began in 1896 in Athens, with London hosting the thirtieth in 2012. Over 200 countries take part in over 300 different events watched by over 4 billion people worldwide. Nations are divided into two groups: those who remain locked by their television sets for the fortnight and those who complain that the Olympics have taken over all other forms of news and entertainment. But love them or hate them, the Olympics grab the attention of many and become a preoccupation of some. The Olympian goal is 'to place sport at the service of the harmonious development of man, with a view to promoting a peaceful society concerned with the preservation of human dignity' (Olympic Charter, 1 September 2004). To achieve this laudable goal, world-class athletes compete on an equal footing for gold medals and for the critical acclaim of their peers and their nation. The Olympian ideal brooks no discrimination, but is based on respect for universal and fundamental ethical principles.

With such a literal level playing field, what could be a better forum for a cross-cultural study?

You may have noticed that during television coverage of the games, when there is no real Olympic news, the channels broadcast seemingly endless commentary. From competitors, trainers, managers, or pundits, everyone has something to say about why this person won or that person lost; why this person failed to live up to expectations or why that person exceeded them. This commentary was the object of a study by Markus *et al.* (2006). They thought that while the competitors may be treated equally on the track, the rhetoric surrounding their performance may not be so uniform. In their study of the language used in such commentaries they contrasted two cultures, American and Japanese.

This **cross-cultural** comparison differs in style from the classic studies of the early to mid twentieth century. Cross-cultural comparisons tended to take an **etic** approach, identifying common features of societies as viewed by outsiders, for example scholars (contrast this with **emic** in the Glossary). These usually compared 'simple' societies with the industrialised West. One example is Mead's **ethnographic** account of Samoan lifestyle (1928). Other researchers took a more **experimental** approach, such as Deregowski *et al.* (1972), who showed that susceptibility to some visual illusions differs between cultures.

In contrast, Markus *et al.*'s cross-cultural study compared data from two industrialised nations, two major world economies, who have more in common with each other than do those contrasted to our own Western culture by Deregowski, amongst others. However, in spite of globalisation, the communications revolution and the World Wide Web, these two nations still have very different cultures and each has a distinctive ethos. Markus and colleagues looked at these differences by comparing the language used to discuss each country's athletic performance in the Olympics. Such a comparison of two technologically similar societies means that any differences found are purely cultural and not simply a product of different stages of social and industrial development.

Established cultural differences were the starting point for their comparison. There is a wealth of literature that shows that East Asian cultures are less likely than Western societies to attribute behaviour to individual personality traits. Attributions are more likely to be made to the situation rather than the individual. If someone does well, people in the East may attribute this to the circumstances or the timing of events. Those in the West are more likely to point to the individual. Markus *et al.* suggest that to consider the individual as a single entity, a disposition or personality, is misleading. They argue that it is better to break down the different aspects of an individual – such as history, motivation, goals and circumstances – and treat them as separate components.

The authors are interested in what are termed 'sociocultural models'. These are ideas and values that are embedded in the surrounding society and culture. Members of the society acquire these as part of the socialisation process. These ideas and values may come from the dominant ideologies of the society, and they act as a framework for the types of explanations and attributions in common use. The particular focus of their research was to explore the ways in which the two societies being studied talk about activities and achievements, and the language that is used to explain their outcomes, which the authors refer to as the 'construction of agency' (2006, p.104).

The authors argue that agency is construed in the USA as a separate or 'disjointed' component of the individual. It is seen as distinct from not only circumstances but also from other components of the person such as history, abilities, or state of mind.

By contrast, countries in South-East Asia are more likely to take a holistic view. They see agency as part of and affected by other personal attributes, and by the environment. As the two cultures are diverse, it could be problematic finding equivalent situations from which to draw comparisons. Activities taken from everyday life would have been affected by those very sociocultural values under investigation, and this would hamper any subsequent comparison. The authors neatly overcame this potential problem by using the common context of the Olympic Games. While the selection and training for the games may be culturally determined, once in competition, athletes, by definition, perform a standardised activity. Therefore, an examination of the language used to describe this common activity should identify any sociocultural differences in the construction of agency, which was the **aim** of the study.

The first section of their paper describes an **observational study**. Some people refer to this style of study as **indirect observation** as the researchers are not observing behaviour as such but rather analysing information that has already been collected for another purpose altogether – in this case, broadcast news. **Data** such as these, that have been gathered for a purpose independent of, and prior to, the study in question, are usually referred to as **secondary data**. The authors examined television and printed sources to compare coverage in the two countries. They predicted that while American explanations of Olympic performance would concentrate on the personal characteristics of the athletes, Japanese accounts would include other aspects of the individual such as history, subjective state and also the context of the performance. Therefore, the first **null hypothesis** was that the number of themes found in the two cultures would be the same; the first **alternative hypothesis** was that more themes would be found in the Japanese coverage than in the American. The second hypothesis was to do with the ways in which these themes were evoked, the prediction being that American commentary would cover more positive than negative features, while there would be no such distinction in the Japanese material.

Going for the Gold: Models of Agency in Japanese and American Contexts

Markus, H.R., Uchida, Y., Omoregie, H., Townsend, S.S.M. & Kitayama, S. (2006). *Psychological Science, 17*(2), 103–112

Method 1

The first task for Markus *et al.* was to collect the coverage, and for this they identified 342 athletes competing in the summer Olympics of 2000 and the winter games of 2002. Of these, 77 were Japanese and approximately 1 in 4 won a medal. They collected coverage on these individuals from major television networks, newspapers and magazines in each country. As you can imagine, this produced a large amount of qualitative data – the task then was to turn this into a form that was amenable to analysis and that allowed the hypotheses to be tested.

The first step in this process was to develop a **coding frame**, which is a means of identifying different categories of the types of explanation used in the coverage. For this, selections of the English-language television coverage were watched by two American coders and by two bilingual Japanese coders who also viewed selections of the Japanese footage. Their task was to undertake a **thematic analysis** which would identify and then categorise all the commentary on the athletes and their perfor-mance, whether by journalists, commentators or the athletes themselves. From this preliminary step, 124 specific themes were identified and therefore became the cod-ing frame. The second step of the process required the coders to examine the remain-ing coverage on the target athletes and code all the commentary using these specific themes.

In order to use these data to test the hypothesis, through discussion, the 124 spe-cific themes were grouped into seven major categories, and then a percentage calcu-lated, initially for each athlete and subsequently for each country. This percentage figure represented the frequency with which each concept was used as part of the total commentary, and allowed the percentage use of each concept to be compared between countries.

Results 1

The seven categories are listed in Table 19.1 in the order of frequency of occurrence for the sample as a whole. 'Personal characteristics' was used more than any other category in both countries although it was used **significantly** more frequently by the Americans. References to the competition itself were also used significantly more frequently by the Americans. Four of the remaining categories were used signifi-cantly more frequently by the Japanese; only the reference to motivational states did not differ between the two countries. Thus the American commentary focused on two areas of explanation while the Japanese one was broader, tending to use four categories more frequently.

Table 19.1. Frequency of themes used

Category	Content	Percentage used American	Percentage used Japanese
1. Personal characteristics	Mental or physical attributes	32*	24
2. Athletic background	Length of time in sport, previous success or failure	13	20*
3. Competition	Standard of the other competitors and/or the experience of competition	16*	8
4. Other people	Family, friends, coaches or team-mates	7	10*
5. Reaction to Olympic Games	Evaluation of performance or future plans	2	9*
6. Motivational state	Positive attitudes to athletics, motivation to win	4	5
7. Emotional state	e.g. 'Happiest feeling in my judo life' (Markus *et al.*, 2006, p.106)	2	5*

* Used significantly more frequently than in other country.

This appears to provide support for their first hypothesis (H_1), but the researchers chose to explore this further by calculating the **mean** number of categories used by the media of each nation for reporting each athlete's performance. For the United States this was 6.54 compared with Japan's 13.09. The authors conclude that, as predicted, the Japanese draw on a wider variety of themes than do their counterparts in the United States.

■ How Safe Is This Conclusion?

This seems to be potentially an interesting contrast between two cultures, but how safe are these findings? You may have noticed that the sample included very many more American athletes than Japanese, and this may feel as though this would **bias** the results in some way. However, the researchers took account of this and presented, instead, the percentage of each type of comment used rather than the raw figures. This is a neat way of accounting for samples of differing sizes (see Box 19.1).

What about the coding frame – how **objective** is that likely to be? Both nationalities contributed to the coding frame, which provides a degree of balance – but could the coders themselves have been biased by the predictions? Thankfully they were not, because they were kept **blind** to the hypotheses. The researchers briefed the coders about the theories of attribution and agency, but they were not told what this particular study was comparing; therefore there is no reason to believe that they were biased in their categorisation.

Percentages

Percentages can be a useful way of presenting data. They are quite easy to calculate to present **frequency data**. To calculate you divide the frequency of the item by the total for the sample and multiply by 100. If the sample of 270 people includes 54 who own hamsters, then the percentage of hamster owners is 54/270 × 100, which is 20 per cent. We find it much easier to understand the proportion when it is presented as a percentage than when trying to juggle and interpret slightly clumsy numbers. Percentages are often the best way of presenting frequency data. Having said that, they should be used with caution. There are two occasions when percentages help the reader to understand the data:

1. When the sample is large. If **N**>100 then percentages may be helpful, and the larger the sample, the more helpful the percentage. If our population is 436,589 strong and our hamster owners number 87,318, most of us would have difficulty hanging on to these numbers, never mind interpreting them, but we might be able to have a grasp of the data if we are told that hamster owners constitute 20 per cent.
2. When comparing groups of dissimilar sizes (as in the example in this chapter). If our Narnian sample has N=45 and the Lilliputian sample has N= 63, comparisons between them are difficult to grasp. If 17 Narnians and 21 Lilliputians own unicorns, it takes a bit of effort to work out whether unicorn owning is more common amongst Narnians or Lilliputians. Presenting this as frequency information – 38 per cent and 33 per cent respectively – makes interpretation easier.

When calculating percentages it is usually advisable to round to the nearest whole number; knowing that 33.3 per cent of the respondents are cat owners does not tell us any more than knowing that 33 per cent are. Decimal places for percentages are usually only justified when a difference between two figures can only be seen in the first decimal place, for example, comparing cat owners with dog owners who comprised 33.9 per cent of the same sample.

There are two golden rules for using percentages:

1. Always ensure that the N (at least, the overall N) is also presented.
2. Never use percentages for small samples unless comparing between different-sized subgroups. When percentages are used for small samples they can be misleading. If I tell you that in my sample 40 per cent of people said they did not like chocolate you might consider this an interesting finding. If it turns out that my N=5, it is less so.

If you think about the type of commentary that is normally made about athletes, the comments on which these codes were based, another thought may have occurred to you. There would seem to be a striking difference between a comment such as 'She won because she was fit', and 'The reason she lost was because she was unfit'. Each of these categories could be used positively or negatively. What if one culture used a category predominantly in a negative way while the other's use was largely positive? Unless this is taken into account then the results might actually be obscuring more than they are revealing.

Fortunately, the researchers explored this as part of a second hypothesis, which predicted that, while Japanese commentary would be both negative and positive, American commentary would focus on the positive attributes of the athletes' actions. In this context, positive comments included strengths and successes, as well as positive emotional or motivational states; negative comments comprised weaknesses, failures and negative emotional or motivational states. They compared the use of negative and positive comments by the two countries. Over the sample as a whole, positive comments were used significantly more than negative comments in each country. There was no significant difference between the countries in their use of positive statements, but the Japanese made significantly more negative attributions.

The authors conclude that this provides evidence to support their second hypothesis (H_2) and that this finding is in line with past research that has shown American culture is more likely to focus on boosting the individual, or, as the authors put it: 'revealing the self-enhancing attributional style common in American contexts' (2006, p.108).

From Observation to Experiment

In order to extend this research, Markus and colleagues moved from using observation to the next phase, an **experiment** using **survey methods**. This is a good example of testing the **validity** of the findings. Having established an apparent difference in extant materials, namely news reports, these findings can then be tested by adopting a completely different research approach.

Method 2

This time, instead of using existing materials, the authors created their own materials and presented these as the **stimuli** in their experiment. They recruited a sample of 120 students, 60 from each country. They used a **vignette study**, namely they presented the **respondents** with an account of a fictitious athlete, a marathon runner, changing her name to fit the cultural background for each of the two groups. This account comprised 40 statements about the athlete, representing nine categories of response, which were developed from the themes identified in the first study. The **participants** were asked to select the 15 statements that they believed to be most relevant, five of which they were to identify as 'indispensable'. The hypotheses for this second study were the same as for the first, namely that the Japanese would choose more themes and that the Americans would focus primarily on positive attributes.

Results 2

Six of the nine categories of commentary showed a **significant** difference in ratings between the two countries. The Americans were more likely to identify statements relating to personal attributes (e.g. 'remarkable', 'interesting and energetic') and to uniqueness (e.g. 'she stood out from the crowd'). In contrast the Japanese selected statements relating to her coach or team-mates (e.g. 'helping her develop her strategy'), her motivation, emotion and doubt. This finding provides further support for the first hypothesis about the tendency of Western culture to focus on the individual. Furthermore, the data showed that American participants selected more positive statements than negative, while the Japanese selected a similar number of each valence. This effect of culture and valence was shown to be significant, thereby providing support for the second hypothesis.

■ How Safe Is This Conclusion?

It may have occurred to you that there is potential for a problem in the interpretation of these results. Consider this: the account of each athlete was the same for both cultures, yet we already know that commentary across cultures differs. Therefore, could the Japanese participants have responded to the athlete's description quite differently from the Americans? For example, as the text used positive and negative comments, this could have had a negative effect on the Americans' appraisal of the athlete. Remember, we know from the first study that American commentary normally concentrates on the positive. For the Japanese the use of both types of statement would have appeared quite commonplace. We have a problem if one group perceived a mediocre athlete while the other saw an elite performer. Such an effect would create a problem for this study; the interpretation of the findings hinges on the stimulus material being the same for both groups. It would mean that we could not safely interpret these results.

The authors, however, took steps to ensure there was no such dilemma. As well as selecting statements from the accounts of the athlete, respondents also had to rate her using a seven-point scale on three dimensions: her likeability, her effectiveness as an athletic role model, and the extent to which she was typical of athletes in their country. There was no difference in the ratings of the two cultures on any of the three dimensions. Clearly both samples came to similar conclusions about the credibility of this athlete. This means that, after all, we can say that the findings support the hypotheses.

What Does This Tell Us About the Cultures?

To explain these findings the authors returned to their description of agency. They argued that their data supported a disjointed view of agency in the United States compared with a holistic view in Japan. Where Americans see the seeds of sporting success within the individual, in Japan the origin of success is perceived to be in the context as much as in the athlete.

What can we infer from this study? The object of research is to learn more about our world; we examine a sample and hope to be able to generalise our findings. What can be generalised from this study? Americans tend to focus on the person and the Japanese take a broader view. Americans avoid negativity but the Japanese do not. There may be some truth in this, but we must not be carried away. These data tell us how the two countries differ in the language used for athletic commentary. It is true that this language is a product of a larger culture. It is also true that the distinction found in the study may be found in other aspects of these two nations. But it would be folly to assume this is so without further evidence. These two cultures have much in common when set against the variety of societies across the planet. It may be that their commonality is greater than their differences. The average American has a lifestyle that is closer to that of the average Japanese than can be found in many other countries. Our global economy has meant that there are many common features in industrialised and developed countries. Indeed, many argue that such countries are becoming homogenous. The major cultural differences lie between the developed and the developing or underdeveloped nations. Nevertheless, Markus and colleagues have shown us how two developed nations may vary in their view of a common activity.

● How Effective Is This Method?

This study used a **mixed methods** approach in two discrete phases. This means that the data from the second phase can be used to support and **validate** the findings from the first study.

Why Study the Media?

We know that this study did more than just look at the newspapers, but it is a fair question. We are all encouraged to be sceptical about what we read in the papers. Many would argue that we should be equally cautious about news coverage in other media as well. With this level of uncertainty, is it reasonable to study the popular media in this way? Are they a legitimate object of study?

The answer has to be yes. We saw in Chapter 12 how an analysis of one medium, young women's magazines, can contribute to our understanding of how an illness is portrayed. Communication in the media is not a one-way process. The media may influence our society, and our social values. But they also reflect them. A picturesque analogy is that the media are the looking-glass of a society. They reflect back what society projects into them. This is what makes them such a good target for study. They are particularly useful for cross-cultural studies, as consistent differences found in the media must arise from differences in the societies concerned.

Qualitative or Quantitative?

This study used two different types of data: **quantitative** and **qualitative**. Study 2 was mostly quantitative, using rating scales and assigning scores to the different statements selected. The data collected in Study 1 from the media are clearly qualitative in nature. The authors in this study selected articles and broadcast news to analyse, as we can see from the quotes given in the category examples above. Taking extracts of language is one of many forms of this type of data.

But look at the findings of that first study. There were significant differences in the number of themes used. There were significant differences in the use of negative statements too. This might seem like an odd juxtaposition: qualitative data and **inferential statistics**! But what the authors did here was to take the qualitative data, code them and then turn those qualitative codes into quantitative data. There was no magic wand needed for this transformation. Instead it was possible just to assign scores and count frequencies, which is what they did. This is very different from a qualitative approach to data analysis (see Chapters 13 and 17), but similar to that used by Inch and Merali in Chapter 12.

Was This a Survey or an Experiment?

You can see that, in this study, the authors have taken control of the material. The observational phase allowed them to identify the details of the object of their interest: cultural differences in approaches to athleticism. They drew their material from existing sources that were freely available in each country being studied. In the second phase, the material was produced specifically for the study. Then the task was to compare how the two different cultural groups reacted to the material. This second phase was a **quasi-experiment** designed to supplement the information gleaned from the media analysis.

The borderline between **analytical survey** and quasi-experiment can seem a little blurred at times. When is asking people questions to test a hypothesis a form of experimentation? When is it a **survey**? Clearly if a researcher asks your opinion about an object – canned soup, the prime minister, wind farms – then it is a survey. If that researcher just wants to know how people are thinking on a topic of interest it is a **descriptive survey**. If the researcher thinks that people might respond differently depending on some, as yet unspecified, characteristics of their background, then they need to ask a wide variety of people. They would then also need to ask for some further information that would allow them to explore the data by these background **variables**. This, however, is still a descriptive survey.

It becomes an analytical survey if the researcher starts with a hypothesis about people's opinions, for example that men will show a greater preference for canned soup than women will. This is a **one-tailed hypothesis** because it is predicting which of two groups will show the preference. A **two-tailed hypothesis** on the same topic would be: there will be a sex difference in expressed preference for this canned soup. This makes no prediction about which sex might show the greater preference, and that is what makes it a two-tailed hypothesis. In either case, the next step would be to survey a sample that was designed to be representative of the total population, and then compare the answers of the males with those of the females. This would allow the researcher to test the hypothesis and so this would be an analytical survey. You will note that it is the views of two groups that are being compared here in order to test the hypothesis, but the material shown to those two groups is the same.

In Chapter 15 surveys were contrasted with experiments. The study in that chapter used questionnaires to test a hypothesis and this was described as an analytical survey. This is because the tendency to satisfice or maximise is construed as being an inherent characteristic of the individual. By asking people what they might do in a hypothetical situation, the survey is asking about a pre-existing tendency within the person. The scenarios used may be fictitious, but the response sought is how the person would behave in a given setting. Survey methods can be described as self-report methods. Participants are reporting how they do behave, or would behave, or what they would think. Contrast that with what Markus *et al.* did. This was an experiment using survey methods and not an analytical survey because the participants were responding to a novel stimulus. Compare the task for these participants with those described in Chapters 15 and 16 where respondents were asked about themselves. See also Box 15.1.

In short, if a researcher wants to know about what already exists it is a survey. If a researcher presents a novel stimulus to see how people respond to it, it is an experiment.

In the second phase of their study, Markus *et al.* wanted to compare the views of two groups of people about the object in question, in this case, the fictitious athlete. As the fictitious athlete is a novel stimulus, this was an experimental design. Because there is neither **control** nor **random allocation** it cannot be a **true experiment** but is a quasi-experiment.

You may be thinking that they changed the athlete's name for the two groups: in one group she has an English name and in the other a Japanese one; does this mean that the tasks were not really equivalent? The answer to this is no, because the researchers wanted to know how people would respond to an athlete from their own culture. So what alternatives were there?

If they had used the same name in both circumstances, then for one group it would have been a foreign name. The researchers needed to ensure that this was not the case, as it would have introduced a **confounding variable**, that is, one group's views of their own culture's athletes versus the group's views of athletes from abroad. This would make it impossible to interpret the results.

They could have given the athlete a name from another language altogether, Russian, German, or Chinese. This at least would have meant that in both cases the participants were giving views of a foreign athlete, so it would not be a confounding variable. But would the researchers have been getting the information they wanted? If they wanted to know how people perceive athletes from their own country, this would have been little help to them. The views of some of the **sample** might be influenced by their views of that other country, or of athletes from that country.

In which case, there would be unexpected noise in the data, and this would be a case of **random error**, because each group is equally susceptible to it and it could affect things either way.

They could have used a hybrid name, English first name and Japanese surname, or vice versa. But this might have produced problems of its own. Because the combination name would have been unusual, it would have drawn the respondents' attention to it. This could lead to **demand characteristics**, where participants try to work out the aim of the experiment and then respond accordingly. In this instance they might be thinking: 'How should I respond to an athlete of mixed race?' Again this would mean that the data could not be used to test the hypothesis.

The one other alternative would have been to use a cipher for the athlete's name, Athlete X, for example. This would overcome the difficulties inherent in the other three alternatives, although it is likely that the cipher used would also have been culturally determined, so this would take us back to where we were in the first place.

Controlling for all **extraneous variables** in research is not an easy process. As we can see from this example of the athlete's name, sometimes it is not possible to control for everything by the very nature of the research question. In this instance, however, Markus and colleagues wanted their respondents to give their views of an athlete from their own culture, and altering the athlete's name to achieve this was the least bad option.

There are other ways in which cross-cultural comparisons can be made, using **psychometrics**, for example. Anderson (1999) compared scores from Chinese and American students on attribution style, depression and loneliness. He found that the Chinese respondents took more responsibility for failure and also had higher levels of depression and loneliness. This suggests that 'the self-enhancing attributional style' described by Markus *et al.* may be protective. Kurman (2002) used questionnaires to look at the relationship between cultural modesty and self-enhancement in three different ethnic groups: Singaporean, Israeli Druze and Israeli Jews. She found self-enhancement differed between cultures, with the Singaporeans being the most self-effacing and the Israeli Druze showing the greatest tendency to brag. Lockwood *et al.* (2005) compared two ethnic cultures in Canada, European and Asian, using questionnaire methods. They found that while the Asian respondents appeared to be motivated by examples of failure, Europeans were more inclined to be motivated by successful role models. Experimental studies of cross-cultural comparisons are rare these days although theoretically possible. Direct observational studies in this context are likely to be problematic.

Why would case studies be unlikely to be suitable for cross-cultural research?

Why would any form of direct observation be problematic for cross-cultural studies?

Conclusion

In this paper Markus and colleagues neatly combined two different types of research in order to do a cross-cultural comparison. The observational phase gave information that helped design the second phase, the survey. So in this way the first study led to the other. We should not, however, underestimate the importance of the first study; it was more than just a pilot for the second study. The authors combined two different approaches to research for their study. In doing this, they provided evidence from one source that confirms and validates the findings of the other. This is an effective way of building a body of knowledge. Had they only completed phase 1 they would have been open to criticism: it could have been argued that the language of news reports is just that, a specialist language which does not reflect the way that ordinary people speak. Had they just done the second phase, then critics might have suggested that the results reflected different cultural responses to survey techniques. The fact that two different methods tell the same story indicates a firm finding. In this instance, the language of the newspapers appears to reflect the way in which individuals describe and analyse their country's athletes. The models of agency that Markus *et al.* sought to identify appear to be similar through both methodological approaches.

In focusing on an activity that two cultures have in common, this study allows us to see the cultural differences between them. The state of technological development is also similar across the two. In spite of this, differences are evident. The authors summarise this nicely in their conclusion:

> Beyond construing the same world differently, perceivers experience and create somewhat different worlds. (2006, p.111)

The authors' main interest was in the descriptions of how and why people act or behave. They explored the normative accounts of achievement in athletics. They selected athletics as a way of comparing this across cultures. They suggest that their findings could be applied beyond the sporting arena to the broader social values of the two countries. This raises an interesting issue in cross-cultural research. It is clearly impractical for a researcher to compare every aspect of society. Therefore, focusing on one small identifiable component, in this case athletics, is a pragmatic solution. But then to what extent does this justify applying empirical findings more generally across the societies? Just because they differ in the way that they talk about sport, does that mean that the nations have different social values?

It would be difficult to argue that evidence about sport can be taken as evidence of a general cultural difference. However, it is equally impossible to suggest that the language used about athletes is in some way totally divorced from the larger culture. If these models of agency differ, can such differences exist in cultures where all other values are the same? It would seem improbable. Therefore, the extrapolation from these findings, the expansion from the established into the unknown, can be justified as a reasonable supposition. It should not, however, be viewed in the same way as the hard evidence provided here on the subject of athletics. This is how research works, building a picture bit by bit. These authors have shown how these two cultures differ in one dimension. They speculate that this reflects a greater difference between the two nations, that is, different models of agency, different understandings of the way in which we negotiate the world. To what extent that speculation is justified can only be established by further research.

Summary Points	
Design	Cross-cultural study: 1. content analysis 2. quasi-experiment with vignette study
Aims	To identify any sociocultural differences in the construction of agency 1. in the media 2. amongst respondents
Sample	1. Media coverage of 2002 and 2002 (Winter) Olympics 2. Students: American (N=60) and Japanese (N=60)
Materials	1. n/a 2. Vignette designed for this research
Analysis	1. Quantitative content analysis 2. Group differences in scores

Contrasting the Methods

An Overview

The purpose of this final chapter is to look at the different methods discussed in the preceding chapters, to compare them in ways not discussed within each individual topic and to contrast the different approaches they portray. Let us first consider the three different methodological approaches, then review some general issues that apply to all methods.

Experiments

Chapters 3 to 9 of this book all looked at **experimentation** in different forms, from laboratory-based studies to **field experiments**. Most experiments can be placed somewhere on this continuum, with the exception of **natural experiments**, which occur rarely and, by definition, are not within the control of the researcher. It might seem that the difference between a lab-based and a field experiment is obvious, but in fact it is not always that clear. Definitions of what constitutes a laboratory study are rare. Woodman (1979) suggested dryly that it is 'an experiment more appropriately suited to field research' (his definition of a field experiment, incidentally, was one 'that should have been done in a laboratory' (p.93)!). Often laboratory experiments can only be identified almost by omission, by not being a field experiment, rather than by a formal definition. Laboratory experiments do not have to take place in 'laboratory' any more than field experiments occur in a field! Confusing, isn't it?

It is relatively straightforward to recognise a lab study with animal work as the animals are not in their natural environment. To identify a lab experiment involving humans, there are two questions that we can ask:

- Was the participant invited to the premises controlled by the researcher?
- Was the **target behaviour** performed at the researcher's request rather than at their instigation?

When the answer to *both* of these is yes, it is a lab-based study. There are three studies in this book which are easy to classify as lab-based: the animal experiments of McDermott and Hauser (2004) in Chapter 7; the study on the cognitive costs of racial prejudice by Salvatore and Shelton (2007) in Chapter 8; and that on mate-selection strategies by Jones *et al.* (2006) in Chapter 9. These last two may not have taken place in what we might conventionally consider a laboratory; there were probably no white coats and certainly no test tubes. Nonetheless, these would normally be described as laboratory experiments.

Laboratory studies such as those in Chapters 7–9 are sometimes criticised because they lack **ecological validity**. The suggestion is that behaviour in the laboratory may not tell us much about behaviour in the real world. However, these studies were carefully designed, each with their own **controls**. Jones *et al.* showed that the different styles of female photographs affected the way that the males were rated; their design allowed them to identify and measure differences in the **dependent variable (DV)**. The extent to which that DV is representative of real-world behaviour is yet to be determined. They did not claim to have shown mate-choice copying, although that is one theoretical interpretation of their findings. Salvatore and Shelton showed that encountering prejudice affected Stroop performance; again the relationship between performance on a Stroop task and real-world behaviour is unclear. Yet their study design demonstrated a clear effect of **independent variable (IV)** on the DV as measured in the 'laboratory'. Both these studies, along with McDermott and Hauser's work, in their current designs were only suitable as laboratory studies as discussed in the respective chapters.

Contrast these lab-based experiments with those described in the four preceding chapters, which all took place in a real-world or applied setting. Could any of these have been done in the laboratory? It is nonsense even to consider this for the experiment in Chapter 3, telephone support for OCD therapy (Kenwright *et al.*, 2005). The chronic nature of the illness, and the prolonged course of therapy required, meant that this could only occur in the participants' own homes over a period of weeks. For the study described in Chapter 4 (Yung *et al.*, 2003) we could measure the effect of music on artificially induced stress in a laboratory, but this would have fallen short of the impressive effect that music had on the real stress experienced by patients about to undergo surgery. These two studies, both examples of **applied research** and very specific and focused in their design, had no problems with ecological validity.

- Each took place in an applied setting; no invitation from the researcher was required to invite the participants into their own home (Chapter 3) or the operating theatre (Chapter 4).
- The participants' behaviour was not in response to a request by the researcher. In Chapter 3 the behaviour was in response to the intervention, and in Chapter 4, in response to the setting.

As for Chapter 5 (Gucciardi & Dimmock, 2008), it is possible that the strategies for dealing with golfers' competitive anxiety could have been conducted in a laboratory, or at least in an artificial setting, providing that it was large enough to allow putting. Could we be certain that any effect demonstrated in an artificial setting would transfer to the real putting green? Because the study was completed on a golf course, most people would call this a field experiment as it was taking place in an applied setting, even though the behaviour, putting, was done at the request of the researcher.

Chapter 6 includes a series of field experiments by Levin *et al.* (2002). Most of the work on change blindness was conducted outside, on the campus of the university, which means it would count as field experiments. The campus was an applied setting: even though the study was on university premises, the participants were not there at the request of the researcher but for some other reason. Their behaviour was not performed at the request of the researcher. It is true that the researcher asked participants for directions, but giving directions was not the target behaviour, which was, rather, their response to the concealed change of personnel. One study involved recruiting participants to take part and asking them to make their way to a designated venue as though they were taking part in a laboratory study. However, the IV was manipulated (the researchers changed places) when the participants believed themselves to be on the way to the designated venue. This may seem like a borderline case between field and laboratory studies. Participants knew they were about to take part in a study, but did not know that their participation had already begun. If we accept that the definition of a field experiment is one that takes place in an applied setting, where the participants might normally be found, and where the behaviour of interest occurs naturally, then we can see that this, too, qualifies as a field study. The setting may have been en route for the laboratory; it may also have been within the province of the researcher, which makes it sound like a lab study. However, it was also the place at which this type of behaviour would naturally occur (the behaviour being reporting to take part in a study!). Furthermore, the participants did not know that they were, at that point, actually taking part in the study; they only believed themselves to be *about* to do so. Therefore, the target behaviour was prompted by the researcher's actions and not requested by the researcher. Therefore, this study seems to fit more comfortably into the category of a field rather than a lab-based study.

Having noted the commonalities of Chapters 3–5, we should not overlook the differences in the study designs. The **randomised controlled trial** for OCD took place over a period of weeks in the participants' own homes. The IV was the type of telephone support offered: scheduled or on demand. In this experiment, the DV was the OCD behaviour of the individuals concerned, that is their ordinary day-to-day behaviour. This experiment was designed to see whether the chosen **intervention** had a long-term effect on the lived experience of the participants. In the following chapter, the use of music to reduce preoperative stress similarly meant introducing the IV into an existing real situation. Unlike the OCD study, this was a single, one-off intervention for each participant and the DV (their level of anxiety) was, likewise, a single occurrence. Admittedly preoperative anxiety may have an impact on post-surgical recovery, but this was beyond the remit of this particular study. Both of these studies tested a form of clinical intervention designed to provide a therapeutic effect to a group of patients: one long-term and one short-term, the first chronic, the second acute. In both cases the comparison was **between conditions**; one used an **independent groups design**, the other, a **related design** using **matched pairs**.

Compare this with the golfers in Chapter 5. This was also comparing between conditions, but this time using **repeated measures**, another form of a related design. The interventions, in this case, were also designed to help the target population; but this is no longer a matter of health, but of sporting performance. This time the target behaviour, putting, was not naturally occurring, that is to say that it was not part of the golfer's ordinary behaviour. The behaviour in question here was being produced specifically for the study. It is true that the golfers would have resumed putting as part of their chosen sport after the study. They may even have chosen to adopt in their future sporting activities the intervention that they had found most useful. The study design, repeated measures, required the participants to repeat the behaviour, putting, keeping all the other features constant.

The studies in Chapters 6 and 7 both used single sample designs to see how participants responded to a stimulus; both used a series of such experiments to tease out a specific issue. Each step of the process identified the effects of different aspects of the IV, each addressing one **hypothesis**. Chapters 8 (racial prejudice) and 9 (mate selection), by contrast, each used just one experiment to answer several different hypotheses. As a result of this, each of these experiments was very complex. The study in Chapter 8 compared the ethnicity of the participant and of the victim and the type of prejudice. Two of these count as IVs because they were manipulated by the researcher, but the third (participant ethnicity) is a **group difference** and, therefore, strictly speaking, not considered an IV. Chapter 9's experiment was similar in that there were two IVs (the direction of the female's gaze and her facial expression) plus a group difference comparison (sex of participant). The difference between the two chapters' studies is that the design of the racial prejudice study was **unrelated**, with each participant only experiencing one of the four conditions, whereas the design of the mate-selection study was mixed, partly related, partly unrelated. The related elements were the female's expression and the direction of her gaze; the unrelated elements were the sex of the participant, and which of each pair of males was the target. This complex design required **counterbalancing** between conditions. Counterbalancing means that the sample has to be divided into different groups so that each counterbalanced condition was experienced by one of those groups. Be careful, though, because this does not make this element of the experiment a comparison between groups. If the counterbalancing has worked effectively, as it did in this instance, then there will be no significant difference between the conditions. Provided that this is the case, then the effect of the IVs can be measured.

As indicated above, one of the key features of a laboratory study, at least for one involving human participants, is that the participants know they are taking part in research. We need to tell them this much to encourage them to come into the lab or lecture theatre or common room – wherever the study will take place. They may not know the research question or hypothesis; they may even be misdirected about the task in hand. For example, Salvatore and Shelton's participants thought that the cognitive task was unrelated to the earlier task of reviewing hiring decisions. These days, they must be told what their participation involves before **informed consent** is sought. This much would be a requirement when seeking ethical approval for a study. Salvatore and Shelton signed up their participants for two experimental tasks, so all had an idea of what they were going to be asked to do. In many cases, participants cannot be told the full design of the study prior to participation because this might influence their responses. If they know the hypothesis they may respond in a way that they believe to be helpful and thereby produce a **Type I error**. Conversely they may opt to do the opposite of what they think is expected (sometimes referred to as the 'screw you' effect) and thus produce a **Type II error**.

As with the laboratory studies, in applied experiments (OCD and preoperative stress) the respondents were recruited into the study after giving fully informed consent. Similarly, the golfers gave fully informed consent for the study on competitive anxiety. Compare this with the change blindness studies. In these, consent was neither obtained nor sought. The participants had no idea that they were taking part in an experiment at the time (although in one case, they thought they were about to do so). In this respect, this is similar in nature to the study by Piliavin *et al.* (1969) mentioned in Chapter 2. This type of study exemplifies what many would consider a 'field experiment', for in each:

- the participants were not invited to premises controlled by the researcher;
- the target behaviour was performed at the researcher's instigation rather than their request.

To summarise how to interpret answers to the two key questions at the start of this chapter:

- if the answer to both questions is 'Yes', you can consider it a lab experiment;
- if the answer to both questions is 'No', you can consider it a field experiment;
- if there is one 'Yes' and one 'No', it is usually better described as a field experiment.

Observation

Observation is the second major strand of research: simply looking at what is happening around us. As with experimentation, there are different ways to approach observational research, and a variety of designs and methods can be deployed. There are five **observational studies** in this book (Chapters 10–14). Unlike the studies in the preceding chapters, in these studies there is no manipulation, no IV and DV. The researcher is not in control, other than by selecting the material to be observed.

The studies on autism (Macintosh & Dissayanake, 2006), in Chapter 10, cognitive maps (Maguire *et al.*, 2000), in Chapter 11, and face recognition (Abe *et al.*, 2007), in Chapter 14, are all examples of direct **observation**. Macintosh and Dissanayake observed naturally occurring behaviour in a school playground to compare children on the autistic spectrum. Studies using this method may use filming equipment to record the behaviour for later analysis, but Macintosh and Dissanayake chose to use an observational schedule, directly recording behaviour as it happened. As such, it was a very 'low-tech' study requiring the minimum of equipment. This is not to deprecate the study in any way; this is part of a long-established tradition of observational studies. It is interesting to contrast this with the study by Maguire *et al.*, who used highly complex equipment to look at the brains of taxi-drivers and others to see whether the area of the brain used in developing cognitive maps could be identified by physiological changes. This was hardly naturalistic observation. Mostly we cannot determine the shape of people's brains by looking at them! It is only with the technology that has recently been made available that this has become a possibility.

Both of these studies looked at a number of cases in order to make comparisons between classifications of people. The **sample** of 56 children in Macintosh and Dissayanake's study comprised three groups: those with higher-functioning autism, those with Asperger's and those who were typically developing. Maguire *et al.* compared the scans of 16 taxi-drivers with those of 50 non-taxi-drivers. Abe *et al.*, by contrast, report only one case: a woman who has problems with face recognition. Unlike the other studies, this **case study** did not need a **comparator**. The reason for the study was that the patient suffered an atypical abnormality. The implied comparator is normality; the woman is described because her pathology is unusual, and can tell us more about how face recognition occurs in healthy humans.

The chapters describing studies that used **indirect observation** both look at eating disorders. Inch and Merali (2006) looked at the way the eating disorders were reported in the media (Chapter 12), while Giles (2006) examined material from internet chat rooms for people with eating disorders (Chapter 13). The first focuses on how this particular pathology is represented in the media; the second highlights the experience of the sufferers. Both are indirect observation because the material is already recorded and in the public domain. Other types of indirect observation would include other written resources such as archives or public records, or even audio recordings and visual material such as films or pictures.

Observation can take a **structured** approach such as that used by Macintosh and Dissanayake, who developed a schedule in order to record the number of instances of different types of play by the children. Maguire *et al.* also used a structured approach to analyse the scans of the taxi-drivers. Inch and Merali used an equally structured approach to analyse the material in the magazines in their study. In each of these three cases the researchers had to develop a means of structuring a large amount of material in such a way that it provided answers to their research questions. It is necessary to ensure that, in developing such a structure, one is not allowing bias to creep in to the **data**. In each case the structure used could have provided data that presented a different picture had that difference existed in the material. To develop an appropriate structure Macintosh and Dissanayake had to decide which target behaviours were of interest, and how they were to be recognised and classified. Maguire *et al.* had to find a way of measuring the relevant part of the

scans, and indeed they chose two different ways to do this, the two acting as a form
of cross-validation. Inch and Merali had to identify their target material from the
large number of magazines included in the **sampling frame**. To do this they produced a clear inclusion criterion for each article (namely that the disorder had to be
mentioned at least three times). A similar approach was taken by Markus *et al.*
(2006), in Chapter 19, in the first part of their study, when they examined reporting
of the Olympics in America and Japan.

Neither Giles nor Abe *et al.* used a purely structured approach. Giles allowed the
material to determine what should or should not be included in his analysis, as his
focus of interest was on the nature of membership of the group being studied, and
how the contributors were viewed in that community. Abe *et al.* did use some structured methods as part of their case study: they provided a scan of the patient's brain
as well as some **numeric data** from **psychometric assessments**. However, the focus
of interest was on the description of the patient's impairment as it manifested itself
in her relationships with her family members. Some observational studies use only
unstructured methods such as those cited as classic observational studies in the reference list to Chapter 10.

Structured observational methods usually allow the researcher to collect **quantitative data**; when unstructured methods are employed the data are **qualitative**.
To collect quantitative, numeric data without structure would provide data that
appeared to be **objective** but which were in fact **subjectively** harvested. This is likely
to lead to **bias**. Conversely, collecting qualitative material using a fully structured
method is likely to result in impoverished data that fail to tell the whole story.

Survey Methods

The third and final strand of research methodology is covered by the umbrella term
survey methods: asking people, covered in Chapters 15–18. These include **interviews, questionnaires**, and **attitude** or **rating scales**. There are three issues here that
we need to consider: closed versus open questions; qualitative versus quantitative
data; and interview versus written material (by 'written', I am including all types of
questionnaires and rating scales). Generally speaking, closed questions are used for
quantitative data and are often collected through textual methods, and open questions are used for qualitative data and frequently collected through interview.
Unfortunately, as so often in research, it is not always that straightforward!

The first two studies on survey methods, Iyengar *et al.* (2006), in Chapter 15, and
Wei *et al.* (2007), in Chapter 16, both used questionnaires to produce quantitative
data: a maximising score and an Experiences in Close Relationships (ECR) score,
respectively. The maximising score was calculated using a measurement instrument
that had been developed and published in previous research. Its function in the
study was to sort the participants into two groups: those with high and those with
low maximising scores. Wei *et al.*, on the other hand, were developing their measurement and through a series of studies establishing its **psychometric properties**.

In each case, the participants were responding to the items by selecting a scaled response (1–7 with Wei *et al.* and 1–9 with Iyengar *et al.*). These are rating scales, and as such can be considered as examples of **closed questions**. The other questions asked by Iyengar *et al.* were also closed in that the type of response was limited to how many jobs participants had applied for, how many offers they had received and their expected annual salary. Theoretically, there was no limit to the answers that could have been given, but all the answers would have been restricted (in this case, to numbers) by the nature of the question – that is what makes these closed questions. These studies, then, provide classic examples of questionnaires: closed questions and quantitative data.

Campbell and Morrison (2007), in Chapter 17, used **open question**s in their interviews to ask their respondents about the experience of paranoia. They published their interview guide as an appendix to their paper; please note their use of the word 'guide'. This was not a list of set questions to be asked in a specified order in particular wording, but rather a list of issues to be covered in the interview. It includes such prompts as 'Can you tell me what sort of things you have been paranoid about?' and 'What do you think your life would be like if you were not paranoid at all?' These are questions designed to evoke very full responses. This, too, fits neatly into the categorisation: interview, open questions and qualitative data.

Hartney *et al.* (2003), in Chapter 18, used a combination of questionnaires and interviews. The questionnaires were standardised measures of dependency and readiness to change, each of which produced scores (closed questions, quantitative data). The interviews provided qualitative data which the researchers could use to explore the views of this particular group of heavy but non-dependent drinkers. Put together, these two sets of data, quantitative and qualitative, worked well to provide an overview of the sample's habits and behaviours.

The second study, in Chapter 19, used survey methods too, but within an experimental design. Markus *et al.* (2006) used a **vignette study** to explore their participants' views of sporting success. This was evidently an experiment; when the overall design of a study includes the introduction and manipulation of an IV then it should be considered experimental. However, within this **quasi-experiment**, data were collected using survey methods, namely asking people to rate the fictional athlete using a seven-point scale (questionnaire, closed question, quantitative data).

However, interviews can also use closed questions; in interview, we could ask exactly the same questions as those asked, for example, by Iyengar *et al.* Closed questions can be particularly useful at interview as supplementary to the main issue, in order to gain some background information on respondents. Ensuring respondents give closed answers in interview may not be as straightforward as in a questionnaire. Respondents may be more loquacious in interview, and it may take a skilled and persistent interviewer to get the closed answer they are seeking, for example:

I: How many jobs have you applied for?
R: It depends whether you include the ones that I just sent a CV to on spec as well as those that were in response to job ads.

I: Just those that were responses to job advertisements.

R: Well, in that case, there were five last month and three the previous and, let me see, six so far this month, I think.

I: So that's 14 altogether?

R: No wait a minute, I forgot, I did an extra one last week.

I: So that's 15 in total then?

R: Not really because one of them was re-advertised so my application was carried forward – so I suppose that doesn't really count as a separate one, does it?

I: (sigh) So we are settling on 14 then?

This type of exchange could have been avoided by specifying, in the question, exactly what information was being sought. 'How many applications have you made to job advertisements in the last three months, excluding those where your application was carried forward?' Questionnaires can give people more time to think, in this case to actually count up their applications, whereas interviews can seem to require a more rapid response from the participant so as not to keep the interviewer waiting. Certainly, if all the data to be collected can be gathered through closed questions, then questionnaires may be more economical and allow for a greater sample size than interviews. Nonetheless, there will still be occasions when interviews may be preferred – if, for example, there are literacy issues with the intended population.

Just as closed questions can be used at interview, so open questions can be used in a questionnaire. There are times when it is useful and profitable to do this even though it may not be as effective as asking the questions at interview. People's responses may be restricted by a wish to complete the task as quickly as possible or by lack of room on the questionnaire for a fuller response. Furthermore, there is no chance to correct them if they get the wrong end of the stick or begin to wander off the point. In interview, as in ordinary conversation, the researcher has a chance to redirect or bring the interviewee back to the issue as required.

You may believe that survey methods are easy to design and construct; after all, asking questions is what we all do in everyday conversation! Doing it right, however, takes a good deal of training and experience. Moreover survey methods are as labour-intensive as other research designs. Broadly speaking, the less structured the method (e.g. unstructured interviews) the more work there is to do in the analysis. With highly structured methods (e.g. attitude scales) the work is in the development of the method, with the data being easier to analyse.

Methods and Data

In terms of the different methods, we have seen that data collected through observation or survey methods can be either quantitative or qualitative or a mixture of both. Experiments are always quantitative studies; there may be times when qualitative data may be collected, but then they will not be the primary outcome measure of the experiment but, rather, they may be used to gather useful information about the experience of the participants. An example of this can be found in the study on change blindness in Chapter 6, when participants were debriefed after the experiment.

In the narrative chapters we have seen researchers turn qualitative into quantitative data (e.g. Inch & Merali, 2006), studies where both sorts of data are gathered to produce a composite picture (e.g. Hartney *et al.*, 2003; Abe *et al.*, 2007) and those where qualitative data alone are analysed using qualitative methods (e.g. Giles, 2006; Campbell & Morrison, 2007).

However, there is a more important distinction between qualitative and quantitative research than simply the nature of the data. A quantitative researcher who collects qualitative data is a very different animal from a qualitative researcher. The majority of the studies cited in this book are quantitative in style; this is because quantitative studies often seem more off-putting to the budding researcher than qualitative research. Qualitative research is just as demanding and as exciting as any **positivist** research. Nevertheless it seems more immediately accessible to the novice than much of the exacting and often confusing terminology of the **hypothetico-deductive** methods characteristic of quantitative research. Qualitative or critical psychology is a different approach to research: its focus is on discovering the meaning for participants. As such it eschews experimental work and all that this entails, such as hypotheses and numerical measurement; its emphasis instead is on the social meaning of constructs as viewed by participants. The task is not to find representative samples and then generalise to a population; rather, it is to understand the perspective of given individuals. There is not a single or uniform qualitative approach, but rather a group of methods and analyses that all subscribe to this paradigm. It is beyond the remit of this book to discuss these in detail; there are many good qualitative research books available, for example Smith (2008) or Willig (2008), to which the interested reader is referred.

Samples

The studies chosen for this book were varied in order to give an indication of the wide variety of research that is carried out within psychology. The majority (all but Chapters 7, 12 and 13) used human participants, as you might expect in this discipline. There are two **content analysis** studies where there are no human samples. Table 20.1 lists the different samples used.

If we break this down further, we can see that there are four studies where *specific* sub-groups in the population were recruited (taxi-drivers, golfers, heavy drinkers and children on the autistic spectrum); there are a further four studies where the samples are patients. You may have noted that in both these groups of studies, all three methodological approaches are represented; there are three experiments, three observational studies and two surveys. If we look at the other six studies that employed human samples but did not require specific groups, we see that surveys and experiments are equally represented. As there is no match between method and sample types, we can see that different methods may be suitable for a variety of samples.

Table 20.1. Chapter topics and samples

Method	Topic	Sample	Population
O	11. Cognitive maps	Taxi-drivers and non-taxi-drivers	H
E	5. Competitive anxiety	Golfers	SG
S	18. Understanding heavy drinking	Heavy drinkers	SG
O	10. The autistic spectrum	Children (typically developing and those with autism)	SG
O	14. Face recognition	Patient	H
S	17. Paranoia	Patients and students and university staff	SG
E	4. Music and stress	Surgical patients	SG
E	3. Obsessive compulsive disorder	Patients with OCD	SG
E	8. Cognitive costs of racial prejudice	College students	H
S	15. Choices and decisions	College students	H
S	16. Measuring romance	College students	H
O	19. Attributing success and failure	Media	
S		College students	H
E	6. Change blindness	People on campus	H
E	9. Mate-selection strategies	Men and women	H
O	13. Eating disorders – the experience	Internet chat room	SG
O	12. Eating disorders and the media	Magazines	SG
E	7. Acoustic preferences	Cotton-top tamarins College students	NH

Key

Method: E = experiment; O = observation; S = survey methods
Population: H = humans; NH = non-humans; SG = specific groups

It is not method that determines sample, of course, but rather the aim of the study. As we have seen in the preceding chapters, each of these studies had very different aims. However, it is instructive to look at a common aspect of the studies' aims, and that is the **population** implicit in the aim (see the fourth column of Table 20.1). Of these eight studies where the sampling frame, and therefore the subsequent sample, comprised a specific group, six were designed to answer questions that were relevant only to the type of person represented by the sample. In some cases, it is possible that the further studies might show how the intervention could be equally applied to other special groups (e.g. athletes other than golfers, patients other than those undergoing surgery or those with OCD). None of these six studies was designed to tell us more about the normal functioning of humans; they were all applied research. In contrast, the two studies that were neuropsychological in nature (on cognitive maps and face recognition) tell us a bit more about how the human brain functions and develops. In both these cases, the particular people identified for recruitment were selected because their experiences made them special. By studying the abnormal we learn more about the normal – this is a long tradition within neuropsychology.

The remaining six studies involving humans where the sampling frame had no specific characteristics were all intended to answer questions about more general populations. In most cases the population was human beings; only in the cross-cultural study was the population restricted to two nationalities. Take a look at the samples selected, from which we can also infer the sampling frame, for all these six studies. What do you notice? Four of the studies recruited only college students; one study reported only that the participants were people on campus, from which it is reasonable to assume that some, at least, will have been college students. One study merely reported that men and women had been recruited but provided no further details of the sample. None of these studies can really be classified as applied research; each is concerned with finding out how humans, in general, respond to given situations or stimuli. Yet the humans used are nearly all college students. College students also make brief appearances in two other studies: on paranoia and acoustic preferences. In each of these two cases the students were recruited as comparators; comparisons were made between their behaviour and that of patients, or that of cotton-top tamarins! College students are a handy resource for researchers: they are easily available, have little difficulty following instructions and tend to be research-savvy. But does that necessarily make them suitable participants? Are college students really representative of humanity? There has been no agreement about the extent to which this is considered to be a problem since it was identified by Sears in 1986. If you are reading this book because you are studying psychology at university, then it is highly probably that you will be invited to take part in at least one study at some point during your degree. You might like to think about the extent to which you feel you are representative of the population!

Degree of Control

One other general dimension on which research studies can be considered is the extent of control maintained by the researcher. As a general rule of thumb, in observational studies researchers have the least control, and in experiments, the most. Yet within each of these categories there is a good deal of variation.

Of the observational studies, Macintosh and Dissanayake (2006) had the least control over their sample, the children in the playground. The children were behaving naturally, and it was up to the observer to record that behaviour without instigating or interfering with it. Maguire *et al.* (2000) and Abe *et al.* (2007) had considerably more control over their participants, allowing them to make detailed measurements using brain scans and psychometric tests respectively. This control was restricted only to measurement; they had no control over the object of their studies: the development of the taxi-drivers' brains, or the pathology and functional deficits of the elderly woman patient. In this respect these two studies had much in common with the content analysis studies in the two chapters on eating disorders. Inch and Merali (2006) and Giles (2006) had material that was already 'captured'; unlike Macintosh and Dissanayake, their task was to sift the material and identify their sample prior to analysis. Like Maguire *et al.* and Abe *et al.*, neither of them had any control over the production of the material they were studying. This is the defining characteristic of an observational study: observing, without influencing, an existing phenomenon.

The issue of control in relation to survey methods has something in common with observation. Like neurological studies and content analysis, recorded interviews and written measures afford the researcher maximum control of measurement and analysis. Like these studies, survey methods also have no control over the production of the material. For example, the questionnaire may ask 'What is your age?' but the answer may be 'None of your business.' Where they differ from these observational studies is that the behaviour in responding to questions (written or spoken or responses) is instigated by the researcher. In this way surveys may have more in common with experiments. If the target behaviour (responses) is elicited by the researcher, there is always the possibility that it may not reflect real behaviour, an issue of ecological validity, if you like. Here the researcher must be mindful of two potential **confounds: evaluation apprehension** and **social desirability**, either of which may influence the respondent's answers and thereby contaminate the data. Designing and developing questionnaire methods is a lengthy process, as outlined in Chapter 16. Getting interview questions right is an equally skilled process, as demonstrated above. Even then, the researcher has no control over the responses. Arguably, more control is retained in interviews than in questionnaires, as the researcher is able to be more 'hands-on'. We should always remember that with surveys we get information on what people say they do, which may not be what they do!

With experimental studies, control is essential. Without adequate control, cause and effect cannot be inferred nor conclusions drawn. What constitutes 'adequate control'? There is no simple or ready answer to this as each study will differ. Any researcher involving humans needs to be aware of the pitfalls, to guard against the possibility not only of evaluation apprehension and social desirability, but also of **demand characteristics**, or even the **Hawthorne effect**. For this reason, McDermott and Hauser's (2004) study involving primates shows how effective good controls can be. It is salutary to remember that when the authors moved to working with humans they immediately encountered one of these pitfalls! The human experiments also had good controls. Jones *et al.* (2006) and Salvatore and Shelton (2007) had very neat designs and were able to attribute patterns in their data to their experimental design. In each case, they controlled the potentially confounding variables effectively. It is theoretically possible that their findings could still have occurred purely by chance in spite of these precautions; this can only be confirmed or refuted if others **replicate** their work. You may have noticed that these three studies, where control is optimum, are also those we classified as laboratory studies; lab-based work and a high degree of research control are synonymous.

Out of the laboratory and into an applied setting, it is still possible to retain adequate control. Kenwright *et al.* (2005) and Yung *et al.* (2003) both employed control groups with their patients, as did Gucciardi and Dimmock (2008) with their golfers. They had, however, very little control over the events themselves. Kenwright *et al.* followed their patients over an extended period and, of course, experienced a **drop-out rate** as a result. They had no control over how their patients behaved between 'phone calls, or what other events happened to them. Yet they still identified a difference in recovery rate between their groups and, like Yung *et al.*, were justified in attributing this to their intervention. Again only replication will confirm this. The golfers acted as their own controls, and showed different responses to different strategies. How much control did the researchers have over their participants' use of each strategy? It is difficult to be certain here as the IV, the 'behaviour' in question, was not detectable to the researchers; but in establishing a difference between conditions, again the researchers are justified in their conclusion.

The remaining study, the true field study on change blindness, had relatively little control, which is usually the way with field studies. Anything can happen and get in the way of the IV and the DV. Also these were single sample studies, so there were no control groups as such. Nonetheless, Levin *et al.* (2002) were able to manipulate their IV and measure their DV, thereby demonstrating how unobservant we, as a species, can be!

Conclusion

There are many ways in which we can categorise research. The narrative chapters in this book have categorised according to method; this chapter has considered other classification systems. Perhaps the biggest divide is the distinction between qualitative or critical approaches and the positivist or quantitative approach, which this book has only mentioned in passing. It is certainly true that methodological approaches and study designs are as varied as the researchers themselves!

When selecting an appropriate method for a given research question there are many issues to consider, not least the pragmatic issue of viability. We might like to know whether pearl-divers tolerate hyperspace better than others because of their experience of changing pressure through deep-sea diving. Good question. But how are you going to get the resources to test that one?

With quantitative research, we need always to remember those terrible twins: **reliability** and **validity**. If we take two measurements of the same object when there have been no changes, we expect those measurements to be the same. If you get on two sets of scales in turn and get two different readings of your weight, then there is an issue with reliability. At least one of your scales is not working properly and not providing a reliable reading. Likewise, if you are setting out to measure something, you need to be sure that your measurement reflects that target object, that it is valid. If you want to measure health, will taking people's temperature provide a valid measurement? No, it will provide a measurement of their temperature; not everyone who is ill has an abnormal temperature and not everyone with an abnormal temperature is ill.

Research in psychology is varied; no one method is intrinsically better than another; no one design superior. Each is open to review and amenable to analysis. Each is useful when used appropriately. For us to build the body of knowledge that we call psychology, we need to call on all of these tools. As I have suggested in the preceding chapters, every topic benefits from being investigated through a wide variety of methods. We can observe phenomena, we can experiment on them and we can ask people questions about them. Each of these provides building blocks in our understanding of how things work.

I hope that this book has given you a taste of this diversity and has whetted your appetite to know more. I also hope that the Glossary and Key Topics will help you understand a range of other research issues. Finally, I hope that it will help you to take some pleasure in reading, understanding and doing research.

Key Topics

Experimental Design

The types of designs listed here are largely used to describe **experiments,** but there are occasions when this terminology can be used in other types of research such as **analytical surveys, structured observation** and **longitudinal studies**.

The problem with research design terminology is that there is more than one way to describe things. In Figure KT1 the designs listed include the broadest classification (related or unrelated), through the general, to the specific. In each case, common synonyms are included. The figure includes the most likely inferential statistic assuming that the study is collecting **numeric data** (**ordinal, interval and ratio**).

Commonly Used Descriptive Statistics

Below is a list of the most commonly used descriptive statistics for each of the four types or **levels of data, nominal, ordinal, interval** and **ratio**. Measures of **central**

	General	Design	Nonparametric	Parametric	Aim
UNRELATED	Between subjects/groups	Group difference	2 groups: Mann–Whitney	2 groups: independent t-test	To compare differences between existing groups
		Independent samples/subjects/groups	>2 groups: Kruskal–Wallis	>2 groups: One way ANOVA	
RELATED	Within subject/groups	Matched pairs	2 groups: Wilcoxon's matched pairs	2 conditions: Matched pairs/related t-test	To compare differences between treatments/interventions/conditions
		Repeated measures	>2 groups: Friedman's	>2 conditions: Repeated measures ANOVA	
	Associations	Correlational	Spearman's	Pearson's	To look for relationships between variables

Figure KT1 Taxonomy of experimental designs with inferential statistics for numeric data.

tendency tell us where the **data** are bunched, the middle point, and measures of variability or **dispersion** tell us how spread out they are around that central point. For interval and ratio data there are also statistics that estimate how **representative** the sample data may be of the population from which they are drawn.

Nominal data

central tendency   **Mode** is the category with the largest number of cases.

variability/dispersion The notion of variability in nominal or categorical data does not really make sense. Variability can only occur when each case is contributing a number to the data set, rather than just being counted.

Ordinal data

central tendency   **Median** is the value at the midpoint of a distribution of scores arranged in rank order.

variability/dispersion **Min, max** are the lowest and the highest values in the data set. Range is the difference between the lowest and highest scores; if the lowest score was 5 and the highest 20 then the range would be 15.

Interval or ratio data

central tendency   **Mean** is the mathematical average of a distribution of scores. It is calculated by totalling the **data set** and then dividing by **N**, the number of cases.

variability/dispersion **Standard deviation (SD)** is the average amount of distance between each score in the data set and its mean; the larger the SD the greater the variability.

representative data   **Standard error of the mean (SEM)** is a calculation that includes a measurement of variability and the sample size. **Confidence interval** calculates how confident we can be that the sample mean represents the population mean.

Commonly Used Inferential Statistics

Below is a list of some of the most commonly used **inferential statistics** with a brief explanation of what they do.

Nominal data

goodness of fit/chi square (χ^2) goodness of fit tests whether distribution of a single categorical variable conforms to prediction, e.g. χ.

(independent) chi square (χ^2)[1] tests associations between categorical variables, e.g. job and sex; uses frequency data.

Fisher's exact probability: for use instead of independent chi square if the numbers are small.

(binomial) sign: compares changes in condition between **T1** and **T2**. Can be used on numeric data but reduces them to nominal data. For example comparing well-being using a rating scale from T1 to T2. Sign test merely looks at whether the rating has improved or deteriorated between measures.

Nonparametric numeric data

Wilcoxon's matched pairs: tests for *differences* between two measures in a **within subjects design**, for example comparing scale scores from T1 to T2. Can be used instead of sign test as it takes more account of relative size of the change.

Friedman's analysis of variance: as Wilcoxon's but when there are more than two measures.

Mann Whitney (U): tests for *differences* between two groups in an **independent design**. For example comparing scores from groups in experimental and control conditions.

Kruskal–Wallis: as Mann Whitney, but when there are more than two groups.

Spearman's correlation: tests for *relationship* between two numeric variables. For example scores on two different scales.

Parametric data

matched pairs/paired/related t-test: tests for *differences* between two measures in a **within subjects design**. For example comparing reaction times from T1 to T2.

repeated measures ANOVA: as matched pairs t-test but when there are more than two measures.

independent t-tests: tests for *differences* between two groups in an **independent design**. For example comparing reaction times from groups in experimental and **control** conditions.

one-way ANOVA: independent t-test, but when there are more than two groups.

Pearson's (product moment) correlation coefficient: tests for *relationship* between two numeric variables. For example scores on two different types of reaction time tasks.

Scale analyses

alpha coefficient/Cronbach's alpha: tests the **internal reliability** of a numeric scale by looking at the way that the items intercorrelate.

Kuder–Richardson: as alpha coefficient, but when items have Yes/No answers rather than numeric options.

(exploratory) factor analysis[2] identifies underlying factors that account for the variation in responses (see Box 18.1).

confirmatory factor analysis checks whether the factors identified by exploratory factor analysis in one sample can also be found in a different sample.

Why Do We Need Inferential Statistics?

When we collect data in psychology we find that there is always a good deal of **variability**. For example, take a reaction time experiment where we are measuring the time it takes people to respond to a prompt or **stimulus** and comparing data from, say, trials in the morning and in the evening to find out when people are more alert. Suppose we get the following set of numbers (milliseconds) from 10 subjects:

a.m.   44, 45, 46, 47, 48, 49, 50, 51, 52, 53,
p.m.   70, 71, 72, 73, 74, 76, 77, 78, 72, 71

Here we have a convincing case that our respondents were much quicker in the morning than the evening. Everyone is quicker, then, by something between 20 and 30 milliseconds, taking approximately 40 per cent longer in the evening.
   Suppose instead we get this set of numbers:

a.m.   44, 45, 46, 47, 48, 49, 50, 51, 52, 53,
p.m.   43, 46, 44, 48, 45, 47, 50, 54, 52, 51

Here the situation suggests that there is no real difference between the two conditions, some people are quicker in the morning and some are quicker in the evening. There is no consistent trend in the **data**.
   But suppose we get a set of data like this:

a.m.   44, 45, 46, 47, 48, 49, 50, 51, 52, 53,
p.m.   50, 51, 52, 53, 54, 56, 57, 58, 52, 51

It looks at first glance as though people are slower in the evening. But a closer look shows us that there are some trials in the evening in which people are quicker than in some of the **trials** in the morning. And we can also see that although most people were quicker in the morning, the last two respondents did not follow this pattern: one showed no difference and one was actually faster in the evening. So can we state that people are generally faster in the morning? Or do our last two respondents make this statement impossible? Are these data just part of the general variability that we get with human data and show no real pattern?
   Inferential statistics allow us to work out the likelihood of getting this particular set of results *if there were no real difference between morning and evening reaction times*. That is, they work out the likelihood of getting a given pattern of results purely by chance. Such statistics work out the **probability** of getting a given set of results. If the set of findings is likely to occur when there is no real difference between the two

conditions, then the difference is described as not significant. However, if it is unlikely to have occurred if there is no real difference then the finding is termed **significant**. (See 'Probability' below.)

Probability

Probability underlies all inferential statistics. At first it can seem like a very strange notion and it can scare off the unwary- but actually we all have an understanding of probability- although we may not realise that we do! Try putting the following events in order of likelihood, most likely first through to least likely:

1. a dice comes up as a six;
2. a tossed coin comes up heads;
3. it will snow in London on Christmas day;
4. you will fly to the moon on gossamer wings;
5. you will think of elephants while reading this;
6. you were born.

I expect most people would put these events in the following order of likelihood: 6, 5, 2, 1, 3, 4. It is a certainty that you were born, as we have not yet managed to clone adults. The elephants bit is a cheap psychologist's trick; by mentioning it, the likelihood has been deliberately manipulated! Your flying to the moon on gossamer wings is an impossibility, I'm guessing, and therefore ranked as least likely. If you put these events in this order of likelihood, or even approximately this order, you already understand probability. The only difference between probability and likelihood is that we have an exact means of calculating probability.

We can calculate probability when we know (a) the possible number of ways of achieving a target outcome and (b) the total number of outcomes possible. We simply divide (a) by (b). For example:

Tossing a coin to come up heads: one target outcome, two possible outcomes: heads or tails therefore a probability of .5 (i.e. 1/2). But if you toss a coin two times what are the chances of both being heads? One target and four possible outcomes: HH, HT, TH, TT. Therefore a probability of .25 (i.e. 1/4).

Throwing a six with one dice: one target outcome, six possible outcomes. Therefore a probability of .167 (i.e. 1/6).

Throwing an even number with one dice: three target outcomes (two, four, or six), and six possible outcomes. Therefore a probability of .5 (i.e. 3/6).

These simple examples make the calculation of probability quite easy to do. Look at the data cited in the section 'Why Do We Need Inferential Statistics?' above. Would you like to have a go at working out the probability of getting those numbers?! It would be considerably more of a challenge. Luckily we don't have to it; it has already been done for us. That is what inferential statistics do: they calculate the probability for you. Inferential statistics are simply a tool we use to calculate probability. Once we know the probability, we can say whether or not a finding is significant.

The exact probability of an event will always vary between 0 (impossible) and 1 (a certainty) and is expressed as a decimal point as above. According to the British Psychological Society Style Guide, probability should be presented without a zero preceding the decimal point: .05 rather than 0.05.

What Is 'Significant'?

Inferential statistics allow us to calculate the probability of getting a particular result, if the **null hypothesis** is true. For example, if we want to test whether taxmen are more neurotic than other government employees, we would compare the neuroticism scores of our two groups. Suppose our scores for the two groups are 25 and 18 respectively. The question then becomes: is 25 significantly higher than 18? Inferential statistics would calculate the probability of getting these two scores if there is no real difference in the two populations from which these groups were drawn, that is, if the null hypothesis was correct. If these two scores are quite probable, if they could easily occur by chance alone, then there will be no significant difference between groups.

A finding that is *unlikely* to occur by chance alone is significant. This means that we need a criterion for what is generally considered unlikely. By convention this is a probability level of .05. This is called the **alpha level**. There are times when researchers consider it prudent to set a more stringent alpha level, for example .01. If you think of the alpha level as being like a goal mouth, the smaller it is the more difficult it is to get a result within it.

If the chances of getting such a result are less likely than that, we say that the result is significant, and it is expressed as $p<.05$.

If we apply this to the coins and the dice, then we would say that if we tossed a coin and it came down heads, this would not be significant because the $p=.5$ and that is clearly bigger than .05. Likewise the probability of throwing a six on a dice, $p=.167$, also not significant. Both of these options are quite likely to occur.

Careful: this is the only time in research when the word significant is acceptable, because it has come to have this technical and specific meaning, and it should not be used on other occasions. If a finding does not reach a significant level is it described as *non-significant – never* insignificant!

Probability Challenge

What about the chances of throwing two sixes in a row: what are they? Answer at the end of Key Topics.

Research Reports

Because research plays such a large part in psychology, all courses require students to learn how to write reports. This is a particular writing style that does not come easily to most of us. There are formal structures for reports which are common across most courses, but there will also be a good deal of local variation in the detail. This is not surprising; a glance at half a dozen reputable psychological journals will confirm that they, too, have 'house styles' for reports. Therefore, this section is meant as a guide to the writing of practical reports and covers those issues that are most likely to apply to course requirements, but even so may not be applicable to everyone.

This guidance is intended, primarily, for **quantitative** reports. Please note that if you are writing a **qualitative** report the structure and approach may differ considerably from what is given here, particularly the presentation and discussion of results.

Always check your individual course requirements. Generally the listed subheadings are all required, but there will be occasions when some are not necessary.

Style

The report should cover what you did and what you found, written throughout in the past tense, using the third person.

correct	The experimenter asked the participant for directions.
not	I asked the participant for directions.
and particularly not	Then you ask the participant for directions.

Title

This should give the reader a very short but crystal-clear idea about the topic of the report, no longer than one sentence, although you may include colons or semicolons. For experimental reports it is often best to state the relationship between the independent and dependent variables (for example: 'The Effects of Organisation of Information on Recall'). Golden rule: be concise but not cryptic. It is not necessary to begin the title with 'A study into' or any synonymous phrase.

Abstract

This is a very brief summary of the *whole* report. It may have a limit of say 150 or 200 words. These days it is quite common for this to be structured with subheadings. It is much easier to write and to read when it is structured, but sometimes this is not a requirement. If you have no such requirement, try writing your abstract using the following subheadings and then remove the headings and put the abstract together as a single paragraph of text. This should help ensure that you have put in all the necessary information.

- Background
- Aims
- Methods
- Results
- Conclusions

The idea of the abstract is to provide sufficient information for the reader to know what the report is all about, including what the investigation has found. You would normally include the number of respondents in your sample. When it comes to published journals, very often the reader will make the decision whether or not to read the rest of the report based on the abstract. Keep the abstract as brief as possible but still useful and informative. It is normally only possible to write your abstract LAST, that is, after you have written the full report, even though it is presented at FIRST, i.e. at the front of the report.

Introduction

This gives the background to the investigation and will include a review of the relevant literature. The introduction should 'set up' the report (there is little use in writing a long review of literature just to prove that you've read it!). The introduction should put your study into its research context and give the reader some idea as to the reasons for doing the piece of work. You should give enough background information so that the reader can understand the value and importance of the research question, as well as the context in which it arose. In covering the literature, this should be an evaluation of the work in the area rather than a detailed description. (See also 'Evaluation vs Summary', p. 261.)

It is often said that the introduction can be described as funnel-shaped. Don't take this literally: the text should be formatted in the same way as normal! However, it is a useful analogy in that it should start from a fairly broad perspective of how the issue fits into the 'real world'. Then it should review the research, starting with studies relevant to the topic and then become increasingly focused on those that relate to the specific variables under scrutiny. This leads neatly up to the research question behind your study.

You should end this section with a clear statement about the aims of your own study and the experimental **hypothesis** where appropriate. These aims or this hypothesis should not come as a surprise to the reader; rather, it should be possible to anticipate them from the material in the earlier part of this section.

Method

Readers will want to know exactly what you did. It is important that the information here is sufficiently detailed to enable someone to replicate exactly the entire investigation. Remember keep this in the past tense. The method section is subdivided into further sections, usually as below, but again there can be variations from this.

Design

The design section is a short section (i.e. one or two sentences) in which you make a clear and accurate statement of the principal features of your design. It is a FORMAL statement outlining what sort of investigation was used. For example: 'this field study used a repeated measures design'.

Sample/Participants

You should provide a brief description of the critical features of the participants in the study. Who were they? How were they selected? If the number of participants is known prior to data collection (e.g. in an experiment) you should also say how many there were. The reader must be able to assess whether your findings can be generalised and whether there are any confounding variables.

Materials/Apparatus

What sort of materials (e.g. experimental stimuli, testing materials, questionnaires) were used? If using established tests, these must be referenced. Any apparatus used should be described accurately. This does *not* include the hardware or software used for statistical analysis.

Procedure

This should be a description of exactly how you carried out the study, i.e. what happened to the respondents from the start to the finish in enough detail to allow replication. Remember, use the past tense.

Method of analysis

As your analysis is part of 'what you did', you should include a statement of what tests were used and why they were chosen. If you use software for analysis (e.g. SPSS or NVIVO) you should give its details here, including the version used. Some authors also provide the brand and model number of the computer running that software, although this is less common these days as the platforms have become more standardised.

Results

You should start this section with a brief outline of your data by giving a reminder of what the data were. For example: *Response times were recorded in milliseconds for all 30 respondents*, or *A total of 43 questionnaires was returned*, or *During the 15-minute observation period the behaviours of 78 individuals were recorded*. If the number of participants was not known until after the data were collected or collated then that may appear here for the first time. This should be followed by a summary of your results, including **descriptive statistics**. The use of tables and figures alone is NOT sufficient; you need to include some explanatory text.

Raw data are not routinely presented here, although they may sometimes be required in an appendix.

If you are using **inferential statistics** these should come next. For each inferential statistic used, give the degrees of freedom, if appropriate, and the **p** value, and state whether or not it represents a **significant** finding.

A very common mistake in quantitative studies is to confuse the boundary between the *results* section and the *discussion* section that follows. The results section shows what you found (e.g. numerical data and results of statistical analyses); the discussion section focuses on the most reasonable explanation of the findings. However, with some qualitative studies this boundary is flexible.

Discussion

This gives the interpretation of the results, evaluation of the theoretical significance of the findings and a general discussion of the investigation. What has your investigation shown? Why was it important? What theory does it support or contradict? How does it fit in with other studies?

This section would normally begin with a consideration of your findings and the most plausible explanations of them. Why do these explanations make sense? Discuss alternative explanations for your results. Try to avoid direct repetition of information given in the results section.

The next step is normally a theoretical discussion of your findings and how they relate to past research. You should refer to the material you presented in the introduction and build on it. Try to avoid repeating the information you gave there, but rather assume that the reader has read the introduction and has some memory of what was cited there:

correct   These findings are similar to those of Smith and Jones (2004), who also
            found a positive correlation.
incorrect   These findings are similar to those of Smith and Jones (2004). *Their
            sample comprised 40 students who took part in a study on recall and
            recognition,* and they also found a positive correlation.

The information in italics, if relevant at all, should have appeared in the introduction and does not need repeating.

You should give some evaluation of the methodological adequacy of your study. Could there have been any design features that may have affected the results? Do you think the results would be different if you tested different participants, or used different stimulus materials? If so, then say why. Do you think that the results could be generalised to different situations or populations? Give justifications for such conclusions. Discuss any possible criticisms of the investigation – how with hindsight could the study have been improved? Try to avoid saying that the sample size was too small – this is not a useful comment. If it really was too small, then the reader is likely to wonder why you did not choose to use a larger one.

Also, you could comment on what new studies would be necessary in order to test the interpretations and theoretical speculations derived from the results of your present study. This is not just recommending a repetition of the study but without the shortcomings previously identified. Try to think of other and quite different ways of exploring the same phenomena. (It might be useful to look at the end of the chapters where alternative approaches are considered.)

Finally you conclude with a few brief summarising points of the results of the study and their theoretical significance. This conclusion should not contain any new information but rather pull together and summarise the key points from the discussion.

References

You should list all your primary reference sources here, that is those articles, texts or resources that you have consulted. (See also 'Referencing', below.)

Appendices

Do not put results here; sometimes raw data should be presented in an appendix. Some materials MAY be usefully included in an appendix. You may be asked to put the printout of your statistical analyses here.

The general rule is not to include anything in an appendix which has not been referred to in the text.

Referencing

The rationale for referencing is: it must be possible to trace the source of all the names which appear in the text, so that a copy of the material can be obtained, in turn, by the reader, if so desired. There are several ways to present this information, but most have adopted the American Psychological Association (APA) standard (albeit with European dating). The British Psychological Society publishes a very comprehensive Style Guide based on the APA standards, which addresses many situations that are beyond the scope of this text. What follows is largely taken from the BPS Style Guide.

These guidelines affect two areas of any piece of work, the text and the reference section, and cover both printed and online sources.

Citing Printed Sources in the Text

There are two types of reference that you may need to use in the text: (1) primary sources, i.e. those which you have read, and (2) secondary sources, i.e. those which are mentioned in something which you have read.

Primary sources
Cite these throughout by listing the author(s) followed by the date of publication in brackets. The name only goes in brackets when it is not part of the preceding sentence.

thus   Patients will vary in their response to the treatment (Smith, 2005).
or   Smith (2005) suggests that patients will vary in their response to treatment.
never   (Smith 2005) suggests that patients will vary in their response to treatment.

Secondary sources
Cite these by listing the author(s) and the date of publication and then state the author of the text you have read

thus   Recall can be affected by interference (Jones, 1987, cited in Smith, 2005).
or   Jones (1987) found that recall can be affected by interference (cited in Smith, 2005).

NEVER cite a secondary reference as though you had read the original.

Quotations
Please ensure that all quotations are acknowledged – and not overused! Don't forget to include the page numbers of all quotations. All quotations of three lines or more must be indented.

thus   'Health professionals are continually asking patients to alter some aspect of their behaviour.' (Smith, 2005, p.145)

Listing Printed Sources in the Reference Section

Make sure that all primary references appear in the reference section. For the examples given above the only author who would appear in the reference section would be Smith (not Jones, because you have not read Jones's work). References must be clearly listed in alphabetical order. If you keep all the references on index cards as you go along this should be quite easy. Alternatively, there are software packages available these days, but make sure that their output matches the requirements of your course. Use the BPS system of referencing exactly as indicated below, with the second and subsequent lines of each entry indented. Always check that the references are consistent and accurate and complete.

Referencing a whole book

   Davies, A.B. & Evans, C.D. (2006). *How the mighty are fallen*. Cambridge: Cambridge University Press.

Referencing an article in a journal

   Jansen, A. (1996). How restrained eaters perceive the amount they eat. *British Journal of Clinical Psychology, 35(3),* 381–392.

Referencing a chapter in a book containing items by a number of different authors

> Arntz, A. & Schmidt, J.M. (1989). Perceived control and experience of pain. In A. Steptoe and A. Appels (Eds.) Stress, personal control and health. Chichester: John Wiley & Sons.

Citing electronic sources in the text

The reference in the text need not mention that it is an electronic reference. As with conventional sources, this should normally include the author, if that information is available (see first example below.) If no author is specified then the name of the site should be given instead (see the second example below.). You will need to take particular care when referencing something in an abbreviated electronic version which appears elsewhere in full (see the third example below).

Examples in the text

> *William of Occam, a fourteenth-century Franciscan friar, is generally accredited with establishing the law of parsimony, hence the phrase 'Occam's razor' (Hiroshi, 2005).*

> *The British Psychological Society is governed by Royal Charter and describes itself as an organization that is both learned and professional (British Psychological Society, 25.09.06).*

> *Bull and Noordhuizen identified four types of mismatch between applause and rhetoric in political speeches (Bull & Noordhuizen, 2000).*

Listing electronic sources in the reference section

There are two objectives when making reference to an electronically sourced item. First, it is to identify its academic credentials, meaning that we need to know the author, date, title and publication information as before; second, in order to get our own copy thereof, we need to know either its internet address (usually referred to as its URL), or other delivery medium (e.g. online, CD-ROM, etc.) or mode (e.g. WWW, FTP, GOPHER, etc.). If necessary, also include specific terms to type once connected to the appropriate address. It is often important to make deliberate use of upper- or lower-case letters. Cite the sources specifically as you used them.

The information given in the reference section should be integrated alphabetically with all the other references. The first part, i.e. giving the author or site name, date and medium, should reflect the reference given in the text (although with authors their initials will be included here). The general rule is that you add a sentence in the format 'Retrieved [day month year] from [electronic address]'. Again if the only date available is the date that you accessed the site, then it should be presented in full. Here are the three references for the examples given above:

Examples in reference section
For a full text electronic copy of a paper previously published in hard copy:

> Hiroshi, S. (1997). Original title, source, volume, and page numbers of paper. Retrieved 9 September 2008 from http://hepweb.rl.ac.uk/ppUK/PhysFAQ/occam.html

Note that the final sentence here has no full stop, to avoid confusing the address.
For general reference material from a website:

> British Psychological Society (25.09.01). Website homepage content. Retrieved 25 September 2008 from http://www.bps.org.uk/faq/faq.cfm

For a research abstract:

> Bull, P. & Noordhuizen, M. (2000). Original title of paper. Journal of Language and Social Psychology, 19(3), 275–294. Retrieved 9 September 2002 from the OVID database.

Other suggestions

- If no author is given, use title as the first element.
- If no title is given, use the first few words of text.
- If there are multiple authors, list them in the order given in the source, last name first, followed by first and middle initials.
- With the exception of the colon, punctuation is used sparingly in the reference section so as not to be confused with punctuation that is part of an electronic address.

NB: as a general rule internet sources should be used very sparingly in academic work. Those that include either 'ac' or 'edu' in their domain name are part of an educational establishment and should be relatively reliable. Those that have 'gov' in their domain name are government publications and therefore a useful source of background material and statistics. All others should be treated with caution.

In fact there are many other categories of material, and you can find instructions on how to deal with them in the BPS Style Guide at http://www.bps.org.uk/publications/submission-guidelines/submission-guidelines_home.cfm

Writing style

Capitalisation

In order to avoid clumsy descriptions of groups within samples, variables measured or instruments deployed, it is often preferable to develop meaningful names when referring to those objects within the study. For example, in Chapter 15, the study by Iyengar et al. (2006) explored differences between people who scored the highest on a scale designed to measure maximising strategies and those who scored lower on that same scale. To refer in the text to these two groups by this wordy description would have become clumsy with repetition. Thus the two groups in the sample can be named with capitalisation to indicate that the names have been coined for this study, Maximisers and Satisficers. As such it can be considered part of an **operational definition**. (Indeed in the study in question the maximising scores of the sample as a whole were rather higher than had been found in previous studies, suggesting that many of these Satisficers would not be considered satisficers within the population.) Discussion of maximisers and satisficers within the population requires no such capitalisation.

When coining such names for the sake of brevity and clarity, meaningful names should be chosen. Terms such as Group 1 and Group 2 or Group A and Group B should be avoided as the reader has to refer back repeatedly to remind him- or herself which is which.

Evaluation vs summary

When writing a literature review it is a good idea to remember the difference between a summary and an evaluation. Ideally you should try to include an element of each, but the evaluation is more important than the summary. As an example, below there is a summary and an evaluation of the well-known fairy story, Snow White. Both are written within a tight word count of 100 words.

Summary
While Snow White dreamed of a prince her stepmother was told by a magic mirror that the princess's beauty surpassed her own. She instructed her huntsman to murder the girl. He, relenting, released the princess into the forest where she eventually settled as housekeeper to seven dwarves. The queen discovered the deception and, disguised as a pedlar, gave Snow White poisoned fruit. The dwarves returning from the mines chased the old woman to her death. They placed the motionless princess in a glass coffin. Months later she was woken with a kiss by the prince from her dreams.

Evaluation
The story describes the persecution and attempted murder of Snow White by her stepmother, a witch. The princess is saved from death by the tender care of the dwarves for whom she had kept house and finally wakened to life-long happiness by a kiss from the prince of her girlish dreams.

Our heroine is portrayed as a passive victim throughout, with a proclivity for household activities and an aspiration to marry a prince. Her stepmother suffers a competitive preoccupation with her looks which drives her to homicide. Neither of these characters makes a good role model for twenty-first-century feminists.

You will notice that the evaluation includes an element of summary. It does not provide as much detail of the story as the full summary, but enough for the purposes of the evaluation that follows. The key to evaluation is that it includes what the author thinks of the text.

You will not be evaluating fairy stories when you write practical reports, but the principle applies across media. Lengthy accounts of other people's research do not make good literature reviews. Identify the key findings, and consider their relevance.

Technical terms,[3] use with care

Cause

Be very cautious in claiming cause and effect. Experiments are the only research method designed to determine cause and effect, but even then it is wise to be cautious in assuming that a causal relationship has been demonstrated; there is often more than one possible explanation for a given set of findings. (See also 'Logic of Hypothesis Testing', in Chapter 6.) Other methods of research cannot by definition establish cause and effect, although sometimes they may provide data that suggest, but cannot determine, cause and effect . (See for example Chapter 11). Be particularly careful not to suggest that **correlations** identify cause and effect.

Random

A **random** sample is one in which every member of the target population has an equal chance of being included. It should not be confused with systematic sampling where, say, every tenth person is selected. Furthermore, it should never be used as a synonym for haphazard. If you ask your friends, or lie in wait in the foyer to leap on unsuspecting passers-by, this may be haphazard but it is not a random but a convenience sample.

Valid/validity

This means that something has been shown to represent that which it was designed to do. This term should not be used without reference to those procedures. Although face validity can mean that it looks all right to the user, valid does not mean 'I can't see anything wrong with it'. **Validity** takes several forms as defined in the Glossary.

Reliable/reliability

This means that a procedure, if repeated, will produce similar results. This term should not be used without reference to those procedures. Reliable does not mean 'It was there when I needed it'.

Common errors to avoid

Affect and effect

This is more to do with grammar than research, but it causes problems throughout psychological research so here are a couple of handy hints for sorting it out.

Do you want to talk about *consequences* or *influences*? For example the consequences of lack of sleep are that you feel bad-tempered.

influence (verb)   Lack of sleep *affects* you.
consequence (noun)   *The effect* of lack of sleep is that you feel bad-tempered.

In research we are trying to establish cause and *effect*. If we succeed, we can show that A *affects* B.

It is sneaky because how it is spelt changes depending on whether we are referring to a consequence (noun), or the action of influencing (verb).

Postscript. The above are the most common uses and the ones that cause the most confusion. However there are times when *affect* is a noun and *effect* is a verb – *but then they have different meanings*:

Affect is another word for emotion. Your affect may be cross, worried, happy, content etc.

Effect is another word for to achieve or bring about. By turning off your computer when you are not using it you can effect a reduction in your carbon footprint.

So if lack of sleep makes you bad-tempered, we could say it affects you, and that its effect is to effect a change in your affect!

Criterion and criteria
'Criterion' is single, 'criteria' is plural. Thus your inclusion criterion may be that all respondents are students. Your exclusion criteria may be that participants must not be psychology students or have previously taken part in the study.

Data
This is a plural word; the singular is datum – which we do not use very often. Therefore data *were* collated and analysed; data *are* presented in a table.

Comprise
Comprise means 'to consist of' so it should not be followed by 'of'. A sample may comprise students. Or it may be composed of students. Or it may consist of students. But it should never be *comprised of* students!

Things to avoid

Prove
Hypotheses are not proven, they are supported. Neither the presentation of data nor the analysis proves anything. These processes may illustrate, demonstrate, support, indicate etc., but never prove.

Opportunist, or Opportunistic sample
Samples may be described as opportunity samples, if they are those that opportunity presents. But they should never be described as opportunistic, which means without scruples or ethical concerns.

I, me, my, or We, us, our
As with all academic writing, you will usually need to avoid the use of the first person. Nor should you replace 'I believe' with 'The author believes'. This is not a solution.

Identification of places/people
It is not only essential to avoid identifying individual participants by name, but also to refrain from naming specific places from which the sample was recruited.

acceptable examples	A hospital in South Wales; a city department store in East Anglia; a school in the Highlands
unacceptable examples	University of Wales Hospital, Debenhams, St Mary's High School

Various
This word is very imprecise, and normally reflects a lack of thoroughness on the part of the author (e.g. 'There are various studies of this subject'). Try to enumerate where possible (e.g. 'There are five relevant studies'); if it is not possible then at least indicate quantity (e.g. 'Few relevant studies have been published').

Assertions
Avoid asserting something without evidence.

good practice	Asch (1951) has shown that people will deny the evidence of their own eyes so as to conform with others.
bad practice	People will deny the evidence of their own eyes so as to conform with others. Research has shown that people will deny the evidence of their own eyes so as to conform with others.

Question/Item numbers
When referring to a **questionnaire, attitude scale** or **interview schedule** avoid citing items by their number alone. This means that the reader has to flick back and forth to understand.

good practice	Over half the sample said they had central heating (Q4) and all the respondents indicated that they owned their own house (Q5).
bad practice	Over half the sample replied yes to question 4. In answer to question 5 all respondents ticked c.

The same principle applies to hypotheses; referring back to Hypothesis 1 and Hypothesis 2 is seriously confusing. Remember: help your reader to follow what you are saying – don't put obstacles in their way.

Cross-referring
It is not necessary to cross-refer in the report. For example in the discussion section you may wish to reflect on your findings in the light of past research, which you have already outlined in the introduction.

good practice	This contrasts with the results of Kirk (2003), whose whole sample had pointed ears.
bad practice	This contrasts with the results of Kirk (2003), as mentioned in the Introduction, who found all his participants had pointed ears.

FAQs about report-writing

How should numbers be represented in the text – in digits or words?

- Numbers up to nine should be expressed as words, 10 or above as digits, except at the beginning of a sentence, when you should always use the word. The British Psychological Society suggests that where possible you should avoid spelling out long numbers at the beginning of a sentence, preferably by rephrasing the sentence. For example, 'The participants comprised 62 males and 62 females' NOT 'Sixty-two males and 62 females acted as participants'.
- Write ALL numbers as digits if they express percentages, percentiles, or if they are followed by (or follow) units of measurement, e.g. 3m, 50dB, £100.
- Use digits when referring to pages, figures or tables (Table 2; Figure 5).
- Use digits when referring to centuries, e.g. 19th century, the 1980s (note, there is no apostrophe in 1980s).
- Use arabic numbers, unless roman numbers are part of an established terminology, thus: Table 3, Experiment 1, BUT Type I error.
- Use a zero before the decimal point when numbers are less than one, EXCEPT when the number cannot be greater than one, for example levels of statistical significance, correlations, and proportions, thus: r= −.86, p< .01.
  Where it looks wrong, use common sense, e.g. 'three 3-part lists' NOT '3 3-part lists', or 'three three-part lists'.

How should percentages be represented in reports?
The BPS suggests using 'per cent' except in tables, where the symbol % may be used.
Avoid using a mixture of the two (e.g. '%age').

How should graphical information be headed?
Use 'Table' and 'Figure' as headings (i.e. not Graph 1, or Histogram 2).

Where should response/return rates be recorded?
In the results section.

How much detail should be included when expressing statistical significance?
Include calculated value, p value and degrees of freedom if appropriate.

Where should be p values be presented?
There are only four places in a report where these would normally appear: abstract, methods of analysis, results and appendix. If you are thinking of putting them in somewhere else, don't! If you wish to discuss a particular result in the discussion section there is no need to repeat the relevant p value, which should have already been cited in the results section.

*How much detail should be included in the method section about why a
particular test/statistical table is being used?*
Just include the type of data. The BPS suggests that you do not need to cite a reference or rationale for using particular statistics (except for type of data), unless it is uncommon, or you are using the statistics in an unusual or controversial way. Such rationale should be located in the method section (under the subheading 'Method of Analysis').

How should et al. be used?

- If a work has two authors, cite both names every time and link them with an ampersand (&) if the citation appears in parentheses: The original study (Smith & Jones, 1984) or with *and* if in running text: The original study by Smith and Jones (1984).
- If a work has three or more authors, for both first and subsequent occurrences cite only the first author followed by *et al.*
- *Note*: Italicise *et al.* (contrary to APA style).
- ALL names and initials should be included in the references section of your project, unless a work has more than six authors, in which case consult BPS Style Guide.
- Avoid possessive constructions such as 'Smith et al.'s recent study'. Try rephrasing: 'The recent study by Smith *et al.*'.

And finally …

All this may seem like an awful lot to take in, and you may feel at times that you will never get the hang of things. But do not despair; practice really does help. Another useful strategy is to read research papers whenever you can, as this will help you become familiar with the style. Don't worry about the bits of papers that you may not understand, that will come with time. It may help to remember that many more students get good marks for their final-year project than get good marks for their first few reports!

Notes

1 If you encounter a test called just 'chi square' it is a good bet the author will be referring to independent rather than goodness of fit.
2 If you encounter the term 'factor analysis' on its own it is a good bet the author will be referring to exploratory rather than confirmatory.
3 Each of these is defined in the Glossary.

Probability Challenge Answer

These are all the possible options of what can happen if you throw a dice twice:

1&1
1&2   2&1
1&3   3&1   2&2
1&4   4&1   2&3   3&2
1&5   5&1   2&4   4&2   3&3
1&6   6&1   2&5   5&2   3&4   4&3
2&6   6&2   3&5   5&3   4&4
3&6   6&3   4&5   5&4
4&6   6&4   5&5
5&6   6&5
6&6

This shows us that there are 36 possible outcomes and only 1 target outcome. 1/36 means p=.028. So getting a double six from two dice would be classed as significant because p<.05.

Remember that the chance of getting a six with one dice was .167? Guess what you get if you multiply the chances of getting a six with the first dice by the chances of getting a six with the second dice? .167 × .167= .028. Funny thing, probability.

BPS Ethical Principles for Conducting Research with Human Participants

Introduction to the revised principles – BPS copyright

The Standing Committee on Ethics in Research with Human Participants has now completed its revision of the Ethical Principles for Research with Human Subjects (British Psychological Society, 1978). The new 'Ethical Principles for Conducting Research with Human Participants' (q.v.) have been approved by the Council.

The Standing Committee wishes to highlight some of the issues that concerned it during the drawing up of the Principles published below. In the forefront of its considerations was the recognition that psychologists owe a debt to those who agree to take part in their studies and that people who are willing to give up their time, even for remuneration, should be able to expect to be treated with the highest standards of consideration and respect. This is reflected in the change from the term 'subjects' to 'participants'. To psychologists brought up on the jargon of their profession the term 'subject' is not derogatory. However, to someone who has not had that experience of psychological research it is a term which can seem impersonal.

Deception

The issue of deception caused the Committee considerable problems. To many outside the psychology profession, and to some within it, the idea of deceiving the participants in one's research is seen as quite inappropriate. At best, the experience of deception in psychological research can make the recipients cynical about the activities and attitudes of psychologists. However, since there are very many psychological processes that are modifiable by individuals if they are aware that they are being studied, the statement of the research hypothesis in advance of the collection of data would make much psychological research impossible. The Committee noted that there is a distinction between withholding some of the details of the hypothesis under test and deliberately falsely informing the participants of the purpose of the research, especially if the information given implied a more benign topic of study than was in fact the case. While the Committee wishes to urge all psychologists to seek to supply as full information as possible to those taking part in their research, it concluded that the central principle was the reaction of participants when deception was revealed. If this led to discomfort, anger or objections from the participants then the deception was inappropriate. The Committee hopes that such a principle protects the dignity of the participants while allowing valuable psychological research to be conducted.

Debriefing

Following the research, especially where any deception or withholding of information had taken place, the Committee wished to emphasise the importance of appropriate debriefing. In some circumstances, the verbal description of the nature of the investigation would not be sufficient to eliminate all possibility of harmful after-effects. For example, an experiment in which negative mood was induced requires the induction of a happy mood state before the participant leaves the experimental setting.

Risk

Another area of concern for the Committee was the protection of participants from undue risk in psychological research. Since this was an area in which the Principles might be looked to during an investigation following a complaint against a researcher, the Committee was concerned to seek a definition that protected the participants in the research without making important research impossible. Risks attend us every moment in life, and to say that research should involve no risks would be inappropriate. However, the important principle seemed to be that when participants entered upon a psychological investigation they should not, in so doing, be increasing the probability that they would come to any form of harm. Thus, the definition of undue risk was based upon the risks that individuals run in their normal lifestyle. This definition makes possible research upon individuals who lead a risk-taking or risk-seeking life (e.g. mountaineers, cave divers), so long as the individuals are not induced to take risks that are greater than those that they would normally encounter in their life outside the research.

Implementation

The Council of the Society approved the Principles at its meeting in February 1990. There followed a two-year period during which the new Principles were provisionally in operation. In Spring 1992 the Council reviewed the Principles, in the light of experience of their operation. During this period researchers were unable to identify problems in the working of the Principles. Following minor amendment the Principles were formally adopted in October 1992.

The Council urges all research psychologists to ensure that they abide by these Principles, which supplement the Society's Code of Conduct (q.v.) and thus violation of them could form the basis of disciplinary action. It is essential that all members of the psychological profession abide by the Principles if psychologists are to continue to retain the privilege of testing human participants in their research. Psychologists have legal as well as moral responsibilities for those who help them in their study, and the long-term reputation of the discipline depends largely upon the experience of those who encounter it first-hand during psychological investigations.

The Principles

1. Introduction

1.1. The principles given below are intended to apply to research with human participants. Principles of conduct in professional practice are to be found in the Society's Code of Conduct and in the advisory documents prepared by the Divisions, Sections and Special Groups of the Society.

1.2. Participants in psychological research should have confidence in the investigators. Good psychological research is possible only if there is mutual respect and confidence between investigators and participants. Psychological investigators are potentially interested in all aspects of human behaviour and conscious experience. However, for ethical reasons, some areas of human experience and behaviour may be beyond the reach of experiment, observation or other form of psychological investigation. Ethical guidelines are necessary to clarify the conditions under which psychological research is acceptable.

1.3. The principles given below supplement for researchers with human participants the general ethical principles of members of the Society as stated in The British Psychological Society's Code of Conduct (q.v.). Members of The British Psychological Society are expected to abide by both the Code of Conduct and the fuller principles expressed here. Members should also draw the principles to the attention of research colleagues who are not members of the Society. Members should encourage colleagues to adopt them and ensure that they are followed by all researchers whom they supervise (e.g. research assistants, postgraduate, undergraduate, A-Level and GCSE students).

1.4. In recent years, there has been an increase in legal actions by members of the general public against professionals for alleged misconduct. Researchers must recognise the possibility of such legal action if they infringe the rights and dignity of participants in their research.

2. General

2.1. In all circumstances, investigators must consider the ethical implications and psychological consequences for the participants in their research. The essential principle is that the investigation should be considered from the standpoint of all participants; foreseeable threats to their psychological well-being, health, values or dignity should be eliminated. Investigators should recognise that, in our multi-cultural and multi-ethnic society and where investigations involve individuals of different ages, gender and social background, the investigators may not have sufficient knowledge of the implications of any investigation for the participants. It should be borne in mind that the best judge of whether an investigation will cause offence may be members of the population from which the participants in the research are to be drawn.

3. Consent

3.1. Whenever possible, the investigator should inform all participants of the objectives of the investigation. The investigator should inform the participants of all aspects of the research or intervention that might reasonably be expected to influence willingness to participate. The investigator should, normally, explain all other aspects of the research or intervention about which the participants enquire. Failure to make full disclosure prior to obtaining informed consent requires additional safeguards to protect the welfare and dignity of the participants (see Section 4).

3.2. Research with children or with participants who have impairments that will limit understanding and/or communication such that they are unable to give their real consent requires special safe-guarding procedures.

3.3. Where possible, the real consent of children and of adults with impairments in understanding or communication should be obtained. In addition, where research involves any persons under 16 years of age, consent should be obtained from parents or from those in loco parentis. If the nature of the research precludes consent being obtained from parents or permission being obtained from teachers, before proceeding with the research, the investigator must obtain approval from an Ethics Committee.

3.4. Where real consent cannot be obtained from adults with impairments in understanding or communication, wherever possible the investigator should consult a person well placed to appreciate the participant's reaction, such as a member of the person's family, and must obtain the disinterested approval of the research from independent advisers.

3.5. When research is being conducted with detained persons, particular care should be taken over informed consent, paying attention to the special circumstances which may affect the person's ability to give free informed consent.

3.6. Investigators should realise that they are often in a position of authority or influence over participants who may be their students, employees or clients. This relationship must not be allowed to pressurise the participants to take part in, or remain in, an investigation.

3.7. The payment of participants must not be used to induce them to risk harm beyond that which they risk without payment in their normal lifestyle.

3.8.   If harm, unusual discomfort, or other negative consequences for the individual's future life might occur, the investigator must obtain the disinterested approval of independent advisers, inform the participants, and obtain informed, real consent from each of them.

3.9.   In longitudinal research, consent may need to be obtained on more than one occasion.

4. Deception

4.1.   The withholding of information or the misleading of participants is unacceptable if the participants are typically likely to object or show unease once debriefed. Where this is in any doubt, appropriate consultation must precede the investigation. Consultation is best carried out with individuals who share the social and cultural background of the participants in the research, but the advice of ethics committees or experienced and disinterested colleagues may be sufficient.

4.2.   Intentional deception of the participants over the purpose and general nature of the investigation should be avoided whenever possible. Participants should never be deliberately misled without extremely strong scientific or medical justification. Even then there should be strict controls and the disinterested approval of independent advisers.

4.3.   It may be impossible to study some psychological processes without withholding information about the true object of the study or deliberately misleading the participants. Before conducting such a study, the investigator has a special responsibility to

(a) determine that alternative procedures avoiding concealment or deception are not available;

(b) ensure that the participants are provided with sufficient information at the earliest stage; and

(c) consult appropriately upon the way that the withholding of information or deliberate deception will be received.

5. Debriefing

5.1.   In studies where the participants are aware that they have taken part in an investigation, when the data have been collected, the investigator should provide the participants with any necessary information to complete their understanding of the nature of the research. The investigator should discuss with the participants their experience of the research in order to monitor any unforeseen negative effects or misconceptions.

5.2.   Debriefing does not provide a justification for unethical aspects of any investigation.

5.3.   Some effects which may be produced by an experiment will not be negated by a verbal description following the research. Investigators have a responsibility to ensure that participants receive any necessary debriefing in the form of active intervention before they leave the research setting.

6. Withdrawal from the investigation

6.1. At the onset of the investigation investigators should make plain to participants their right to withdraw from the research at any time, irrespective of whether or not payment or other inducement has been offered. It is recognised that this may be difficult in certain observational or organisational settings, but nevertheless the investigator must attempt to ensure that participants (including children) know of their right to withdraw. When testing children, avoidance of the testing situation may be taken as evidence of failure to consent to the procedure and should be acknowledged.

6.2. In the light of experience of the investigation, or as a result of debriefing, the participant has the right to withdraw retrospectively any consent given, and to require that their own data, including recordings, be destroyed.

7. Confidentiality

7.1. Subject to the requirements of legislation, including the Data Protection Act, information obtained about a participant during an investigation is confidential unless otherwise agreed in advance. Investigators who are put under pressure to disclose confidential information should draw this point to the attention of those exerting such pressure. Participants in psychological research have a right to expect that information they provide will be treated confidentially and, if published, will not be identifiable as theirs. In the event that confidentiality and/or anonymity cannot be guaranteed, the participant must be warned of this in advance of agreeing to participate.

8. Protection of participants

8.1. Investigators have a primary responsibility to protect participants from physical and mental harm during the investigation. Normally, the risk of harm must be no greater than in ordinary life, i.e. participants should not be exposed to risks greater than or additional to those encountered in their normal lifestyles. Where the risk of harm is greater than in ordinary life the provisions of 3.8 should apply. Participants must be asked about any factors in the procedure that might create a risk, such as pre-existing medical conditions, and must be advised of any special action they should take to avoid risk.

8.2. Participants should be informed of procedures for contacting the investigator within a reasonable time period following participation should stress, potential harm, or related questions or concern arise despite the precautions required by the Principles. Where research procedures might result in undesirable consequences for participants, the investigator has the responsibility to detect and remove or correct these consequences.

8.3.   Where research may involve behaviour or experiences that participants may regard as personal and private the participants must be protected from stress by all appropriate measures, including the assurance that answers to personal questions need not be given. There should be no concealment or deception when seeking information that might encroach on privacy.

8.4.   In research involving children, great caution should be exercised when discussing the results with parents, teachers or others acting in loco parentis, since evaluative statements may carry unintended weight.

9. Observational research

9.1.   Studies based upon observation must respect the privacy and psychological well-being of the individuals studied. Unless those observed give their consent to being observed, observational research is only acceptable in situations where those observed would expect to be observed by strangers. Additionally, particular account should be taken of local cultural values and of the possibility of intruding upon the privacy of individuals who, even while in a normally public space, may believe they are unobserved.

10. Giving advice

10.1.   During research, an investigator may obtain evidence of psychological or physical problems of which a participant is, apparently, unaware. In such a case, the investigator has a responsibility to inform the participant if the investigator believes that by not doing so the participant's future well-being may be endangered.

10.2.   If, in the normal course of psychological research, or as a result of problems detected as in 10.1, a participant solicits advice concerning educational, personality, behavioural or health issues, caution should be exercised. If the issue is serious and the investigator is not qualified to offer assistance, the appropriate source of professional advice should be recommended. Further details on the giving of advice will be found in the Society's Code of Conduct.

10.3.   In some kinds of investigation the giving of advice is appropriate if this forms an intrinsic part of the research and has been agreed in advance.

11. Colleagues

11.1.   Investigators share responsibility for the ethical treatment of research participants with their collaborators, assistants, students and employees. A psychologist who believes that another psychologist or investigator may be conducting research that is not in accordance with the principles above should encourage that investigator to re-evaluate the research.

Glossary

acquiescent response set *see* **response set**.

action research is 'real-world' research, and may be informal and iterative in style, in which the participants are seen as collaborators with the researcher. The aim is to problem-solve and improve processes or systems.

aim can be defined as the clearly directed intent or purpose of an investigation. All investigations have aims, whether or not they are expressed. When an aim is expressed it should be written as an infinitive with the preposition 'to' (e.g. to test, to examine, to determine etc.). In some cases people prefer to express their aim as a research question. Some studies also have a **hypothesis**. The aim is usually cited in the **abstract** and at the end of the introduction to the report. Aims, questions and hypotheses are compared under **hypothesis** in this glossary. *See also Key Topics: Research Reports.*

alpha coefficient is the name given to the **correlation coefficient** that is used to test **internal reliability** in **psychometric assessments**. A positive correlation indicates that all the items in the scale are tapping in to the same thing.

alpha level is the level of **probability** at which a result is said to be **significant**. The usual alpha level is .05; any probability level below that is deemed to be unlikely to have occurred by chance alone. *See Key Topics: Probability.*

alternative hypothesis is the full name for the research hypothesis, and it is what a study is designed to test; it is the alternative to the **null hypothesis**. It can also be called an experimental hypothesis. *See* **experimental hypothesis; hypothesis**.

analysis of covariance (ANCOVA) is an analysis based on **analysis of variance**, which takes into account the effect of another variable. For example, measuring reaction times in two conditions, it would be useful to take the age of the participants into account as older people tend to have slower reaction times. In this instance, the **independent variable** would be experimental condition, the **dependent variable** would be reaction times and age would be the covariate that ANCOVA would control for in the analysis.

analysis of variance (ANOVA) is an **inferential statistic** useful when an analysis is more complex than simply comparing two sets of scores. It measures the extent to which the **variance** in a data set can be attributed to the experimental design rather than to variation between individuals. The calculated value from an analysis of variance is referred to as F, and as general rule the higher the value of F, the more likely it is to represent a **significant** effect of the **independent variable (IV)**. A simple *one-way analysis* of variance allows comparison of three or more sets of data, i.e. it can compare the scores from three or more different groups (**between subjects**), or from one group on three or more occasions (**repeated measures/within subjects**). More complex analyses are also possible, for example, a *two-way analysis* measures the extent to which the variance can be attributed to two **factors**. This can be either within subjects, when there are two repeated measures or between two groups to compare, or a mixture of the two. The example in Chapter 8 is a *three-way analysis* because it has three between subject factors as there are the pre-existing groups (race) and two independent variables. A *mixed ANOVA* allows you to measure between and within subjects simultaneously. An example of this is described in Chapter 9, where the between subjects factor was the sex of participant and the within subjects factor was the two levels of two independent variables manipulated through repeated measures.

There are two advantages of using an ANOVA. First, it allows you to compare three or more things at once and thereby reduces the likelihood of a **Type I error** (false positive) that may occur with multiple testing. Secondly, it allows the researcher to look for an **interaction** between different levels of different factors. For example, suppose you measured job anxiety and the between subjects factors were sex and profession (GPs and teachers). ANOVA would tell you whether anxiety differed between males and females, and between GPs and teachers. It would also be able to detect an interaction between the two, for instance, if males doctors were more anxious than female doctors, but female teachers were more anxious than male teachers. This would be an interaction between the two factors: sex and profession. NB: ANOVA is a parametric statistic and its use should be limited to data that meet the necessary assumptions of such statistics.

analytical survey This uses survey methods to test a specific hypothesis. E.g. Parents whose children are in primary school are more likely to watch television with their children than parents whose children are in comprehensive school. In this case the sample would usually include, at least, approximately equal numbers of parents from each group. *Compare with* **descriptive survey**.

ANCOVA *see* **analysis of covariance**.

anonymity is the protection of the participant in a study so that even the researchers cannot link the subject with the information provided. In contrast **confidentiality** means the prevention of disclosure of a participant's identity to other than authorised individuals. *See Box 2.1.*

ANOVA *see* **analysis of variance**.

apparatus: equipment (usually hardware, possibly mechanical or electronic) used in studies, normally experiments. When an apparatus is used, it would be expected that 'Apparatus' should be a subheading in the method section of the report. *Compare with* **materials**. *See also Key Topics: Research Reports.*

applied research is research that is designed to address a defined practical issue, to answer a clinical question or solve a specific, pragmatic problem.

archival data are data obtained from existing sources, often public records.

asymmetrical transfer effect may occur when an experiment uses **counterbalancing** in a **within subjects** design to control for **order effects**. When an asymmetrical transfer effect is identified in the data it means that the order of the experience of the conditions has determined the outcome. For example, a study comparing recall of emotive versus neutral words would have half the participants given the neutral wordlist first while the other half received the emotive wordlist first. This is **counterbalancing**. An asymmetrical transfer effect could then look as in Table G1 below. The data show that the average number of words recalled was higher from the emotive wordlist for one group and from the neutral wordlist for the other group. In this example both groups do better with the first list. *See also* **symmetrical transfer effect**.

Table G1

	Group 1	Group 2
First list/mean recalled	emotive/15	neutral/ 16
Second list/mean recalled	neutral/ 11	emotive/13

attitude scale is a survey measure designed to produce an overall score representing a respondent's attitude to an issue or object. They usually comprise a list of statements, rather than questions, and the task is to indicate how much you agree with each statement in turn. Half the statements will be positive about the issue or object and the remainder will be negative. For example, measuring attitudes to structure: 'I hate to change my plans at the last minute' and 'I enjoy being spontaneous'. There are several different scaling measures, but the three most common are **Likert**, **forced choice**, and **visual analogues**. In order to be sure that the scale is measuring what it purports to measure, the **psychometric properties** of the scale need to be evaluated. *Compare with* **questionnaires**. *See also* **rating scales**.

attrition rates/drop-out rates refer to the number of people who drop out of a study once it has started. Attrition rates are higher for lengthy and complex studies and represent a particular problem for **longitudinal** and **time-lag studies**.

baseline measurement is the measurement(s) of the **dependent variable** taken in a study before the manipulation of the **independent variable**. *See Chapter 9 for further information.*

between conditions is a research design where the focus of the research is to compare different conditions. This may be an **unrelated design** with **independent samples**, or a **related design** which would either be **matched pairs** or **repeated measures**.

between groups/between subjects design is an **unrelated** or **independent** design where the analysis compares two groups. The focus of the design may be to compare different pre-existing groups, **group difference** design, or to compare between conditions using **independent samples**.

bias occurs if we fail to be entirely objective. The dictionary definition of bias is a predisposition or tendency, especially a personal or sometimes unreasoned judgement. Bias can creep into the scientific method at any stage of the process and is a result of the difficulty that humans have in remaining entirely neutral at all times. In **quantitative** research, there are several techniques designed to reduce bias cased by **experimenter effects**, such as **blind** techniques.

Other forms of bias can occur if conditions or **stimuli** in a study are erroneously assumed to be equivalent. This type is best avoided by following a clearly defined research **protocol**. In **qualitative** research, bias is not seen as problematic provided that it is recognised; researchers need to acknowledge their personal input into the research process.

biased sample occurs if a subgroup of a population is over-represented. Psychology itself has been criticised for having a biased sample, as psychology students seem to be somewhat over-represented in the research process.

binomial sign test *see Key Topics: Commonly Used Inferential Statistics.*

bipolar scales are designed to measure both positive and negative responses to the subject of the scale. The 'zero' response in a bipolar scale is the middle response, denoting a lack of strong feelings one way or the other, for example:

Happy   *Sad*

(+2)   (+1)   (0)   (−1)   (−2)

Contrast this with a unipolar rating scales which only measure the extent of the single variable in question, for example:

Not at all   *Very anxious*
anxious   *indeed*

(0)   (1)   (2)   (3)   (4)

See also **Likert scaling; attitude scale.**

blind is a general term meaning that the person participating in a study is not aware of the nature of some, or all, of the details of the study. If someone is kept 'blind' to the research aim, it means they are not told the specific aim of the study. An example of this can be found in Chapter 8. A *single blind* study is one where the participant does not know what stimulus s/he has received or to which experimental condition s/he has been assigned. This may be appropriate if the researcher has no involvement with the participant throughout the study, for example in a study where stimuli are presented and responses recorded by computer in a single session. A *double blind* experiment is where neither the participant nor the person collecting the data knows to which experimental condition the participant has been assigned. They may, in some instances, not even know which **treatment** the participant has received. This is an important and frequently used way to reduce **experimenter effects.**

carry-over effects *see* **order effects.**

case study is when a single case is studied and reported. This can be an individual of particular interest (there is an example of this in Chapter 14), or it can be a case study of an institution or organisation. Occasionally more than one case is reported within a case study. Case studies are not designed for generalisation, but provide insights and information nonetheless. It is a largely observational method of research.

categorical variables/data *see* **nominal data.**

ceiling effects occur when a task or assessment produces a large number of high scores and, thereby, fails to distinguish between cases. *See also* **floor effects.**

central tendency refers to the way in which data are distributed. A measure of central tendency is a **descriptive statistic** that gives an indication of the shape of a data set by identifying where the data congregate. There are three main such measures: **mean**, **median** and **mode**.

chi square (χ^2) is a statistic that forms part of the calculation of several inferential statistics including the **independent chi square** and the **chi square goodness of fit**.

chi square/goodness of fit *see Key Topics: Commonly Used Inferential Statistics.*

clinical trials are research studies designed to test new treatments or medications. There are three phases of clinical trials that need to be completed before a medicine is marketed. Phase I checks the safety of the different doses of the medicine on a small group of healthy volunteers. Phase II comprises screening studies with a larger group to see if the drug is effective and to continue to evaluate its safety. Phase III is the authoritative **randomised controlled trial**.

closed questions are questions with a limited number of possible answers. In **questionnaires** this usually means that a range of answers is provided for the respondent to select one, for example 'Yes/No' or 'Always/Sometimes/Rarely/Never'. In **interviews**, as in ordinary speech, a closed question is one where the range of possible answers is limited, for example 'How old are you?' 'Did you go on holiday this year?' 'What is your favourite TV programme?' *Compare with* **open questions**.

cluster sample is when a sample is drawn from a designated place or institution that is known to have an appropriate population. For example, if the population of interest was psychology undergraduates, it is unlikely that a list of all such students in the country would be available. Recruiting instead from a number of universities would provide the researcher with several cluster samples.

coding frame/schedule is a list of the target behaviours to be categorised in structured observation; these are identified and defined prior to the start of data collection.

coefficient is a figure that is achieved through a statistical procedure that measures the relationship between two sets of numerical data. The calculated figure ranges from −1 to +1. Coefficients near 0 suggest that there is no correlation, while a figure nearer +1 suggests that the two variables have a *positive correlation*. A figure nearer −1 indicates a *negative correlation*. However, the critical value that the coefficient must reach to be significant depends on the number of cases in the sample: the bigger the sample, the lower the threshold for significance. For example, a correlation of .3 is not a significant correlation for a sample of 20 people but it is if there are 40. There are two common correlation statistics that produce **correlation coefficients**, Pearson's (product moment) correlation coefficient and its **nonparametric** equivalent Spearman's correlation. *See Key Topics: Commonly Used Inferential Statistics.* Coefficients are also used in measures of **reliability**. *See also* **alpha coefficient**.

cohort is a sample that is defined by a time band. A cohort of children, for example, may be defined by an age group, or a cohort of students may be defined by the graduation year. This term is most commonly used in **longitudinal**, **time-lag** or **cross-sectional** studies.

cohort effect is a potential problem when two different cohorts in a study have had different experiences other than that which is the focus of the study. For example, if we wanted to compare first-year students' attitudes to higher education in 2005 and 2015, the cohort effect would be that the second sample were affected by the raising of the school leaving age to 17, which may affect their responses.

comparator is a group of cases or an individual case that provides researchers with a standard or measurement against which it is possible to compare **data** taken from a **sample**.

concurrent validity (in **psychometrics**) is when the results of a psychometric assessment are compared with results from other established assessments taken at the same time. *See Chapter 16 for an example.*

confidence interval is a **descriptive statistic**, a measurement of how representative the sample is of the population, usually recommended for use with **interval** or **ratio data**. *See Key Topics: Commonly Used Descriptive Statistics.*

confidentiality means the prevention of disclosure of a participant's identity to other than authorised, and specified, individuals. In contrast, **anonymity** is the protection of the participant in a study so that even the researchers cannot link the subject with the information provided. *See Box 2.1.*

confirmatory factor analysis is a form of factor analysis that is designed to test whether the data fit a particular specified model. It is often used in the development of psychometric assessments to confirm the factor structure identified in an early data set. *See Chapter 16 for an example.*

confounding error is the result of a **confounding variable**.

confounding variable/confound is a variable not under the control of the researcher that varies *systematically* within the study design, decreasing the researcher's ability to isolate cause and effect. It can affect the **independent** or **dependent variable**. Confounding variables can produce **Type I** or **Type II errors**.

construct validity means that the operational definition or psychometric assessment has successfully encompassed the target construct. *See the example under the heading 'How Effective Is the Study Design?' in Chapter 10.*

content analysis is a broad range of approaches to analysing **qualitative data**. At one end the analysis can be quantitative (*as in Chapter 12*) or it may be a **qualitative analysis** (*as in Chapter 13*). The data may have been collected using **survey methods** or unstructured observation, or they may be **secondary data**.

content validity (in **psychometrics**) refers to the extent to which the whole of the target area is covered by the assessment. For example, if an assessment is designed to measure visual memory then it would need to include assessments of long- and short-term memory.

continuous data/continuous variable describes a measurement where there is no limit to the number of subdivisions that could be made to increase accuracy. The only restriction on the number of those subdivisions is the accuracy of the measuring equipment. For example, grams can be split into micrograms (100,000th part of a gram), nanograms (1,000,000,000th part of a gram) or even smaller. Continuous variables are a subgroup of **interval** or **ratio data** only. *Compare with* **discrete data/discrete variable**.

control (noun) is a standard of comparison for checking or verifying the results of an experiment or it can refer to an individual or group used for the purpose of comparison in an experiment.

control (verb) is the keystone of experimental research as the study needs to control all relevant **variables**, i.e. the **independent variable** and all **extraneous variables**.

control condition is the condition with which the **experimental condition** can be compared. For example, if you want to measure how sleep deprivation affects performance, it is not enough simply to deprive your sample of sleep prior to measuring performance unless you also had a control condition in which performance was measured without sleep deprivation.

convenience sampling involves recruiting participants because they are convenient; for example, experimenting on psychology students or recruiting acquaintances to complete questionnaires. This is **non-probability sampling**. *Compare with* **opportunity sampling**.

correlate is a statistical measurement technique that tests whether there is a relationship between two numeric variables. For example, if you correlate height and weight in a given sample of children you are likely to find there is relationship between the two. That relationship is expressed as a **correlation coefficient**.

correlation is a term used in statistics to refer to a relationship that exists between numeric variables, that is, whether they co-relate. Where two variables have a *positive correlation* it means that as one increases so the other does. For example, calorific intake and body weight are correlated: the greater the number of calories consumed, the greater the body weight; thus calories and weight are positively correlated. A *negative correlation* is when one variable increases while the other decreases. For example, annual income and incidence of illness: wealthier people have fewer illnesses than poorer people; therefore money and ill health are negatively correlated. If two variables show no evidence of being correlated, this is referred to as a *zero correlation*, for example IQ scores and shoe size.

correlation coefficient is the outcome of a statistical technique that measures the strength of the relationship between two numeric variables. This coefficient can vary from +1 (a strong positive correlation) through 0 (no correlation) to −1 (a strong negative correlation). For example, a coefficient of .987 is a very strong positive correlation, a coefficient of −.567 is quite a strong negative correlation and one of .012 is so weak as to be non-existent. If two variables are so perfectly related that the coefficient is +1 or −1, it is termed a *perfect correlation*.

correlational design/research is when a study determines the extent to which two or more variables are **correlated**. It will require taking two (or more) measures from each case in the sample. Correlational design does not establish cause and effect.

counterbalancing is a way to control for order effects in a **within subjects design**. In its simplest form: half the participants experience condition A followed by condition B; for the other half, this is reversed. Counterbalancing is more complicated when there are more than two conditions. Consider an experiment with three conditions: A, B and C. The trick in

Table G2

	First presentation	Second presentation	Third presentation
Group 1	A	B	C
Group 2	B	C	A
Group 3	C	A	B

counterbalancing is to make sure that each condition appears in each position an equal number of times. An example of how this might be counterbalanced is given in Table G2. Note that all three conditions are performed once for each group in the order which controls for the order of presentation across all three conditions.

covariance is the amount of variation or **variance** that two **numeric variables** share.

criterion validity (in **psychometrics**) is the extent to which the measurement correlates with an external criterion or **variable** of the phenomenon under study.

Cronbach's alpha *see* **alpha coefficient**.

cross-cultural study is a study that compares two different cultures or societies. It differs from an **ethnographic** study where the researcher is aspiring to learn about a different culture and is attempting not to bring in to the research the trappings and values of her or his own culture. *There is an example of a cross-cultural study in Chapter 19.*

crossover trial is a clinical trial in which all participants receive both treatments, but at different times. Halfway through the study, one group is switched from the experimental to the control treatment, and the other group is switched from the control to the experimental treatment.

cross-sectional study involves comparing different groups in the population at a single point in time. For example, to explore children's development a researcher might select three samples: 5-year-olds, 8-year-olds and 11-year-olds. *Compare with* **time-lag** *and* **longitudinal studies**.

data (plural) are measurements or observations. *Datum* (singular) is a single measurement or observation, often called a score or a raw score.

data set a collection of measurements or observations.

debrief is when participants in a research study are provided with further details of the study design or aim that they could not be told prior to taking part, as it would have affected their behaviour/response. In the experiment in Chapter 6, for example, participants had to be debriefed in order to find out whether they had noticed the change in their conversational partner. In the Milgram study in Chapter 2, participants were debriefed when they were introduced to the 'Learner' whom they had believed to be unconscious.

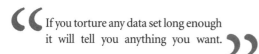

If you torture any data set long enough it will tell you anything you want.

deduction is the process of reasoning in which a conclusion follows necessarily from the stated premises or **theory**. (The word can also refer to a conclusion reached by this process.) **Quantitative** research uses deductive reasoning. *See also* **induction**.

demand characteristics means that aspects of a research programme or of a researcher's conduct, or even appearance, may cause the subject to try to guess the aim of the study and therefore, possibly, to attempt deliberately to confirm or refute what they believe to be the experimenter's hypothesis. Some argue that demand characteristics are inevitable in most forms of research involving humans as it is an innate tendency to try to make sense of a situation.

demographic variables mean the characteristics of a population. These can include sex, race, age, income, educational level, home ownership, or employment status, for example. Demographic details are often sought of a sample to ensure that it is representative of a population of interest. They are sometimes needed to ascertain whether there is a **mediating** and potentially **confounding variable**.

denominator is the figure below the line in a fraction or formula. For example, with ¾, the four is the denominator; the three is the **numerator**.

dependent variable (DV) is the variable that is being investigated and on which data are collected during the study. It is assumed to be affected by the **independent variable (IV)**. This type of terminology is most suited to an experimental design, but it is used in other research settings too. *The IVs and DVs are identified and listed in the summary grid at the end of each of the six chapters on experiments.*

descriptive statistics are statistical procedures used to summarise, organise and simplify data. *See Key Topics: Commonly Used Descriptive Statistics.*

descriptive survey aims to provide a description of a specified population on a particular attribute, for example discovering which television programme is favoured by parents (20 per cent favour *Blue Peter*, 25 per cent *The Simpsons* and 55 per cent *Dr Who*). *Compare with* **analytical survey**.

directional hypothesis *see* **one-tailed hypothesis**.

discourse analysis is a means of analysing spoken communication which assumes that people use words to construct the world as they experience it. It is a form of **qualitative analysis**.

discrete data/discrete variable refers to a type of measurement that is not amenable to subdivisions. For example, the score on a **psychometric** scale, or the number of children in a family, or the number of words recalled from a list. (Please note that subdivisions may be used when looking at averages, but not individual cases. The average number of children in a family may be 2.4, but no family of that size exists as there is no such thing as 0.4 of a child.) *Compare with* **continuous data/continuous variable**.

discriminatory power is the extent to which a psychometric assessment, or an item therein, is effective in placing individuals on the continuum that is being measured. For example, if a test is intended to measure state anxiety, we would want to know how successful it was in sorting individuals into a rank order from highly anxious to not at all anxious.

dispersion/spread/variability all refer to the way in which a set of numeric data is spread around the central point. There are different **measures** to represent this. *See Key Topics: Commonly Used Descriptive Statistics.*

distracters are employed in experimental research when the task is to identify or recognise the target stimulus. If the task is to recognise an object previously presented in a memory test, then that object may be presented with say three different but similar objects to see if the participant can select the target object. *For an example, see Chapter 6.*

double blind *see* **blind**.

drop-out rates *see* **attrition rates**.

ecological validity when findings can be generalised from the specific study to the real-world setting in which the behaviour in question is likely to occur. In general, ecological validity tends to be higher in observational studies and field experiments than in laboratory studies.

emic is a term describing views of the world, ideas, or constructs that members of a given culture accept as real, meaningful, or appropriate, but which are not universally found across cultures. *See also* **etic**.

empirical/empirically (adjective and adverb) relating to collection of data which demonstrates orderly relationships.

empirical methods the collection of data from which conclusions can be drawn or **orderly relationships** established.

error is the variation in the data that has not been controlled or manipulated by the researcher. *See also* **Type I** and **Type II**.

ethical to do with **ethics**.

ethics are rules of conduct for behaviour, especially research. *See Chapter 2 for an outline of ethical theories and principles, and also BPS Ethical Principles for Conducting Research with Human Participants for more details.*

ethnography/ethnographic approach involves the researcher in studying a group that shares a common culture over a prolonged period of time and producing a qualitative account of that culture. The expectation is that researchers should immerse themselves in the culture and should attempt not to allow their prior expectations of the culture to influence their report. This is a **qualitative** method.

etic is a term describing views of the world, ideas or constructs that researchers transfer from their own culture to other cultures; the point of view of a cultural outsider such as a scholar or tourist. *See also* **emic**.

evaluation apprehension is when a participant's response is governed by what s/he believes the researcher will infer about her/him rather than by her/his own natural behaviour pattern. The effect on the response may be either towards or away from conforming to perceived social norms. For example, in an experiment designed to test how people respond to unexpected events, a participant might refuse to respond for fear of being judged in some way by that response. *See Chapter 7. Compare with* **social desirability**.

event-sampling is one method for sampling data in **structured observation**. It occurs when the aim of the study is to examine a particular type of, or target, behaviour. For example, observing children playing the researcher may only be interested in solitary play and so focuses observation on each of these events within the playground. This will normally require recording behaviour if there is any possibility that two target events could occur at the same time. *See also* **point-sampling**; **time-sampling**.

ex post facto (literal meaning: after the fact) is a **quasi-experimental** design where the researcher does not have control over the **independent variable**; rather, changes in the **independent variable (IV)** have already occurred before the research starts. Therefore, it is not usually possible to determine cause and effect, but collated evidence over a series of ex post facto studies may be conclusive. Ex post facto studies are useful when there are groups who differ on an implied IV and the researcher wants to explore the effects; for example, students who have a second language and those who do not (IV) could be followed to see whether there is a difference in grades achieved in English examinations. This design can also be used when groups differ on a **dependent variable** and the researcher wants to look at possible explanatory IVs; for example, students who drop out of college and those who graduate could be investigated to see whether there were clear differences in entry qualifications, domestic circumstances etc. Ex post facto studies can be **prospective** or **retrospective**.

exclusion criteria are the attributes of potential participants which would make them unsuitable for inclusion in a particular piece of research. One exclusion criterion, for example, could be if a potential participant was aware of the aims of the study. *See also* **inclusion criteria**.

experiment is a controlled test or investigation of a **hypothesis**. It will involve the manipulation or control of at least one variable (the **independent variable**) and the measurement of at least one other (the **dependent variable**). *See also* **field experiment; natural experiment; quasi-experiment; true experiment**. *There are examples of experiments in Chapters 3–9.*

experimental condition refers to the condition in an experiment which is the focus of the study, unlike the **control condition** with which it is being compared. For example, if you want to measure how sleep deprivation affects performance, in one condition you would require your participants to go without sleep – this would be the experimental condition; you would compare their subsequent performance with that of the control condition.

experimental error refers to uncontrolled sources of variability in a data set which occur randomly during the experiment and may be due to individual differences among participants.

experimental hypothesis (H$_1$), like the **alternative hypothesis**, is a statement of cause and effect that an **experiment** is designed to test. For example in Chapter 3, H$_1$: one form of telephone support would be more effective than the other. The final decision once the experiment is completed is always given in terms of the **null hypothesis**. We either 'Reject H$_0$' or 'Do not reject H$_0$'. We never say that we 'Reject H$_1$', nor that we 'Accept H$_1$'. When the null hypothesis is rejected, we can only say that the experimental hypothesis *may* be true. *For a further discussion of this logic, see Box 6.1.*

experimental manipulation refers to the change that a researcher deliberately produces in an experiment. For example, in Chapter 6, the experimental manipulation was the change of conversational partner; in Chapter 7, it was the type of sound played to the monkey.

experimental method is a general term used to refer to the scientific method for studying cause-and-effect relationships between variables. It is not really different in meaning from the terms **experiment** or **experimentation**, but it tends to be used in different contexts where the emphasis is on the methodological approach.

experimental paradigm in the behavioural sciences this is an experimental set-up (i.e. a way to conduct a certain type of experiment) that is defined by certain fine-tuned standards and which often has a theoretical background. A paradigm in this technical sense, however, is not as strict a way of thinking as it is in the epistemological meaning. *See also* **paradigm**.

experimentation (1) is a type of research characterised by the manipulation of one variable and the measurement of another.

experimentation (2) is the act of carrying out an experiment.

experimenter effects are the influence of the experimenter's behaviour, personality traits, or expectancies on the results of his or her own research. *See also* **experimenter/researcher expectancy**.

experimenter/researcher expectancy is a particular form of experimenter effect where the researcher's knowledge of the experimental design, or of the anticipated outcome, affects the data. This is not to suggest that the experimenter deliberately intervenes to distort the data, but rather that the influence is inadvertent. The influence of expectancy was famously demonstrated by Rosenthal and Jacobson (1968) in a study where teachers were told which children would be higher achievers although the children identified had been selected at random and there was no evidence that the children would improve their performance more than other children (those in the control condition). When all the children were tested at the end of the study, those identified by the researcher did show greater improvements than those in the control group. This effect could only be attributed to their teachers' expectations of improvement.

exploratory factor analysis *see Key Topics: Commonly Used Inferential Statistics.*

external reliability is the extent to which the findings of a study could be repeated across time, or samples, or circumstances; also known as **test-retest reliability** when applied to **psychometric assessments**. *See also Box 16.1.*

external validity refers to the extent to which a given finding can be generalised to other cases in different contexts. This is also referred to as the *stability* of a measure.

extraneous variables All variables that are not under the control of the researcher and may therefore interfere with the interpretation of the findings. Extraneous variables can have a random effect, producing 'noise' in the data and making it difficult to draw any conclusions (**random error**) or a systematic effect which may lead the researcher to a spurious conclusion (**confounding variables**).

face validity (in **psychometrics**) refers to the degree to which an assessment appears to measure what it purports to measure. For example, a measurement of stress should comprise items that focus on stressful situations or responses.

factor is a term which usually refers to the **independent variable**, but can also be used to refer to pre-existing group differences or variables that are controlled in the study. For example in Chapter 9 there were four factors: the woman's facial expression (the independent variable); the sex of the participant (group difference); which male face in each pair was the target; and which of each pair was smiled at (two variables controlled across the sample).

factor analysis *see Key Topics: Commonly Used Inferential Statistics.*

factor structure refers to the hypothetical constructs that underpin observed behaviour. This is most commonly cited in **psychometric** assessments, where there are assumed to be underlying attributes that influence an individual's responses. *See Box 18.1.*

false positive/false negative *see* **Type I/II errors**.

field experiment takes place in an applied setting where the participants might normally be found and where the behaviour of interest occurs naturally. Despite its name, this does not have to happen outdoors: it may be in a factory, a shop, a school or a hospital, for example. As it is an experiment it will involve making changes to one variable to see how this affects another variable. *Compare with* **natural experiment**.

field study is a more generic term which includes field experiments as well as other forms of research such as observation, or in some cases survey methods.

Fisher's exact probability *see Key Topics: Commonly Used Inferential Statistics.*

floor effects occur when a task or assessment produces a large number of low scores and, thereby, fails to distinguish between cases. *See also* **ceiling effects**.

forced choice responses are sometimes used in questionnaires or attitude scales where there is no midpoint option representing a neutral response; thus respondents are forced to make a choice in favour of or against the object in question. Forced choice responses can be used with a variant of **Likert scaling** or with a different array of evaluative responses. Researchers usually favour four options over two to allow for gradations in response (e.g. very good, quite good, quite poor, very poor).

frequency data refers to the number of cases in particular categories within a **data set**. For example the study in Chapter 4 provides frequency data on the type of surgery for which each patient was scheduled.

Friedman's analysis of variance *see Key Topics: Commonly Used Inferential Statistics.*

fully structured interview is an interview where the order of the questions and their wording are the same for each participant in the study. This usually means that the interviewer should not deviate from the prepared interview schedule. It also means that the interviewer has some prepared responses if the interviewee queries the meaning of any of the questions. For example, the rejoinder might be 'There are no right or wrong answers; we are interested in your opinion.' *Compare with* **semi-structured** *and* **unstructured interviews**.

funnelling technique is way of organising questions in either an interview or a questionnaire when the researcher leads gently to the key issue. This is normally used to see whether a respondent raises the key issue in their response to preliminary questions. It provides participants with an opportunity to mention spontaneously target items prior to direct questioning. *For an example, see Chapter 6.*

generalising/generalisation is the process of inferring from **sample data** an effect or phenomenon that will also be found in the **population** from which the sample was drawn. Generalisation is often considered a cornerstone of **quantitative** research but it is not so often the aim of **qualitative** research. *See also* **representative** *and Box 17.1.*

goodness of fit/chi square (χ^2) goodness of fit *see Key Topics: Commonly Used Inferential Statistics.*

grounded theory is an **inductive** approach in **qualitative** research. It means that the theory is built from what emerges from the data. Contrast this with a **quantitative** approach, the **hypothetico-deductive method**. *For example, see Chapter 18.*

group difference study is a study design where the comparison is between two (or more) existing groups in the population. As such it cannot be a true experiment as clearly the **independent variable** (the grouping variable) is not within the **manipulation** of the **experimenter**. There is an example of this in Chapter 8 where there were two groups of different ethnicity.

H_0 abbreviation for **null hypothesis**.

H_1, H_2 etc. abbreviations for first, second **alternative/experimental hypothesis** etc.

habituated means to have become accustomed to or used to something. It is commonly, but not solely, used in experiments involving animals and refers to how they respond to the repeated presentation of what was initially a novel stimulus.

Hawthorne effect is the effect on human behaviour or performance caused by the knowledge that the behaviour or performance is being studied. The name comes from a study, in the first part of the twentieth century, of factors affecting productivity at the Hawthorne plant of the General Electric Company in the USA. A team of researchers found that all changes to conditions on the assembly line improved production and had beneficial effects – even opposing changes, such as increasing the lighting to maximum and later reducing it to little more than moonlight. It was concluded that the increase in productivity was caused by being studied. The workers were responding to the interesting new process of being the subject of a scientific investigation – a cautionary tale!

homogeneity of variance means two or more sets of data having a similar amount of variability. This is a requirement for some **parametric inferential statistics** and can be assessed using statistical measures. If one set of data varies a great deal more than a second set, this may require caution in the use of some parametric tests of difference.

hypothesis (plural **hypotheses**) is a clear but tentative statement of a relationship between two or more variables, which can be tested by empirical methods: **experiments**, **survey methods** or **observation**. Hypotheses should not be confused with research questions or **aims**. For example, an aim might be: To develop a model of factors influencing dietary choice. The research question might be: Are such influences different across generations? The hypothesis might be: Age affects perceptions of a 'healthy diet'. *See also* **null hypothesis**; **one-tailed hypothesis**; **two-tailed hypothesis**.

hypothetical construct is an explanatory variable which is not directly observable. For example, the concepts of intelligence and memory are used to explain phenomena in psychology, but neither is directly observable or directly measurable; therefore an **operational definition** is required. *See* **psychometrics**; **reliable/reliability**; **standardisation**; **valid/validity**.

hypothetico-deductive method refers to the scientific method of attempting to test or falsify a hypothesis derived from observable phenomena. This involves observing phenomena, devising a theory that would explain the relationship between the observed variables, and developing from this a hypothesis to test the theory. *See also Box 7.1.*

idiographic means relating to or involving the study of individuals. Therefore individual research focuses on understanding the individual experience rather than seeking to generalise. Idiographic research is largely **qualitative**. *Compare with* **nomothetic research**.

inclusion criteria are the attributes of potential participants which are required for inclusion in the research. One inclusion criterion, for example, could be that all participants are fluent in English. *See also* **exclusion criteria**.

independent chi square (χ^2) test *see Key Topics: Commonly Used Inferential Statistics.*

independent design/sample/subjects/groups is a research design where two or more separate groups are used and their results compared. The focus of the study may be on a pre-existing variable on which these two groups were considered to differ (**between groups** design), or the groups may be artificially constructed from the existing sample and then assigned to separate experimental set-ups (**between conditions** design).

independent t-test *see Key Topics: Commonly Used Inferential Statistics.*

independent variable (IV) is the variable that the experimenter manipulates in order to observe the subsequent effect. It is assumed that the independent variable will have a direct effect on the **dependent variable (DV)**. This type of terminology is most suited to an experimental design, but it is used in other research settings too. *The IVs and DVs are identified and listed in the summary grid at the end of each of the six chapters on experiments.*

indirect observation is a method of observation of existing material rather observing people (or animals) directly. Data are not collected for the research but rather the aim is to analyse materials such as **archival data**, statistics, publications or any form of media or recordings (*for examples, see Chapters 12 and 13*) or even graffiti (e.g. Klofas & Cutshall, 1985).

induction/inductive research infers a general conclusion or orderly relationship from a specific observed phenomenon. Induction means drawing theory from the data, rather than seeking data to test an existing theory. It is used largely in **qualitative research**. *See also* **deduction**.

inferential statistics/statistical tests are a set of mathematical manipulations which allow the researcher to decide whether or not their findings are **significant**. They allow the researcher to take a sample from a population and then, using **probability**, to draw *inferences* about the characteristics of that population.

> Most people use statistics the way a drunk uses a lamp post – more for support than illumination. (Mark Twain, author, 1835–1910)

informed consent refers to participants agreeing to take part in a study after they have fully understood what participation involves. It is a common requirement set by ethics committees prior to approving a study.

interaction *see* **analysis of variance**.

inter-judge reliability *see* **inter-rater reliability**.

internal reliability is the consistency of a measure within itself. For example, a measurement comprising 20 items on anxiety would be expected to show that each item taps into anxiety. Internal reliability is measured by correlations between the items; it usually involves either **split-half method** or **alpha coefficients**.

internal validity refers to the successful manipulation of the **independent variable** within a study, such that cause and effect can be safely inferred.

inter-observer reliability measures the extent to which two or more sets of independent observations produce the same results. Inter-observer reliability can be measured statistically, using a **coefficient**. When inter-observer reliability is poor, it suggests that **subjectivity** or **bias** has crept into the observation and it may be a result of inadequate observer training, or the **operational definitions** may have been inappropriate or flawed.

inter-rater/inter-judge reliability measures the extent to which two or more sets of independent ratings produce the same results. It is often used interchangeably with **inter-observer reliability**. Rating, however, is different from observations as it involves a numerical rating of a target behaviour or object, rather than a categorisation or description. Like inter-observer reliability, inter-rater reliability can be measured statistically, using a **coefficient**.

interval data are data where each point in the scale is the same interval from its adjacent point, but where there is no absolute zero. Temperature is a good example of this: each degree on a scale is the same size, and the difference between 34 and 35 degrees is exactly the same as the difference between 35 and 36 degrees. However, zero degrees does not mean no temperature but is simply a designated point on the scale. You can add and subtract interval data, but you cannot multiply or divide them. Half of 34 degrees is not half as hot! Likewise, the time is recorded in interval data: 14.10 and 14.15 and 14.20 each have the same size interval (five minutes) between them; 00.00 does not mean 'no time', it means midnight! Contrast this with timings which are recorded in **ratio data**. Some **standardised scales** produce interval data, for example IQ tests. In most statistics, however, interval data are treated in the same way as ratio data. *See also* **nominal data**; **ordinal data**; **ratio data**.

intervention is a procedure or *treatment* that is intended to prevent or treat a condition. The term comes originally from **clinical trials** but is now sometimes used in more general **experimental manipulations** affecting the participants or their environment. An alternative term with a similar meaning is treatment, a controlled technique or action applied in a specified process or **experiment**. Although it has medical connotations, it can also be used in non-clinical research.

interview is a process whereby the researcher asks the respondent questions or encourages her/him to talk about particular issues. The respondent's answers may be written by the interviewer or alternatively recorded electronically. Interviews may be **fully structured, semi-structured** or **unstructured**. *Compare with* **questionnaires**. *There are examples of interviews in Chapters 17 and 18.*

interview schedule is the briefing document used in interviews. In **semi-structured interviews** this might only be a list of general questions or topics to be explored during the interview. In **fully structured interviews** a schedule will have the precise wording of each question, prompt and supplementary, set out in the order in which they are to be asked.

item analysis is a means of checking each item in a scale or **psychometric** assessment to ensure that it **correlates** with other similar items and/or with the total score. This is assessed by using an **alpha** (**Cronbach's**) **correlation**. *For examples, see Chapter 16.*

known groups validity (**psychometrics**) is the extent to which the measurement successfully shows a difference between two groups of cases which are known to differ on the variable in question. For example, developing a measurement of attitudes to vegetarianism, you could compare the scores of, say, the vegan society and those of livestock farmers.

Kruskal – Wallis *see Key Topics: Commonly Used Inferential Statistics.*

Kuder – Richardson *see Key Topics: Commonly Used Inferential Statistics.*

levels (in **factors**) are the number of conditions or groups identified in the factor. If the factor is sex, there are two levels: male and female. If the factor refers to two experimental conditions and a control it would be said to have three levels.

levels of measurement refer to the four different types of quantitative data that can be collected: **nominal**, **ordinal**, **interval** and **ratio**. Understanding what each level of data means is an important step towards understanding what statistics to use. *See Key Topics: Commonly Used Descriptive Statistics* and *Commonly Used Inferential Statistics.*

Likert scaling is a form of scaled response often used in questionnaires, or attitude scales, where the participant is asked to indicate her/his degree of agreement with an evaluative statement. The responses are given a numerical value and this enables the calculation of a total response for the overall questionnaire or attitude scale. Traditionally a five-point scale is used; however, some advocate using a seven- or nine-point scale. The number of options is normally odd in order to allow a midpoint to represent neither agreement nor disagreement. *See also* **forced choice**.

literature review is a synthesis of past research evidence relevant to a particular study, and serves as part of the introduction to the report. *See Key Topics: Research Reports.*

longitudinal study involves following a sample over time. For example, to study child development, a researcher might recruit a sample of 5-year-olds and follow them over the next six years of their development, taking measurements at predetermined intervals. Short-term longitudinal studies are more common than long-term studies as the latter are expensive on resources and suffer high **attrition rates**. *Compare with* **time-lag** and **cross-sectional studies**.

manipulation in an experiment, the researcher manipulates the **independent variable** to see whether it affects the **dependent variable**. Manipulation has been considered the essence of experimentation and this often distinguishes it from other methods. When there is manipulation, it will be an experiment. But be careful; not all experiments include manipulation: for example, **natural experiments** or **group difference experiments** may not; *see Chapters 8 and 19.*

manipulation checks are a means of testing whether the manipulation of the independent variable has been successful. It can be built into the study design as a precaution, but may alternatively be included at the end of the study in the **debriefing**. The nature of the manipulation check varies with the type of research. For example, in a **Phase II clinical trial** the manipulation check may involve taking blood tests to ensure that different doses of the drug have been appropriately administered. *There is an example of a manipulation check in Chapter 8.*

Mann Whitney (U) test *see Key Topics: Commonly Used Inferential Statistics.*

matched pairs design is where respondents in a study are assigned to one group or condition by being paired with an identifiable and equivalent individual in another. It is classified as a **within subjects** or **related design**. *There is an example of this in Chapter 4.*

matched pairs t-test/paired t-test/related t-test *see Key Topics: Commonly Used Inferential Statistics.*

materials are tools used in studies, often referring to psychometric measures, questionnaires or similar survey style items. When used in a study this is often a subheading in the study report. Compare with **apparatus**. *See also Key Topics: Research Reports.*

max *see* **min, max.**

mean is a **descriptive statistic**, a measurement of **central tendency** usually recommended for use with **interval** or **ratio data**. *See Key Topics: Commonly Used Descriptive Statistics.*

measures are instruments, devices, assessments or methods that provide data on the quantity or quality of the **independent** or **dependent variable**.

median is a **descriptive statistic**, a measurement of **central tendency** usually recommended for use with **ordinal data**. *See Key Topics: Commonly Used Descriptive Statistics.*

median split is a method of dividing a collection of data into two equal groups around the midpoint, or **median**. It is commonly used to divide respondents into two groups, those scoring high on one particular variable and those scoring lower. While it is common practice, it is not without its critics because it can produce a false dichotomy, as the midpoint in the data may be a distortion of the construct depending on the **sampling procedure** used. *There is an example of the use of a median split in Chapter 15.*

mediating variable is a variable that may explain the observed relationship between the **independent** and the **dependent variable**. It can be a variable that is a predictor of the dependent variable(s), and simultaneously predicted by the independent variable(s). For example, in Chapter 3 we saw that a regular schedule of calls resulted in effective treatment. It is possible that the regular schedule did not directly affect treatment, but rather encouraged people to stay in the trial, which in turn affected treatment. If this were the case then staying on the trial would be the mediating variable.

meta-analysis is the systematic analysis of a set of existing research papers in order to draw general conclusions about the topic in question. Unlike a **systematic review**, this incorporates analyses of the published **data**.

min, max is a **descriptive statistic**, a measurement of **variability** usually recommended for use with **ordinal data**. *See Key Topics: Commonly Used Descriptive Statistics.*

mixed design refers to studies, usually experiments, that include both **within group** and **between group** comparisons. Usually this means that both comparisons are made within the same trial, rather than as separate phases of the same study. *There are examples of this in Chapters 8 and 9.*

mixed methods means that a study has used more than one method to collect data. *See, for example, Chapter 18.*

modal is of, or to do with, the **mode**. A modal value is the number of cases in the mode. For example, where there is a sample of 100 people, only 35 of whom are female, then the mode is male, and the modal value is 65.

mode is a **descriptive statistic**, a measurement of **central tendency** usually recommended for use with **nominal data**. *See Key Topics: Commonly Used Descriptive Statistics.*

N is a standardised abbreviation for the number when stating how many cases were in a study or a group, e.g. N=20.

N=1 design *see* **single case design.**

naive, in research, refers to participants who have not previously taken part in the study and do not know its aim. This quality is independent of how cynical or experienced the participants may be in real life!

natural experiment happens when an event is taking place in the real world that allows a before and after comparison. It is an experiment in name only as the manipulation of the independent variable is not within the control of the researcher. For example, if we wanted to see whether students find examinations stressful, we could measure their stress levels mid-term, and then again at the start of the examination period, a so-called 'naturally occurring' stressor! *Compare with* **field experiment**.

naturalistic refers to a type of study in which researchers look at the behaviour of persons or objects in their usual or natural environment – not to be confused with naturist!

negative correlation *see* **correlation**.

nominal data/nominal level of data, also known as **categorical data**, are data that are simply frequency counts of classifications of cases. Collecting nominal data means that a researcher has a number of categories of interest and counts the frequency of the occurrence of each within their sample, thereby producing **frequency data.** Examples would be categories determined by **demographic variables** (Males and Females), by behaviour (Smokers, Ex-Smokers and Non-Smokers) or by responses to a question (Yes and No) or an experimental task (Completers and Non-Completers). This is the simplest form of data and it is not **numeric data**, as only classifications are taken from each case, rather than a number. *See also* **interval data**; **ordinal data**; **ratio data.**

nomothetic means relating to or involving the search for universal principles. Therefore nomothetic research is that from which generalisations to the relevant population can be made. Nomothetic research is largely **quantitative**. *Compare with* **idiographic.**

non-directional hypothesis *see* **two-tailed hypothesis**.

non-directive interview is an interview where the interviewer does not direct the course of the interview and remains non-judgemental. This type of interview is more common in therapy than in research although it can be used in this context too.

nonparametric statistics make no assumptions about the underlying **parameters** of the **population**. **Inferential statistics** for **nominal data** are nonparametric, as are those for **numeric data**, which require the data to be ranked. *See Key Points: Commonly Used Inferential Statistics and also* **parametric statistics.**

non-participant observation is where the researcher's role is purely observational. This usually involves **structured observation**, where the behaviour is either recorded for subsequent analysis or noted at the time using a systematic sampling technique, **time**, **point**, or **event sampling**.

non-probability sampling refers to sampling strategies that fall short of **probability sampling**; it is where the probability of a case from the population being selected is unknown. Nearly all experimental research uses non-probability sampling methods, which include **convenience**, **opportunity**, **purposive**, **self-selected**, **snowball**, **systematic** and **volunteer sampling**.

non-significant is the correct term to describe a finding when inferential statistics fail to reach **significance** (usually **p**<.05). It is unwise to describe such a finding as insignificant.

normative data are those that represent what is shown to be statistically normal as a result of collecting **data**, usually using a **psychometric assessment**, from a large number of people, part of the process of **standardisation**. A standardised assessment may have normative data for different sectors of the **population**.

norms are statistical measures of **central tendency** on a performance of a well-defined group that serves as a reference by which to gauge the performance of the other individuals who take the test. Most norms tables show, in descending order, various test scores and the percentage of people in the reference group who scored below each score level. Thus, knowing an individual's score, you can quickly determine how he or she compares with the reference group.

null hypothesis (H$_0$) is the opposite of the **experimental** or **alternative hypothesis**. If the experimental hypothesis is that age influences perceptions of a 'healthy diet', the null hypothesis would be that age has no effect on these perceptions. The null hypothesis is a statement that the **independent variable** has no effect on the **dependent variable** or that there is no association between **variables**. The null hypothesis is usually only inferred in research reports, and rarely stated. *For another example, see the discussion under the heading 'How Can We Locate the Failure?' in Chapter 6, and Box 6.1.*

numerator is the figure above the line in a fraction or formula. For example, with ¾, the three is the numerator; the four is the **denominator**.

numeric data/scores/variables are when each case in the data set contributes a number or score (e.g. IQ tests, rating scales, reaction times) as opposed to **nominal data**, when each case is merely classified into a category (e.g. sex, occupation, group).

objective means free from bias in judgement; in particular, objective measures are those that are easily verifiable such as in the physical sciences (e.g., weight, length, time etc.). It may take me 10 minutes to get ready to go out, which is an objective measure. This may seem an unreasonably long time to some, a **subjective** assessment.

objective data/measurements are measurements that are capable of being verified by another, for example physical measurements, response times. *Compare with* **subjective data**.

observation is a research technique in which the variable(s) of interest are merely watched and recorded. It may be used in any form of **empirical** study.

observational study/research/design is a study using observation as its only, or at least primary, method of data collection. There are three main types: **participant, non-participant** and **indirect**. The observations may be **structured** on **unstructured**. It is a method of gathering information that involves watching the behaviour of interest, without interfering, in the natural setting in which it occurs. The advantage of an observational study is that it allows the researcher to look at naturalistic behaviour; the disadvantage is the lack of control over the environment. *There are examples of observational studies in Chapters 10–14.*

observer bias occurs when the characteristics of the observer have an unwanted influence on the data. From the psychology of perception we know that each person's view of the world is unique; without meaning to deceive, the observer may over- or under-record behaviour or events of interest. Careful checks can be employed to reduce this.

Occam's razor is the principle that, all else being equal, simpler explanations of phenomena should be preferred over more complex ones. It was devised by William of Occam, a fourteenth-century British philosopher. It is also known as the principle of **parsimony**.

one-tailed hypothesis predicts the direction of the results; for example, males will have faster reaction times than females. Also called a *directional hypothesis*.

one-way ANOVA *see Key Topics: Commonly Used Inferential Statistics.*

open questions are those that allow a wide range of possible answers. For example: What did you think of the play? How would you tackle this topic? *Compare with* **closed questions**.

operational definition is a means of defining and identifying the measurement technique of a **variable** or construct.

operationalise means to define and measure a **variable**. For example, if you wanted to measure perceptual speed you might operationalise this as the number of letter Ps that can be deleted from a block of text in 90 seconds. This provides both a definition and a way of measuring the variable: perceptual speed.

opportunity sampling is when participants are recruited into a study by dint of their already being gathered together. Examples include: students in lecture theatre, attendees at a conference, patients in a waiting room. *Compare with* **convenience sampling**.

order effects, sometimes called **carry-over effects**. In a **within subjects** design each participant experiences each condition of the experiment. Order effects means that the order in which those conditions are experienced will affect the outcome, possibly either through learning or improving with practice, which favours the second condition, or through fatigue or confusion, which favours the first. This can be controlled for by **counterbalancing**.

orderly relationships is a neat turn of phrase to describe what quantitative researchers seek: orderly relationships between two (or more) known variables.

ordinal data are numbers that can be put in rank order (1st, 2nd, 3rd etc.). Comparisons of greater and lesser can be made, in addition to equality and inequality. An example would be the results of a race which say only who arrived first, second, third etc. but provide no time intervals. Many measurements in psychology produce ordinal data. It is generally considered safer to assume that all scores from scales, unless **standardised**, provide ordinal rather than interval data. *See also* **interval data**; **nominal data**; **ratio data**.

outcome measure/variable is the measurement taken that is used to test whether, or how, the **experimental manipulation** worked. It is often used interchangeably with **dependent variable (DV)**, although usually the outcome measure is an **operationalised DV**. For example, 'H_1: examinations cause anxiety' is tested in a study by asking respondents to complete the State-Trait Anxiety Inventory. In this case the dependent variable is anxiety, but the outcome measure is the score in the inventory.

outlier is any value that is markedly smaller or larger than other values in a set of **numeric data**. For example, in the **data set** 31, 35, 34, 29, 38, 2, 36, 35, 33, 30, the outlier is 2. Outlier in a clinical context (*for example, Chapter 11*) is a case that is more extreme on some measure than the general trend in the population.

p is an abbreviation for probability and is used when reporting the results of **inferential statistics**. p<.05 means the result is **significant**, p>.05 means the result is **non-significant**. *See also Key Topics: Probability.*

paired t-test/matched pairs t-test/related t-test *see Key Topics: Commonly Used Inferential Statistics.*

paradigm is a set of practices that define a scientific discipline during a particular period of time and may include the following points: what is to be observed and scrutinised; the kind of questions that are supposed to be asked and probed for answers in relation to this subject; how these questions are to be structured; and how the results of investigations should be interpreted.

parameter is a value, usually a numerical value, that describes a population. It may be derived from a single measurement or from a set of measurements from the population.

parametric statistics a group of inferential statistics that rely on certain qualities in the **parameters** of the variable being tested. Parametric statistics are more effective than **non-parametric** statistics in detecting effects but are limited because data are not always suitable for their use. Parametric statistics are normally only used with data that are either **interval** or **ratio** and are not suitable for **ordinal** or **nominal data**. *See Key Topics: Commonly Used Inferential Statistics and also* **nonparametric statistics**.

parsimony is the principle that the simplest explanation, the one that requires the fewest hypotheses, or the smaller number of processes, is the one most likely to be correct. *Also known as* **Occam's razor**.

participant is a person who take part in a research study. This word is preferred these days to **subject**. It can refer to any person taking part in any form of research, unlike **respondent** which is normally restricted to survey methods.

participant observation requires the researcher to take part, that is to act in the same way as or in a complementary way to, the people s/he is studying. By its nature this is unlikely to be **structured observation**. In *fully participant observation* (e.g. Festinger *et al.*, 1964; Rosenhan, 1973) the researcher does not disclose her/his true identity; in *participant as observer* (e.g. Whyte, 1945) the research is not a secret but is not overtly discussed; in *observer as participant* the researcher is accepted into the group as observer and taken into confidence (e.g. Frankenberg, 1957). The added advantage of participating in this manner is the development of the relationship between observer and observed, which can also prove to be a disadvantage, depending how events pan out. Another problem is the effect that the observer has on the sample.

participant variables are those variables that participants bring to the research process. They may cause variability in the data which may result in a **Type II error**; alternatively if there is a systematic effect, participant variables could even cause a **Type I error**; for example, if one group in a study happened to be predominantly female while the other was predominantly male.

Pearson's (product moment) correlation coefficient *see Key Topics: Commonly Used Inferential Statistics*.

perfect correlation *see* **correlation coefficient**.

Phase I, II or III *see* **clinical trials**.

pilot study/piloting/pilot work is the preliminary use of a research procedure designed to identify problems and omissions before the main study. It can also include exploratory work to identify relevant issues prior to the design of the **data**-collection process or instrument. It can test the feasibility of a design and can also be used to provide for item analysis with **psychometric assessments**.

placebo is a dummy treatment, or an inactive substance administered to a control group, to compare its effects with a real substance, drug or treatment. This is designed to control, or at least minimise, the influence of participants' expectations on the research process.

point-sampling is one method for sampling data in **structured observation**. It occurs when the observer records the type of behaviour of each individual in turn then moves on to the next. *See also* **event-sampling**; **time-sampling**.

population is a set of individuals or units of interest in a particular study. In research, a population is somewhat different from the geographical sense (for example, the population of Birmingham). A population means the types of cases under study, so a population could be 3-year-olds, expectant mothers, healthy adults, Hell's Angels or cotton-top tamarins, for example.

positive correlation *see* **correlation**.

positivism/positivist is the doctrine that emphasises the role of scientific and empirical methods of enquiry and argues that the only real object of scientific study can be numerically measurable phenomena.

post hoc means literally 'after this'. A *post hoc* between groups comparison (as in Chapter 6) is one where the groups can only be identified after the **data** collection. *Post hoc* analysis is the use of inferential statistics after the experimental hypothesis has been tested, an analysis that is prompted by the findings of that initial analysis.

power calculation is a statistical calculation of the ability of an experiment to avoid **false positive** and/or **false negative results**. Power calculations allow researchers to determine how large a **sample** will be needed to demonstrate an effect, if one exists. Power calculations involve a measurement of expected **variability** in the **data** – the greater the variability, the larger the required sample.

predictive validity is the extent to which a variable predicts the measurement of a second subsequent variable. For example, if an assessment of ability has predictive validity it should be able to predict how children will do in school assessments.

pre-/post-design, also called *pretest – posttest* design, is a study that examines whether or not participants in an **intervention** change during the course of the intervention, and then attributes any change to the intervention. If used without a **control** group, there can be problems in determining whether changes in the **dependent variable** (DV) are caused by the intervention or by time, alone. This can lead to erroneous conclusions about the effectiveness of the intervention.

probability refers to likelihood; in statistics it is the likelihood of achieving a certain set of results. **Inferential statistics** are used to calculate probability and, by convention in psychology, if the chances of something occurring are less than 1 in 20 it is considered to be **significant**. *See also Key Topics: Probability*.

probability sampling is a form of sampling where each case in the population has a known, and usually equal, chance of being selected. **Random sampling** and **stratified sampling** are both examples of probability sampling.

procedure is the formal title in a research report used to describe the way that a study is carried out. *See Key Topics: Research Reports*.

prospective studies are those that follow a sample over a period of time. This may not necessarily be a long period of time, as in a **longitudinal study**. The **independent variable**, or presumed cause, is identified at the start of the study and participants are measured at some future point to observe the dependent variable or effect. *Compare with* **retrospective studies**.

protocol is a predefined written method or procedure in the design and implementation of an experiment.

psychometric assessments/tests/measures are designed to quantify or assess some psychological **variable**, or **hypothetical construct**, such as knowledge, intelligence, ability, personality or mood. *There is an example of how a scale may be developed in Chapter 16.*

psychometric properties are the properties of a **psychometric assessment** which need to be established during its development including **reliability**, **validity** and its **factor structure**.

psychometrics is the area of psychology concerned with the theory and technique of measurement of **hypothetical constructs** such as knowledge, achievement, abilities, attitudes and personality traits. It involves developing the construction of instruments and procedures for measurement; as well as the development and refinement of theoretical approaches to this measurement. (The word is derived from 'psycho', to do with the mind, and 'metrics', meaning measurement.)

purposive sampling is the selection of a particular sample on purpose. The variables that determine the criterion for inclusion are analytically and theoretically linked to the research questions.

qualitative analysis comprises a group of qualitative methods for exploring **qualitative data**. There are many different ways of doing qualitative analysis, for example, **discourse analysis**, **grounded theory**, interpretative phenomenological analysis (*see Chapter 17*), **thematic analysis**, and membership categorisation analysis (*see Chapter 13*).

qualitative approach/research explores and tries to understand people's beliefs, experiences, attitudes, behaviour and interactions. It generates non-**numeric data**. The best-known qualitative methods of enquiry include in-depth interviews, focus groups, documentary analysis and unstructured observation. It is an **inductive** rather than a **deductive** method of research.

qualitative data are unstructured **data**, such as text, speech or visual images.

quantitative analysis is the use of statistical techniques, **descriptive** or **inferential**, to understand **quantitative data** and to identify relationships between, and among, **variables**.

quantitative approach/research is a systematic attempt to define, measure and report on the relationships between variables. It generates **numeric data** or **data** that can be converted into numbers, and tends to use **deduction**. *Compare with* **qualitative research**. *See also Chapters 12 and 13, which make this comparison.*

quantitative data are those that can be measured or counted in some way and are represented using numbers.

quartiles are the three data points that divide an ordered **data set** into four equal parts. For example in the following data set the quartiles are underlined: 10,11,11,12,<u>13</u>,14,15,16,16, <u>17</u>,18,19,19,20,<u>21</u>,22,23,25,25,26.

quasi-experiments The word 'quasi' means *as if* or *almost*, so a quasi-experiment is almost a true experiment. There are many types of quasi-experimental research designs; for example, it may be that a **random sample** or **random allocation** are not possible. The distinguishing feature is that the researcher does not have the full control of all the **variables** that is characteristic of the **true experiment**.

questionnaire is a set of questions that are read and answered by the **respondent**. Questionnaires used always to be pen-and-paper measures, but these days many are computerised. Questionnaires can comprise **open** and/or **closed questions** *Compare with* **rating scales** *and* **attitude scales**. *There is an example of a questionnaire study in Chapter 15.*

quota sample is where researchers are set quotas of different types of respondent for their sample, for example 20 women aged 18–21 years. The method of selection of potential respondents is unspecified but is not random. Once the quota is full, recruitment stops. This is a **non-probability sampling** technique. *Compare with* **stratified sampling**.

random means having no specific pattern, purpose, or objective. In research methods it does not, however, mean haphazard, as it does in common speech.

random allocation/randomly assigned means that participants are allocated to groups or conditions through the use of random number tables, or through a random number generator on a computer. For example, if I have 30 participants, I might get the computer to generate 30 random numbers, one for each participant in the order in which they are recruited into the study, and then assign all those with an odd number to one condition and all those with an even number to another. Random allocation is considered to be safer and less subject to bias than **systematic allocation** (e.g. alternating between conditions).

random error has no specific pattern, purpose, or objective, and produces an overall effect on the **data** that may mask the orderly relationship under study. *See also* **Type II error**. Random error may be caused by **participant variables** (individual variation), the conditions or context of the study, situational variables, or the condition of the person at the time. *Compare with* **systematic error**.

> Remember the generalised iceberg principle: seven-eighths of everything is hidden from view.

random sampling means that each person in the **population** in question has a known chance of being recruited into the study. All sampling techniques are subject to **bias,** but with random sampling there is a theoretical framework against which the chances of bias can be calculated.

randomisation is the process of assigning cases to conditions or groups on a random basis. *See also* **random allocation**.

randomisation protocol is a step-by-step plan of how randomisation will be achieved.

randomised controlled trial (**RCT**) is a study in which people are randomly allocated to receive one of several **interventions**. One of these interventions acts as a comparison to provide a benchmark. *There is an example of this in Chapter 3.*

rating scales/scales are means of producing a numerical measurement of a characteristic, or a set of responses. Some **psychometric assessments** comprise rating scales. Rating scales may be **attitude scales**, or may be used to measure a set of unconnected characteristics. *See also* **unipolar scales** and **bipolar scales**. *Compare with* **questionnaires**. *There is an example of how scales are developed in Chapter 16.*

ratio data, like **interval data**, are data where each point in the scale is the same interval from its adjacent point, but, unlike interval data, ratio data have an absolute zero. All physical measurements (height, weight, heart rate etc.) are ratio data. Note that with ratio data you can multiply and divide and keep the relationships constant: 4 metres is twice as long as 2 metres, and 8 metres is twice as long as 4 metres; 250 grams is half of 500 grams, which, itself, is half a kilo 1000 grams). Likewise timings are recorded in ratio data, whether they are recorded using a stopwatch or as part of a computerised task. Contrast this with the time which is recorded as interval data – the difference being that in timings (ratio data), 0 milliseconds really does mean 'no time'. In most statistics, however, interval data and ratio data are treated the same. Some **standardised scales** produce ratio data. *See also* **interval data; nominal data; ordinal data.**

raw data means untreated data. Therefore raw data may be, for example, the completed questionnaires collected in a survey. 'Raw' can also refer to **descriptive statistics**, for example a raw mean, especially if these are data are subsequently changed or transformed in some way.

recruitment is the method used to invite prospective participants to take part in a research study.

reflexivity involves reflecting on the way in which research is carried out, the role the researcher has played in the formation of the data and understanding how the process of doing research shapes its outcomes. Reflexive analysis may be part of a report on a qualitative study.

related design is a generic term where two measures are taken from each case in the sample. The simplest way of achieving this is for the same individual to provide both measures (**repeated measures design**, or **pre-/post-design**). Where this is impractical, a **matched pairs design** may be used, where individual cases in one condition are clearly matched with a specific case in the other condition(s). These include **within subject/within group** comparisons and **correlations**. *See Key Topics: Experimental Design.*

related t-test/paired t-test/matched pairs t-test *see Key Topics: Commonly used Inferential Statistics.*

reliable/reliability refers to the consistency of a measure, instrument, observer or effect. There are several types of reliability, including **inter-observer/rater/judge reliability, internal reliability, external reliability**. Reliability is an important factor in **psychometrics** and there are two types of reliability that really only occur in this context: **test-retest reliability** and **split-half reliability**. *Compare with* **validity**.

repeated measures ANOVA *see Key Topics: Commonly Used Inferential Statistics.*

repeated measures design is a related research design where the aim of the study is to compare between two (or more) different conditions within the same individuals. It means that at least two measurements are collected from each individual. It is classified as a **within subject** or **related design**. *There is an example of this in Chapter 5.*

replicate means to carry out a study in exactly the same manner, and with an equivalent sample to one that has already been completed. It can be seen to be an important part of the research process as replication **validates** earlier results.

representative sample is one that represents the **population** from which it is drawn. This may be a very large population or a small subgroup within that population. There are two ways to attempt to achieve this. (1) Use **random sampling** to reduce **bias** in **sample** selection – a **quantitative approach**. Here, the aim is to be able to **generalise** to the population. (2) Identify key cases that represent particular characteristics central to the research aim – a **qualitative approach**. The aim, in this case, is to provide insight into particular experiences. *For a further discussion of this see Box 17.1.*

respondents are those people who take part in a survey methods research. Unlike participants, this word is only used for this type of research. It is preferred these days to **subjects**.

respondent validation is used in qualitative survey methods when the researcher summarises and analyses the data and then asks the respondents to review this outcome and comment, or correct, as appropriate.

response rate refers to the percentage of invited **respondents** in a survey who accept the invitation and answer the survey. It is calculated by dividing the number of people who answered by the number of respondents invited. For example, if 200 questionnaires are distributed, and 90 are filled out and returned, the response rate would be 45 per cent.

response set/response acquiescence/acquiescent response set is when a **respondent** falls into a pattern of responding to a **questionnaire** or **scale** and appears not to be considering each item individually. For instance they may begin by ticking the box on the left of the page and then continue ticking down the same column of boxes irrespective of the content of the item. This is why reverse items are normally included so that this type of response can be detected and, maybe, discarded.

retrospective studies are studies that trace the histories, or explore the past experiences or behaviour, of a **sample** prior to their recruitment into the study. *Compare with* **prospective studies**.

samples are a set of selected cases from a target **population** from whom it is hoped to draw inferences that apply to the population as a whole, or shed light on a particular issue. Samples can be human, animal, or inanimate (such as passages of text or examples of products). 'Sample' is usually one of the headings in a report. *See also Key Topics: Research Reports.*

sampling bias is an over-representation of one particular category in a sample. Some have claimed that research is biased because it uses volunteers. Certainly, much research uses students, and psychology students at that! The extent to which this creates a problem depends on the intended population and the characteristics under study. For example, if the study is examining reaction times in a healthy normal population, then the over-representation of psychology students in a sample might not be too much of a problem; we have no reason to believe that psychology students' reaction times would be different from those of other comparable age groups in the population. However, if the study were a survey of adults' attitudes to university fees, then students might not represent the views of the general population.

sampling frame is a listing of all the possible and accessible elements or cases in the **target population** under study. For example, if you wanted to access all voters in an election, your frame might well be the electoral register.

sampling strategies/sampling procedures are the mechanisms used for selecting a sample. The two main strategies are **probability sampling**, and **non-probability sampling**.

scales *see* **rating scales**.

scoping study is the first level of a study that is performed to see whether the topic or approach is viable and merits further investigation.

scores *see* **numeric data**.

SD *see* **standard deviation**.

secondary data are those that have already been collected for some purpose, independent of the study in which they are used.

self-selected sample refers to those participants who are selected as a result of their own actions. This includes volunteer samples, but other samples too, such as when **data** are collected in a particular public place which by definition only some people will have elected to attend.

semi-structured interviews are those where there is a predetermined list of topics to cover but the sequence in which they are covered and the way in which questions are asked, or prompts used, is not specified; rather it arises from natural conversational style. *Compare with* **fully structured interviews**.

sign/binomial sign test *see Key Topics: Commonly Used Inferential Statistics.*

significant has a specific meaning when used with **inferential statistics**. These statistics calculate the **probability** of obtaining a specific set of results if there were no real effect in the **data**. If the chances are less than 1 in 20, the effect in the data is taken to be significant, that is it signifies a real effect. For example, in Chapter 7, the researchers compared the differences in experimental conditions over four trials. In each trial the two conditions produced different measurements, but for only three of the four was the difference large enough to be called significant. For the other condition the difference could easily have occurred by chance. When this is the case the findings are said to be **non-significant** (never insignificant). *See Key Topics: Probability.*

single blind *see* **blind**.

single case design is where the sample comprises one individual. This may be a case study (*as in Chapter 14*), or in exceptional cases it can be experimentation, for example, Ebbinghaus (1850–1909), who tested memory capacity by learning lists of nonsense syllables. Sometimes called N=1 design.

single group/sample design is one where **data** are collected from one group of people in one condition, and is therefore distinct from unrelated and related designs. This may be appropriate in a preliminary or **scoping study**. It can also be used when data are collected to compare to an expected distribution or an existing datum such as a published **norm**, for example, measuring the reading age of a group of 8-year-olds to see whether it is in line with that expected for their age. *An example where a single sample design was effective in its own right in an experiment is given in Chapter 6.*

snowball sampling involves recruiting participants into the research through contacts of the researcher or other participants. Snowball sampling can be a form of **purposive sampling** where critical cases are required for the study.

social desirability can influence people's behaviour or responses in research, which may mean that **data** are inaccurate. For example, in a survey designed to find out about criminal behaviour people may be reluctant to admit to having engaged in such behaviours because they know that the socially desirable response is to deny that they ever behaved in such a way. Social desirability is most likely to be a problem in **surveys**, although there are times when it can affect responses in **experiments** or **observational studies** too. *See also* **evaluation apprehension**.

Spearman's correlation *see Key Topics: Commonly Used Inferential Statistics.*

split-half method is a way of measuring the **internal reliability** of a **psychometric** assessment. The process compares the scores on two equal halves of the assessment, which can be produced either by dividing the items **randomly** into two or alternatively by halving by odd and even numbers.

spread *see* **dispersion**.

stability *see* **external reliability**.

standard deviation is a **descriptive statistic**, a measurement of **variability** usually recommended for use with **interval** or **ratio data**. *See Key Topics: Commonly Used Descriptive Statistics.*

standard error of the mean (SEM) is a **descriptive statistic**, a measurement of how representative the sample is of the population, usually recommended for use with **interval** or **ratio data**. *See Key Topics: Commonly Used Descriptive Statistics.*

standard score is a form of measurement from a **psychometric assessment** that expresses how far a given score is from some reference point, typically the mean of the relevant **population**. There are three common types of score: **stanine scores**, **T scores** and **Z scores**.

standardisation is the process whereby a psychometric assessment is **standardised**.

standardise to collect data for a **psychometric measure** from a large number of cases in order to identify the average scores for the **population** from which those cases are drawn. Standardisation is often carried out on more than one type of sample, for example, different age groups. *See Box 14.1.* An assessment that has been standardised may be taken to produce interval data.

standardised assessments/scales/tests are **psychometric measures** that have been **standardised** on appropriate samples representing the **populations** for which the measurement is meant.

standardised procedure is a way of ensuring that repeated measurements or assessments within a study are delivered in exactly the same way at each occurrence.

stanine score is a form of standardised score used in some **psychometric assessments** that expresses how far a score is from the mean. It describes performance on a nine-point scale ranging from 1 to 9; scores of 1–3 are often interpreted as being below average; 4–6 as being average; and 7–9 as being above average.

statistical tests/inferential statistics are a set of mathematical manipulations which allow the researcher to decide whether or not their findings are **significant**.

statistics are a set of methods and rules for organising, summarising and interpreting information.

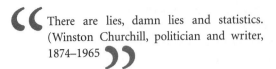

There are lies, damn lies and statistics. (Winston Churchill, politician and writer, 1874–1965

stimulus (plural **stimuli**) an agent, action, or condition introduced by the experimenter to elicit or accelerate a physiological or psychological activity or response.

stratified sampling is a sample drawn from different layers (*strata* in Latin) of the population to ensure that all such layers are represented. For example, if a society as is perceived to have five socio-economic classes, then the sample should have representatives from each of those classes. The size of each of stratification should be proportionate to its representation in the population. Therefore if a society is 25 per cent unskilled manual labourers, then the sample should also be 25 per cent unskilled manual labourers. Within each subgroup or layer, cases are selected on a random basis, which makes this a **probability sampling** technique. *Compare with* **quota sampling**.

structured interview is one where the wording of the questions, subsequent prompts and the order in which they are asked are established prior to data collection and are, therefore, uniform across the sample.

structured/systematic observation is when the categories of behaviour to be observed are clearly specified and classified prior to data collection. This is a **quantitative approach** to observation. *There is an example of this in Chapter 10.*

subject is an individual taking part in experiment. NB: traditionally, in psychology, anyone taking part in research was called the subject, but today there is a move away from this objectifying terminology, and the term **participant** is preferred. However, in the case of animal studies, 'subject' is still common terminology. Furthermore, in experimental design and in inferential statistics it is still customary to refer to **within subjects** or **between subjects** designs.

subjective assessments/measures are those which are not open to external scrutiny, for example personality questionnaires, self-reported behaviours.

subjective data/measurements are individual responses to measurements which are not amenable to verification from another, for example, responses to an **interview** or **questionnaire**. *Compare with* **objective data**.

subjectivity means existing in the mind, based on individual judgement or discretion; a subjective evaluation may be no more than a personal opinion.

survey is the product of a data-collection technique involving **survey methods**, usually a large-scale **questionnaire** study.

survey methods are a group of procedures that involve asking people questions. They include questionnaires, attitude scales, rating scales, checklists and interviews. Survey methods may be the overall design of the study or they can be used within a different design such as experimentation. NB: there is no real consensus about exactly what constitutes survey methods; some researchers would restrict the use of the term to large-scale **questionnaire** studies, while others use it in its broadest sense, meaning any type of research that involves asking people questions. To complicate matters further, some people, usually not psychologists, use the term 'survey' for an observational study. This text has used this term in the broadest sense to incorporate all such interrogative research strategies thereby including all research that is neither observation nor experimentation. *There are examples of survey methods in Chapters 15–19.*

symmetrical transfer effect means that the order of the experience of the conditions, in a **repeated measures** design, has had a direct and equal effect on the outcome. This can occur when an experiment uses **counterbalancing** in a **within subjects** design to control for **order effects**. For example, a study comparing recall of emotive versus neutral words would have half the participants given the neutral wordlist first while the other half received the emotive wordlist first. This is **counterbalancing**. A symmetrical transfer effect could then look like the data in Table G3. These show that the average number of words recalled was always higher for the emotive list, but that for both lists the second recall was better than the first. *See also* **asymmetrical transfer effect**.

Table G3

	Group 1	Group 2
First list/mean recalled	emotive/15	neutral/9
Second list/mean recalled	neutral/11	emotive/17

systematic allocation is when participants are allocated to condition or group systematically, for example, alternately. It is a less effective method than **random allocation**.

systematic errors are those that produce a result that is consistently distorted across the sample. These errors result from biases introduced by instrumental method, or human factors. A systematic error can be a **confounding variable** that can either mask a true effect (**Type II error**) or produce a spurious effect (**Type I error**).

systematic review is a synthesis of the research evidence on a particular topic, obtained through an exhaustive literature search for all relevant studies. The criteria for including studies in the review are explicitly stipulated. A systematic review is more thorough than a **literature review**, but does not use the statistical techniques of a **meta-analysis**.

systematic sampling is when a sample is drawn from a sampling frame using a systematic selection such as every fifth name on a list, or every fourth house on a street. It is a form of **non-probability sampling** but it removes some of the **bias** found in other non-probability strategies although it is not as effective in this respect as random sampling.

T score is a form of standardised score used in some **psychometric assessments** that expresses how far a score is from the mean. It has a midpoint of 50, meaning that scores above 50 represent above-average performance while those below 50 indicate below-average performance. *See also* **standard, stanine** and **Z scores**.

T1, T2, T3 etc. are abbreviations used to represent the occurrence of events in a research study (Time 1, Time 2, Time 3 etc.). In an **experimental** study T may refer to the presentation of **stimuli** or to **trials** and may be separated by anything from milliseconds, to hours or even days. In an **observational** study, T may be used to refer to different periods of observation, whereas in a longitudinal survey T may refer to different rounds of data collection, and these may be separated by a period of months or even years.

target behaviour refers to the behaviour that is under study and that is seen as part of the aim. It is likely to be part of the **operational definition** and in experimentation it may be the

dependent variable. Target behaviour is a term most often encountered in either observation or experiments.

target population is the population to which the researcher would like to generalise her or his findings, based on analysis of a sample. Consequently the **sample** is selected from a target population.

test-retest reliability a measure of consistency for **psychometric assessments** and refers to the extent to which that measure would produce the same results if used again with the same, or a similar, sample under the same, or similar, conditions; sometimes known as **external reliability**. The closer the scores are, the more reliable the test. NB: not all measures need to be reliable; those measuring transient states (e.g. anxiety) are expected to fluctuate over time. *See also Box 16.1.*

thematic analysis is a type of **qualitative analysis** where a theme is identified based on its recurrence and forcefulness. Major themes are those that permeate the **data** in different sections and that are formed by different **respondents**. It is a way of understanding how the respondents (in survey methods), or the sample (in secondary data), interpret and evaluate phenomena.

theory is a set of statements or principles devised to explain a group of observed facts or phenomena. When a theory has been repeatedly tested, or is widely accepted, then it can be used to make predictions about natural phenomena.

time-lag study involves taking similar samples at different time points. For example, a study of child development might involve recruiting a sample of 5- or 6-year-olds in 2010, 2015 and 2020. As you can see, this is an expensive process and likely to suffer from high **attrition rates**. It is sometimes managed retrospectively, however, using **archival** or **secondary data** to compare with contemporary data. *Compare with* **longitudinal** *and* **cross-sectional studies**.

time series study is a study in which periodic measurements are obtained prior to, during and following the introduction of an intervention or treatment, in order to reach conclusions about the effect of the intervention. What distinguishes time series from other similar designs is that a series of measurements is taken prior to the intervention and then again after it.

time-sampling technique is one method for sampling data in **structured observation**. It means that the observation periods are defined by time; thus each target may be observed for, say, a one-minute period before the observer shifts her/his attention to the next. It can also be used when all behaviours occurring during a designated amount of time are recorded. *See also* **point-sampling**.

treatment *see* **intervention**.

trial (1) can be used synonymously with **experiment** to refer to whole study, for example **clinical trials, randomised controlled trials**.

trial (2) an experiment can be composed of a series of trials where each trial represents one **respondent** completing one turn through the experimental design.

true experiment is an experiment where the researcher has full control over all the variables, both **independent** and **dependent variables**, as well any known **extraneous variables**; if the experiment uses **independent subjects**, they are **randomly allocated** to conditions; if it uses

related subjects the order of the conditions is either randomly allocated or **counterbalanced**. *See also* **quasi-experiments**.

two-tailed hypothesis makes no specific prediction about the direction of the results: for example, that there will be a sex difference in reaction times. Note, in this case, the **hypothesis** does not state which sex will be the faster. Also called a *non-directional hypothesis*.

Type I error/false positive occurs when a study appears to produce a significant effect when no such effect really exists. *Mnemonic*: <u>one</u> thinks <u>one</u> has something when really <u>one</u> does not! *See also* **extraneous variables**.

Type II error/false negative occurs when a study does not produce a significant effect when in reality such an effect exists. *Mnemonic*: this means <u>to</u> overlook a real effect! *See also* **extraneous variables**.

unipolar scales are a type of rating scale where a 'zero' response means a lack of that characteristic. *See also* **bipolar scales**.

unrelated design is a generic term for all studies where **participants** in one group are not matched specifically with those in other group(s). It is also called an **independent**, a **between subjects** or a **between groups design**. *See Key Topics: Experimental Design*.

unrelated subjects are those subjects in an **unrelated design**. They may be part of a **group difference** study or **independent groups design**. *See Key Topics: Experimental Design*.

Unrelated t-test *see* **independent t-test**.

unstructured interview is an interview that has no predetermined plan about its course – generally only the overall topic is decided in advance. The **respondents** are encouraged to talk freely and the researcher follows the path set by the interviewee rather than the other way around. It should be distinguished from a *non-directive interview* with a therapeutic intervention intended to allow the client to choose what to talk about without the judgement or advice of the therapist.

unstructured observation is the unplanned, informal, watching and recording of behaviours as they occur in a natural environment. It can be **participant** or **non-participant**. *For examples, see the references for Chapter 10.*

valid/validity refers to the extent to which a measurement actually measures, or detects, what it is supposed to measure. (*See discussion under the heading 'How Effective Was the Study Design?' in Chapter 10 for an example.*) There are several sorts of validity that can be applied to all types of research: **construct**, **ecological**, **external**, **internal**, and **predictive validity**. There are some types that are generally only used with psychometric assessment, including **concurrent**, **content**, **criterion**, **face** and **known groups validity**. *Compare with* **reliability**.

validate means to test whether a study, assessment or measure is valid.

variability *see* **dispersion**.

variable is used to refer to a measurable factor, characteristic, or attribute of an individual or a system that varies across cases and/or over time.

variance is a statistical measure of the extent to which a sample of scores varies.

vignette study is a study where the stimulus material is a short description or story and participants are asked questions about the story. A neat early example is the work of Luchins, who gave his participants one of two versions of a short story (approximately 200 words) about a fictional character's day. The events in the two versions were the same, but the order of them differed. Luchins wanted to see whether the order of presentation of information had an impact on the way participants judged the lead character in the short story, which it did.

visual analogue scales are scales that are designed to provide a relative measurement of the topic. For example, to measure pain a visual analogue might look like this:

Table G4

No pain at all	Worst pain imaginable

volunteer sample is when the participants volunteer to take part in the research study. This may be in response to an advertisement or an invitation or even a plea! Much experimental research has involved volunteer samples when, logistically and ethically, other types of sampling are less appropriate.

Wilcoxon's matched pairs test *see Key Topics: Commonly Used Inferential Statistics.*

within subject/within group comparison is a related research design where the aim of the study is to compare between two different conditions, or to compare two variables within the same individuals. It means that at least two measurements are collected from each individual. The two forms of a **within subjects** design are **repeated measures** and **matched pairs**. *See Key Topics: Experimental Design.*

Z score is a form of standardised score used in some **psychometric assessments** that expresses how far a score is from the mean. It has a midpoint of 0. Scores above the mean will be positive and those below will be negative scores. Nearly all Z scores will fall between -3.00 and $+3.00$; for this reason Z scores are normally presented to at least two decimal places.

" There are 10 kinds of people in the world … those who understand binary, and those who don't. "

zero correlation *see* **correlation**.

References

Chapter 2. Ethics

Beauchamp, T. & Childress, J. (1994). *Principles of biomedical ethics.* Oxford: Oxford University Press.

British Psychological Society (2005). *Code of conduct, ethical principles and guidelines.* Leicester: BPS.

Milgram, S. (1963). Behavioural study of obedience. *Journal of Abnormal and Social Psychology, 67,* 371–378.

Piliavin, I.M., Rodin J. & Piliavin, J. (1969). Good Samaritanism: An underground phenomenon? *Journal of Personality and Social Psychology, 13*(4), 289–299.

Slater, M., Antley, A., Davison, A., Swapp, D., Guger, C., Barker, C., Pistrang, N. & Sanchez-Vives, M.V. (2006). *A virtual reprise of the Stanley Milgram obedience experiments.* http://www.plosone.org/article/info:doi/10.1371/journal.pone.0000039

Zimbardo, Philip G. (1999–2005). *The Stanford Prison Experiment: A simulation study of the psychology of imprisonment conducted at Stanford University.* http://www.prisonexp.org

Chapter 3. Obsessive Compulsive Disorder

Kenwright, M., Marks, I., Graham, C., Franses, A. & Mataix-Cols, D. (2005). Brief scheduled 'phone support from a clinician to enhance computer aided self-help for Obsessive Compulsive Disorder: Randomized controlled trial. *Journal of Clinical Psychology, 61*(12), 1499–1508.

Math, S.B. & Janardhan Reddy, Y.C. (2007). Issues in the pharmacological treatment of obsessive-compulsive disorder. *International Journal of Clinical Practice, 61*(7), 1188–1197.

Patel, S.R., Carmody, J. & Simpson, H.B. (2007). Adapting mindfulness-based stress reduction for the treatment of obsessive-compulsive disorder: A case report. *Cognitive and Behavioral Practice, 14*(4), 375–380.

Wu, K.D. & Carter, S.A. (2008). Further investigation of the Obsessive Beliefs Questionnaire: Factor structure and specificity of relations with OCD symptoms. *Journal of Anxiety Disorders, 22*(5), 824–836.

Chapter 4. Music and Stress

Cooke, M., Chaboyer, W., Schluter, P. & Hiratos, M. (2005). The effect of music on preoperative anxiety in day surgery. *Journal of Advanced Nursing, 52*(1), 47–55.

Choi, B.-C. (2008). Awareness of music therapy practices and factors influencing specific theoretical approaches. *Journal of Music Therapy, 45*(1), 93–109.

Gillen, E., Biley, F. & Allen, D. (2008). Effects of music listening on adult patients' pre-procedural state anxiety in hospital. *International Journal of Evidence-Based Healthcare, 6*(1), 24–49.

Glass, D.C. & Singer, J.E. (1972). *Experiments on noise and social stressors.* New York: Academic Press.

Spitzer, M., Rath, F. & Groen, G. (2005). Music and subjective well being: Preliminary results on use of a sound bed in depressive patients. *Nervenheilkunde: Zeitschrift fur interdisziplinaere Fortbildun, 24*(3), 198–202.

Thompson, R.G., Moulin, C.J.A., Hayre, S. & Jones, R.W. (2005) Music enhances category fluency in healthy older adults and Alzheimer's disease patients. *Experimental Aging Research, 31*(1), 91–99.

Walworth, D.D. (2003). The effect of preferred music genre selection versus preferred song selection on experimentally induced anxiety levels. *Journal of Music Therapy, 40*(1), 2–14.

Yung, P.M.B., Szeto, C. K., Lau, B.W.K. & Chan, T.M.F. (2003). The effect of music in managing preoperative stress for Chinese surgical patients in the operating room holding area: A controlled trial. *International Journal of Stress Management, 10*(1), 64–74.

Chapter 5. Competitive Anxiety

Beaudoin, C.M. (2006). Competitive orientations and sport motivation of professional women football players: An internet survey. *Journal of Sport Behavior, 29*(3), 201–212.

Bell, R.J. & Thompson, C.L. (2007). Solution-focused guided imagery for a golfer experiencing the yips: A case study. *Athletic Insight: Online Journal of Sport Psychology, 9*(1), 1–15. http://www.athleticinsight.com/vol9iss1/golfimagery.htm

Fradkin, A.J., Cameron, P.A. & Gabbe, B.J. (2007) Is there an association between self-reported warm-up behaviour and golf related injury in female golfers? *Journal of Science and Medicine in Sport, 10*(1), 66–71.

Gucciardi, D.F. & Dimmock, J.A. (2008). Choking under pressure in sensorimotor skills: Conscious processing or depleted attentional resources? *Psychology of Sport and Exercise, 9*, 45–59.

Jones, J.W., Neuman, G., Altmann, R. & Dreschler, B. (2001) Development of the Sports Performance Inventory: A psychological measure of athletic potential. *Journal of Business and Psychology, 15*(3), 491–503.

Neumann, D.L. & Thomas, P.R. (2008) A camera-based scoring system for evaluating perform-ance accuracy during a golf putting task. *Behavior Research Methods, 40*(3), 892–897.

Chapter 6. Change Blindness

Baddeley, A. (2007). *Working memory, thought, and action*. Oxford: Oxford University Press.
Davies, G.M. & Hine, S. (2007) Change blindness and eyewitness testimony. *Journal of Psychology: Interdisciplinary and Applied, 141*(4), 423–434.
Levin, D.T., Simons, D.J., Angelone, B.L. & Chabris, C.F. (2002). Memory for centrally attended changing objects in an incidental real-world change detection paradigm. *British Journal of Psychology, 93*, 289–302.
Simons, D.J. & Levin, D.T. (1998) Failure to detect changes in a real world interaction. *Psychonomic Bulletin and Review, 5*, 644–649.
Smilek, D., Eastwood, J.D., Reynolds, M.G. & Kingstone, A. (2008). Metacognition and change detection: Do lab and life really converge? *Consciousness and Cognition: An International Journal, 17*(3), 1056–1061.
Symes, E., Tucker, M., Ellis, R., Vainio, L. & Ottoboni, G. (2008). Grasp preparation improves change detection for congruent objects. *Journal of Experimental Psychology: Human Perception and Performance, 34*(4), 854–871.
Varakin, D.A., Levin, D.T. & Collins, K.M. (2007). Comparison and representation failures both cause real-world change blindness. *Perception, 36*(5), 737–749.

Chapter 7. Acoustic Preferences

British Psychological Society (2005). *Code of conduct, ethical principles and guidelines*. Leicester: BPS.
Garber, P.A., Gomes, D.F. & Bicca-Marques, J.C. (2008). Experimental field study of hand preference in wild black-horned (Cebus nigritus) and white-faced (Cebus capucinus) capuchins: Evidence for individual and species differences. *Animal Cognition, 11*(3), 401–411.
McDermott, J. & Hauser, M. (2004). Are consonant intervals music to their ears? Spontaneous acoustic preferences in a non-human primate. *Cognition, 94*, B11–B21.
McDermott, J. & Hauser, M.D. (2007). Nonhuman primates prefer slow tempos but dislike music overall. *Cognition, 104*(3), 654–668.
Rentfrow, P.J., Samuel D. & Gosling, S.D. (2003). The do re mi's of everyday life: The structure and personality correlates of music preferences. *Personality Processes and Individual Differences, 84*(6), 1236–1256.
Russell, W.M.S. & Burch, R.L. (1959). *The principles of humane experimental technique*. UFAW special edition, 1992.

Chapter 8. Cognitive Costs of Racial Prejudice

Johnson, D. (2008). Racial prejudice, perceived injustice, and the black–white gap in punitive attitudes. *Journal of Criminal Justice, 36*(2), 198–206.

Lin, M.H., Kwan, V.S.Y., Cheung, A. & Fiske, S.T. (2005). Stereotype content model explains prejudice for an envied outgroup: Scale of anti-Asian American stereotypes. *Personality and Social Psychology Bulletin, 31*(1), 34–47.

Salvatore, J. & Shelton, J.N. (2007). Cognitive costs of exposure to racial prejudice. *Psychological Science, 18*(9), 810–815.

Tomic, A. & Jahn, K. (2008). Case dismissed: Police discretion and racial differences in dismissals of felony charges. *American Law and Economics Review, 10*(1), 110–141.

Chapter 9. Mate-Selection Strategies

Bercovitch, F.B. (1991). Mate selection, consortship formation, and reproductive tactics in adult female savanna baboons. *Primates, 32*(4), 437–452.

Cobb, N.P., Larson, J.H. & Watson, W.L. (2003). Development of the attitudes about romance and mate selection scale. *Family Relations, 52*(3), 222–231.

Husseneder, C. & Simms, D.M. (2008). Size and heterozygosity influence partner selection in the Formosan subterranean termite. *Behavioral Ecology, 19*(4), 764–773.

Jones, B.C., DeBruine, L.M., Little, A.C., Burriss, R.P. & Feinberg, D.R. (2006). Social transmission of face preferences among humans. *Proceedings of the Royal Society* (doi:10/1098/rspb.2006.0205).

Le Roux, E., Scholtz, C.H., Kinahan, A.A. & Bateman, P.W. (2008) Pre- and post-copulatory mate selection mechanisms in an African dung beetle, Circellium bacchus (Coleoptera: Scarabaeidae). *Journal of Insect Behavior, 21*(3), 111–122.

Smahel, D. & Subrahmanyam, K. (2007) 'Any girls want to chat press 911': Partner selection in monitored and unmonitored teen chat rooms. *CyberPsychology & Behavior, 10*(3), 346–353.

Zajonc, R.B. (1968). Attitudinal effects of mere exposure. *Journal of Personality and Social Psychology, 9*, monograph supplement no. 2, part 2.

Chapter 10. The Autistic Spectrum

Goodall, J. (1986). *The chimpanzees of Gombe.* Boston: Houghton Mifflin.

Hoeppner, B.B., Goodwin, M.S., Velicer, W.F. & Heltshe, J. (2007). An applied example of pooled time series analysis: Cardiovascular reactivity to stressors in children with autism. *Multivariate Behavioral Research, 42*(4), 707–727.

Levy, E.T. & Fowler, C.A. (2005). How autistic children may use narrative discourse to scaffold coherent interpretations of events: A case study. *Imagination, Cognition and Personality, 24*(3), 207–244.

Macintosh, K. & Dissanayake, C. (2006). A comparative study of the spontaneous social interactions of children with high functioning autism and children with Asperger's disorder. *Autism, 10*(2), 199–220.

Roseman, B., Schneider, E., Crimmins, D., Bostwick, H., Visintainer, P., Jaskow, P.A. & Accardo, P. (2001). What to measure in autism drug trials. *Journal of Autism and Developmental Disorders, 31*(3), 361–362.

Williams, G., Sears, L. & Allard, A. (2006). Parent perceptions of efficacy for strategies used to facilitate sleep in children with autism. *Journal of Developmental and Physical Disabilities, 18*(1), 25–33.

Participant Observation – Classic Studies

Festinger, L., Reickman, H. & Schachter, S. (1956). *When prophecy fails: A social and psychological study of a modern group that predicted the destruction of the world.* London: Pinter & Martin.

Frankenberg, R. (1957). *Village on the border.* London: Cohen & West

Rosenhan, D.L. (1973). On being sane in insane places. *Science, 179,* 250–258.

Whyte, W.F. (1943). *Street corner society: The social structure of an Italian slum* (4th edn. 1993). Chicago: University of Chicago Press.

Chapter 11. Cognitive Maps

Kearney, A.R. & Kaplan, S. (1997). Toward a methodology for the measurement of knowledge structures of ordinary people: The Conceptual Content Cognitive Map (3CM). *Environment and Behavior, 29*(5), 579–617.

Maguire, E.A., Frackowiak, R.S.J. & Frith, C.D. (1997). Recalling routes around London: Activation of the right hippocampus in taxi drivers. *Journal of Neuroscience, 17*(18), 7103–7110.

Maguire, E.A., Gadian, D.G., Johnsrude, I.S., Good, C.D., Ashburner, J., Frackowiak, R.S.J. & Frith, C.D. (2000). Navigation related structural changes in the hippocampi of taxi drivers. *Proceedings of the National Academy of Sciences of the United States of America, 97*(8), 4398–4403.

O'Keefe, J. & Nadel, L. (1978). *The hippocampus as a cognitive map.* Oxford: Oxford University Press.

Singer, R.A., Abroms, B.D. & Zentall, T.R. (2007) Formation of a simple cognitive map by rats. *International Journal of Comparative Psychology, 19*(4), 417–425.

Wray, M.K., Klein, B.A., Mattila, H.R. & Seeley, T.D. (2008). Honeybees do not reject dances for 'implausible' locations: Reconsidering the evidence for cognitive maps in insects. *Animal Behaviour, 76*(2), 261–269.

Chapter 12. Eating Disorders and the Media

Ahern, A.L., Bennett, K.M. & Hetherington, M.M. (2008). Internalization of the ultra-thin ideal: Positive implicit associations with underweight fashion models are associated with drive for thinness in young women. *Eating Disorders: The Journal of Treatment & Prevention, 16*(4), 294–307.

Inch, R. & Merali, N. (2006). A content analysis of popular magazine articles on eating disorders. *Eating Disorders, 14,* 109–120.

Mond, J.M., Myers, T.C., Crosby, R.D., Hay, P.J., Rodgers, B., Morgan, J.F., Lacey, J.H. & Mitchell, J.E. (2008). Screening for eating disorders in primary care: EDE-Q versus SCOFF. *Behaviour Research and Therapy, 46*(5), 612–622.

Moriarty, C.M. & Harrison, K. (2008). Television exposure and disordered eating among children: A longitudinal panel study. *Journal of Communication, 58*(2), 361–381.

Chapter 13. Eating Disorders: The Experience

British Psychological Society (2007). *Guidelines for ethical practice into psychological research online.* Leicester: BPS.

Freedman, G., Liechner, P., Manley, R., Sandhu, P.S. & Wang, T.C. (2006). Understanding anorexia nervosa through the analysis of thematic content of letters in an adolescent sample. *European Eating Disorders Review, 14,* 301–307.

Garner, D.M., Olmstead, M.P. & Polivy, J. (1983). Development and validation of a multidimensional eating disorder inventory for anorexia nervosa and bulimia. *International Journal of Eating Disorders, 2,* 15–34.

Giles, D. (2006). Constructing identities in cyberspace: The case of eating disorders. *British Journal of Social Psychology, 45,* 463–477.

Hogg, M.A. & Vaughan, G.M. (2007). *Social psychology* (5th edn.). London: Prentice Hall.

Inch, R. & Merali, N. (2006). A content analysis of popular magazine articles on eating disorders. *Eating Disorders, 14,* 109–120.

Ogden, J. & Greville, L. (1993). Cognitive changes to preloading in restrained and unrestrained eaters as measured by the Stroop task. *International Journal of Eating Disorders, 14,* 185–195.

Silverman, D. (2004). *Doing qualitative research: A practical handbook.* London: Sage Publications.

Smith J.A. (Ed.) (2008). *Qualitative psychology: A practical guide to research methods* (2nd edn.). London: Sage Publications.

Chapter 14. Face Recognition

Abe, N., Ishii, H., Fujii, T., Ueno, A., Lee, E., Ishioka, T. & Mori, E. (2007). Selective impairment in the retrieval of family relationships in person identification: A case study of delusional misidentification. *Neuropsychologia, 45,* 2902–2909.

Firestone, A., Turk-Browne, N.B. & Ryan, J.D. (2007). Age-related deficits in face recognition are related to underlying changes in scanning behaviour. *Aging, Neuropsychology, and Cognition,14*(6), 594–607.

Hawley, K.S. & Cherry, K.E. (2004). Spaced-retrieval effects on name-face recognition in older adults with probable Alzheimer's disease. *Behavior Modification, 28*(2), 276–296.

Hochhalter, A.K., Sweeney, W.A., Bakke, B.L., Holub, R.J. & Overmier, J.B. (2000). Improving face recognition in alcohol dementia. *Clinical Gerontologist, 22*(2), 3–18.

Rizzo, S., Venneri, A. & Papagno, C. (2002). Famous face recognition and naming test: A normative study. *Neurological Sciences, 23*(4), 153–159.

Chapter 15. Choices and Decisions

Garst, J., Kerr, N.L., Harris, S.E. & Sheppard, L.A. (2002). Satisficing in hypothesis generation. *American Journal of Psychology, 115*(4), 475–500.

Iyengar, S.S., Wells, R.E. & Schwartz, B. (2006). Doing better but feeling worse: looking for the best job undermines job satisfaction. *Psychological Science, 17*(2), 143–150.

Reader, W.R. & Payne, S.J. (2007). Allocating time across multiple texts: Sampling and satisficing. *Human–Computer Interaction, 22*(3), 263–298.

Schwartz, B., Ward, A., Monterosso, J., Lyubomirsky, S., White, K. & Lehman, D.R. (2002). Maximizing versus satisficing: happiness is a matter of choice. *Journal of Personality and Social Psychology, 83*, 1178–1197.

Chapter 16. Measuring Romance

Dewitte, M. & de Houwer, J. (2008). Adult attachment and attention to positive and negative emotional face expressions. *Journal of Research in Personality, 42*(2), 498–505.

Doumas, D.M., Pearson, C.L., Elgin, J.E. & McKinley, L.L. (2008). Adult attachment as a risk factor for intimate partner violence: The 'mispairing' of partners' attachment styles. *Journal of Interpersonal Violence, 23*(5), 616–634.

Fortuna, K. & Roisman, G.I. (2008). Insecurity, stress, and symptoms of psychopathology: Contrasting results from self-reports versus interviews of adult attachment. *Attachment & Human Development, 10*(1), 11–28.

Gormley, B. (2004). Application of adult attachment theory to treatment of chronically suicidal, traumatized women. *Psychotherapy: Theory, Research, Practice, Training, 41*(2), 136–143.

Quirin, M., Pruessner, J.C. & Kuhl, J. (2008). HPA system regulation and adult attachment anxiety: Individual differences in reactive and awakening cortisol. *Psychoneuroendocrinology, 33*, 581–590.

Spielberger, C.D. (1983) *State trait anxiety inventory*. Palo Alto, Ca.: Consulting Psychologists Press.

Torgersen, A. M., Grova, B.K. & Sommerstad, R. (2007). A pilot study of attachment patterns in adult twins. *Attachment & Human Development, 9*(2), 127–138.

Wei, M., Russell, D.W., Mallinckrodt, B. & Vogel, D.L. (2007). The Experiences in Close Relationship scale (ECR) – short form: Reliability, validity, and factor structure. *Journal of Personality Assessment, 88*(2), 187–204.

Chapter 17. Paranoia

Campbell, M.L.C. & Morrison, A.P. (2007). The subjective experience of paranoia: Comparing the experiences of patients with psychosis and individuals with no psychiatric history. *Clinical Psychology and Psychotherapy, 14*, 63–77.

Coombs, D.R., Penn, D.L., Chadwick, P., Trower, P., Michael, C.O. & Basso, M.R. (2007). Subtypes of paranoia in a nonclinical sample. *Cognitive Neuropsychiatry, 12*(6), 537–553.

Corbin, J. & Strauss, A. (2008). *Basics of qualitative research: Techniques and procedures for developing grounded theory* (3rd edn.). London: Sage Publications.

Cresswell, J.W. (2007). *Qualitative Inquiry and research design: Choosing among five approaches* (2nd edn.). London: Sage Publications.

Gracie, A., Freeman, D., Green, S., Garety, P.A., Kuipers, E., Hardy, A., Ray, K., Dunn, G., Bebbington, P. & Fowler, D. (2007). The association between traumatic experience, paranoia and hallucinations: A test of the predictions of psychological models. *Acta Psychiatrica Scandinavica, 116*(4) 280–289.

Moritz, S. & Laudan, A. (2007). Attention bias for paranoia-relevant visual stimuli in schizo-
    phrenia. *Cognitive Neuropsychiatry, 12*(5), 381–390.
Shryane, N. M., Corcoran, R., Rowse, G., Moore, R., Cummins, S., Blackwood, N., Howard, R.
    & Bentall, R.P. (2008). Deception and false belief in paranoia: Modelling theory of mind
    stories. *Cognitive Neuropsychiatry, 13*(1), 8–32.
Silverman, D. (2006). *Interpreting qualitative data: Methods for analysing talk, text and inter-
    action* (3rd edn.). London: Sage Publications.
Smith J., Jarman M. & Osborne M. (1999). Doing interpretative phenomenological analysis.
    In M. Murray & K. Chamberlain (Eds.) *Qualitative health psychology*. London. Sage
    Publications.
Thewissen, V., Bentall, R.P., Lecomte, T., van Os, J. & Myin-Germeys, I. (2008). Fluctuations
    in self-esteem and paranoia in the context of daily life. *Journal of Abnormal Psychology,
    117*(1), 143–153.

Chapter 18. Understanding Heavy Drinking

Augustin-Normand, C. & Consigny, M. (2007). Alcohol abuse in young people: An emer-
    gency room survey. (French). *Alcoologie et Addictologie, 29*(3), 267–269.
Hartney, E., Orford, J., Dalton, S., Ferrins-Brown, M., Kerr, C. & Maslin, J. (2003). Untreated
    heavy drinkers: A qualitative and quantitative study of dependence and readiness to
    change. *Addiction Research & Theory, 11*(5), 317–337.
Hartney, E., Orford, J., Dalton, S. (2004). Untreated heavy drinkers: A qualitative and quanti-
    tative study of dependence and readiness to change (Letter). *Addiction Research and
    Theory, 12*(2), 191–193.
Hazelton, L.D., Sterns, G.L. & Chisholm, T. (2003). Decision-making capacity and alcohol
    abuse: Clinical and ethical considerations in personal care choices. *General Hospital
    Psychiatry, 25*(2), 130–135.
Heather, N., Rollnick, S. & Bell, A. (1993). Predictive validity of the Readiness to Change
    Questionnaire. *Addiction, 88*, 1667–1677.
Keyes, K.M. & Hasin, D.S. (2008). Socio-economic status and problem alcohol use: The posi-
    tive relationship between income and the DSM-IV alcohol abuse diagnosis. *Addiction,
    103*(7), 1120–1130.
Markowitz, J.C., Kocsis, J.H., Christos, P., Bleiberg, K. & Carlin, A. (2008). Pilot study of inter-
    personal psychotherapy versus supportive psychotherapy for dysthymic patients with
    secondary alcohol abuse or dependence. *Journal of Nervous and Mental Disease, 196*(6),
    468–474.
Paschall, M.J., Bersamin, M., Fearnow-Kenney, M.D., Wyrick, D.L. & Currey, D. (2006).
    Short-term evaluation of a web-based college alcohol misuse and harm prevention
    course. *Journal of Alcohol and Drug Education, 50*(3), 49–65.
Raistrick, D., Bradshaw, J., Tober, G., Weiner, J., Allison, J. & Healey, C. (1994). Development
    of the Leeds Dependence Questionnaire (LDQ): A questionnaire to measure alcohol
    and opiate dependence in the context of a treatment evaluation package. *Addiction, 89*,
    563–572.
Rollnick, S., Heather, N., Gold, R. & Hall, W. (1992). Development of a short 'Readiness to
    Change Questionnaire' for use in brief, opportunistic interventions among excessive
    drinkers. *British Journal of Addiction, 87*, 743–754.

World Health Organisation. (2001). *Alcohol Use Disorders Identification Test – AUDIT* (2nd edn.). Retrieved from http://www.who.int/substance_abuse/publications/alcohol/en/

Wu, P., Hoven, C.W., Okezie, N., Fuller, C.J. & Cohen, P. (2007). Alcohol abuse and depression in children and adolescents. *Journal of Child & Adolescent Substance Abuse, 17*(2), 51–69.

Chapter 19. Attributing Success and Failure

Anderson, C.A. (1999). Attributional style, depression, and loneliness: A cross-cultural comparison of American and Chinese students. *Personality and Social Psychology Bulletin, 25*(4), 482–499.

Deregowski, J.B., Muldrow, E.S. & Muldrow, W.F. (1972). Pictorial recognition in a remote Ethiopian population. *Perception, 1*, 417–25.

Kurman, J. (2002). Measured cross-cultural differences in self-enhancement and the sensitivity of the self-enhancement measure to the modesty response *Cross-Cultural Research: The Journal of Comparative Social Science, 36*(1), 73–75.

Lockwood, P., Marshall, T.C. & Sadler, P. (2005). Promoting success or preventing failure: Cultural differences in motivation by positive and negative role models. *Personality and Social Psychology Bulletin, 31*(3), 379–392.

Markus, H.R., Uchida, Y., Omoregie, H., Townsend, S.S.M. & Kitayama, S. (2006). Going for the gold: Models of agency in Japanese and American contexts. *Psychological Science, 17*(2), 103–112.

Mead, M. (1928) *Coming of age in Samoa.* New York: Harper Perennial Modern Classics (reprinted 2001).

Chapter 20. Contasting the Methods

Abe, N., Ishii, H., Fujii, T., Ueno, A., Lee, E., Ishioka, T. & Mori, E. (2007). Selective impairment in the retrieval of family relationships in person identification: A case study of delusional misidentification. *Neuropsychologia, 45*, 2902–2909.

Campbell, M.L.C. & Morrison, A.P. (2007). The subjective experience of paranoia: Comparing the experiences of patients with psychosis and individuals with no psychiatric history. *Clinical Psychology and Psychotherapy, 14*, 63–77.

Giles, D. (2006). Constructing identities in cyberspace: The case of eating disorders. *British Journal of Social Psychology, 45*, 463–477.

Gucciardi, D.F. & Dimmock, J.A. (2008). Choking under pressure in sensorimotor skills: Conscious processing or depleted attentional resources? *Psychology of Sport and Exercise, 9*, 45–59.

Hartney, E., Orford, J., Dalton, S., Ferrins-Brown, M., Kerr, C. & Maslin, J. (2003). Untreated heavy drinkers: A qualitative and quantitative study of dependence and readiness to change. *Addiction Research & Theory, 11*(5), 317–337.

Inch, R. & Merali, N. (2006). A content analysis of popular magazine articles on eating disorders. *Eating Disorders, 14*, 109–120.

Iyengar, S.S., Wells, R.E. & Schwartz, B. (2006). Doing better but feeling worse: Looking for the best job undermines job satisfaction. *Psychological Science, 17*(2), 143–150.

Jones, B.C., DeBruine, L.M., Little, A.C., Burriss, R.P. & Feinberg, D.R. (2006). Social trans-mission of face preferences among humans. *Proceedings of the Royal Society* (doi:10/1098/rspb.2006.0205).

Kenwright, M., Marks, I., Graham, C., Franses, A. & Mataix-Cols, D. (2005). Brief scheduled 'phone support from a clinician to enhance computer aided self-help for Obsessive Compulsive Disorder: Randomized controlled trial. *Journal of Clinical Psychology, 61*(12), 1499–1508.

Levin, D.T., Simons, D.J., Angelone, B.L. & Chabris, C.F. (2002). Memory for centrally attended changing objects in an incidental real-world change detection paradigm. *British Journal of Psychology, 93*, 289–302.

Macintosh, K. & Dissanayake, C. (2006). A comparative study of the spontaneous social interactions of children with high functioning autism and children with Asperger's dis-order. *Autism, 10*(2), 199–220.

Maguire, E.A., Gadian, D.G., Johnsrude, I.S., Good, C.D., Ashburner, J., Frackowiak, R.S.J. & Frith, C.D. (2000). Navigation related structural changes in the hippocampi of taxi driv-ers. *Proceedings of the National Academy of Sciences of the United States of America, 97*(8), 4398–4403.

Markus, H.R., Uchida, Y., Omoregie, H., Townsend, S.S.M. & Kitayama, S. (2006). Going for the gold: Models of agency in Japanese and American contexts. *Psychological Science, 17*(2), 103–112.

McDermott, J. & Hauser, M. (2004). Are consonant intervals music to their ears? Spontaneous acoustic preferences in a non-human primate. *Cognition, 94*, B11–B21.

Piliavin I.M., Rodin J. & Piliavin, J. (1969). Good Samaritanism: An underground phenom-enon? *Journal of Personality and Social Psychology, 13*(4), 289–299.

Salvatore, J. & Shelton, J.N. (2007). Cognitive costs of exposure to racial prejudice. *Psychological Science, 18*(9), 810–815.

Sears, D.O. (1986). College sophomores in the laboratory: Influences of a narrow data base on social psychology's view of human nature. *Journal of Personality and Social Psychology, 51*(3), 515–530.

Smith, J.A. (Ed.) (2008). *Qualitative psychology a practical guide to research methods* (2nd edn.). London: Sage Publications.

Wei, M., Russell, D.W., Mallinckrodt, B. & Vogel, D.L. (2007). The Experiences in Close Relationship scale (ECR) – short form: Reliability, validity, and factor structure. *Journal of Personality Assessment, 88*(2), 187–204.

Willig, C. (2008). *Introducing qualitative research in psychology*. Buckingham: Open University Press.

Woodman, R.W. (1979). The devil's dictionary of behavioural science research terms. *Academy of Management Review, 4*, 93–94.

Yung, P.M.B., Szeto, C.K., Lau, B.W.K. & Chan, T.M.F. (2003). The effect of music in manag-ing preoperative stress for Chinese surgical patients in the operating room holding area: A controlled trial. *International Journal of Stress Management, 10*(1), 64–74.

Glossary

Festinger, L., Reickman, H. & Schachter, S. (1956). *When prophecy fails: A social and psycho-logical study of a modern group that predicted the destruction of the world*. London: Pinter & Martin.

Frankenberg, R. (1957). *Village on the border*. London: Cohen & West.

Klofas, J. & Cutshall, C. (1985). Unobtrusive research methods in criminal justice: Using graffiti in the reconstruction of institutional cultures. *Journal of Research in Crime and Delinquency, 22*(4), 355–373.

Rosenhan, D.L. (1973). On being sane in insane places. *Science, 179*, 250–8.

Rosenthal, R. & Jacobson, L. (1968, 1992) *Pygmalion in the classroom: Teacher expectation and pupils' intellectual development*. New York: Irvington.

Whyte, W.F. (1943). *Street corner society: The social structure of an Italian slum* (4th edn. 1993). Chicago: University of Chicago Press.

Index

Bold numbers refer to entries in the Glossary.